FIELD OF VISION
THE BROADCAST LIFE OF
KENNETH ALLSOP

Field Of Vision
The Broadcast Life of Kenneth Allsop
◊
Mark Andresen

TRAFFORD

© Copyright 2004 Mark Andresen.
All rights reserved. No part of this publication may be reproduced, stored in a retrieval system, or transmitted, in any form or by any means, electronic, mechanical, photocopying, recording, or otherwise, without the written prior permission of the author.

Note for Librarians: A cataloguing record for this book is available from Library and Archives Canada at www.collectionscanada.ca/amicus/index-e.html
ISBN 1-4120-2407-2

Offices in Canada, USA, Ireland and UK
This book was published on-demand in cooperation with Trafford Publishing. On-demand publishing is a unique process and service of making a book available for retail sale to the public taking advantage of on-demand manufacturing and Internet marketing. On-demand publishing includes promotions, retail sales, manufacturing, order fulfilment, accounting and collecting royalties on behalf of the author.

Book sales for North America and international:
Trafford Publishing, 6E–2333 Government St.,
Victoria, BC v8t 4p4 CANADA
phone 250 383 6864 (toll-free 1 888 232 4444)
fax 250 383 6804; email to orders@trafford.com
Book sales in Europe:
Trafford Publishing (UK) Limited, 9 Park End Street, 2nd Floor
Oxford, UK OX1 1HH UNITED KINGDOM
phone 44 (0)1865 722 113 (local rate 0845 230 9601)
facsimile 44 (0)1865 722 868; info.uk@trafford.com
Order online at:
trafford.com/04-0235

10 9 8 7 6 5 4 3 2

CONTENTS

List of Illustrations	7
Introduction by Colin Wilson	9
Foreword by Tristan Allsop	15
Prologue - True to Nature	21
1. *Chapel and Stone*	27
2. *Co-Ops*	39
3. *Holbeck to Isleworth*	55
4. *The Great West Road*	72
5. *The Elusive 'Otter' Man*	95
6. *Wide, Open Spaces*	107
7. *Betty*	131
8. *LAC 915084*	135
9. *'Everything is Forward'*	151
10. *Common Wealth*	180
11. *Sanctuaries*	200
12. *Spying and Selling*	227
13. *Barwythe*	239
14. *'Picture Post' Years*	267
15. *Henry and the Grey House*	307
16. *'This is Kenneth Allsop...'*	321
17. *'Tonight'*	353
18. *Betty, Again*	381
19. *On the Road*	385
20. *'24 Hours'*	399
21. *The Merton Term Retreat*	426
22. *The Allsop Spirit*	453
23. *Defending West Dorset*	483
24. *Out of Time*	509
Epilogue - The Irrepressible Peregrine	531
Bibliography	539
Acknowledgements	540
Index	543

Illustrations

p. 19   Four-year-old KA with mother Mary. Yorkshire, 1924.
p. 20   KA, same age, with father John and grandmother.
p. 70   John and KA holidaying in Devon, 1934.
          Another shot of Kenneth...
p. 94   How the fifteen-year-old KA would have appeared to the Williamsons'...
p. 129 KA and BA's wedding...
p. 178 KA and BA in the back garden of 100, Mount View Road, c. 1945.
          KA convalescing on the same day.
p. 198 The Allsops' with first child Andrew, c. 1947.
p. 225 KA in rustic gear... c. 1949.
          KA showing Andrew his shotgun...
p. 237 'Barwythe'
          KA and BA outside 'Barwythe,' c. 1949. (2 shots)
p. 265 KA in Dirk Bogarde chic... 1950.
p. 266 Allsops' on holiday in Devon, 1950.
p. 319 KA interviewed Louis Armstrong on three occasions...
p. 352 October 1960: a new man joins 'Tonight.' (*BBC*).
p. 397 Feeling the pressure... (*BBC*) 1965.
p. 424 A hopeful HW... (*BBC*) 1967.
p. 425 KA being enrobed... 1969.
          Amanda, Tristan, BA and Fabian...
p. 451 KA takes over the helm at '24 Hours.' (*BBC*) 1969.
p. 482 Looking out for marauders... 1972.
          A campaigning DWD flyer, 1972.
p. 529 'Mr. Pencil,' summer, 1970. (*Peter Ryan*).

*All photographs copyright The Kenneth Allsop Estate,
except where otherwise stated.*

INTRODUCTION
by Colin Wilson

I am delighted that a biography of Ken Allsop has appeared at last. He was a friend for whom I felt considerable affection and, since his death, always experienced a feeling of sadness when I thought about him. Now, at least, Mark Andresen has created a permanent memorial to a unique writer.

In May 1956, when I was 24, my first book *The Outsider* appeared, and sold out its first edition in a few days. Ken wrote of me; 'not since Lord Byron has a writer awakened to such instant fame.' This was partly because I was classified, with the playwright John Osborne, as an Angry Young Man. It was a vertiginous and not entirely unpleasant experience; a little like being drunk and then hung over for days at a time. Ken Allsop recognised my disorientation, and became the kind of elder brother I never had. He was also sympathetic when the inevitable reaction came, and the critics panned my second book.

I met Ken in the Soho bookshop of a delightful, vague man called David Archer, famous for his eccentricity. He once gave a party for Dylan Thomas after publishing Thomas's first poems, and the next morning asked Thomas if he had enjoyed himself. 'You forgot to invite me,' said Thomas. I found Ken instantly fascinating; not simply because he had such modesty and charm, but because he was obviously highly literate and intelligent. Also present was a colleague of Ken's: Dan Farson. They had worked together on *Picture Post*, and it was Dan who had contacted me to ask if he could interview me for a series he was writing on young writers for *The Daily Mail*. When I mentioned that I was about to go on holiday in the West Country with my girlfriend Joy, Ken suggested giving us a lift there. He and Dan intended to go and see Dan's father Negley, who, in the mid-1930s', had achieved overnight fame and bestseller-dom with his autobiography, *The Way of a Transgressor*.

Which is how, on a brilliantly sunny morning, we came to be driving down to North Devon in Ken's open-topped roadster. I recall that we kept seeing dead rabbits, and Ken remarked, 'myxamatosis,' which led me to ask, 'what's myxamatosis?' I had spent most of my time, for the past few years, absorbed in books and seldom read a newspaper. As Ken - slightly incredulous at my ignorance - explained about it, I realised that he was exactly the kind of person I had always wanted as a friend. Someone who knew all the things I needed to know about now; that I had suddenly emerged from years of immersion in literature and ideas, and into the world of people and events.

Negley and his wife Eve lived in a house - The Grey House - on a cliff top not far from Croyde. Woolacombe was about a mile's walk along the beach to the north. And Negley and Ken had in common one thing that gave them instant rapport - a leg injury. Negley had been involved in a flying accident in the First World War, and he had a great hole in his shinbone that still needed cleaning and disinfecting every day. But, he enjoyed swimming in the sea. When Negley urged Ken to come and join him, it was obvious that Ken was worried and nervous. But, he finally unscrewed his leg and, supported by Negley, hopped down the beach and into the sea. From his exhilaration when he came out, it was obvious to us that this had been a breakthrough experience.
  On that visit Ken also intended to go and see the author, Henry Williamson, who lived a few miles from Negley; but he had to keep his intention a secret, for Negley detested Henry. The latter, an immensely handsome man with a blonde moustache was, unfortunately, a maniacal egoist and, like most egoists, neurotic to the point of paranoia. He also behaved very badly towards women. For years he had been having an affair with the daughter of the poet, Edward Thomas, but unable to marry her because he was already married. But, on the day his divorce came through, he met a pretty schoolteacher on the beach, and married her without further ado.

The incident that had brought about the break from the Farsons' was trivial but amusing. Henry had gone over to The Grey House to read the latest installment of his multi-volume novel, *A Chronicle of Ancient Sunlight* and, since his hero was, basically, himself, Negley inclined to chafe at this preening of Henry's ego. (Henry had the habit of keeping the latest chapter of the book in his inside pocket, and pulling it out at a moment's notice, to read to any captive audience. He often did it in The Savage Club, of which we were both members.

On this occasion, Henry was reading to Negley and Eve when their dachshund, Albert, began to demand attention by rubbing itself against Henry's foot. Without even glancing up, Henry lashed out with his toe and Albert flew across the room. Henry continued reading, until something in the nature of the silence struck him, and he looked up to find Eve standing there, unable to speak with rage and pointing at the door. She finally managed to gasp, 'get out of my house!'; which is why Ken had to keep his intended visit a secret.

The four of us went: Ken, Dan, Joy and myself. Henry lived in a house like a prefabricated barn. His pretty new wife was there; a shapely teacher of gymnastics (who, shortly after, left him). Henry produced the latest chapter of the Madison Saga, and read on, long after we were due back for dinner. None of us felt we could interrupt. We finally arrived home very late - Ken was sure Henry had done it deliberately - and had to make lame excuses about not noticing how quickly the time had flown by in the pub.

Ken told me he had been deeply influenced by Henry's nature books, like *Tarka the Otter* and *Salar the Salmon*. (Negley had nicknamed Henry 'Tarka the Rotter'). Ken's novel *Adventure Lit Their Star* (1949) was about birds, and is a classic; his other nature book, *The Sun Himself Must Die* (also 1949) is almost as good. The problem was that Ken could not make a living from such books, no matter how highly they were esteemed by critics. Henry had written *Tarka* in a farm cottage with the baby on his knee much of the time. Then, Henry (and, more important, his wife Loetitia), was willing to put up with poverty. But, Ken said he was not so ascetically inclined, and liked to drive a good car and have a bottle of whisky in the cupboard. So, he had been forced to slave in Fleet Street and forgo the kind of writing he much preferred.

*

Ken wrote the first book about the Angry Young Man phenomenon, *The Angry Decade*, in 1958. In it, he defended my second book, which had been so violently damned by the other critics, arguing that part of the reason was that its predecessor - *The Outsider* - had not been understood. He grouped myself and my two close friends - Bill Hopkins and Stuart Holroyd - together in a chapter called 'The Law Givers.' The truth was that Ken had no real sympathy for my own preoccupation with the question of whether human existence is ultimately meaningless yet, I think, respected the obsessive nature of my concern with the problem. This probably explains why he signed a copy of the book; 'For Colin, who is not exactly the Hero of this book, and only partially a Villain, but certainly one of its main Begetters.'

This demonstrates something of the close sympathy between us, and why I valued his friendship so much. He signed the book in January 1959. I subsequently sent Ken the typescript of my novel *Ritual in the Dark*. He made some extremely valuable comments, including rewriting for me a passage that was supposed to be a newspaper report about the crimes - based on the Jack the Ripper murders - that are the subject of the book.

One day, Joy and I went to see Ken and his wife Betty at their home north of London. Ken played us *West Side Story*, which was breaking records on Broadway; he particularly liked the number 'Gee, Officer Krupke.' Now, I never hear this without thinking of him. In fact, Ken loved American culture - especially jazz - and was fascinated by the bootleg era. When he was writing the history of the period - *The Bootleggers* - I lent him my copy of *The Tax Dodgers* by Elmer L. Irey; the man who finally nailed Capone.

Joy and I moved to a cottage near Mevagissey, in Cornwall, in the spring of 1957. I had to install electricity in order to play my records; for music has always been for me an absolute necessity. Partly under Ken's influence, I had been discovering jazz and, when he came down to interview me there, we talked a great deal about jazz and jazzmen, for I had bought myself all kinds of books on the subject and listened to it a great deal. Ken's knowledge was encyclopaedic; I asked his opinion about everyone from Ma Rainey to Charlie Parker. I was enthusiastic about Miles Davis, but Ken disliked him, finding the tone controlled to the point of constipation. He also disliked the Modern Jazz Quartet, because he felt there was something affected about the way they came on stage in business suits and refused to acknowledge applause. I asked him later what he thought of The Beatles, fairly certain he would be uncomplimentary. But, to my surprise, he thought they were brilliant musicians and he enjoyed their music. After that, I even bought some of their records, although I must confess I never really came to enjoy them as much as Louis Armstrong or Charlie Parker.

He was in Cornwall, I seem to recall, to follow up on a story about an accident that had confined me to my armchair. This was entirely my own fault. Trying to light a fire that had gone out several times, I rushed outside to grab a drum that I thought contained paraffin. In fact, it was a *mixture* of paraffin and petrol that I used for the generator. I smelt the petrol as I sloshed it onto the fire, and tried to jump backwards. I was too late; there was a roar, and I was blown halfway across the room. The explosion blew out the glass from one side of my spectacles, took some skin off the side of my face, and burned my hand. I could only thank my guardian angel that it was not *pure* petrol, and that I did not burn down the cottage.

Now, it so happened that our spare bedroom - we had two - was permeated by the unpleasant smell of a dead rat. We had put down poison for some of the rats that overran the garden tip, and one of them had obviously crawled indoors to die. We searched the bedroom, but there was no sign of it. However, the smell gradually decreased and, when Ken came down, it was just bearable, provided the window and door were left wide open. In his subsequent article, Ken talked about visiting me in my 'rat-infested cottage.' My father was infuriated and upset, for he liked boasting about my country cottage to his friends in the pub, and now they went out of their way to wound his vanity by joking about the rats.

Years later, we learned the answer to the mystery of the smell. Then, tenants who moved into the cottage decided to throw out a giant pile of mattresses that occupied a corner of the bedroom. Between two, near the bottom, they found the skeleton of the rat. I had glanced at the mattresses when searching for the source of the smell, but dismissed the idea that anything could have crawled into something so tightly packed.

Now, I lived so far from London I saw far less of Ken than I would have liked. Then we bought a house not far from the cottage, and even bought a black and white television, so I was able to watch him on *Panorama*. But, although I liked him as a Presenter and interviewer, I felt that his rather well-bred voice was not ideal for television. When he moved onto programmes on the environment, I became less interested.

I had gathered from friends in Fleet Street that Ken was something of a womaniser, which surprised me since he seemed such a well balanced family man. But then, I think that it went with his love of fast cars and America's bootleg era. And I never forgot his comment about how much he envied Henry Williamson for being able to go on writing the kinds of books he wanted to write. I suspect that the womanising was a symptom of some nagging dissatisfaction with his life. Yet, when I heard of his death, and then the rumours of his suicide, I completely discounted them, for I felt he was much too sane and controlled a person to kill himself. And, I continued to feel the same in subsequent years. It was not until I read Mark Andresen's book that I learned of the overwork of those last years, and the anxieties about his job and his health - to understand the reason - and finally came to accept that his death was self-inflicted. If Ken's spirit is somewhere around, I hope he will accept this Introduction as a small mark of my continuing affection.

Colin Wilson,
Cornwall
31st October, 2004

FOREWORD
by Tristan Allsop

My father died in 1973. In the three decades that spanned what was, by any measure, a hugely successful career, he was lucky to be in at the start of an extraordinarily exciting transition in journalism. In the late 1950's and early 60's the increasingly hungry maw of television Current Affairs sucked in a stream of established Fleet Street journalists to feed the needs of the BBC's Lime Grove Studios, and the still new ITV. *Picture Post* magazine alone supplied at least a dozen of the most successful television current affairs, cameramen, producers and presenters. One of these was my father.

Largely due to the opportunities television gave him he became a commentator for and of his time, both on the screen and in print. Undoubtedly his on-screen fame opened journalistic opportunities for him and over the course of the next quarter-century he was published in *The Sunday Times, The Spectator, The New Statesman, The Daily Mail, The Evening Standard,* as well as the now-defunct *Evening News, Nova, Listener, Punch* and many others.

He became an icon, for some as famous for his sartorial style as for his journalism. He was the Jeremy Paxman of his time. But he was a man who was ultimately despairing of his own and of Man's condition. He killed himself on May 23rd 1973 in his Dorset home whilst my mother and sister were in London at the Chelsea Flower Show.

Like any individual he was full of contradictions and complexities often unfathomable to others. He could be irascible, demanding, unreasonable – with himself as much as his children and his colleagues. Undoubtedly he made enemies. But he was also a man of great warmth, charm and wit, with a wonderful sense of humour, and an insatiable curiosity for knowledge. (He deeply regretted never going to university and was determined his children should do so).

He had a great number of first class and long-time friends. Some, such as George Hilton, feature in this account of his life, but many others, notably his closest friend David Malbert, City Editor of the *London Evening News,* are long dead and could not contribute to the book or offer insight to the private man. But no one could maintain so many lasting friendships without being a man of worth and value. John and Marjorie Edwards are an American couple, still resident at the Californian address they were at when my father first encountered them in Copenhagen airport in 1957. They remember a man "with great curiosity, a marvellous sense of humour, a belief in the equality of all people and races, who was open to new ideas, and tolerant of your ideas so long as they did not run afoul of his ideals".

David Brend, who was, and is, *my* closest friend remembers him from the perspective of a teenager:

"I was probably thirteen and, I recall, nervous about meeting him. He was by far the most famous person I had encountered. What I hadn't expected was the accessibility, warmth and humour. That, and being treated as an equal. I didn't think TV personalities did that to their sons' teenage friends. Yet there was always a slight sense of danger. It was implicit in the way others deferred to him; his sharpness when he encountered inept grammar or the way he could crush a poorly expressed argument. But the rewards were considerable. Conversations over the kitchen table, or late at night in his office, never faltered, constantly testing the boundaries of our knowledge while remaining inclusive. He introduced us, me certainly, to a calibre of thoughtful humour I hadn't experienced and that remains with me to this day."

Although best known for his television work he detested the term 'Television Personality' and regarded himself first and foremost as a writer anchored in the print journalism of Fleet Street. He would have been appalled at the recent BBC edict forbidding their staff journalists to write for the printed press. As well as being a serious threat to his own income, he would have seen it as an artificial separation of complementary skills and the denial of a vital training ground for high quality television writing.

All journalism is essentially ephemeral, yet even more so was television in the years he dominated current affairs with David

Dimbleby, Ludovic Kennedy and Cliff Michelmore. Nightly live programmes and no VHS recorders then. Few enough programmes remain in the archives of the BBC, but my father's written journalism survives - in newspaper archives and in the cuttings books stored in my loft.

Writing was a source of both pain for him - the agonising process of teasing out yet another weekly column for *The Daily Mail* - and of intense pleasure - especially in his later books *Bootleggers* and *Hard Travellin'*. Yet his output was prodigious. In 1972 alone, the last full year before his death, his articles filled three fat ledgers. A crude estimate suggests over five thousand column inches containing maybe one hundred and fifty thousand words in that one year. There are twelve more such volumes and several boxes of cuttings in the loft above my head. In *Scan*, a collection of his journalism published in 1965 he reckoned he'd thus far turned out a million-and-a-half words as a journalist (excluding his dozen books). A further eight years of undiminished output that followed must have added another million to that total.

The range of his writing was catholic to say the least: regular jazz and book reviews, especially as literary editor of *The Daily Mail* for eight years (then, under editor Mike Randall, a respected newspaper), interviews with key public figures of the time, commentary on social trends and mores, and some intensely personal pieces (on 25 years of living with pain for example). Unlike Paxman, however, he generally steered away from political stories. He had an overwhelming dislike and mistrust of organised politics.

His writing style was distinctive, even idiosyncratic; not always an easy read, but invariably rewarding. And his love for the English language was demonstrated not solely in his writing; it was communicated to his three children with passion and with an intolerance for sloppy grammar and lazy speaking. The richest language in the world, he believed, deserved nurturing and respect.

The same literary panache was clear in his television scriptwriting. This was at a time when the majority of television journalists had learned their literary craft in Fleet Street before they transferred to television. If my father was still alive I have no doubt that he would consider the quality of writing for television today to be generally atrocious. Lazy, repetitive, with little regard for the power of the visual image it accompanies, and a tabloid vocabulary stooping to the lowest common denominator. He would be appalled.

His printed words provide a lasting, if now unseen, memorial to his life. Yet while the public memory of him may have faded, ours (mine, my sister's, my brother's) has never dimmed. He remains in my mind a dominant, warm, affectionate father who worked too hard and spent too little time with us. More than thirty years after his death I still miss him, and my everlasting regret is that my wife and children never knew him, nor he them.

Tristan Allsop,
London
25th January, 2004

Four-year-old Kenneth with mother Mary, Yorkshire, 1924.

Kenneth, same age, with father John and grandmother.

Prologue:
True to Nature

On the last morning of his life, the journalist and broadcaster Kenneth Allsop described himself as reduced to a mechanism 'broken down at full steam.' Film star looks and a characteristic iron will had finally succumbed to three decades of restricting pain from a body permanently tainted by TB. Unavoidable pressure on the nerve-exposed region, all this time, offered no concession when, finally, it was most needed. There were ongoing environmental campaigns with new ones queuing for the cachet afforded by his name. But, unknown to everyone, he'd since withdrawn, spiritually, beyond recall. A driven idealist, a failure to perform was foreign territory, reflecting what he thought he saw in those unwilling to continue the cause. But, crucially, his influence had affected others, closer to him, who remembered him as a martyr to it. Only this wasn't the point: or his.

The main misconception about Kenneth Allsop, fostered since his death in 1973, has been based upon a solely romantic notion; that here was a man, despondent at the destruction of nature around him, seeing no future for a mankind that prioritised enforced change for individual profit over independent, organic growth. But such a view was what Kenneth himself feared by the start of 1973. Interviewing fellow Dorset resident John Fowles for a January *Sunday Times* of that year, the author of *The French Lieutenant's Woman* thought his questioner felt he'd increasingly bore the weight of a responsibility he hadn't asked for; that he'd become, in his words, 'an ombudsman for all things natural.' The Green Belt building, first witnessed by Kenneth as a Middlesex schoolboy in the 1930s', had become an issue for countless other organisations; in number, over two thousand by this year. Meanwhile, Friends of the Earth had coalesced and begun to protest by their own instinctive means. Kenneth cared, and deeply, but also very much on his own terms. Inevitably, this posture divided those on the receiving end of rural change. Many village locals saw him merely as an interfering 'townie' with more compassion for animals than for people – *their* people - whom they had to abide by. While the environmental Establishment continued in wilful ignorance, seeing him – as they do to this day – 'not one of us' if they recall him at all; a privileged individual, not a pack animal, and happy to remain so.

Perhaps both definitions are correct; that he was a 'townie' and that he was elitist enough to snub simply joining another's pressure group when he could lead his own. He'd certainly brought it upon himself. But, the assumptions arising from these views remain wide of the mark. Today, his legacy appears almost profoundly neglected. But it is not one of a safe, easily definable, BBC and Fleet Street man with a melancholy, romantic soul who sought out the green between the grey like some 20th Century William Blake. Rather, the real story to tell is of an idealist, and one of stark contradictions: stylish yet insecure, cerebral but petulant, remotely stoic but highly sensitive, a good advisor but poor taker of advice, refuter of celebrity while a shameless self-publicist, a casual philanderer and lover but obsessive adherent to discipline at home.

From 1935 to the end of Kenneth's life, Henry Williamson - the nature writer and author of *Tarka the Otter* - directed a seemingly unconscious but pervasive influence of which the younger man became strangely obsessed. It was not obsession, so much, with Williamson's personality (though this, alone, could intrigue most witnesses) but with what he represented as a plausible, alternative way of living; a sustainable bridge between past and future.

The fifteen-year-old had acquired a taste for wide, open spaces from the borderless back gardens of his last two homes, and his father's own preoccupation with outdoor sketching. Williamson's eccentricity and political naivete initially puzzled and later exasperated Kenneth, whose own character was cerebral and self-disciplined. (Doubters need only read his profile on William Burroughs, or ongoing literary wrestling with his own conscience in support of Colin Wilson's 'outsider' writings, to see how he judged solely by the accepted guidelines of good English criticism, rather than some romanticist kinship). But, gripped by the combined ideals of writing on, off, and by, the land, young Kenneth was certain of its cyclical, seasonal dominance over the daily restrictions imposed by the inadequate pen-pushers upon urban life.

Journalist, broadcaster, author, historian and prolific 'ideas man,' Kenneth Allsop was, in his day, a publicly well-known face and intellectually respected. A man – admirably, in my view – whose intellect recognised no boundaries, (even if this, occasionally, left him out of his depth), due to his being almost exclusively self-taught. Born in January 1920, he'd find himself at least five years senior to most like-minded contemporaries, while significantly younger than those to whom he felt particular affinity. This affinity – conscious or otherwise – stemmed from a generation-old Edwardian age, when libertarianism, suspicious of cant and dogma, was represented by the works of D.H. Lawrence, and party political allegiances were more fluid and not cast in stone.

Likewise, entering middle age, Kenneth came to be accepted as the BBC's 'voice' by its viewers and listeners; but never 'The Voice of the BBC' by his employers there. Not that Kenneth would have had a problem with this. Previous to 1973, this view offered him the autonomy, as a freelancer, he had always desired. Between 1951 and 1972, he'd managed to negotiate favourable contractual terms with Press, TV and Radio, biannually, above the standard rate, keeping his own head just above the murky waters of excess debt. Conversely, such autonomy, by this year, was the very position by which he would become sidelined. The pervading mood of the new Conservatism, elected to power six years later, would be that those who lived, so died, upon swords of their own making.

Always having to look ahead, he had recently been showing an increasing interest in his family's past. Dubious health and a leg lost through TB-related *sarcoidosis* during the World War II, had afforded rare chances for personal research. The BBC's half-hearted commitment to Ken's springtime environmental / current affairs TV programme, *Down to Earth*, resulted in it being pulled the previous August, just before the final edition. Ken was now in the position of being effectively frozen out of regular, future commitments by the BBC hierarchy. Their view was that Allsop no longer called the tune, so long as they could call upon replacements half the cost, half the age and, if trainable, half the talent.

While unlikely the BBC Controller or his colleagues announced this to his face, the sidelining, after he twice put their noses out of joint, in public, in June '72, was telling enough for him to have got the message. So, mid-August, he casually announced his semi-retirement - from regular broadcasting - in *The Sunday Times*: the paper he was about to join. It wasn't as if he'd had a choice. Ever the diplomat, no headline baiting blame was apportioned for his new employer; only an acceptance that he desired more personal space. The cliché of 'spending more time with the family' applied but, also, followed through.

In April '73, his long-suffering wife, Betty, accompanied him on a weeklong assignment to Kenya. In mid-May, they both went to the annual West Country Writers Conference in Exeter, with another mutual engagement in South Wales the following weekend. It was a period of reconciliation for the couple. But it would be their last.

Connections with the BBC should have been irretrievably severed from here. But, Ken was resigned to the fact that, as a long-term freelancer with appetites greater than his earnings, he lacked the luxury of options. With cold resignation, he could accept the least shallow programme formats offered, and whistle for preferential scheduling. He was not about to appear, primetime, again.

So, it was a tired, disconsolate and disenfranchised Ken who lunched with Fowles and his wife, Elizabeth, that post-Christmas day in 1973. Less than six months later, alone in bed at his Dorset mill house, on a rain-soaked morning when he was due to leave for Television Centre for rehearsals renewed pain from his nerve-raw stump – a torture inflicted for thirty years - pulled his raised torso back onto the mattress. At a time he was bestowed with renewed respect, he questioned the will to carry on. For the first time, the following chapters relate the character that informed the choices made, and his journey there.

1
1889 – 1904:
Chapel and Stone

Large slabs of tough millstone grit, bifurcated cleanly in the sawmill, were transported to an area of the quarry ready for the Allsop brothers of Mexborough, West Yorkshire. Precision and resilience: the two most desired qualities of the Yorkshire quarryman. Accuracy and a strong, deft touch: an expected prerequisite. For trimming of a stone's outer edge, a huge T-square, chisel and hammer efficiently finished the job, cleaving at right angles, cracked areas swiftly discarded by instinctive eyes. It was then readied for a final rubdown to a smooth, clean surface. Shaped as though pre-packaged for convenience and aesthetic appeal alone, the neatly piled stones were then carried by steam locomotive to builders merchants from the North to the South of late Victorian Britain. Consequently, according to Willie and Sam Allsop's youngest brother, John, 'Knowledgeable people can recognise Morley Stone wherever they see it.'

Quarrying could be a dangerous business; perhaps not in the same league as the coal mining that also maintained the West Yorkshire communities, but with blind risks of its own. Blasting a stone wall with gunpowder was the first, a handkerchief the only shield. Picks glancing off a sheer stone surface, early morning, when muscles remained slack, embedding themselves above the knee, were regular occurrences. John junior's elder brother, Tom, was a victim of that, although home treatment seemed sufficient. His other brother, Sam, standing in a rail wagon, arranging a load of slabs, was crushed beneath a swinging cargo held by a crane high above his head. Of course, it very nearly killed him, but he somehow survived through a drawn out combination of home care and regular visits from the local GP. John JR recorded what he saw, heard and smelt when he visited the quarry during school holidays.

The 'swish-swish of the mighty saw in the mill,' the large wagons, locomotives trundling slowly to collect the finished slabs and 'puffing ponderously away' again. The deep green lake that had formed across the base when he felt brave enough to peer over the brink of the gouged-out stone basin. The ten feet square stone built hut with its centre stove to which the men brought their food and tin-canned tea. The smell of the bacon, fried by elder brother Walter, and the anecdotal conversation of the men, regularly punctuated by swearing.

Their father, John Allsop Senior, was site manager for *Messrs. Pawson Brothers, Morley*, coming across as a stern but fair employer. Failures to discharge duty were severely challenged, but he appears no hypocrite, always willing to lead the men by example. John Jr. claims he 'enjoyed his position and the feeling of power.' He doesn't say if there was a ceiling to this or if it ever went to his head, though a relative lack of enforced discipline at home would suggest otherwise.

Talk was 'free and open' with interests clearly mutual between the males. The evening peace was occasionally disturbed by visiting sub-managers or their colleagues, for consultations with John Sr. on concerns or grievances held by the men, safety issues, or updates on deliveries. Otherwise, reading dominated 'til lights out, with a few 'banned' writers on the sons and daughters lists. 'Father probably knew this, but winked an eye.'

The boys' Georgian, Derbyshire-born grandfather, Samuel,

reputedly illegitimate by one Mr. Tempest, denied all responsibility. 'So, Samuel took his mother's name; 'Allsop.' In the minds of local fraternity, it was obvious when Samuel grew up that kin Tempest, son of a local publican, was daddy.' He followed the trade that, locally, was deemed most secure, and quite literally, as the railway ventured North, for building assignments on walls and bridges, becoming a stone mason, working at the Yorkshire quarry of Bramley, which he later managed. His son, John (Sr.), born in this town in 1850, followed in what was to become the family trade, here and at Horsforth. Between the early 1870s' and late 1880s', John and his Leeds-born wife Louisa (*nee* Hustwaite) were to slavishly follow the Victorian 'biblical injunction' of large families, bearing seven children here between them; Martha, (known affectionately as Pattie), Samuel, (Jr.), William, (Willie), Thomas, (Tom), Jane, Walter and Louisa (Jr.). A move from Bramley to Mexborough – another Yorkshire quarry town – produced an eighth and last, John (Jr.), on 19th February 1889.

The address was a cottage on a hill made up from discarded quarry stone, furred over, presumably, by soil and grass. While all the boys had at least some grounding in, and by, the quarry, the girls would find mutual support in weaving, sewing, and a genuine interest in well-made clothes; but nothing so vulgar or 'su'thern' as mere fashion. Son John evocatively recalled a typical evening at home:
'When dressmaking started, the large table was cleared, there was a flurry of cottons, silks, patterns; 'trying on' accompanied by excitable comments – with pins in mouth, approval or disapproval – "a bit out here," "it's too long," then finally, "Ah! That's it."'
Sardonic rejoinders shot from the brothers in the corner chairs, heads buried in theoretical texts relevant to their work, in Geology and Management. Accents were sing-song, mildly fey, with a world weary descant spoken

through the side of the mouth, or what the Leeds-born playwright, Alan Bennett, would bluntly refer to as sounding 'rather wet and lackadaisical' on return visits to the city. As a class, the Allsops' were of an aspirational lower middle but sociologically tough to pin down.

John Sr., outside his management duties at the stone quarry, was a Methodist lay preacher at the local chapel. Methodism had a history of being almost its own class, hermetically sealed from other aspects of Christianity in the community. Practising Methodists ranged from the working classes to the gentry in a proactive way that the Church of England could only envy and rarely muster. As an orator, John Sr. had a distinct speaking voice with, no doubt, that world-weary accent which a low burr would effectively accentuate as coming from one that had seen The End and accepted his fate. An effective performer, since attendance's at Ebenezer Methodist Church (Morley's Chapel) were consistently high. Standing in the pulpit, he struck a round-faced, burly, bear-like figure of medium height, an inner strength suggested and augmented by dark, round eyes, straight back and thick but trimmed beard.

'Stone and Chapel were always in evidence,' son John recalled, 'our lives were largely governed by quarry talk when under-managers called in the evenings, or the Minister came to discuss chapel affairs.' The Sunday School in Mexborough had afforded the youngest son a chance to exercise his talent for English. It is strange that this seems never to have been actively encouraged by his father once the talent was revealed. Not that there is any clear evidence of discouragement, but it was not a subject he was initially schooled in or taken under wing at Morley. A combination of Bible readings and local advertising hoardings fostered intriguing misspellings in the boy's mind with the alphabet never formally taught. Yet, 'I seemed to sense the word as a whole (while) spelling, too, came almost instinctively.' And he had arrived at the town with a parting gift from his Sunday School teacher; what could be described as a coffee-table book, *Great Events*; 'a beautifully illustrated historical production.'

Of John Sr.'s wife, Louisa, little is recalled. She seems to have died here, at Mexborough, of a fatal illness, in her late thirties. John Jr. suspects the sister named after her may also have taken after her; 'dark, petite, deep blue eyes, saucy smile' who was also 'very self-contained' in character and 'disliked teasing.' Perhaps it was the harboured, oppressive atmosphere of too many memories, which caused the further move, around 1894, to Morley, when John Jr. was five.

He recalled its geography as 'a town of about twenty five thousand inhabitants...fairly self-contained (and) influenced to some degree by the larger cities within a seven mile ring; Leeds, Bradford and Wakefield. Leeds more particularly as a social attraction with its theatres and restaurants.'

The sole means of getting there was by boarding the rail carriages of the Great Northern or London & North-West lines. Bonds inevitably strengthened at this new start. John Jr. recalls growing especially close to Pattie, the eldest, through his early years of puberty. Excursions with her from Morley into Leeds were through country and mainly on foot: out of necessity, as there was no public transport until the outskirts of the City were reached. For John, this leant an opportunity for observation previously taken for granted, while satisfying one further curiosity.

'I was very fond of exploring and found a great joy along the country lanes, looking for birds nests and wayside flowers and fruits. One wild thistle plant's silky flower provided 'tobacco,' and acorn for the pipe-bowl, a straw for the stem, and we had our first 'smoke.' Shocking aroma accompanied by the guilt of doing something secretly.' Nature provided other dubious treats for the lad; catapults from Y-shaped branches, hedgerows – whip-stocks, while 'an *umbelliferous* plant stalk made a fine blowpipe,' its ammunition provided by the berries from a thorn bush, and the inevitable throwing-stones for the competitive target practice game of 'big duck.'

Unselfconsciously, John Jr. uses the word 'love' to describe the knowledge he was acquiring of the local flora, fauna and bird population. The whole of the South and West Yorkshire region fast became his subject of authority, as he found shortcuts over hills and valleys to towns like Batley, Dewsbury, Ossett, Bramley and Pudsey, observing and absorbing the patterns of wildlife along the way. Whatever the future held for John, it was quite obvious that he was not about to add to the proud, ancestral, Allsop ranks of quarry slabmen.

Walter was the brother closest in both age and interest. 'Whatever he did, I tried to emulate. If I was threatened or bullied I would say, "I'll tell our Walter," confident that this would avert the threat.' Walter challenged those local village lads with a penchant for bullying by walking 'with a slightly arrogant swing, giving an impression of forcefulness,' inadvertently becoming the last of the Allsop quarry boys, as a 'rapper,' aged thirteen. This entailed standing perched upon a platform, four feet square, over the quarry basin, tapping out a series of signals on an iron plate hung from the guard rail, understood by the men as meaning 'lift' whenever a stone was ready for heaving up by the crane standing by. But this limited duty was shared with acting as messenger between their father, John's, office and that of the secretary in the town.

Sometime later, John Jr. must have been given access to the former, probably during those school holiday visits to the quarry. Seeing all the paperwork, required reading and documentation requiring his father's signature in that neat, careful script, planted a seed for future consideration. The youngest brother also found common ground in collecting particular comics and 'yellowbacks' of the day from the local Co-Operative Library. '...We obtained *Boys Own Paper*, bound editions, *Strand Magazine*, ditto. School stories were a favourite, the 'derring do' type, too. *Hal Harkaway*, a paperback edition, bought out of pocket money, if any. This was rather frowned upon by father, not being up to 'standard.' *Midshipman Easy*, Jules Verne *Adventures of a Three Guinea Watch*, W. W. Jacobs...*Sexton Blake*; for myself from the early days, *Chips*, *Comic Cuts*, later *Jester*, *Ally Sloper*, Rider Haggard, Fenimore Cooper, Talbot Barnes Reed...'

John JR referred to 'standards.' This appears to have been his father's favourite word, also used as a system of progression at his youngest son's school. Perhaps John SR valued these as desirable goals above the more anal and hypocritical 'discipline' and 'restraint' so typical of the period. Here, standards are an attainment, not an imposed directive. So, there is this constant, barely articulated, feeling about the Allsops', that one must always look up and out, beyond the restrictions of your class to a Jerusalem beyond; quite what this was may not have been known, even to John SR. Certainly, he did not feel the need to home in on and exploit his youngest son's personal strength in English.

To be fair, his youngest was turning out to be a thoughtful, quiet, lad. Vocal dissent before his father was never really on the cards, so it is doubtful his son clearly articulated what he wanted. John JR had been progressing well at school and his father had been earning enough to offer the boy a choice of Grammar Schools at Batley or Leeds. It must have been some relief to him that his quiet son did not push for the more expensive of the two. John was not that wealthy. 'So, I sat at Batley.' Passed by his examiners, the poor boy faced a six mile daily walk – three miles each way – to a town considered not quite far enough to justify public transport.

Here, his attraction to English finally received some

encouragement and he was introduced to the Sciences. The courses were now more specialised, taught by men with degrees. But this opportunity for attainment was, initially, marred by bullying. His new cap was used as a football while he, personally, was often slung unceremoniously over the school wall. With his quiet demeanour, the boy was 'asking for it' to the kind of thugs who wouldn't have got one over on brother Walter. But spare no sympathy; he had been taken by surprise. As quarrymen, Allsops were no weaklings. 'After these baptisms I settled in quite well, taking my share as an 'old' boy in inflicting the indignities on later 'new' boys.' Heartened by this new found, toughened exterior, John Jr. went on to gain a 'Cambridge Local' certificate.

In his mind, his youngest son was working his own way out. It was not *literary* learning that John JR was warming to, anyway. It had been his comics' *visualisations* of stories and his gift book *Great Events*, marrying picture, text, and pictorial text, which brought on an exhilaration of the senses. Shape and sound fascinated more than meaning. But he was reminded, more than once, of the importance of an occupation.

'I got the notion to be a commercial traveller influenced, largely, by a Mr. Benson who lived near by. He seemed to me to live a free and prosperous life, always well dressed, debonair and sociable. My father asked him to call and give his advice. To my disappointment he poured cold water on the idea. I don't know why! So, the next on my 'list' was a clerical worker...I became an office boy.' The relief from manual labour this environment seemed to offer, had not been unknown to John JR, having watched favoured brother Walter on his jaunts between 'rapping,' while the youngest son almost certainly sat in with his father between classes.

It was about now, in 1903-4, that John Sr.'s health had begun, noticeably, to fail: gastritis causing the hands on demands of quarry management to take a back seat. Unfortunately, his greater reliance upon office administration had not really helped as, throughout, he'd still maintained his chapel duties. With no immediate break from the family in sight, John Sr. offered his youngest son daytime work with him, in the office. John JR reported that as he progressed, his father gave him private lessons in Pitman's Shorthand, clearly showing a new interest in his various courses of study. It is also likely that he witnessed a burgeoning restlessness that needed an outlet. John JR was leaving his boyhood behind.

'At about age fifteen or sixteen, boys of my association, getting restless of the limitations of attending Sunday School and feeling that they were over the junior children's class, drifted away, taking walks in the country lanes on Sunday afternoons... After Sunday evening's service, in small groups, it was the thing to parade the town main street. There, they would meet girls of the same age, also seeking some freedom from home restrictions.'

Morley's Annual Carnival of 1904, held in the Cricket and Football Grounds, was the meeting place for pubescent expressions of celebration, or 'parading.' A rare, much sought after excuse for meeting girls, this was still the Edwardian era where, outside the showing off, 'we knew the limits beyond which we didn't venture.' Transformed into a public park, a brass band played odd, instrumental segues of Music Hall numbers and the more up-tempo Christian hymns. Apparently, they were a mainstay of such events, rather than just background ambience, being taken quite seriously as shows in themselves across the West Riding. At this event 15-year-old John met a round faced girl of the same age named Mary Halliday. 'A bonny lass, chestnut-brown hair in ringlets, and the loveliest brown eyes, which spoke volumes.' (Of what, he doesn't recount).

With the same group of mates, who had themselves been

parading and courting with the girl's friends, John met Mary on their own West Yorkshire turf of Beeston; in Old Lane and Cross Flatts Park. By the time they were sixteen, the gang had split into fours, (of two men and two women) and, inevitably, into couples.

Mary had accompanied her mother, three sisters and one brother from Horwich, Lancashire about seven years before, when her father had died, to the little Millshaw Cottage, Beeston. Little is known about Mr. Halliday, other than he divided his life, while there, between earning his keep as engineer at a cotton mill and playing cricket, professionally, for the Lancashire County team. His widow, Sarah, consequently moved back to the town her forebears knew better than any other: Beeston. The familiarity of the town turned out, not only to be a form of reassurance for her, but a place of employment for her daughters, 'helping the family budget.' This at a time when the working woman was – still - a novelty.

Most of the Hallidays' relations were trades people. Mary's grandparents ran their home as the village store, 'using the tiny front window as a show place.' Uncles, on her mother's side, ran a blacksmith shop. They, with various cousins, shared responsibility in a carpentry / joinery family firm. Mary, herself, printed upon patent leather at the local tannery. As with Mary's late father, Cricket was the Hallidays' favoured sport and pastime and, even if distant relations weren't close, it is likely that they bumped into each other at Yorkshire – Lancashire matches on a semi-regular basis. This, then, was a community so close-knit as to be an oligarchy in miniature. In 1904-5, when John Allsop Jr. was introduced to Mary's family, Beeston had remained structurally unaltered since the mid-18th Century, but soon paid the price of sleepy complacency. 'A cluster of old cottages, a church – St. Mary's – two public houses, a few larger, detached houses...It still retained its rural aspect. A brick air vent in the fields gave evidence of former coal-mining activity, an old mill, tumbledown now; a tannery on the edge of the hamlet, were the only signs of industry. The farmlands took over the rest of the area.' John suggests Leeds Council – only two miles away – suddenly woke up to its picturesque and accessible potential, making it popularly residential within the next five years; a portent too prosaic to raise much vocal concern.

2
1904 – 1919:
Co-Ops'

On the cusp of manhood, John JR struck an almost priest-like figure; a slender, rangy frame topped by a calm, gentle expression, slender nose and cheekbones, very pale, deep-set and quietly observant light blue eyes, with brown hair swept back from the temples. A benevolent, reassuring presence, which would only increase with the years. Mary Halliday succumbed instantly. John was non-threatening, respectful and fairly well educated compared with most of the local lads whom she found loud, vain and intrusive. It is not clear what made the attraction mutual enough to really mean something for John. She certainly caught his attention, but he never expands on this. There is a sense he resigned himself to a fate he neither asked for nor felt single-minded enough to reject. 'What will be, will be.' A maxim followed by his ailing father in the pulpit.

During 1905, his girlfriend's family left the small Millshaw Cottage for a terraced house, no larger, in the nearby village of Holbeck. 27, Cross Flatts Grove sat as one of a like-minded line off the main road to Leeds. John found the village 'an uninspiring, sprawling collection of factories, small dwellings, railway and canal systems.' However, the maintenance of the fatherless family budget had not been interrupted en route. John still saw them as 'very closely-knit...mother and home pre-eminent. A warm welcome greeted relatives and friends, a table of good Yorkshire fare always provided.' John melded into their company, without realising Mrs. Halliday's approval might have been an issue, such was the hit he made with them. Sarah was most likely relieved that Mary had chosen the courteous, upwardly mobile John, rather than another Beestonite lad. So, it was, 'he'll do,' as soon as he passed through the front door. With the insurance of a prospective wife, John remained at home, now alone and closer to his weakening father. John seemed to gain courage from this new intimacy and John Sr. had time for his youngest, showing at least a glimmer of interest in his administrative courses. 'Father was not demonstrative, but one felt he was concerned in one's well being' and 'quietly proud of the name I was making at the office,' John states with characteristic tact.

During 1906 – 07, John's desire to break out in his own right found a home he could somehow relate to. Growing up with two such close family units as the Allsops' and Hallidays' had instilled in him a feeling of sanctuary that was now second nature. Far too conservative to ever actually rebel, John, at eighteen, stumbled upon a compromise that seemed to offer both the independence he was seeking and a sense of mutuality with common purpose.

One day he flicked through a copy of *Co-Operative News*: the Co-Operative Society's organ. He may have been partly inspired by his stepmother, who was a member of her local branch. Among the advertisements for 'managers, buyers and others,' appeared a vacancy for office secretary. John applied to such posts on numerous occasions until the offer of an interview finally arose. He accepted with a festering impatience, only to find it led him down a, possibly, dead end route of filing and form-signing that is the dread off all attracted to the office environment. But, with a limited amount of travelling, acting as rep., beyond Leeds bounds, it had compensations. 'I learned to meet people and to have confidence in moving out of what had been...a close-knit community.'

Perhaps his new employer had missed the point, but John

wanted something more, of which this job represented just a part.

The next three years in John's life appear vague and short on extant detail. The disappointment of his first job was alleviated by continuing home courses in administration and a safety net opening for the post of junior clerk at the office of the local Co-Operative Society.

'The salary was 5/- a week but, having shown extra merit at the test examination, I was engaged at 6/- a week, to my pride and joy!' He learned to type in the office during the day while his father, now too immobile to commit, had hired a private tutor to continue with John's Pitman's shorthand course, one evening a week. (Clearly, this soon frustrated him, as he took up its study again some eight years later). Subsequent Passes in book-keeping, management, and 'Public Auditorship,' confirmed John's faith in his own abilities, this latter making him, without a hint of smugness, 'one of thirty-seven successful candidates out of the whole of Britain.'

In 1911, aged twenty-two, came a watershed in John's life that, in many ways, defined him as a man and potential careerist while changing his home life forever. Still intent upon a secretaryship, he'd had more interviews at co-operatives' at Earley, Grimsby and Coventry, but each ended as 'we'll let you knows'. Then, early autumn, a letter dropped through John SR's door, from someone his son had never applied to, but who'd clearly been made aware of him. It was an invitation for interview at Ealing Tenants Ltd., in London. The prospect of 'my leaving home, the last of the children to do so, may have given father a feeling of sadness, but we both assumed an air of inevitability. My own regrets were more than covered by an exhilaration of achievement. For a few years I had ambitiously looked forward to a secretaryship, and the prospects in the co-partnership organisation were good.' There was no going back.

The question, now, concerned Mary's reaction. Just as John was once 'expected' to join the role-call of Allsop quarrymen, so it would have been assumed by the Hallidays' that Mary would age, an 'old Beestonite.' Could she really make the break? Discussions between them are not recorded but she would not have gone south willingly, even for the man she loved. John wasn't voraciously career-orientated as it was, but Mary was even less so, very much accepting of her role as homemaker, with her mother and sisters reassuringly close to hand. Any initial, genuine excitement for her future spouse would undoubtedly have been tempered by subsequent feelings of imminent loss. Giving him up, though, never appeared an option. Love had solidified into partnership; John's preferred state of affairs.

John records the November day he arrived in London as 'dull, heavy, misty, not at all inspiring.' He notes the change of scenery from Morley, 'with its mills and chimneys and compact streets of dwellings,' to 'emerging into Haven Green (where) I had an impression of spaciousness, cleanliness, and graciousness, so different to the scene I had left behind...' From Leeds to London, he then boards the new tube service from Kings Cross to Ealing Broadway. Much of his enthusiastic, descriptive language gives a fictional feel to the following account, but his love of landscape art rings true.

'Arriving at the offices in the Garden Village, Brentham, where the interview took place, I had absorbed, quickly, the beauty of the tree-lined streets, the beautifully designed cottages, the gardens still flowering...' There is a suggestion John was offered the post on the spot with a significant rise in wages – particularly for the time – to 35d., from the 24d. he had been earning in Morley, rising a further 5d. after the obligatory three-month trial. It was a proud man who returned to Mary at Beeston, with a start date of January

1912. Christmas was enhanced for them, still further, with the announcement of their engagement, with the proviso – most likely from the determinedly staid Mary – that John completed the three-month trial.

'The Society let us have a small flat in Holyoake Walk, (Ealing), and there we began our new life together. The impact upon Mary of her home and surroundings was, at first, disturbing; away from the family and friends, contacting strangers and different living conditions did take some adjusting.' Added to this would have been the isolation felt of living in, what was then, a ground floor flat. The couple kicked up enough of a fuss for the Co-Operative to move them to 'a small cottage with a garden, front and back' before the summer. This new address, 70, Meadvale Road, was near Brentham; home to the Garden Village Movement and the offices in which John was now at work. He describes their new home in glowing terms as if it were a little part of the West Riding made flesh.

' 'Every man his garden' – the precept of the founders of the Garden Village Movement, were faithfully adhered to, with a result gratifying to the eye and, no doubt, to one's physical fitness. Come spring and the blossoming of cherry almond trees along the pavements presented an unforgettable picture. Acacia's pendulous fingers - apple and pear bloom - gave added beauty.'

Such an aesthetic sense would soon be passed on. Mary may well have become infected by John's new sense of communal worth and slowly taken to this new life from here. Certainly, Holbeck had become a rather drab and run-down village by the reign of Edward VII, with demolitions and re-buildings occurring on a semi-regular basis. One street, off Old Lane, offered terraces with bay windows, as a cursory nod to middle class gentility, but this was its limit of aesthetic intent.

The previous year saw the introduction of Land Values Duties. These were having a negative effect on the acreage of land that could be released for development. Consequently, over the next four years, London lost more accommodation through demolition than could be replaced. From 1914, the accepted family unit would no longer be united, physically, for Government consideration, so widening the gulf between them still further.

During the summer of 1912, enthused with his significantly increased wage packet of 40d. a week, John bought a piano for Mary. A rather austere, old-fashioned, woman tutor was brought in for lessons; fingers clasped, elbows protruding, her skirts sweeping down the garden around her, and formally bowing as she entered their small hallway.

'Mary sang the popular songs of the day. Occasionally we would try a duet, but as I have no musical sense...the result was not encouraging.' No: John preferred combining the aesthetic and literary pleasure to be had from 'learning the rudiments of floriculture.' On a sunny afternoon, he could be seen lounging in a hammock, reading, and then working on their meagre, but beautifully disciplined little garden of roses and fuchsia. From this back garden - situated on a sixty acre estate of soccer and cricket pitches, tennis courts and clubhouse -John could view what he charmingly describes as 'a picture of flannelled, soft-shoed activity.' Here, on occasion, he'd 'slip down to the bowling green...to play this old English game at which I was a fair exponent.'

During the week, he continued boning up with extra-curricular study, ever restless to better himself. First, with a swiftly disregarded course of 'a remarkable lack of direction' at Ealing College, followed by one on Statistics run by the Co-Operative Union HQ at Leman Street, East London. Just as he once familiarised himself, on foot, over the West Riding, so John saw nothing unusual in purposefully taking the long way home to familiarise himself with the City.

Evenings were taken up with a home course in his pet ambition of 'Secretaryship,' the exam of which he past, enabling enrolment as a member of the Co-Operative Services Association. This was a key development in John's life, and the most crucial shift in fortune since his move down here from Yorkshire. Now, he was no longer administrating as office assistant but taking a part in making decisions on the Society's development. He was, in effect, a chartered surveyor in his own right, acting as an agent between the house-builder and house-buyer, in these days before the Housing Association. Ultimately, his own man:

'One felt to be in a creative operation; studying lay-out plans, house plans, then to watch workmen carrying out the actual building of homes, (then) discussing with prospective tenants their new homes, arranging the financial terms, and seeing them taking up occupation... This also (applied) to the work of dealing with investors when capital was raised.'

Although not a Site Manager of the partnership, he had, in effect, overtaken his father in responsibility if not in status. No doubt John Sr. would have been proud, but his Morley based presence no longer registers after his son's departure, suggesting his responsibilities through ill health had finally claimed him. His provincial son and daughter-in-law had faced a certain amount of Home Counties snobbery on arrival due, mainly, to their Yorkshire dialects. Middle-class themselves, John and Mary were clearly working-class northerners to the ears of those that worked in London, but resided on its neighbouring estates. They were not assisted, as might have been assumed, by the Co-Partnership's Mancunian Secretary or Devonian Chairman. While the builders, many of whom were part of the Management Committee, spoke Birmingham 'Brum.'

By contrast, some prospective buyers could embarrass by their gratitude. One eccentric woman refused to be palmed-off by the handshake alone, regaling the Allsops with gifts of gloves and sherry, often draining the contents alone during enforced social visits to Mary. Refusing proffered favours herself, the woman then placed a continuous order with a local tradesman, who left a daily bottle on the Allsops doorstep alongside their milk. 'What passers-by and neighbours thought, we shuddered to think!' exclaims John with suburban unease. On another occasion, a woman would call on rent day, clearly reliant upon quiet John's brand of diplomacy, demanding to speak only to *'Mr. Alsep.'* This woman, 'who considered herself a class above most and adopted a high-pitched, commanding tone of voice and Girton accent, would, as a preliminary to dipping into her purse, very carefully and deliberately doff her gloves, finger by finger, not quite covering the fact that they were riddled with holes!'

By 1913, the Allsops' had settled into their new life. John, accompanied by Mary, began showing visiting brothers and sisters around the London landmarks he'd made a picturesque, mental note of over the previous year.

'We, in turn, spent holidays back in our home town, glad to see familiar faces and places.' Sister Pattie was impressed enough by the setting and way of life to entice husband Tom down from their home in Nelson, Lancashire, to buy a house. This was most likely achieved through John himself, as they landed just eight doors down from her brother to No. 86. When Tom was offered a job as carpenter on the building programme, a new Allsop community was born. But he quickly proved too set in his ways to 'muck in' with the communal approach, so stayed in London, finding work elsewhere. At weekends, John, Mary, Tom and Pattie, picnicked in the semi-rural country of Horsenden Hill, Perivale, Harrow-on-the-Hill, Hangar Hill and Park Royal. Led, no doubt, by John, who wondered how best to capture the beauty of the landscapes he was witnessing, while quietly munching on a sandwich.

August 1914 would slap tranquil Edwardianism across the face from a peace - and pace - to which it could never return.

'Along with most males who had not voluntarily joined the Forces, I attested under the Derby scheme. This allowed us some time for adjustment; when the call-up came it was less of a shock.' John was posted to the Queen's Royal West Surrey Regiment, and trained at Hounslow, Guildford and Crowborough; 'thoroughly hating the whole set-up, but resigned to the inevitability of it.' At Crowborough, in Sussex, he found a way of temporarily maintaining his link with nature. It isn't recorded as to who instigated the idea of adorning the barrack room with locally gathered blooms, but John discovered several local, like-minds at the base.

'As civilians they were, naturally, farm hands, gardeners, domestic workers. Instinctively, they were attracted by the Sussex countryside's flora.' While awaiting the draft to France, the lads returned from weekend rambles with armfuls of collected flowers, to be displayed in tins and jam jars salvaged from the camp's rubbish tip. The fragrance wafting through the barrack room made a welcome contrast to the sweat, fag-ash and boot polish odours other troops were taking for granted. Wild woodbines wound around the rafters, *celandine* covered the windowsills, limiting the space for the 'ladies smock' and *campion*, also found alongside the country roads and byways. What the officers thought of all this isn't recorded. It is unlikely they feared they'd not return, as the War was not predicted to last more than a few months, and the depravity of the front line was not foreseen. But, there is something oddly moving about decking a last point of call, at peace, in flowers before a conflict overseas; an act that could only happen today if it was known that change were irredeemable and the past, non-returnable.

The poor quality diet the men had endured at base brought on, in John, a bout of gastritis that lasted several weeks. The misery was compounded by the journey, aboard the troopship, that left Folkestone for Bologne. Added to this must have been the knowledge of his father's fate at its grasping fists. Drill and bayonet practice was endured through it, as he did his best not to lag behind. Tummy ache was not something destined to inspire sympathy with a war on.

'All the way up the front line I was told, "no-one went sick here." Pale and puffing, inexorably, the Medical Officer attended at the last moment he was assigned to attend the front. According to John, treatment and an improvement in his diet did not stop the seriousness of his former condition finally sinking in with his commanding officers, where, one morning, he awoke to find a tag attached to his night-shirt with 'walking case, Blighty,' penned on the label. Almost immediately, he was on a steamship back to a hospital at Stoke-on-Trent, aftercare at Rugeley, Staffordshire, before returning with the West Surrey lads at Gore Court, Sittingbourne.

Originally directed back 'on draft' to France, a group of 11 from his Regiment were seconded to Mesopotamia. Viewing this preferable, exotic location as an opportunity to break out of conditions he saw as cold and stark, John put himself forward to replace one of the chosen who seemed fearful of disease and, possibly, not seeing home for years.

'The Captain, preferring a volunteer...to a reluctant soldier, agreed. So, in a very short time, after a few days draft leave, I was aboard a troopship heading for Basrah, in the Persian Gulf.' John found his fellow occupants had shared his feeling that a puncture from a vaccination needle was far less a wound than penetration from exploded shrapnel. Life appeared far easier going than he'd anticipated on arrival at the Basrah camp. In fact, 'there was no drill or parades.'

With this extra time he began writing letters back to Mary, doubtful that the majority would be received. Serendipity struck a second time for John when his Staff-Sergeant strode through the barrack's 'doorless, palm-leaved huts,' demanding 'Anyone 'ere used to clerical work?' Six men got up and two were eventually chosen after an obligatory typing test, of which John was one. Reporting to Baghdad's Military Governor, Brigadier-General Hawker, installed in a large mud-brick building overlooking the Tigris, he was eventually posted (after yet more tests) as an administrative assistant to the Staff Captain 'whose duty it was to accompany the Governor, whether in the office or on outside duties.' John, with his shy sense of near-disbelief, found himself sharing his office with the two most powerful white men in the city.

While John's life may have begun contemporaneously with that of D. H. Lawrence in the neighbouring county, his life from here reads closer to that of T.E. Indeed, John recalls that 'constant movement between VIPs' and the two Governors brought us in (indirect) contact with eminent visitors; we heard of the exploits of Miss Bell and a young man who later became known as Lawrence of Arabia.' Whether he expected it or not, Mexborough's John Allsop was now a servant to the British Empire's elite. Being instinctively Conservative, this wouldn't have posed a problem. With a war on, it wasn't an issue demanding attention, in any case, from the rank and file.

Had it been possible to be so wise before the event, John and a fellow Sergeant, returning one night to their billet from the city, might have avoided an attack from an Arab wielding a knife. Grabbing the Sergeant from behind, he raised the weapon above his head, and was about to plunge it into his neck when a military policeman appeared.

'Our assailant dashed off, lost in the dark, murky bazaars,' according to John. Although straight from the annals of Buchan, John's archaic, fiction-like choice of wording does not discount its authenticity. The tension caused by unresolved matters of land rights, adjudicated by the unwanted but all-powerful British, around 1916, made token expressions of martyrdom inevitable, as John later describes:

'The main fear came from dissident Arab tribes. It was difficult to differentiate loyal and disloyal tribes. On the surface it was calm. People of many nations mixed freely in the City. Occasionally, a spy was caught. It was a grisly spectacle to witness a public execution, which took place at the Citadel, but was done purposely to impress the populace with the power of British might.' After which, 'my friend Bert (Morris) and I...kept within the City limits; it was safer.'

The growing, mutual distrust had led to an increase in incidents of Arabs silently entering the doorless billets and deftly removing rifles and ammunition from the stores. John suspected the regularity at which this occurred was due, in part, to their Bashran night guards being in league with the raiders. It was becoming increasingly difficult to know whom to trust. One morning, John was in the office with the Governor and Staff Captain when a servant brought in the coffee as requested. The sudden, inexplicable death of the Captain soon after put the kibosh on this, with the Governor viewed as the intended target.

Amidst such instability, John's continued appetite for self-improvement was pushing him up the ranks. Now a Sergeant, he was paid thirty rupees a month more than as a Corporal. Gerard, his Lieutenant, became the new Staff Captain, and John, with six other 'rankers' found himself in charge of his own office behind the legend, Market Control. 'I handled the Bills and accounts and office routine; the staff dealing with ration vouchers. The people employed...were a mixed crowd; friendly Arabs, Armenians, Caucasians and Jewish.' John enjoyed a newfound respect beyond all expectation. One of his 'rankers,' a former farm labourer called Bill Cranham, shyly confessed to John about his dyslexia. He felt he had little choice, since he was desperate to write home to his wife. John agreed. He doesn't clarify whether he dictated Cranham's words or wrote from his own head but 'his wife must have been surprised to receive such...endearing missives.'

Pitman's shorthand remained an obstacle to be overcome. Eight years after he dropped its study, he takes it up once more, this time in the company of Hall, 'a footman in civilian life – a quiet, decent lad.' But progress was still slow and inconsistent. Consequently, Lieutenant Gerard, impressed by John's attempt but with no knowledge of his success rate, had told the Governor whose own, trained, shorthand writer had gone sick. A very nervous John told Gerard about his lack of speed in this area but he waved this away with, 'just do your best.' He had nowhere else to turn. 'Every word had to be interpreted into Arabic or, vice-versa, to English. What with...the Arabic names of the accused and witnesses, I could only get down scrappy notes.' John said he was sure this meant transference back to his regiment, disgraced, but the Governor appeared understanding and imposed no penalty. This experience may have put him off Pitman for life. On paper, at least, he never refers to it again.

The Armistice of 11th November, 1918 compelled a need for patience in the men, intent upon returning to their families, they could not be expected to feel.

'The order of demobilisation was classified in order of importance of trades at home.' This 'advantage' proved double-edged. As his Regiment's only former administrator to a housing co-operative, John was fortunate to find himself prioritised, falling within the same category as the builders. But, he found his discharge ticket had to act as a Pass on a return journey to England he was expected to make alone. And, even as one of the first to be relieved of duty, he still had to wait some five long months before reaching Meadvale Road. 'I had to attach myself to any unit on the way, so that I had rations and a place to bed down.'

Fortunately, he wasn't the only priority coming home. At Karachi, India, he squeezed into an already packed troopship of relieved and restless men, continuing on through Suez, Mediterranean, the Gibraltar Straits, Biscay Bay, to the English Channel and Southampton. Relieving himself of his Army gear and discharge / reserve details at Crystal Palace, he stopped overnight, before taking the early morning train bound for Ealing on the Good Friday of 1919. 'Glorious weather and a glorious feeling that a new era had commenced. Mary was home as I had managed to let her know that I might get an early discharge, but it was overwhelming to see me so soon.' So overwhelmed was Mary that, before spring was out, she fell pregnant.

John and Mary were now 30 years of age. The mystery surrounding just what constituted their relationship is about to resume with a vengeance, as it probably did for them both at this time. Neither appear especially sexually responsive - Mary seemingly unperturbed by this - the recent War testing the temperaments of most newly wedded couples. But a sense of nagging dissatisfaction on her part (or, rather, dissatisfied nagging) can only account for the couple's movements over the next five years. For now, the priority was the unborn child.

Without his knowledge, John was being short-listed for promotion. A national demand for new housing helped increase his salary at Brentham to around £7 a week, with a share in the Co-Operative's bonus scheme. As a consequence, John completely refurbished their Meadvale Road home in time for the projected birth. Then, perhaps with only a fortnight to go, the nurse-midwife they'd engaged fell sick and cancelled her commitment to them. Amidst the panic of renewed enquiries through the Christmas of 1919, no-one else appeared forthcoming.

Finally, 'Mary settled the difficulty by promptly packing her suitcase and head(ing) for Beeston, where her mother took care of her. She was quite an experienced midwife, having attended many neighbours in that capacity.'

She remained at 27, Cross Flatts Grove, Holbeck, on 29th January 1920, until Mary's mother, Sarah, delivered them a big-eyed baby boy to the applause of cold, torrential rain and storm-force winds battering Leeds and the rest of Yorkshire. Telegraph cables and overhead tram-wires collapsed across the county, causing structural damage and, at least, two fatalities, including a railway guard in Wakefield and woollen mill worker in Huddersfield. The county had already been snowed under during John and Mary's search for the replacement midwife, through clearly inaccurate predictions of an early spring.

3
1920 – 1929:
Holbeck to Isleworth

The boy was christened 'Kenneth' in Holbeck by a registrar named Wordsworth on 3rd March, 1920. Apt, considering the baby's future. Local press reports of the time highlighted the brace of Yorkshire miners – six years before the General Strike - descending upon Downing Street to push home their demand to Lloyd George for the nationalisation of their pits. While Prohibition – the American concern - was already a matter of some debate in the Letters section of *The Yorkshire Post* – the Allsops regular delivery. Forsaken for Mary's recovery in the Entertainment section was a cornucopia of Variety: John Hart's Grand Annual Pantomime was playing *Tom, Tom, the Piper's Son*, this day, at the Leeds Grand. Mona Vivian – 'London's latest star' – had *Aladdin* at the Theatre Royal. While, 'Messrs. Green, Smith and Sleight' presented *FIZZ!* – 'a revue of the finest vintage' at The Queen's.

Amongst advertisements for *Decca*'s portable gramophone, *Sensola*, the 'soft-textured underwear,' and '*Tatcho* Hair Grower,' sit touching postscripts to the Great War. Army huts, cut price, rarely missed an issue, while a Leeds worker who'd endured months of pain from a poisoned leg outlined the miraculous cure he'd undergone thanks to regular applications of *Zam-Buk* Ointment: a hangover from Edwardian naivete.

The boy's parents had produced an infant, startling in his dark, Mongol-oval eyes, widely spaced, within an equally broad cranium, which, at first glance, combined traits of Mary with the late John SR. His name had not been an uncommon choice for the middle-classes of Edwardian Northern England: on a par with John around Leeds. Now it was more associated with the budding theatrical impresario and Tory MP: all upwardly mobile in character and intent.

Meantime, the Co-Operative planned to open a new estate near Guildford, Surrey. One Lord Onslow, supportive of the Garden Village Movement, proposed this next Garden Village to be established on a six-hundred-acre site. The existing land, Wilderness Farm, would be confirmed as part of the intended estate, supplying the residents with farm produce. Bricks, for the new houses, would be produced on the estate itself.

'There was a clay deposit confirmed by experts as suitable for brick-making.' This rural expanse was also accessible via Woking and the main line, London – Portsmouth. Ever hopeful of finally attaining a Secretaryship after fifteen years of trying, John was interviewed and offered the post of Assistant Secretary. (Ever the bridesmaid...) But, at least it afforded 'a wider field of operation' than he was experiencing at Brentham.

With Mary recovered and back from Holbeck with baby Kenneth, they took the train from Meadvale Road to inspect the area as a possible future home. The Co-Operative first drew their attention to two old cottages sitting on the highest part of the estate, known as The Fort. A legacy of the Napoleonic era, the view was breathtaking but hardly realistic for Mary, whose only form of transport was the new pram she'd have to push up, and restrain on the way back. No, they would bide their time until one of the new houses was complete. Sensible enough, considering the recent refurbishment's at Meadvale Road, but as John was now working around here, it would mean, each day, travelling back to Ealing. He put up with this for a year, maintained only by his resolve to see this intriguing project to its conclusion. It was worthwhile. With several new roads opened up to this development, Mary returned to cast her eye, once more, over a prospective property. John recalls;

'We fixed upon a semi-detached house...open to the farm lands at the back, with a splendid view at the front of the undulating estate.'

With Onslow Village – named after its benefactor – complete by 1921, John and Mary, with baby Kenneth, moved in. As with the first move from Holbeck to Ealing, Mary was not happy. <u>Still,</u> she felt distanced from the familiarity of related Hallidays' – with only one-off, housewarming visits by the curious – and the new neighbours made no effort. Also, the paths into Guildford's, then, only shopping centre, were still too steep for her with the loaded pram. Cryptically, John adds that he was 'fully occupied by office work and had very limited time for relaxation and home life.' Words of a tactful man, silently fuming. He could not have been pleased with his wife's response. As he adds; 'Board meetings were hectic, management plans scrutinised and criticised, creating an atmosphere tense and trying.'

While the estate was completed, post-war shortages of building materials – enforced by new Government restrictions – dashed hopes for further developments. The Co-Operative's Board temporarily arrested all future plans until conditions became, in their eyes, more favourable. Now a holding company, staffing levels had to be reduced to a minimum. As a clerical worker – albeit senior – John was made a victim. He doesn't put it so bluntly. But, without doubt, he was sacked. Mary now saw her chance. They would return home – to Holbeck.

John doesn't say how defeated he felt, having to return to Leeds during 1922. It must have winded him, spiritually, even in the knowledge that the whole country was suffering economic insecurity. The Great War passed with an unspoken, nationwide consensus for self-determination impossible up until 1918. The military's treatment of its own men had ensured that. In this context, a decade's worth of co-operative experience had placed John in an advantageous position. On his pride-battering return to Holbeck, John only generalises about the 'friendly welcome (easing) any anxiety we had' and this period being 'a time of stress and strain.' Once again, Sarah Halliday offered him and her daughters' shelter at her Cross Flatts Grove home. Mary was back where she felt she belonged but, like most men in this position, John could not be kept.

To some extent he had to start again, specialising in one of the many aspects his past duties. A sideline at the Ealing office had been to advise incoming tenants on insuring their property and entering into the most appropriate form of life assurance. So, on his next tram ride into Leeds, he called in on the city's Co-Operative Insurance Society:

'This office conducted all classes of insurance business, but were making an effort to build up the 'industrial' class. To an agent, this was the most rewarding, although the work entailed daily canvassing, door-to-door, in residential areas.'

John was not a natural salesman, too modest and sincere to act his way through a telephone directory's worth of clients. But he did not enjoy the luxury of choice. The wife and toddler could not be supported on his bank account indefinitely. Concentrating on what he saw as 'the better type of business called 'O.B.', and for general class such as 'Fire, Motor, Third Party,' he collected 'a modicum of policies, quite good from a commission angle.' Adding morning canvassing to his afternoon and evening shifts impressed his District Manager, a Mr. Southers, enough to promote John to his Assistant on a salary of £7 a week. Financially, he was where he was three years before and, perhaps the irony wasn't lost on John, still an assistant, with no longed for 'secretaryship' in sight. Still, he was back as a member of staff with a co-operative, so he could plan ahead from a solvent position. He and Mary, between them, were able to apply to Leeds Housing Department for a new home. John must have been particularly relieved to leave the caring, but stifling, atmosphere of Sarah and her daughters' when the offer came through of a semi-detached at Meanwood, in Leeds' rural north-east.

A time of stability settled on John and Mary. Both seemed happy here. Mary remained relatively near her mother and sisters, while John's staff job at the Co-Operative Insurance in the city centre brought, as he put it, 'many privileges.' Young Kenneth was a serious, observant toddler, with straight, baby-blonde hair and an expression of thuggish porcelain. The holiday season of 1923 saw the Allsops taking a much-needed break, in Scarborough. A surviving photograph shows John on the beach with Kenneth, sitting astride a donkey, the boy with a glum expression suggesting foiled superiority. 'Why am I doing *this*?'

John claims he and Mary had taken for granted that they would remain at Meanwood for the foreseeable future. Certainly, they needed a damned good reason to move yet again. It transpired that John, on leaving Ealing three years before, had kept in contact with at least one member of the Co-operative there. So it was, some time in 1925, when a letter arrived asking if he and Mary would like to return to Ealing. The premise was that, with economic conditions looking more favourable than when they had left, several of the Directors had formed a building company – *Building Enterprises Ltd.* - along the lines of the Garden City ideal, and were in the process of estate development, east of Lampton, in Middlesex.

'Temptingly,' recalls John, 'they offered me a leading office position at an increased salary with the promise of a house when built.' Although settled at Meanwood, the dormant idealist in John jumped at the chance to return to 'the work of estate and housing development' which door-to-door canvassing, however benign the company, couldn't hope to eclipse. Mary was more positive about the idea than he might have hoped. It isn't clear why she was willing to leave Meanwood. Perhaps her priorities had changed now she had Kenneth to consider. Perhaps she felt he needed a more urban and accessible environment. And John's former instincts had proven him right. Also, she did get on with John's sister, Pattie, who still resided at 86, Meadvale Road, with husband Tom. Maybe, Mary simply didn't realise how much she'd miss the area until she'd gone. Either way, by the beginning of 1926, the Allsops had packed up – for the fourth time in six years – and headed South.

As the finishing touches to the Middlesex estate were made, the Allsops stayed a while with Tom and Pattie. Upon its completion the family were offered a small semi-detached, situated in Spring Grove, at 83, Spring Grove Road, Isleworth, the Co-Operative making a gift of the deposit, and the balance coming as a mortgage from the local Council. Perhaps to salve his conscience and Mary's, he named it 'Cottingley,' – a favourite, rural Yorkshire village - as a reminder of their roots. John's Ealing office was walking distance away but, having now learnt to drive, he was also meeting prospective buyers further afield, at another new development; Langley, in Buckinghamshire. A sylvan period commenced for the family with John, a man of means, Mary, more at home in the South than she had ever been, and a son, now brown-fringed, Chinese-eyed, bony-legged, and endowed with a precocious curiosity his mother felt only too willing to appease.

John appears to have been a reluctant lover; at least in relation to Mary. So, Kenneth, from birth, was viewed as the prize of their union. Consequently, no material expenditure was deemed too great or unnecessary in Mary's eyes.

Audrey, John's niece by brother Willie, who was living in Beeston's Tempest Road, remembers Kenneth at High Tea Sunday visits to Holbeck, as 'attractive-looking' and 'studiously inclined,' while taking him 'proudly for a walk in his new, white sailor suit' as the grown-ups chatted. A multitude of 'posh' clothes, sweets and new model bicycles were showered upon the boy during and after his toddler years. Par for the course for today's middle-class parents but, here in the mid-1920s' – on John's relatively modest income and with Mary having left work behind at the Beeston Tannery – a major, personal sacrifice to attain. The sheer number of gifts given, each week, to arouse the boy's sensual gratification points – paradoxically – to a suspected ignorance of his spiritual needs. It is possible neither John nor Mary really knew how to handle him.

What the boy did inherit from his father, that pleased John no end, was a growing fascination for the countryside. It may have been on one of these walks that Audrey Allsop, in her unofficial capacity of big sister and an only child herself, saw Kenneth innocently carry home an owl in his school jacket lining to keep as a prospective pet. Like his father before him, Kenneth was assuming an 'outdoor temperament' and a head for retaining, then reviewing, images that intrigued him, wanting to find and follow them from their source.

'Spring Grove' – redeveloped by *Building Enterprises Ltd.* of High Holborn as part of the new Lampton Estate in Isleworth, Middlesex - represented an England on a point of no return: where urban development meant social renewal and rural stasis, social depression. This was the stark choice facing those, whose occupations now disregarded the old class distinctions. (1924 had seen the first Labour

Government initiate the Wheatley Housing Act, which provided Ministry of Health subsidies for a programme of public housing with an ultimate target of 200,000 new properties each year up until 1940).

Months passed and what the instinctively conservative John saw as 'a political group' in the area had begun to suspect a stitch-up between the reigning councillors and their apologists. John, himself, was backed into the fray, appalled to learn of a road-widening scheme, approved of by their Urban District Council, which appeared to slice off a band of the Allsops' front garden. As well as the encroachment upon their privacy, there was the question of the effect on the future desirability of the house to consider. Their civil servant neighbour, Wilfred Turner, asked John if he would join him in calling a residents' meeting to discuss the Council's ill-considered plans.

'Recognising that we had much support and a case, the plans were re-examined. To our satisfaction, an amended scheme was adopted.' Consequently, other residents on the Lampton Estate, on the back of this victory and the prospect of a heard voice, formed the Lampton Ratepayers Association. Voted in as Chairman, the gentle, fair playing John regularly found himself caught between a barrage of newly empowered citizens. 'Some bought personal problems, others (brought) party politics up for discussion.'

Adopting as neutral a position as he could, John's objectivity paid off when he was voted in as the Heston and Isleworth U.D.C.'s first Conservative councillor. In his own way, John Allsop had played a small, but key, part in this period of change that saw the re-development and resettlement of the appositely named Home Counties.

By September 1926, the child was installed at Wyndham & St. Andrew's College - the local Prep School. An eight-year period of dissatisfaction, boredom and frustration was to follow. The boy's interests were beginning to reflect those of his father at the same age; words and pictures holding the same fascination he felt compelled to express in English and Art. But the other subjects, and their teachers, were not challenging his flowering intelligence. Consequently, he was not mixing well and his circle of real friends was small. An inability to simply and confidently express himself was assured. If not a regular victim of the local bullies, the boy was in danger of turning into himself and his own desires:

'I was a holy, prudish child. My first experience of what I later could identify as a sexual tremor, came when I was six or seven.' Kenneth's parents had taken him on a visit back to his ubiquitous grandmother at Cross Flatts Grove. 'I was already then aware of uncomfortable differences between me and the local children...I was a stranger, but worse, a foreigner, and they were the aboriginals' with a native tongue and mysterious local customs, and I was an... intruder who was already conscious of speaking differently and wearing peculiar clothes, such as the orchidaceous red and black school cap and a badged blazer.' Kenneth's recollection of his first return visit to Holbeck less than two years after leaving, sounds woefully elitist and snobbish. But this wasn't penned from a perspective of class so much as of the inability to interact. For him, 'playtime' during the family gatherings was consisting of quiet, voyeuristic, dissections. He may not have been happy being apart, but it had its advantages. He was once 'uneasily' in the company of local boys and girls with 'their flat, Yorkshire voices,' and on disused shrub-land. It could have been Cousin Audrey he accompanied here who presented him to her friends. Feeling awkward and cautious, the outsider was only half-heartedly accepted into the group. The air was stifling from the sun and, after a session of hopscotch 'on an arena chalked on the flags,' they fell back exhausted, in a row, against the neighbouring garden wall. Suddenly, 'it was a little girl who started the dares. She volunteered, with taunting audacity, to take off her shoes and socks and walk, barefoot, across to the hedge and back. It was a distance of no more than 15 feet. Until that moment, I think, I had not been conscious of any difference between boys and girls. She undid her plimsolls and showed off her socks, and she skipped across the sharp stones, her grimy bare legs...' Frustrating in its own way, the anecdote cuts off here, a probable second page of notes missing. The clear upshot is of arousal to a gradual revelation that often begins a boy's initiation to the sexual experience.

When his father bought his first motorcycle as a way to avoid changing tube trains over the relatively short distance to his office, John couldn't have foreseen the second obsession in his son he was about to inspire. Quickly disillusioned by its maintenance demands and sheer weight, John was soon trading it in for a 'brand new Raleigh-type' cycle for Kenneth. Having taught the seven year-old the basics of pedalling and road sensibility, Kenneth struck fear into his parents hearts by managing to leave the house for extended periods with the clear disadvantage of being too small to reach the pedal at its furthest point from the saddle. On his daily ride to school, 'Mary and I had palpitations knowing that he had to dismount at Thornbury Road Crossing, and somehow had to remount to continue his journey.' Once his feet touched the ground, John bought him 'a French Racer-type,' which Kenneth would customise with coloured tape and shorn mudguards as he became an intent young ornithologist, seeking out the wildlife of his new, local hunting ground; Osterley Park. Conveniently situated en route to the boy's school - at the top of Thornbury Road – the acres surrounding Osterley House comprised a wood, lakes, playing field and sports ground.

While Mary may have overcompensated on her willingness to please the boy, John was forming a particularly close bond. With increasing demands upon his time in Ealing, John looks to have made the most of when he was around. Actively encouraging his son's wide-ranging interests, boxing gloves were bought and play-fights were shared. An acquired love of the new, silent Hollywood films – particularly sophisticated by 1928 - sparked off a desire in Kenneth to act out at home, and amongst his few school friends, characters and situations he had just witnessed in the darkened stalls of the local flicks, most likely in nearby Hounslow. John and Mary would help him dress up as the latest, on-screen, swashbuckling heroes – *a la* Douglas Fairbanks - with the help of his mother's second hand clothes and his father's makeshift accessories. Surviving photographs from the summer of '28, taken by John in their back garden, show Kenneth as a Roman villager, army sentry, and mob hoodlum. He especially related to these gangster and Western movies and their hedonists' spirit of adventure. Here was a way of life that left behind the reassuring cosiness of comics such as *Film Fun* and *The Champion* to seek the immediacy of danger inherent in being an outlaw or explorer on foreign territory. Having already felt what it was like to be the outsider looking in, he now found something heroic in the position. He could never relate to the crowd, anyway, so here was his vindication.

Mary's token nod at escapism was musical. On Sunday evenings, John accompanied her 'rich and dulcet voice' on their front room piano. Kenneth recalls hearing recitations of popular parlour songs of the day, such as 'Drink to Me Only With Thine Eyes,' 'Indian Love Lyrics' and Jeanette Macdonald numbers from incoming 'talkies' like *Beyond the Blue Horizon*. For him, this merely punctuated a pervading sense of loneliness around his mother that seventeen years away from Yorkshire had still yet to relinquish. In fact, an uncomfortable feeling prevails that both parents remained victims of south-east snobbism; while mutual expressions of love are as remote as ever.

Kenneth's second subtly erotic experience occurred around this time. Perhaps believing their son actually enjoyed these Sunday evenings, or from guilt at his exclusion, John and Mary hired a piano teacher for weekly lessons. She might have been in her twenties, dusky, but certainly French and married. As this short-sleeved wonder reached up for some exercise books, the boy felt a brief cold sweat pass over as a thick, black, hirsute patch flowered out from between her armpit as she stood, domineering, over him. But, in the lessons at least, he showed little interest and often made a beeline back to Osterley Park en route. His mother, of course, quite understood.

While John was away, Kenneth divided his time, like most precocious children, between an imaginative life of 'sketches, story-writing, or 'dressing-up' in his bedroom, and scouring Osterley Park, clutching his new found *Natural History Journal*. Clambering up trees, nest high, he'd carefully scoop out and study his latest acquisition for pastel-coloured birds' eggs. (A mildly illicit but not illegal practice, then). Aware of their import to the mother, the nests would not be left empty. The *frisson* of this only added to his intense but, perhaps, also unshared interest in nature.

Between the ages of nine and fifteen, Kenneth seems bereft of a soul mate in this obsession. Certainly, he had acquired friends at Wyndham & St. Andrew's; the local Prep School he was attending – a mile away off Thornbury Road – with whom he'd exchange visits to bedrooms and compare heroic acquisitions. But no one of an entirely like-mind. So, he reverted back into his own, back into an escapist, intellectual pursuit for which his *Natural History Journal* served a dual purpose.

'Books became my air-route,' he recalls. 'Even this wasn't very accessible. First, my mother had a beady suspicion and resentment of reading; she could not forbear to snap her disapproval if one hunched for too long over a book. "Your eyes will drop out. Always got your head buried in a book."' This wasn't something a potential tradesman did, but for a trades*woman*, completely taboo. A first suggestion of dissent to Kenneth from a mother who'd idolised him. She might have feared him turning out a bit too 'arty' and soft-headed as her husband was in danger of becoming since he had recently returned to carrying his sketch book on motoring holidays to Devon, recently discovered, and return, familial visits to Yorkshire. Yet, this summit of her concern reflects just how good life was for them now. 1930 commenced three years of comparative wealth for the Allsops.'

John's almost accidental entry into local politics had the upside of 'a strong social element and club life.' But, the inevitable elites were forming, while travelling expenses to business-related dinners were proving a drain. Consequently, he claims his supporters, boosted by the influence that accompanied a new-found voice, decided he also should become more accountable to them, appointing a sub committee to dissect the council's agenda and also 'advise' John on how to vote at council meetings. Not surprisingly, the independently minded Allsop found this intolerable, and continued to vote the way he saw fit.

'This did not improve my popularity with the small committee!' he reflects. 'I would not be deflected and pursued my own way until an election became due, when the U.D.C. became a Borough Council.' Declining a further nomination, John cryptically states that he 'ceased public life' as a consequence. We may never know whether the disagreements were political or if he was simply, unceremoniously dumped in the Council's transition of June 1929. Either way, John could now afford to bear such disappointments. He had become a respected figure from his years of service with the Co-operative, and, through continuing involvement in the developments required for a swiftly swelling population, found himself wealthier than he had ever been. As the people continued to pour in, so the demand for housing increased.

The Edwardian era was well and truly over as the country attempted to meet the demands of a people who were marrying earlier, living longer and travelling easier, thanks to a long awaited and coherent system of public transport. Between 1921 and 1935, the population of Heston and Isleworth would be seen to double. Meanwhile, nearby Hounslow was growing in popularity with a new, commuter set buying and selling in ever-greater quantities. Distribution links for the import and export of related goods and services was prioritised at both Government and local levels. Before 1929 had ended, John would have heard about the proposed underground rail link at Osterley, to serve the Piccadilly Line and directly connect Spring Grove Road to what was fast becoming the most important trade route in England. And new housing developments north of Hounslow were allowing for ease of access to it. So, John was once more looking north, but he didn't have to look too far in that direction to see where his family's future lay.

John and Kenneth holidaying in Devon, 1934.

Another shot of Kenneth on the Devon holiday, 1934.

4
1930 – 1935:
The Great West Road

The post-war, literary middle-classes despised the Great West Road. Transcending party politics, the half-articulated consensus was of a 'tarmacamid slash' slicing through Blake's England, and purely for the shallow, exploitative needs of commerce. The playwright, J.B. Priestley, John's contemporary from the West Riding, felt it 'looked very odd. Being new, it did not look English. We might suddenly have rolled into California.' He could not comprehend the line of new factories, flanking either side, looking so unlike those of his own Yorkshire boyhood, and more like displays from 'the Franco-British Exhibition.'

Fellow writers queued-up to wrinkle their noses at what they saw as they motored down this never-ending dual carriageway. 'Pass on to High Wycombe, where industrial vulgarity is in supreme command,' wrote Howard Marshall. S.P.B. Mais's heart sank at 'the long suburban street...indifferently labelled,' but also pondered on what 'the aesthetic outlook of children born in the new houses that border the Great West Road will be like? Here is neither town nor village, but an aggregation of row upon row of houses that are presumably fitted with every labour-saving gadget, but lack any semblance of character.' But Mais also found what must have initially struck John; the saving graces of the London Passenger Transport Board's sports ground and club house, and the Art Deco appearance of factories such as *Firestone Tyres*, and the carved stone entrance and orange-gold tinted facing brickwork of the brand new *Jantzen* Knitting Mills; both companies from the U.S.A.

There is little doubt that John's decision to move there was a mainly commercial one. It is likely he was personally involved in the developments being built alongside the new five and a half-mile extension that passed through Osterley. As the chartered surveyor he now was, he did not share the middle class's disdain for new public properties. The quality of workmanship was what mattered. Besides, had he not grown up with a fascination of English from the pictorial quality of words writ large upon advertising hoardings? By the spring of 1930, John had apparently convinced Mary of the wisdom in moving.

Still unhappy in the South, she was, nevertheless, resigned to this looming commercial prospect outweighing any parochial-sounding preferences she might voice. She half-heartedly consoled herself to Kenneth that it had 'plenty of life' from 'the ceaseless hurl of anonymous, non-local traffic – especially on fine Sunday mornings.' Never gregarious herself, Mary may also have tired of the effects that the small town, sectional infighting, by the self-appointed sub-committee, had upon John on his late night returns home.

Kenneth was not complaining. He would now be even closer to Osterley Park, just a short dash north up nearby Ridgeway Road to its outskirts. Upon its completion, John, Mary and Kenneth became the first residents of a house named 'Roxburgh,' and its exceptionally high number of 717. There is an ominous metaphor apparent in John's attempts to paper over the blandness of their new home, with a veneer of cut-price, rather facile, grandeur, clear from first glance. Kenneth later evoked memories of the short path up to the front door, which was 'crazy-paved – apparently, perfectly good York stone had been deliberately smashed to get the desired pixy look and healed by cement sutures,' while ill-disguised 'paperish wood, which had warped, concave-like shavings, were nailed together and stained black to create a dim William Morris-ish, Tudor cottage, effect,' and displayed on the frontage above a front door already featured with 'small, chunky squares of frosted glass.'

In response to the disappointment he had endured as a Councillor, John determinedly began scouting round for vacant floor space from which to run his own concept of a business. He had, after all, gained enough allies and all-round knowledge of both the administrative and practical sides to property building and selling as a foundation upon which to build his own career as a chartered surveyor. Equally, he was approaching middle age and tired of taking orders, as the sub-committee debacle had revealed. Based in Hounslow High Street, over the next two years John would take advantage of the new prosperity by opening no less than three well-situated offices in the region; a second in Hounslow, one back at Spring Grove Road, (No. 49), and one in the Great West Road itself, sharing directorship responsibilities with two Co-Operative colleagues; W.S. Gaiger and A.G. Morris. With grim defiance for greater things, they founded the operation as *'SUPREMACY CONSTRUCTIONS LTD. BUILDERS & PUBLIC WORKS CONTRACTORS.'* Kenneth later described how John saw himself at this time:

'My father was, in the early 30s', one of the new generation to which the *Daily Express* was beginning to make its coruscating appeal. Indeed, the very class it was instrumental in creating: the pre-Gambol suburbanite, the acquisitive, small business entrepreneur, the pusher on the underground...My father saw his own hopes and problems reflected - graphically - in the Little Man. He voted for the Conservative Party because (I infer) it seemed to represent what his aspirations were and what his expectations might reasonably be, and also because he was strenuously – and not easily – escaping from what should...have been his life as a man who worked with his hands in the stone quarries of Yorkshire...'

There is a photograph of the Allsops' in 1931, taken outside the Middleton home of Jack Halliday, Mary's brother. Their background – in both meanings of the term – contrasts sharply with their appearance. Each of them is particularly well dressed. John, typically reserved, but particularly tanned and confident. Kenneth, smugly grinning, baize-suited with a cravat, handkerchief and *Brylcreem*ed parting across his broad brow, completing an effect of Lord Snooty precocity. Between and behind both, upon the crumbled remnants of a garden wall, sits Mary, with a smile identical to her boy's, her left hand firmly gripping her 11 year-old son's right elbow for all she is worth. They do not look like a family a mere twelve months away from the devastating effects of the Great Depression.

How the Depression specifically effected John's business isn't personally recorded. But he had overreached himself. The consequences swiftly threatened ruin, just as he and his colleagues were gaining ground. He could only continue by cutting his rented space by half. One of the Hounslow offices and that at Spring Grove – open barely two years – had to close, leaving John only the Registered Office in Hounslow High Street and that at Great West Road. Stoically, he was to retain this address, but had little choice but to spend more of his time working from home. Kenneth's frustration with school was compounded by a deteriorating relationship with Wyndham & St. Andrew's: a privately owned and cheaply run public institution, in a state of disrepair – spiritually as well as structurally, in his son's view.

Never demonstrably close – even for the period - the onset of the Depression and middle age affected John and Mary's relationship quite badly. A coolness developed between them; the once regular piano recitals the first casualty. Conversation dwindled to monosyllables. John developed an ulcer, soothed only by a glass of warm milk, sipped after an eerie evening of silent withdrawal into his account ledgers. Kenneth later suspected he was constantly adding up the same figures. Feelings of failure must have surpassed those of eight years earlier, as he had fallen from a considerably higher plateau. Three now unaffordable cars sat idly in a large, purpose-built, asbestos garage at the bottom of their garden, partially hidden by ever-lengthening stems of Virginia Creeper. Inevitably, two were soon sold. Meanwhile, Mary would silently leaf through a copy of *Picturegoer* under the broad-leaved shade of what she called her 'stag plant,' lost in her own thoughts.

Amidst this domestic atmosphere, Kenneth continued to please himself. For some time his father had been teaching him the rudiments of painting at the dining table, last thing before bed. But that was during the good times. His parents' inability to articulate put paid to this, causing an introspection more than ever concentrated upon his reading. Left to his own devices, he also acquired a love of jazz from listening to the wireless set, that was 'originally a speaker decorated with dried poppy pods, later replaced by a *Pye*, with the rising sun in fretwork relief as fascia for the speaker, which swung on a turntable so as to adjust finely with the fingertip to improve reception of the Western Brothers or Lew Stone, via the Daventry station.' During bird-watching jaunts through Osterley Park, he began showing off to his friends by miming the instrumental performances of well-known jazz musicians or singing in their style.

These theatrical re-enactments were symptomatic of the nullifying boredom and frustration he was feeling at school. Nothing inspired him. Its Edwardian attempts at discipline had no goal or sense of purpose in his eyes. Consequently, the course work he was producing looked uninspired and mediocre. In class, although no regular troublemaker himself, he found his attention often wandering to, and being amused by, the class's 'black marker'; the boy notorious for talking, joking, and often ordered out of lessons. Only at English did he show a natural ability that his teacher, here, was ill equipped to advance. But, in this, Kenneth required no encouragement. Set poems and short stories were opportunities snatched from heavy-lidded efforts at concentration and turgid reciting. Of less instinctive interest, his illustrative skills were gaining good reports; thanks, mainly, to his father's earlier tutoring. It was the other subjects that were the problem. It was clear that Kenneth had a special gift for words and pictorial description that negated extra learning.

Mary's response to this was odd but not unprecedented for the time. She simply kept him home; and on a fairly regular basis. As someone with only a basic grounding of formal education herself, there was little guilt attached. Besides, she had an additional motive. Her Kenneth was not a healthy lad, right now. Flu, repetitive colds, and recurring 'sties' over the eyelids replaced each other on an almost fortnightly basis. He was entering puberty paying for an imbalance in diet caused by his mother's continued smothering supplication. What Kenneth wanted, Kenneth invariably got. She had bowed to his expectation of sweetmeats over red meat or greens without question. And, even if he was about to enter manhood, such acquiescence wasn't about to end now.

John realised that his son remaining home - only to be spoiled - was not a position with any future. Perhaps he could school Kenneth in the ways of office administration, as his father did for him thirty years before. Although, not surprisingly, the boy had shown no interest in his father's affairs, Kenneth was his only heir and likely to remain so.

So, to whom else could he pass on the business? He pondered on this as 1933 came to a close.

On Christmas Day, amongst the smart shirts, shoes, and gorging supply of chocolate and coconut-ice that continued piling up around the 13-year-old through these otherwise lean years, a slim, leather, brown-backed, *Charles Letts* diary, decorated on the inner facings by a well-wrought and colourful landscape painting of birds. This diary – seventy years on – survives, and is well worth close study. Since the move to this address in 1930, Kenneth's life revolved around a quintet of school chums. Clifford Read has the most mentions, as do his parents, whose Hounslow address points to them being friends of John and Mary from their days at Spring Grove. Frank Childs lives with his, and not far from the Allsops', at a house along the Great West Road curiously named 'Minehead.' John Collins brings an element of dangerous adventure into Kenneth's life, through late evenings of exploration for local girls along the Road, while Roy Summerhayes makes sporadic appearances for appointments made but rarely kept. Ron Waldren appears belatedly on the scene, while his sister, Margaret, was quietly heading toward a more superior score in her English finals than anyone else in the school, including her brother's new, clever-clever, friend. Kenneth has acquired a small terrier he calls Boy; a stray he picked up that had followed him from Osterley Park one day in 1932.

It is a place of boyish liberties, taken on property made recently – but not obviously - private, as Outer London's rural fields become encroached upon by the brickwork boundaries of the new light industries. Kenneth on his customised, French-style bike and his fellow cyclists seek out the bird-life where they can, the diversity of which, if not the number, remains bountiful. (It is hard to picture Kenneth being anywhere but out at the front, making sure he leads these expeditions). They speed across the cabbage fields adjoining Osterley Park, the flat allotment land of Harlington Road and Bath Road, the scrub land frequented by gypsies next to Brentford, the path parallel to its tube line that runs south alongside the Great West Road and between its new factories built upon former sports fields. The school-capped, blazer-wearing lads running the gauntlet of irritable adult cyclists, occasional motorist and threatening site owner. For Kenneth, at least, an exhilarating burst of adrenaline much needed between the omnipresent, debilitating lack of dietary fibre.

On New Years Day, 1934, he awakes with toothache; no doubt from the sugar-laden diet over Christmas. On the 29th, his 14th birthday, 'a frightful sty on my right eye.' The following day the tooth was pulled at last by a local dentist. 'He gave me 4 shots of cocaine. It hurt. But I was determined <u>not</u> to holler out.' The day after this: 'My sty's as big as a football.' And again: 'in afternoon had tummy-ache. *I don't know what I'm made of:* styes' (sic), toothache, indigestion.' Officially, he'd returned to school on Wednesday 10th January, but once all these symptoms had finally passed, rather than going back, he was helping his father, down the Road, or bussing to the office at Hounslow High Street, acting as gopher for John's partner, George Morris. 'I'm getting quite efficient,' Kenneth announced. On 22nd February a concerned son confided; 'Dad a bit worried about business. He wants me to go into the office <u>now</u>...' On the Sunday morning of 4th March, a further disablement. Attempting to climb over a fence of spiked railings with John Collins, he slips and almost impales himself. An aggrieved visiting uncle (probably Tom, with Auntie Pattie) gives him 6d. for his pains.

The following day, Kenneth relates his very first anecdote; 'On the radio a man was to give a speech on the national character, but when he came to the mike he said, "I was to deliver a speech, but as I resent the way in which the speech was cut by the BBC, I will give the full speech to the press," and he went away...' That Saturday, the Reads visit the Allsops. Kenneth's voice had presumably broken by now, attaining a slightly nasal, but low, burr since, 'We played at broadcasting. I pretended I was Cab Calloway. Cliff and lots of others say I'd make a good rhythm singer.' The following day he followed homework with cutting and pasting pictures 'of movie stars and aeroplanes' in his bedroom. On Tuesday 20th March, he ponders that, 'the traffic on the Gr(ea)t W(est) Rd makes one wonder where it all came from...'

The 21st heralds the start of the bird-nesting season. But Kenneth has already acquired examples of eggs from one hundred different specimens, seeing no need to clear the nests. On Saturday 24th he arrogantly proclaims that he, John and Cliff 'beat up a couple of fresh ducks.'

Meanwhile, John JR seems genuinely pleased by his son's contribution to the business. With insurance a continuing, lucrative sideline, he gives Kenneth six shillings & six pence for his help. The 25th was a prematurely sweltering day, upon which Kenneth cycled to the opening of Osterley Station, built as a route to the Piccadilly Underground. On the 5th April he finds two robins building their nest in the toolbox of his father's shed. With rare but genuine humility – almost out of kilter with the rest of the diary – he quietly adds, 'I hope they are not disturbed. It will be nice and sheltered for them.' This robins' nest becomes the boy's main object of concern over the rest of the month as he makes for the shed each evening to watch its completion with the addition of eggs and chicks. On 10th April, at Osterley Park, he, Cliff and John find a haystack, throw down their bikes, and drag it up a nearby tree to build a nest of their own. 'Had a ripping game in it,' he exclaims, announcing their gang was now called, with a jazz-like allusion, 'The Kenonian Trio.' Here ensued illicit talk of local girls, smoking of *Park Royals*, and reading of the sacred book.

Olympia had become a venue the Allsops attended annually. On Tuesday 2nd January, Kenneth marvelled at the touring Bertram Mills Christmas Circus. Later, still buzzing, he sees a display, which ignites within him a 'flesh-creeping awe' that will remain for years.

'After the performance, I cajoled (my mother) into a lengthy tour of the sideshows, the distorting mirrors, pinball machines and shooting galleries installed in that concrete and girder cavern...I came to a stop before a huge and ugly car, a saloon constructed like a tank: ...it was a 40 h.p. V8 Cadillac, custom-built in 1928, at a cost of £6,000, for Mr. Capone... There was a placard on the dais...announcing: THE CAR OF SCARFACE AL CAPONE, KING OF THE GANGSTERS. Alongside there was a gallery of photographs of the king himself and his courtiers, many of them flash-lit in uncomfortable postures, damp with their own blood in gutters and on the bullet-ripped upholstery... Presiding over the exhibit which had, I later learned, been bought by a British speculator after Capone's enforced retirement from gang-rule in 1931, was a young man in chalk-stripe flannels, a sports coat with pleated pockets, and a bow tie. Business was slackish, and while pattering away with the spiel about the car's lurid history, he lifted me into the driving seat...and said: "Imagine, kid, that you're driving through Chicago with a rival gang after you going *rat-a-tat-a-tat-a-tat-a-tat*." I did... Then came (the diary's) awed footnote: 'I actually handled a real Thomson sub-machine gun."

Kenneth wrote this in 1961. It reveals a cool, amoral interest at full throttle for a time at which it had only just ignited. He adds that soon after this revelation, a visit to his Aunt Pattie at Ealing, sparked a further expansion in interest of Americana. Passing an open-fronted comics' shop, amongst the hoped for copies of *Gem*, *Magnet* and Nelson

Lee Library, were American pulp magazines, such as *True Confessions* and *Real Detective*. Alongside are picture-covers of women 'in black stockings and kami-knickers hanging upside–down off divans to talk on the telephone' and 'smudgy photographs of corpses, police line-ups...and gangsters' molls... I began, somewhat furtively, to buy these. Parental opposition apart, even to me they looked rancidly morbid – but none the less fascinating.' The culture shock experienced by John and Mary must have reflected badly upon Kenneth at the time, but this is not recorded. What is certain is that here was the darker, closer-to-home, territory of the hero he could relate to. The movies offered the glamour; these magazines, the illicit spice and sensuality his burgeoning manhood could rightly covet. Kenneth could never quite re-capture such delicious interest from the Olympia. He still had responsibilities to maintain as an only son, expected to follow his father. On the 12th April, the Ideal Homes Exhibition was staged. 'Heath Robinson's house was a scream...We saw some glass-blowing being done...Saw Sidney Barnes and his band there.'

Early the following week, John told Kenneth that he was so impressed by his help over the previous month that, as from Wednesday, he would take him on at the Great West Road office as an unofficial employee. On the Saturday a previously proud Kenneth was deflated to report that having received his first wage, 'I only got 5/-; ½ crown for me and ½ for Ma.' (While he had become 'posh' since leaving Leeds at age 5, he is still referring to Mary colloquially, rather than using 'Mother' or 'Mummy').

Deterred enough by this to concentrate more on his own paperwork than his father's, Kenneth sneaks use of the office typewriter to complete a short story he's been working on. Before the week is out it is complete. In his own mind, he has become a part of the adventure. 'My pen name is Val St.

John, pronounced Sijon.' Set in August 1917, 'Cameo of the Air' concerns a dogfight between Air Corps fighter ace, John Stone, his compatriot, Jack Meyers and their 'Hun' enemy, Karl Visdecht. In spite of the occasional, naive spelling and confusion – on Kenneth's part – as to who is 'Jack' and who 'John' – there is an ingenious use of character informing the plot's resolution as the British men cruise 'slowly to and fro' over German lines, and association of guilt through a similar 'recklessness' in the past. After successfully downing Stone's plane, it is the same recklessness Meyer characteristically used that lands the wicked Visdecht into British hands, where the latter had mistakenly expected to land amongst those of his own people. Inspired by, but a literary advance on, the strip-fiction in *Gem* and *Magnet* he weekly devoured. It is more knowingly Buchanesque in feel and pace. He is exploring a newfound love of the language, indulging in adverb, adjective and pronoun in a way that was to alter very little through his life. Witness how 'John heard the *staccato revvings* of some German 'Mercedes' engines,' and 'he threw the ship out of that first *treacherous* burst,' while 'strut-wires *shrieked like stricken demons*': a burgeoning voice alliterative and precise.

Two days on from its completion, he celebrates, buying himself a leather pilot's jacket for 2 guineas and his first cigar, which he immediately lights up. On 1st May his robins' eggs hatch and his nest is emptied. By Saturday the 5th, he is still smugly buzzing over his successful fathering to Cliff in the Reading Room of Hounslow Public Library. 'Cliff says that birds are my second friends. He's right too.'

While Kenneth, once again, takes eager advantage of English homework with another creative rush, John discusses with Mary the viability of a ten day holiday to Devon in late June. It isn't clear whether they had been before as a family, but John, at least, would have familiarised himself with the County, since the all-too-short golden days of (what would now be termed 'networking') from the Ealing office. Paignton edged out Teignmouth as their final choice. Kenneth was decked out in another new wardrobe for the occasion; this of a pre-Ben Sherman style shirt with matching tie, 'like the Americans,' a second brown striped shirt and a pair of brown and white brogues. On the 20th June they took the train from London to a hotel near the sea front. The next ten days were spent at different locations along the coast. Kenneth swam, canoed, and suffered the effects of ultra-violet over-exposure. During the last three days the Allsops' visited Ansteyes Cove.

'It's too beautiful for words,' wrote a spellbound Kenneth, 'what a height we were,' and Goodrington Sands, where the Tunners' - former neighbours from Spring Grove Road - now lived. After returning home on the 30th, Kenneth states that he would not be going back to the office, but wait until the start of the new term of his next school. John must have seen it coming since his son's only consoling point of interest in the job had been use of the typewriter. In August, John bought a new car; a Hillman Straight 8. '20 H.P. & 8 cylinders,' writes his enthusiastic son. 'We were giving it a polish over. It goes beautifully. Simply hums.'

John had to replace it within three weeks. The effects of the Depression still hung over him, and this attempt at bolstering a feel-good factor that accompanied the family in Devon proved somewhat premature. Thus, a more modestly sized Austin 10-4 replaced the roomy Hillman. On Monday 20th August, Kenneth starts at Pitman's Private School. Named after the founder of the shorthand system of writing his father struggled through for so long to reach his current position, John probably thought he was doing his boy a favour. Kenneth's entry for this day suggests he may have chosen well.

'It's a fine school. I've got my cap badge and locker. We had entrance tests. The mistress said my English paper was the best. I nearly got lost in the passages...'

Time would reveal that Kenneth was no happier here than he'd been at Wyndham & St. Andrew's. The site was made up of two mock medieval, late Victorian mansions, with an intervening wall hastily demolished. Classes were in half gloom, the walls were left to multiplying layers of grime and dust, while the desks and chairs were almost certainly contemporary to the original occupiers, worm-rotted and slightly unstable. Kenneth later recalled the general air of neglect as being heightened by that equal to it, outside, where the shrubbery 'swarmed in sinister profusion.'

Kenneth almost certainly exaggerates the Gothic Melodrama with the benefit of tainted hindsight. But, there is little doubt that the school, if reassuringly traditional in appearance, was left dilapidated for eventual closure, which occurred less than a decade later. The headmaster was 'An immensely tall, shambling man with the most harassed, haunted face I have ever seen on a human being... His head was always so bowed that his chin rested inside his soiled collar, his gown was as theatrically tattered as a young barrister's...I was mortally afraid of him.' His teachers appeared to arrive and leave on a semi-regular basis. One of the few favourites was a Mr. Cholly, whom he describes as 'a cynical, debauched playboy in ginger plus-fours, who always tiptoed, frailly, into the classroom in the morning with a raging hangover.' Collapsing into his seat, he'd groan over his folded arms, at his desk, for the first twenty minutes of each lesson. On receipt of a long-awaited cheque he was replaced by a make-up wearing, 'out' homosexual, swiftly let go after an affair with the school's rugby captain. 'In they came and out they went...on their uppers and down at heel, their references bad but their accents good, to linger a little while to bore us with facts that it bored them to repeat...'

Only his eccentric, elderly history master stayed long enough to gain an iota of respect. As did the slightly sadistic

Mr. Hunter, who 'induced in me a passing stammer and a paralysed terror of saying anything spontaneous that could be seized upon...' Lessons were more specialised. Inevitably, shorthand was chosen as part of the curriculum and allied to bookkeeping. Only mildly diverted by the latter, he remained about as keen on the former as his father at his age. Still, 'Miss Mallard, the English mistress, is quite decent, though rather prim.' Here, Kenneth acquires Grade As' for his writing exercises as if he were vacantly re-doing the same piece. His actual attention was on a schoolmate; a Canadian girl named Joan Taylor. Possibly without the wise counsel of John Collins, Kenneth hung around outside 22, Kings Avenue, Ealing, an evening, only to discover, a month later, she lived elsewhere. On the 7th September he found it, subsequently leaving a note for her at school, asking her if she liked him. 'I didn't see her read,' worries the lovesick lad. 'I wonder what will happen tomorrow.' On the 12th, he plucked up the courage to ask her and found the feeling bashfully reciprocated. 'She speaks very queer. All the 'A's short.'

Further nightly, occasionally vain, vigils outside schoolgirls' houses with John Collins follow, as relief from the semi-regular shorthand tests he began passing with ease. 'I'm in (Section) D now,' he writes with a distracted inevitability. 'Got 'A' for English.' He also acquires another sty over an eye; fast becoming accepted as a permanent fixture of his face. On 21st November he reports Miss Mallard wanting him to go for the RSA English Exam, set for the following May. Two days later – the bane of both the bright and the dense – he is sent out of the shorthand class for 'mucking about with Carter.'

On the 24th, as he returns to the station from the Engineering Exhibition at Olympia with a friend, he sneaks into a second hand bookshop and picks up two novels by Jules Verne and a bird book, possibly by Richard Jefferies.

This begins a heightened period of interest for Kenneth, as if Pitman's had, infuriatingly, managed to distract him from a genuine interest. December is spent acquiring bird books with a vengeance; from swapping his fifty-six volumes of *Story of the Nations* for Francis Pitt's *British Animal Life* at a second hand stall at Hammersmith, to icy evenings endured at the newly discovered library at Ealing. His interest in girls already matures. Miss Lane, another teacher at Pitman's is trailed by Kenneth and Waldren, his old St. Andrew's chum. Again, without John Collins they struggle to find the right house. The 13th reveals him ending the year as it had begun:

'Didn't go to school. I've got a whacking great sty on my eye.' But he is well enough to dig the new jazz, many numbers from the wireless, some accompanying the films he saw as double features at the local Dominion or Empire; 'Stars Fell On Alabama' by Harry Roy, 'Smoke Gets In Your Eyes,' 'My Heart Was Sleeping,' 'Leena' and 'I'm Lost In a Fog.' He was experiencing Nocl Coward's dictum about the potency of cheap music just before exposure to adult cynicism made such appreciation taboo.

The Christmas presents outshone those of the previous year. On the 22nd, Kenneth bought Mary a box of Du Barry perfume, while John received one hundred cigarettes and a rolled, gold pin from Mary. During these exchanges, John sprang what might have been the best surprise of all for his son, albeit one with conditions; 'Dad knows the editor of the *Axis* & I'm going to write a nature article and get it published.' On the 23rd, Kenneth received some early gifts, with the obligatory confectionery store; '2 fine nature books, a tie, a pair of slippers, a box of 12 *Mars*, toffees, orange & lemon slices, a box of choc. biscuits & a new diary. On Christmas Eve, he and Boy watched a kestrel hovering low above their heads for several minutes during a walk, followed – on Christmas Day itself - by a gathering of nine friends and relatives, including the Reads and, possibly, Tom and Pattie, with a further showering of sweets for Kenneth. His spoiling is a matter of debate, but there is no doubting the selflessness his parents continued to bestow while times remained tough. John, in particular, resigned to his son following a path he had not himself trailed, comes across as supportive and proactive on his behalf.

It was clear that Kenneth was committed enough to describing what he saw on paper, to earn some kind of future living. John, himself, could have taken such a route had the opportunity arisen soon enough to discard the demanding requirement of shorthand. From now – as the entry for the 22nd December reveals – John endeavours to make some connections, sounding out colleagues in Spring Grove's Ratepayers' Association. Kenneth, meanwhile, divides his allegedly 'free' time between the reading rooms of Ealing and Hounslow Public Libraries. Compensating, increasingly, for the lack of inspiration in class, he spends darkening, late afternoons through January and February 1935 tolerating freezing feet, hands and accompanying heavy bladder in their vaulted, cold stone rooms, searching out an ever growing head-list of nature titles even he could not, collectively, afford. Amidst a line of already familiar spines, Kenneth pulls out one title and squintingly makes out *The Lone Swallows - Henry Williamson*. Years later, Kenneth whimsically recalled 'a cloud of wonder that there was actually another person living who felt as I did about birds and the countryside, and who could express in words the agonising, poignant, inexplicable yearnings I felt.' He opened it in the midst of the title story to read "The beautiful swallows, be tender to them."

What the 15-year-old experienced is hard to gauge seven decades on. It is not romantic nostalgia alone. The boy expresses a genuine, half-articulated compassion for creatures whose domestic habits he had grown up with and witnessed at first hand without the accompanying cutting remarks or cynical dissent of adults. But it is unlikely he had seen or heard expressed such pure and simple observations from them either. In an unsourced letter from 1970, Kenneth claimed the book 'must have mistakenly strayed from the fiction section...' With its short, conversational sentences and poetic descriptions, an easy mistake for a grown-up librarian to make. Then, Williamson was and, perhaps, always will be, best known for his 1927 children's novel, *Tarka the Otter*, of which the 15-year-old must have heard.

It is a great pity that the 1935 diary is missing. The first six months could have collectively revealed how the initial impact of this author manifested itself in the pastimes of Kenneth's daily life. What is clear is that *The Lone Swallows* somehow awoke and connected the once distinct categories of fact and fiction in his mind. Between the parochial chuckles of his comics and the dangerous glamour of Hollywood and Chicago, there was little to relate to.

What spoke to him about his life, now, around the Great West Road? This was the missing link. This was the England of hungry, tousle-haired, middle class boys, as drawn by C.F. Tunicliffe in the 1933 edition and subsequent titles. A world of white shirts, rolled sleeves, fawn tunic and plus-fours, chocolate knee-length woollen socks and laced boots, and peering with naive intensity at blue, brown-speckled bird's eggs, reached from a nest set within the bole of an ancient oak, halfway up its length, as his mate enviously waits below, gazing up at him from its roots. In the text, Williamson was describing his Devon hermitage but he could have been describing the still undeveloped fields around the Harlington and Ridgeway Roads or even Osterley Park itself:

'The kestrel is considered by some naturalists to be the most scientific hoverer of our British hawks. Certainly, he uses with great skill the winds of heaven for his livelihood. He leans upon the moving air, sometimes slipping sideways and losing height, but reassuming poise by quick beats of his chestnut pinions...

The hovering of the kestrel is weak, delicately balanced; that of the buzzard clumsily weighty, and only managed in a strong air current; the peregrine falcon cuts into the gusts, controlling his flight with instant power, unheeding the wind's vagaries.' Beautifully compared, excitingly described. 'I went in the afternoon to a place near to the awful hill where Tom and I rushed down on our cycles three years ago, at 40-60 m.p.h. I went with Terence. We had a very strong headwind against us. We frequently saw large flocks of plovers in the green meadows. They ran about on the ground very fast, and suddenly digging their beak into the ground, ran away again. I saw 4 or 5 flocks, each of a thousand I should think...' (p. 82-83). Kenneth had been living this, breathlessly, since he was six.

'When I was irritably tapped on the shoulder by one of the turnstile matrons and told that the library was closing, I walked, still dazed, with the book held tight, reluctant to allow it to be stamped in case it should (escape me) and strapped it on my carrier and pedalled home fast through the winter night, to reach the privacy of my bedroom where I could start again, more slowly, to assimilate the marvel that had been vouchsafed me.'

'During the following months I gorged myself on Williamson. I read *The Old Stag* and *The Peregrine's Saga* and *Tarka the Otter*, and then I discovered that this magical man had also written novels, and I got hold of the first two of *The Flax of Dream* tetralogy, *The Beautiful Years* and *Dandelion Days*. It was a period as extrapolated from normal experience, as hallucinatory and iridescent and beatific as the start of an adult love affair...' (Ibid).

Extrapolated but still connected. The adult Kenneth can't

help but write of this period with a stylised, Edwardian pretension that masks what was, in reality, an over-compensating, pubescent obsession. As with most obsessions that occur at this most vulnerable age, it transgressed accepted boundaries of interest to become almost possession.

In spite of the glove of parental security that enclosed him – or perhaps because of it – Kenneth felt himself to be a hollow shell and one waiting to be filled. By what he was never very clear. But there were already intimations. Mary's confection affection revealed this.

'I don't know what I'm made of,' he had written the previous year, puzzled by his ailments. He still had his small circle of friends to share the locale with but no one, really, on his level. For Kenneth, Williamson's hermitage was read as a plausible means to an end; a destination at which he could arrive on his own terms, if imitating Williamson's proved implausible.

Meanwhile – with Easter over – the long awaited, final term was about to start. While the revelation of Williamson connected to his own life, it wasn't about to offer him work. He felt this during his most recent piece of English homework: 'Thoughts of a Boy Returning Home from School on an Evening.' A stream-of-consciousness double-sided page hesitantly typed on his father's office machine. Kenneth explains that his thoughts are written in the exact sequence by which they occurred. A section highlights an ominous awareness of what he must imminently lose:

'One advantage of the house facing the North – Rooms always cool. Bit too cool in winter. Hang my Mac up. Just look at Boy; full length in the hearth. Pat his lazy hide. Roll him over. Curse, (?) why does he always squeal when you touch his paws. Go under, you bad dog. Wonder where mother is? Switch on the radio...Oh, here's the *Daily Express*...Radio: National, 5.15. The String Sextet conducted by Jan Mowkowski. Probably comes from Poplar. Why don't they feature Teddy Joyce anymore?... Shoot upstairs. Step on the carpet as I open the door, so it won't catch. What a mess my shelves look. Books everywhere. Wish I could get that shelf up by my bed, then I could have all my bird books there and there would be plenty of room for all the others. Wonder if the embryo solvent will have dissolved the contents of that pheasant's egg I tried to blow on Sunday. Open the drawer carefully. Nasty-looking mess: all black. I'll blow it after tea. Just have another look at my eggs. I reckon my birds of prey drawer looks much the best. Gosh, I heard the sparrowhawks catch as I pulled the drawer out. Don't want to bust that. That's the ripper I got at Oxshott two years ago. Wonder why it is that looking at my eggs always makes me feel sad. Memories of happy days spent and gone, I suppose. Sickly sentimentality. I wonder what I shall do when I've started work. Can't very well go nesting then. Somehow I dread the thought of it. Wish I had the courage to do what Henry Williamson did, when he chucked everything and walked and walked to Devon where "the sun was the only master and the only clock." But he believed in himself, implicitly. I'm a coward. There's Ma calling. Whiz downstairs singing. I'm as good as Crosby, in fact better. What's for tea...?'

How the fifteen-year-old Kenneth would have appeared to the Williamsons' on his first, foiled attempt to meet Henry.

5
1935:
The Elusive 'Otter' Man

During Monday 13th May 1935, T.E. Lawrence – the Lawrence of Arabia still in hiding under the post-war sobriquet of 'Shaw' – swerved his motorbike to avoid two, young cyclists, peddling side-by-side. He was returning to his Clouds Hill cottage, Bovington Camp, from the local post office, where he had arranged to send a telegram to his friend, Henry Williamson. The previous week, Henry had written to Lawrence asking if he could visit for a stay the following Tuesday. Aware that his reply might not reach his friend before the suggested time, Lawrence hurriedly arranged the assenting wire. But the 'swerve' caused the infamous crash, leaving him comatose in the camp hospital, the skull irreparably fractured.

The following morning, Henry heard the news over the wireless. He wrote that 'about an hour after hearing this news, I began to ache in the breast; while my thoughts before this were only of myself...' On the morning of the following Sunday, Lawrence died. 'Sad,' Henry wrote in his oddly detached style, 'and now he will be a legend forever. The one bright creature of our age <u>untarnished</u> by any rumour, failing, weakness.' Henry had known Lawrence – on and off – for only the last six years but, in terms both literary and ideological, had warmed to him as the protege to his tutor.

According to Anne Williamson's affectionate chronicle, *Tarka and the Last Romantic*, Henry's 1935 diary remained – from this point – ominously blank on <u>any</u> personal detail. As if he could only manage his grief-ridden isolation by throwing himself, wholeheartedly, into completing his current project, being, in this case, what became the children's novel *Salar the Salmon*, kick-starting a fitfully fruitful period for this strange, impulsive man.

  Standing straight-backed at six feet six, narrow hipped and shouldered, sunken-cheeks connected by a long upper-lip beneath the largest, darkest, most sadly beautiful saucer-eyes gazing balefully above a trimmed, moustache, Henry cut a figure of benevolent command. Charmingly undermining were his baggy, knee-length, countryman plus fours, lending an aspect that might be described as droll stillness. A reedy-soft, melancholic voice came into its own when reading out loud his poetry in the front room of his home or down the local public house - an acquired taste among those locals that heard it. At this time, Henry, his wife Loetitia, and their five young children – William, (nicknamed 'Windles'), John, Margaret, Rosemary and Robert – were living in Shallowford Cottage, near South Molton in the county of Devon. Situated around twenty miles east of the family's previous address at Georgeham, this long, white-walled, farmhouse-like building, stood as rented accommodation on the Castle Hill estate of Earl Fortescue, close by the fishable River Bray. By the summer, Henry began to feel jaded: not a healthy way to slide out from under the weight of depression from Lawrence's death to commitment to the new book. (Loetitia was also expecting a sixth child – Richard – before the summer was out). This had turned to boredom by the end of the year.

 'I was forty years of age,' he wrote: 'What to do with myself..? Day after day was the same; walking to the Deer Park bridge, staring at the flood waters, walking up the river bank, seeing the spraints of the otter...seeing the same old heron rising with leisurely alarm three hundred yards away up river, to beat his wide grey wings to the oak-trees at the bottom of Bremridge Hill...No stimulation left in the valley;

all the excitement of staring at salmon, and discovering about them, and the river, was in *Salar."* (*The Story of a Norfolk Farm*, 1942)

It was in such a mood that he most likely forgot about the letter he had received from a bright young lad, asking if he could visit him, since he and his parents took their annual holidays in Devon. On the promised day, the fifteen-year-old cycled his way there, alone, in the open-necked tweed jacket and plus fours his mother had bought him for his burgeoning manhood. But if he had dreams of a Stanley-Livingstone type encounter, the boy was about to be disappointed. On hearing of his arrival, Henry sent 'Windles,' his eldest, to chaperon the lad around the bullrush grounds of Shallowford. Since 'Windles' was only nine, had better things to do, and cycled, audaciously, out ahead of the elder lad, a quiet, mutual annoyance ensued. But, the visitor stayed long enough to absorb the beauty of his surroundings, perhaps desperately hoping for a last-minute appearance by his new idol. It never came. But while Henry wanted out, Shallowford was to leave a lasting impression upon Kenneth Allsop as an ideal for living he might, one day, recreate for himself.

On the same day Loetitia Williamson bore Richard, their fourth son, Henry received a letter from Germany. It was signed 'John Heygate': a fellow writer and long term friend of Lawrence's. Henry's response to it kick-started a permanently tainted reputation that lives on to this day. Heygate had been working for two years at Berlin's *Ufa* Film Studios as scriptwriter on British version's of their movies, but had to leave through ongoing complications with his health. Now he was inviting Henry to join him, in September, for a motoring holiday that would take in this year's National Socialist Rally at Nuremberg. He added that they would be escorted by Herr Chemnitzer; a head from the

Direction of German Writers. Henry accepted, in dire need of a break, but only after Heygate's sweetener to 'arrange everything.' Heygate generously paid Henry's passage on the Bremen, which departed Southampton Docks on September 2nd. He relates the following events in his next book, *Goodbye West Country*. Not a publication due for reissue, it painted an intriguing view of pre-war posturing.

On arrival at Berlin, Henry met Heygate for an evening meal at a large local restaurant, where he expresses surprise at the number of wealthy Jews around him. The reader is assured that the reaction is simply to the Press's 'distortional magnification' and 'reiteration of hostile criticism of the Nazis...' The next day he visits a Jewish-owned department store; an occasional victim of picketing. There, a local confronts him as to why he bought from here and not a German-owned store. At this stage, Henry merely relates his observation. Progressively, he drops in pro-Hitler asides – the banning of rubber truncheons carried by the police - ending on how, 'everywhere, I saw faces that looked to be breathing extra oxygen; people free from mental fear. Would there be another war, I asked again and again, and received the same answer, No: Germany was now strong, and would create her own destiny, no more crowd hysteria or mass-panic, no more political parties fighting for power...no more irresponsible, newspaper scare-stuff.'

Henry and Heygate befriend a Nazi, Henry, naively, inviting him to lunch at the local Jewish *Trocadero*. Moving off to a smaller eatery in a side-street, Henry notes the young man's split personality when he reacts to the price of pork on their bill; 'one, the grown-up small boy of the (Great) War period, rather naïf and unsophisticated; the other, animated by his built-up National Socialist will.' He adds a remembrance of Lawrence – 'our nearest approach to Hitler' – allegedly having to shoot a man at point blank range, triggering a similar change in character.

One afternoon, Henry visits the *Ufa* Studios to watch Heygate at work and the same scene being played out before the cameras in German, French and English by the actress, Lilian Harvey and her three European leading men. Each play the same character but with the nuances felt most appropriate to each country. The following Saturday morning, Henry, carrying his leather-cased, *Rolliflex* camera, Heygate and Chemnitzer were racing down the Avus dual carriageway at 82 m.p.h., the former excited by the sight of the grey uniformed marching troops they passed en route, 'each soldier wearing a flower in helmet or tunic.' Henry heroically likens it to a march through Surrey he made during the 14-18 War with 'the gifts of apples and flowers from cottages.'

By dusk the party arrived at the outskirts of Nuremburg, proclaimed by an explosion of fireworks. Passing the checkpoint, their M.G.'s battery falters and bed down in a dining wagon. At dawn, Henry reads that Adolf Hitler was to speak in the *Luitpold-arena*. Alighting from a bus he reports, in awe, that 'the arena was vast, miles and miles of continuous benches arising around the oval. Banners stretched up behind us, each 200 ft. high and about 80 wide, great red roller-blinds with swastikas.' Elbowed across from his chosen seat by a hawk-faced Reverend from Oxford, he then witnesses 'a flutter of cries and a stir moving, like a tide, round the oval: down below a minute black car gliding, followed by another, another, another, a whole string of them. People on their feet, a roar of 'HEIL HITLER!' No, not a roar, an eager gladness, everyone happy and welcoming that tiny figure on the dais down there, with outstretched right arms.' Henry checks his growing excitement, almost guiltily, with an intimation of disappointment at the consequent rant. 'I felt that Hitler was imitating his earlier self in his speech, in so far as the white-heat of declamation was concerned...The Hitler of *Mein Kampf* was the same in spirit; but the sapling was now the oak tree.' As if in solace, he later returns to what originally galvanised his belief:

'Clerks, farm labourers, waiters tram conductors, sons of generals and princes, newspaper boys, boxers, poets, writers, unemployed, wounded soldiers – these heard him in those early days, and were shocked into a new way of thought, and gave up all for an Idea, and bound themselves together for their beliefs...'

His excitement re-builds with a parroting of *Mein Kampf* itself when he re-asserts that the rightful heirs to the future are the strong in defeat of the weak. It is only natural that 'one set wished to restore the old German fabric, to re-design it on its ancient foundations; the other said it must be razed to the ground, a new building international in design, geometrical, concrete, must replace it.' (An interesting question is whether or not he knew Hitler was inspired by the very Empire – 'the old German fabric' - he refers to and, ultimately, bore down on him).

Later that day, he sees the unintentionally comic figure of Goring, grinning and posing for various rehearsed photographers. 'He seemed to be popular, to be regarded as a jester, but they liked him.' Goebbels appeared to him next, only to receive a more forced cheer. Beginning to tire of the endless procession, Henry's attention wanders to the mutual reaction of a member of the old Prussian guard - 'a smallish, very dapper man in greenish-grey uniform' - with the 'tall, red-faced' new boys. The aristocrat looked and sounded quietly angered and defeated while the younger, lower middle-class Nazis' smiled between themselves. 'An isolation of the old world in the new,' states Henry: a telling moment.

Back in his room at The Adlon Hotel, a 'hollow-feeling' Henry, flaking out and the worse for champagne from a tour around the Berlin bars, directs his *Rolliflex*, mid-shave, at his mirror and clicks. The result is intriguing. His shaving foam has cut off either end of his moustache and his hair has been hurriedly parted. A pleasingly ironic gaze reflects back an impersonation that many, less well disposed toward the target, would be copying in four years time, only with less personal insight or admiration.

Even considering the turn of events alongside Henry's incorrigible eccentricity, it is still hard to love the man who constantly refers to an apparently pragmatic English reporter on the scene as 'Star Liberal,' unthinkingly aping Lawrence's contempt for humanism. But, this is tempered by the nagging feeling, throughout the text, that Henry is a basically good man enamoured with, and influenced by, the cult of personality. Perhaps, a clue to the real Henry was voiced by a well-travelled stranger he fell into conversation with, where he was staying, at the Adlon Hotel. It has a chilling subtext. The stranger reported that the American Ambassador was granted a forty-minute audience with Hitler on the question of the Jews' persecution:

'The Ambassador spoke for thirty-nine and a half minutes, giving the President's official views, the President's personal views, the viewpoint of Congress. Hitler listened to all of it. Then he said, 'Mr. Ambassador, if I had my way, there would not be a Jew alive in Germany today.' (The stranger:) What do you think of that?' (Henry:) I said it was just a silly and mischievous story. 'Is it true?' I asked the ex-naval officer who had been our host on the tour. 'No,' he said quietly. After some more, this cosmopolitan chap asked me what I did, what was I doing in Berlin. 'Oh, just looking around.' 'You're a fascist, I suppose?' No, just trying to 'see things truly, as the sun sees them, without shadows.' 'Oh, I get you. You're a Liberal sentimentalist.' '

Historically intriguing, *Goodbye West Country* manages to feature some of Henry's most pedantic prose. It is as if his well known, well-loved, aesthetic sense has crumbled to reveal a proletarian operator. There is a constant sense of a once half-articulated, partially defined idealism, first taken and glamorised by Lawrence, then goaded and magnified by Hitler. Or, rather, galvanised by him in a way so uncompromising as to be adrenal. The Fuhrer's goal-centred intent mistaken for pure integrity.

If too much of an eccentric and loose cannon ever to be taken seriously as a party spokesman or trustee, as Anne Williamson suggested, there is little doubting the true source of Henry's fascist sympathies. She explains that, as a former soldier on the front line during the 1914-18 War,

'Henry took a great deal of interest in what was happening in Germany at this time, understandably since he had German blood from his paternal grandmother, Adela Luhn; and his love for the Romantic music of Wagner gives the main clue to his inner being. His acceptance was also coloured by his cathartic experience of the Christmas Truce in 1914 when he had discovered that the ordinary German soldier thought, as the ordinary English soldier did, that he fought for the good of his country and that God was on his side – a revelation which was to be such a profound influence on Henry's life and beliefs.'

Henry was a part of a pre-World War II sensibility that related to Adolf Hitler as a former working-class soldier made good. Who, through a single-minded determination to elevate his country out of the apologist position it had signed up to in 1919, had vision, guts and - often sidelined - the gathering support from the majority of his people. Up until 1938 the Conservative Government and the majority of Fleet Street tabloids were in support of Hitler's populist efforts. Of course, such a perspective seems incredible now, and almost appeasement in itself. But just as Orson Welles's *War of the Worlds* broadcast of this year convinced enough Stateside listeners of alien invasion to cause minor panic, so the British newsreels unwittingly fostered a mood of iconic identification. But, this was the year when the press finally lost its innocence; a crossover point where 'fact' became opinionated as propaganda and one image was more telling to most than any diatribe in tiny print. And Henry just loved 'the talkies.'

Soon after the encounter with the well-travelled stranger, Henry sat, penniless, at a table in the lounge of The Adlon, his sciatic nerve – a legacy of the Flanders plain – burning the issue in his right thigh. Options for returning to Southampton were negligible; sales from the sole, German, translation of *Tarka* did not justify an approach and Heygate had already shown generosity in getting him here. It took his host 'from the Propaganda Ministry' to enter the lounge, hear of his quandary, and covertly pass over a wad of 150 marks. Henry celebrated that evening on Rhine Wine with Heygate and his party, so numbing the physical pain enough for him to make the journey home. Back home, he eagerly wrote the foreword to *The Flax of Dream*: the manuscript currently with his publisher and awaiting a New Year release. 'I salute the great man across the Rhine, whose life symbol is the happy child,' he wrote, unaware of how history would unfold and treat such a statement.

Mid-October, *Salar the Salmon* was published to generally favourable reviews. However, Henry countered queries about the 'stuffed bream in a glass case' that appeared in his Writing Hut as being a gift from the Sitwells', awarded for The Worst Novel of the Year.' Late December, the 'bored and stale' (Ibid). author jumped into his black Alvis Silver Eagle, and drove his way to London's Savage Club. To alleviate such boredom, he often pushed down hard on his accelerator when the narrow, open country road appeared clear before him. Henry compared the feeling of the driver's seat to an aircraft's cockpit. 'It was fast, doing 85 mph when flat out, and it covered 24 miles to the gallon.' He adds in justification; 'These mechanical facts interested me, as once the precision of words had occupied all my time.' Such adrenal bursts were still rare in 1935.

Arriving at the Savage, Henry took a call from Richard de la Mare, who invited him for a few days recuperation. The de la Mares' lived at East Runton, near Cromer, North Norfolk. According to Anne Williamson, Henry then unburdened himself of 'his feeling of stagnation and frustration and fears for the future.' In response, his wife apparently suggested he move out to the area and that she knew of a local farmhouse currently up for sale.

The following day, Henry accompanied them to view Old Hall at Stiffkey with its accompanying 235 acres of farmland. Straight away, he saw that it was 'far too large' and, on closer inspection, 'half-decayed and gloomy.' Inside he describes an atmosphere of an abandoned castle and a pervading melancholia. Hardly the recuperation he was after. De la Mare was disappointed by Henry's reaction. 'I wanted sunlight, air, and soundness about me: not darkness and decadence. The rafters seemed almost entirely rotten, and were hung with bats. I wanted to get out into the air.' (*Story of a Norfolk Farm*). Characteristically, he daydreamed half-serious possibilities that made connections and convinced. It was a wonderful place for the children. In his own boyhood, he had pondered upon life as a farmer. Now, out left field, the possibility re-occurred. 'Of course, I said, I wasn't really serious; yet the farm was in a beautiful position, with its hills and woods and meadows.' He talked it over with 'Dick' en route back to his cottage. Another visit was arranged. Then, Henry bought it. While it wasn't that swift a decision, it did not take much for Henry to change his mind, once the initial doubts were assuaged. His romantic claims to the land do not ring quite as true as him being told that the area boasted a fashionable hotel a couple of miles away and the finest small shoot in the county, 'which, of course, means England.' (Ibid) In *Story of a Norfolk Farm*,

Henry portentously compares his decision to a much larger picture. 'Was this the way out? Would an active life rid me of the periods in which life seemed but vain endurance, for some purpose I saw dimly in the future as an inner call or urge to be of use to a new England?'

6
1936 – 1939:
Wide, Open Spaces

Kenneth awoke to January 1936 with little to look forward to. At sixteen years of age, he was in danger of being regarded as the classic non-achiever. Far from turning his attention to seeking work, his extended cycling expeditions around Osterley, Hounslow, and now, further afield, were making him a stranger at home. He had no intention of going on to college, expecting a magnification of school life, and a further interruption to his own personal studies, which – with no alternatives in sight - were gaining in importance. This did not bode well for his relationship with John and Mary.

Monday the 6th saw the start of another new term. 'Didn't go to school today,' he wrote with a touch of defiance. 'So, in afternoon, I took Boy for a very long walk.' The previous Autumn he had submitted his, then, most recent Pitman's essay - 'Thoughts of a Boy Returning from School...' – to *Unity* magazine, run by the Spring Grove Ratepayers Association. But while its editor, Gould, promised him its appearance in the November cover issue, it was absent. Gould wrote him an apologetic letter, ending, 'I can definitely tell you that it will be published in our Dec. number...' but there was still no room. A good result in his Art exam, with an excellent accompanying reference, resigned Kenneth to sitting an entrance test at the R.C.A. in May. He passed, but still held out. John could not have been pleased. Unemployment for a middle-class sixteen-year-old of above average intelligence in 1936 was taboo and not a consideration. Reluctantly, on his parents' insistence, he resigned himself to a further year at Pitman's. It was not all despair. One morning, the head mournfully announced at assembly that his most detested teacher, Mr. Hunter, he of the 'loud hectoring voice and...refined technique in sarcastic bullying,' had crashed his Morgan three-wheeler against a bank behind the playing fields, the previous evening. It had ended up on its roof, crushing and killing him instantly.

'This episode provided me with the only tangible fruit of all my school years; a temporary faith in the justice of God.'

Also, and with a little more temperance, a discovery of the Reverend Gilbert White's *Natural History of Selborne* inspired, on Good Friday (10th April), a Williamson-like cycling expedition to the village with friend Ron, where respects were paid at the naturalist's grave.

In recent months, Kenneth had been wooing a girl, met during a dance at the tennis club adjoining the local recreation centre, known only as 'Poppy.' Little is known about her except that she had almost certainly claimed his virginity by this time and 'went' with Kenneth on those few evenings when she wasn't second place to the Park. The annual, family car journey to Devon went ahead in June; this year, the narrow, winding, high-hedged country lanes taking them to stay on a farm near Barnstaple. Kenneth, exploring the grounds alone, now had possession of an air-rifle with which he would stalk and shoot the occasional rabbit. He claims he killed few, but that the farmer was grateful for those he took, as his gin-traps were unreliable.

Back at Osterley, John's highly chequered career in the housing business took another risky turn as he advertised his abilities as a 'business broker' in the local press; more out of desperation than as a positive career move. He was the lone proprietor, now, with the one remaining office at 433, Great West Road. 'Genuine businesses of all trades urgently required for waiting purchasers,' he advertised with a touch of quiet desperation. No longer had he the luxury to pick and choose clients with a social conscience.

Kenneth was spending 'idle' time, passing on the dusty Victorian tomes of Jeffries, W.H. Hudson and White, giving sole attention to the more contemporary Williamson titles. First, *The Old Stag*, *The Peregrine's Saga* and *Tarka the Otter*; subsequently, the novels *The Beautiful Years* and *Dandelion Days*, that began *The Flax of Dream* tetralogy. The texts often suggested inspiration from the same writers and for the same reasons as affected him. This realisation must have made Henry's non-appearance at Shallowford the previous Summer all the more frustrating. At least once a fortnight, he was managing to sneak into his exercise book a review of one of these titles, on the pretext of that week's English assignment. On 10th September, he *precised* a recent piece on *Patriot's Progress*. He ends with the claim that,

'I think there is no other book which preaches so clearly, yet subtly, against war.' It was a line he would re-use in future reviews, but his teacher was already unconvinced. 'There are many,' she insisted in her marking, adding an ungracious 'minus' to his Grade 'A..' On 2nd November, he gave his reasons for his new obsession; '...he writes about nature in a way that I admire and understand; not the "a combat of our feathered friends on nature's great stage" style, but (with) a feeling, honest and sympathetic style. Yet, not flowery, nor gushing, nor pretentious.' He goes on, 'I feel I should like Mr. Williamson, personally. He is, I think, a person to whom I could talk, and who would understand me.' He adds that his other attraction is the variety of subject matter on which he writes, and considers *The Gold Falcon*, 'a masterpiece' ill-judged by the critics.

Not yet a convincing interpreter, Kenneth was, at least, flowering as a reviewer of texts. Allied to this was a growing need to articulate the dissent he felt at the changes being instituted around him in the name of commerce. There is a sense that Osterley Park was fast becoming a haven for this young exile; literally, a wildlife *sanctuary* protected from the tarmac and concrete he saw enclosing, surreptitiously, around him on his nightly returns home. On the second Wednesday of November, he left school, taking the tube to Piccadilly to visit the *Sunday Times* Book Exhibition at Dorland Hall, Lower Regent Street. Before picking up a couple of titles from one of the stalls, he and John attended an upstairs lecture there, being given by 'the farmer-author' A. G. Street. With a naive generalisation, Kenneth summed-up Street's remarks; that 'land must not be divided into "penny-packets," but must, as in the old days, be presided over by feudal lords. Or better still, it must be National. That is the only way to stay the hand of the *jerry-builder*.' A favoured term of John's, used to describe houses constructed solely for quick profit, and with no co-operative input, like those in the neighbouring new towns of Whitton and Staines.

A modest, but genuine, opportunity arose, albeit not one that Kenneth would have chased, left to his own devices. In the course of daily business, one of John's clients turned out to be the son of Percival Marshall, a local publisher. After reminding the son about the imminent expiring of his car insurance, John got to chatting socially with him and brought the conversation around to his own, extolling his talent. Marshall mooted journalism as an option. John would not have been keen but harboured any dissent. He left Marshall who promised to ask his father if there were any current vacancies. On the 22nd November, Marshall replied that his father wanted examples of Kenneth's writing by which to gauge his strengths. On the back of this, Marshall Sr. might then be in a position to steer him to the preferred post. He ended that 'My father and I would be very pleased to see your son and heir sometime, and have a chat with him, and put him wise so far as we can as to his best way of graduating into modern journalism.'

Over the next week John managed to procure a couple of examples from Kenneth, who probably felt by now he had little to lose. On 1st December, he cautiously wrote back to Marshall with their enclosure; '...you will gather that he is keenly interested in Ornithology. I quite realise that this may not be the means of making him a living, but it is something to have an interest.' He added that he believed finding the right atmosphere could only serve to develop his gifts; typical restraint from John in a near desperate situation. At a subsequent meeting with them both there were smiles all round but, ultimately, little to show. It wouldn't be until the middle of the following year that the first of three events occurred, in quick succession, to cancel out the despondency from the vainly raised hopes of these last eighteen months.

While John was supportive of his son wanting, badly, to write for a living, in the short term it was the living itself that mattered. If Kenneth didn't want to become a draughtsman, then he'd have to use the only other experience already gained. Searching through his records of contacts from younger days, John found the home address and number of a former colleague from his time in Mesopotamia, during the 1914-18 War, who may well have been the then Governor at Baghdad, Brigadier-General Hawker. 'Hawker,' in turn, found John's idle son a job as a shorthand and copy-typist clerk for the Iraq Legation of the Diplomatic Service, situated at 22, Queen's Gate, South Kensington, just off the Cromwell Road. (The defeated Mesopotamian territories of the Ottoman Empire had the newly independent 'Iraq' granted as a mandate to Britain by the League of Nations in 1920).

'The only relief was that it was near the Natural History Museum,' a gloomy Kenneth recalled. Also, the prestigious address didn't hide the fact that the post was not dissimilar to that overseen by his father for the last two years. It isn't known how long he was here, but John was clearly asking for trouble if he expected any long-term commitment.

It was likely around this time – stuck in an office, but still influenced by the discipline – that Kenneth warmed to the idea of reporting as the most realistic way out. Having digested all the available Williamsons,' he was now discovering the writings of the foreign correspondent, Negley Farson, whose autobiography – *The Way of a Transgressor* – had been published at the end of the previous year. Observation required movement and travel; twin demands administrative ties could never fulfil. He saw what he was missing by the briefings and de-briefings of the diplomatic envoys leaving for, and returning from, their latest missions abroad. Always on his mind was that any deviation from the life that had, inextricably, become his love, would be an unbearable wrench. He had too little interest in his artistic talent, and had failed at everything else. He saw no other choice but to make the writing work for him. This had to mean journalism.

Both John and Mary were of one mind when he voiced this, and tried to dissuade him. John seems to have been encouraging Kenneth's writing in the vain hope that the boy might become attracted to publishing, although it is likely he had, all the while, feared the worst. Journalism was not the rather cheap and sensationalist level of verbiage he was hoping Kenneth would descend to. Surely, he could aim higher? While voicing this concern, John submitted Kenneth's latest story to *Unity*, entitled 'The Poachers.' A light appeared at the end of this terminal tunnel; they published. Kenneth was jubilant, no doubt added piquancy coming from his father's continuing support. This sudden lifeline ignited a sudden rush of adrenaline, which manifested itself in job applications to twenty-five separate newspaper editors. But, rejection from each and every one swiftly dragged him back down.

Meanwhile, quietly evident was a burgeoning maturity in his prose, the exercise book reviews influenced by the absorbed poetry. A surviving essay from March 1937 highlights what reads like an ownership of Williamson's ruminative, romantic style, but one becoming incorporated into Kenneth's experience;

'Once again Spring is round! It seems but a few months since last the harbinger cuckoo was heard on the Heath, and the first swallow seen coursing the reeds by the lake, that rainy, warm afternoon...' ('Nature Notes,' March 1937, unpublished) With personal opinion;

'The rooks have now been back at their colonies for several weeks, and many of the black stick nests contain squaking (sic) young. They are an industrious, noisy crowd, these rooks, but always ready to pilfer anything that they think there is any chance of getting away with. In fact, they remind me of the residents of a big city. They are the gregarious townsfolk of the bird world.' (Ibid)

This is the first time Kenneth relates human attributes to animals in a social context; the voice, that of a reporter. The disreputable rook and crow – also mentioned in the piece – are holding a strange fascination for him, to become a regular motif over the next decade. Ever answerable to his own rules, Kenneth 'pilfered' the crow, keeping it as a pet for the next two years.

On 11th June 1937, Frank Lawrance, the editor of *The Slough Observer*, – Middlesex's largest local daily – followed up a letter of 5th February that had been one of Kenneth's twenty-five negative responses. His application had not been forgotten. This second reply by Lawrance stated that, if he were still looking for a post on a local paper, then an interview could be arranged at a mutually agreeable time. The meeting was set for the following week and went very well; Lawrance finding himself struck as much by the seventeen-year-old's slender, well-spoken presence as by his writing. Its conclusion was more than Kenneth could have expected. Lawrance would give him a try-out, up to the following spring, as a regular contributor on 12s. 6d. Per week.

On the 21st June, Kenneth was authorised a permit onto the Staines and Littleton reservoir works 'for the purpose of wild bird observation' by its Chief Engineer, and a small space for 250 words was made available for a weekly, Friday column. Four weeks later sees Kenneth finally making some progress from 'The Poachers' the previous year, with publication of the first of his 'Country Log's. Tellingly subtitled 'A weekly glimpse of the changing rural scene, viewed through the eyes of a young nature-lover,' Kenneth embarked upon nine months of Williamson-influenced introspection; two paragraph essays on an idealised England a world away from the Great West Road. So, it is ironic that those not written from the reservoir works were written from the remaining greenery between its factories and the depths of Osterley Park.

First published on 16th July, 'The Fullness of Summer' is an unashamedly sensual celebration of basking on a hot July afternoon, while naively, self-consciously, peppered with the same use of adjective and adverb first experimented with in 1934. Spring has a 'sapply-greeness,' (sic) the atmosphere is 'brassy-hot,' while the wild doves crooning is described as 'slumberous.' By the following Friday's 'Log' – 'Summer Night' – he had noted the self-conscious use of adjective and removed them: a mature reflection. Dusk approaches and, sitting on a bank made up of rabbit hole diggings, Kenneth describes the waking duties of an owl and its mate and the intrusion of a third. The result is one of the simplest, most undemanding, pieces he would ever write. But, the former descriptive excesses could not be permanently suppressed. Such usage was to become an increasing elaboration in

Kenneth's writing.

This *Observer* was founded on 6th May, 1883, by the independent printing press of one Charles Luff in Buckingham Gardens. The press was small but already big on intent, incorporating Slough, Eton, Windsor, Maidenhead, Colnbrook and Uxbridge on its masthead, with separate editions for the first and final three. Edward Luff, inheriting the business on his father's death, brought Frank Lawrance in as a partner in 1933. Lawrence subsequently took over the business in 1946.

Quite what Kenneth's brief was here, and how intentional the poetic license, is unknown. Perhaps he was expressing what he wanted to see or simply heightened what was already there. A subsequent autobiographical note recalls, 'the longing, then, for a richness of flowers and birds I'd never known but read of in Richard Jeffries, H(enry) W(illiamson), Frances Pitt's E(vening) N(ews) articles and *The Nature Lover*...' What mattered was that through consuming Henry's prose style over the previous two years, he had, quite sublimely, made his mark.

The one review he received was the only one that mattered, and marked the second major event. Upon the Allsop's doormat dropped a typewritten postcard from Henry Williamson himself, from the farm at Stiffkey, Norfolk. It had taken Henry just over two years to respond to Kenneth's 1935 letter. Its precise content is lost, but the date suggests Henry had read his protege's first *Slough Observer* pieces and returned congratulations. Its receipt made Kenneth excitedly dizzy and dry-mouthed. This was vindication – the *only* vindication – that mattered.

'I examined and re-read the card many times, with intense excitement and wonderment...,' Kenneth wrote years later. 'For the postcard was the first direct and physical contact with a god of my private mythology, a man who had become so close to me in my imaginative life as companion and mentor – a doppelganger brother – that it seemed almost eerie to hold in my hand this evidence that he existed as a separate flesh-and-blood entity.' With no imminent employment to interrupt his inner life, the re-enthused Kenneth required no further motivation to complete his commitment to the paper.

Still only seventeen, Kenneth remained a freelance contributor and not in the full-time staff post he had desired. Through the remainder of 1937, he would impress his commitment to Lawrance, endeavouring to become just that. The crow reared its ugly head again for him, with the newly-discovered plover, on the 30th July, an observation inspired by this year's family Summer jaunt to Devon materialised on the 6th August, with the home ground of the local Estuary featuring the following week. On 19th November, 'The Climb' harked not-so-far back to the golden days of his covert, boyhood treks, with a description of a nest hunt:

'First of all, the "bunk." The boy got as firm a hold as possible on the flaky bark and heaved upwards. Gripping hard with his knees round the slim bole, he gave another jerk towards two branches jutting out each side of the fir. His feet scrambling, desperately, for a toe-hold sent down showers of bark dust on to the long claws of bramble growing at the base.' Once at the targeted level, he spies the nest; ' "Eggs!" he yelled down. "How many?" a voice instantly reached up almost at screaming point. There were five...There was a smile on his lips and he felt jubilantly happy, and at the same time strangely contented up here in the tree tops with no sound but the soft hissing of the green tips in the wind...Presently, he bent over to the eyrie and picked out two of the best — both were blotched and smeared with a lovely red. He undid his coat, placed one in each empty pocket, and wrapping his legs round the trunk, half-climbed, half-slithered, to the ground in a black cloud.'

By December, he'd found a way to expand the expected

word-count with a two-parter on the wildlife scouring Hounslow's dilapidated Powder Mills. There, he saw a 'curious, rather sinister area of abandoned country around which the council estates, new arterial roads, and railway lines swilled; bordered Hounslow Heath, a degenerate and desolate spread of scruffy common land...roamed by gangs of rather rough, tough small boys who rather frightened me, and who rough-rode their bikes up and down the switch-backing, coiling track of the Butts, overgrown with thorn and furze.'

But, the settled birds stronger will enticed him on; 'several pairs of red-backed shrike nested in the Butts despite the persecution; woodlarks on the open country and stone chats, reed buntings in the reedy fields on the edge of the heath...' Kenneth's curiosity drove him on to the 'little side' of the Mill itself, through to the end of a long tunnel and out onto 'scruffy, semi-marshy, abandoned, marginal land,' so rewarded by nesting wild duck and kestrel 'in the low, hedgerow tree, from which 8 or 9 eggs were taken day by day, (but) she went on laying.' On the 'big side' – an old wood – stood the conically-shaped remnants of the Powder Mill itself; skeletal from an infamous explosion, allegedly, during gunpowder production for the Crimea.

While his weekly contribution to *The Slough Observer* provided the tantalising foretaste of what he wanted to do, it still did not, on its own, provide the living his parents expected. The third event occurred when John helped negotiate a position at a new magazine specialising in a pastime once close to both their hearts. For in High Holborn, London, WC1, in one of two tiny offices taken over eighteen months earlier, four sweating and dishevelled-looking men made up the editorial staff of a small, troubled, weekly paper called *The Bicycle*.

The Kenneth who joined *The Bicycle*'s staff, in the autumn of

1937, was fast becoming physically cut out for such a hothouse of limited room and resources. He was taller now, standing at five feet seven inches, thinner and generally rangier, like a racetrack athlete. He was also quite pasty-faced; a noticeable pallor that was to stay while he remained in England.

Its continuance was assured at *The Bicycle*. Kenneth described the magazine's shaky foundations from its inability to acquire proper advertising revenue and the three libel suits already to its name since its first issue on 25th February 1936.

'The offices were in a grimy backwater of High Holborn, sandwiched between the business premises of a body-building expert and a delicatessen... while upstairs, three middle-aged and extremely badly dressed men and a blowsy young woman produced, irregularly, a magazine called *Modish Man*." It is questionable as to whether there was ever an *advertised* vacancy. 'From the start, the exact definition of my job was a little hazy. But after a few weeks, I dropped into a routine of typing letters, occasionally reporting bicycle and sports meetings, and completely re-writing articles contributed by impoverished freelancers, so that the interesting facts could be retained while the original manuscript was returned with an "Editor Regrets" slip.'

The atmosphere was a literal hothouse, the thickly humid air the result of the launderette and its' wringing machine below. If the one, cracked office window was opened for relief, blackened dust blew coldly in from the factory opposite. Kenneth was stationed opposite a man of similar age, whom he recalled as 'lean' and 'earnest' and suffering from the type of heaving, sawdust breathing the ambience here could only maintain. The Features Editor oversaw next door. A fortuitous position in that the paper's continued support appears to have stemmed, solely, from the popularity of his sightseeing column. Kenneth seems to have envied him touring out of London in his saloon for the purposes of research, the results regularly including 'a few witty barbs aimed at the motorist class.' He claims contributors expecting payment were sent direct to this editor and leave – ten minutes later – not only without satisfaction but often with tail between legs. Kenneth calls it 'his magnificent aptitude for lying,' but a touch of jealousy on his part might account for an equal talent in persuasion.

Sharing this space with the Features Editor was an ex-Fleet Street journalist, long down on his luck after a burst of youthful success, now suffering from the inevitable drink problem and precarious heart, and referred to as 'Davis.' At a quiet moment during the day, Davis would often wander through from next door and sit astride the corner of Kenneth's desk. This bald-headed, sweat-soaked, thickset and world-weary figure then related his professional rise and fall. Having never worked on a national daily, his anecdotes initially intrigued the seventeen-year-old, but he soon became an apparition of dread when he found Davis to be repeating himself, verbatim, from the day before. Of course, the rest of the staff were well aware of Davis's circuitous reminiscence, but took some amusement in the new boy finding this out for himself.

'Always he would conclude, "Well, I began life on a sporting paper, and I am afraid I've completed the cycle.' So was everyone else. Despite this, Kenneth retained what he called a 'secret compassion' for him, as Davis was more relishing the description of his woes than indulging in negative self-pity.

Kenneth would leave these cloying conditions each evening, returning to his bedroom to read his latest acquisition of Williamson and write up his observations from the latest weekend cycle rides. His acquaintances may have gotten older, but his boyish enthusiasms remained.

A sense, not yet verbally expressed, was building within of

powerlessness at the covert take-over of Osterley's fields and undeveloped land. In his early teens, he had already witnessed skeletal constructions swiftly materialising along the Great West Road, backing, ever closer, onto once accessible territory. In 1930, when he'd accompanied his parents here as a ten year old, barely half a dozen companies had completed sites; America's *Firestone Tyre and Rubber Company* had been opened just eighteen months, accompanying the *Isleworth Winery, Pyrene Factory* and soon-to-be-opened *Macfarlane Lang's Imperial Biscuit Works*. The brand new *Packard Cars* and *Jantzen Knitting Mills* remained stylishly idle for the following few months. But by 1938, the likes of *Henly's* showroom ('Britain's biggest motor agency') and the rationalised *Gillette Razor and Blade* works, compounded Kenneth's sense of increasing marginalisation. The official declaration – 'PRIVATE PROPERTY' – had paralleled this over the previous eight years. In the pillaging crow he found a natural ally. A beast whose rebellious, even anarchic, instinct brought some much needed disorder to an increasingly ordered environment.

George Orwell did not share the disdain of his more right-wing contemporaries. With a characteristically cooler head he observed such growth as the shape of things to come. The Great West Road was fast representing 'the germs of the future England' in its car-accessible strip of light industry. Of its inhabitants, the Allsops' now represented just one example of the new income, 'but it is the same kind of life being lived at different levels...It is a rather restless, cultureless life, centring round tinned food, 'Picture Post,' the radio and the internal combustion engine...they are the indeterminate stratums at which the older class distinctions are beginning to break down.' (*England Your England*, (1941)). These Allsops' were as indeterminate a middle-class as their forefathers had been.

On the 25th March, 1938, 'Trout Poachers' described the river-keeper's killing of a heron. The perspective is not from one who either sympathises or dissents from the act, but simply an objective description of the kill:

'The heron...was thrown several feet by the impact of the shot. It caught him almost solidly...under the wing where it joined its body. Clawing violently at the air with his one whole pinion, the trout-poacher fell heavily towards the water. A second chance shot blew off his head.' The writer is as interested in the aftermath, as simply a work of nature, as he is by the act itself. 'Before long (the fish) were back nosing and nibbling curiously at the heavy object which was floating half in, half out, of the shallows.'

On the 27th May, the crow makes his third headlining appearance in the column. (By now, Lawrance had extended Kenneth's obligation to the paper to the end of the year). On August 12th, Kenneth introduces us to 'Kwuk'; the one-eyed owl. A point of interest here is the continuing suggestion of personal experience in the prose. Kenneth, in reality, was rarely fearful of handling animals that anyone with pre-learned experience, today, may deem well intentioned but irresponsible. Having been surrounded and attacked by a flock of rooks, Kwuk is left injured. He is found in this state by 'the boy,' who removes his jacket and 'pounces' on it, but is slashed by a claw on his exposed hand, the owl then escaping. But Kwuk lived to fight another day and a return visit in 'They Soared Beneath The Clouds' ten weeks later. By September 23rd's 'Drear, Damp Night,' Kenneth's observations are maturing further with a voice, recognisably, his own, discarding the Williamson similes for more instinctive, personal description:

'Dawn broke the colour of a dead fish and the sun poked over the still dripping trees on the mamelon like an inflamed eye. The marsh was a scene of desolation, with everything flattened into a soddened mash. (sic) At the further end, over the pulped bank, the river swelled a dirty grey brown.'

Apparent are turns of phrasing that Kenneth would utilise much later; the previous revelling in language, tempered and disciplined by the need for occasional convention. 'Dirty grey brown' sounds comparatively pedantic to his earlier excesses.

In early November, Frank Lawrance was impressed enough by his reliability and quality of work to offer him the long-awaited full-time post. The 12s. 6d. he had been on the previous sixteen months, as a contributor, was about to rise to a staggering 30s. as a member of staff. Lawrance introduced him to the rest of the team that included Laurence Thompson, Leslie Tunks, Anthony Foye, Jack May, Michael Gardner, Don Humphreys and Ted Jones. The youngest of the team, Kenneth found like-minds dissatisfied with the local education system, and hungry for a less parochial future. All apart from Frank Lawrance; a traditionalist who maintained an editorial distance by calling him 'Allsop.' To the others, the new cub reporter became, simply, 'Ken.' He fitted in with the knockabout air of positive cynicism. This, he achieved, not by joining it, but through challenging their assumptions he found all too easy to share. He found some, like Leslie Tunks, further entrenched in the Left than he, with others, like Jack May and Mike Gardner, less politically committed, but sympathetic. Subsequent correspondence, exchanged during the War, suggests Kenneth's advice was always deemed the most insightful, if not always agreed with.

Here, he took full advantage of his new status, able to exercise, for the first time in public, his reconciliation of country pursuits with arguments from his left-leaning perspective. 'Is There A Good Reason For Hunting Wild Animals?' was published on 11th. Initially inspired by Lawrance as an overview on 'the rights and wrongs of

Beagling,' after a local protest meeting, held the previous Friday, against the Eton College Beagle Hounds hunt, Kenneth set out his stall:

'The fight against the hounding of small animals is based almost solely on humanitarian grounds...Is it in accordance with our "advanced civilisation" that people SHOULD BE ALLOWED to get a thrill from seeing a wild animal ripped and torn by hounds which are trained from birth for that one purpose?' He concedes that, while he has never hunted, 'I...have often walked the fields with a shot gun. There IS a definite zest in sighting a rabbit near the blackthorn, stopping and quietly bringing the gun to your shoulder...' but that Man should rise above such instinctive urges and redirect them 'in proper channels.' Equally, he recognised that a controlled hunting of certain species was a necessity for their continuance, but that this should be overseen by Government and not unilaterally by a hunt. 'The English fauna is small enough already and has been seriously depleted during the last century. Surely it would be worth preserving the otter and the badger...Not as fugitives which are put up with only for the sake of the hunts, but as inhabitants of our island...as living creatures which have more right in this land than we have ourselves.' More tellingly, he identifies how the nature of the hunt has changed, where once the working class tradesmen hunted alongside the squire but that, today, 'the average hunter spends the week in a Piccadilly flat and the weekend in watching the throat of the pregnant vixen torn out.'

Of the local shooting parties, he adds; 'I have met a number of hunting people: the typical male has, probably, plenty of room to spare in his head, for his brains do not occupy much space; the female has, in all likelihood, a packet of nails where her heart should be.' His case 'for and against' was proving top-heavy, ending with the intriguing question, 'Are these birds and animals worth preserving for their own sakes only?' His response, 'If not, they should be exterminated quickly and mercifully,' is defiant, upset and purely adrenal. Hardly a balanced argument, then, but Kenneth was in dire need of voicing the intrusions he was witnessing into the natural order of things; his natural order.

In the spring of 1939, Kenneth began interviewing for his first series of articles as *The Slough Observer*'s new reporter. As if in response to his new, independent status, he emphasised his taste in Americana still further by adopting a fedora – slanted at a *louche* angle – with a bright yellow tie and suede shoes. He was also growing his hair, just onto the collar, a lank cowlick hanging lazily down by his right temple. Entitled 'Industries In Our Midst,' the new Slough Trading Estate, its factories and their produce became his subjects. Such exotic hot spots as *A. Meek & Co. Ltd's Brooches and Ornaments, Be-Ze-Be's Jam* and *Peter Field's* suspender-less sock manufacturers were his assignments. The series collective tone suggests he had little genuine interest or input. His ideas were well above this station. Primarily, its purpose was as comparatively innocent propaganda for the locale, inspired by a colonial protectionism by the Home Counties, against the backdrop of social unrest festering in Europe.

On 27th April 1939, the Tory Government announced the call-up of all men aged twenty and over; relief for the nineteen-year-old Kenneth. Between the journalists there was mutual agreement that, if they had to join a military service, then the RAF seemed a safer, cleaner bet than the severe grafting and regimentation expected in the British Army. However, the announcement also ensured a sadly premature parting with colleagues like Leslie Tunks, Ted Jones and Mike Gardner. Kenneth saw out his remaining months of liberty making the most of his parochial stories, which suddenly took on a greater significance. On the 1st

September, Kenneth was extolling the virtues of the collection and delivery service of the Slough and Langley Laundry, 'whose vans cover 2,000 miles in this district in one week...' Hardly heady stuff, but the complacent local press were resigned to the inevitable after Hitler invaded Poland some forty-eight hours later. Slough's reporters' were given, with provisos,' a comparatively free hand as part of the War Effort. Kenneth excelled, as a consequence:

'To you, the petrol rationing may mean the end of your weekend spins in the car,' he opened in an article later this month, with what was fast becoming a trademark, accusatory prelude. 'But to some Slough people in the service station trade it means unemployment and financial disaster.' After procuring the recent experiences of local garage owners, a wistful Kenneth concludes that 'traffic in the evenings is almost nil. The writer of this article walked two miles across Slough in the moonlight at about 9.30 p.m. on Monday, from Farnham Road to Wexham Road, and only met two cars, two buses and a few bicycles. It was an almost uncannily peaceful scene.'

A maternity home for expectant mothers, away from their soldiering husbands, and in the midst of short-notice renovation, is reported with only partial attention, yet with some genuine concern. But, Kenneth was not yet immune to influence through his own ignorance. A look at the drainage of Slough's evacuees, and the heart-rending excuses used by the children's natural parents for their return, is naively frowned upon by the reporter.

'In some instances, parents have insisted on taking their children back on the most trifling pretexts. One father who bundled his little boy back to London was most indignant because the householder with whom the boy had been staying had not warmed the milk before pouring it on his cereal! Another example of parents making mountains out of molehills is this case. On receiving a complaint from a parent, a Town Hall official visited the house where the child was billeted and found it to be a most comfortable residence; the food was good, varied and plentiful. Yet, the irate parent was insistent on having the billet changed because she thought her child's underclothing was not being looked after properly.'

He was listening to the editor to whom he was so indebted. His feet are on firmer territory when he lifts his eyes to the skies. Under the heading, 'Now We're Remembering The Stars,' he ponders over the consequence of the regular blackouts as citizens are forced to forsake neon and electric lighting to 'wonder at the loveliness of natural night.' Apparently, this has overcome Britons' natural reserve to the extent that Kenneth finds himself chatting incessantly with total strangers. Towards the end of the year, Kenneth exhibits his physicality in accepting a challenge from the Rector of St. Mary's Church parish magazine to climb the forty-three steps of its spiral staircase to the very top of its belfry; something no visitor had achieved in the past decade. Kenneth had to climb farther.

'(I) mounted a spidery and rusty iron ladder to a narrow balcony, almost 400 feet high, around the slim cone of the steeple – the first visitor in ten years to venture to this height.' With this boast, he describes standing upon the timbers directly over the huge bells, clambering over the swaying wooden wheel and swinging up on to the narrow iron ladder, leading to an equally narrow balcony. With his seasoned, calm steeple-keeper, Alfred Bateman, ahead, Kenneth looks out on Slough and the surrounding country with 'Windsor Castle predominating to the South.' Immediately below, the town itself with its Trading Estate and 'jagged background' of pointing chimneys. Kenneth was exuding a confidence in danger of appearing arrogant. We can picture the loose-limbed, dark-haired, pale-skinned nineteen-year-old, surveying the landscape with wide-set eyes and more than a hint of superiority. He knew he was better than any of this and deserved much more. It is not as if his mother could have failed to remind him. If only the right opportunity arose he could prove it. But, at the back of his mind was the obstacle of a new War; he was already running out of time.

Soon after their son was offered the full-time post with *The Slough Observer*, John and Mary agreed to leave Middlesex and return to Yorkshire. Since he was now in a position to support himself, and the county had become so much more his home than theirs, they virtually gave him 'Roxburgh.' (In response, Kenneth said a ceremonial farewell to his boyhood by giving his now immense collection of birds' eggs, in trust, to Hounslow Library. Both, after all, were responsible for where he was now, and an influence on where he intended heading). In his own mind, John had failed in his long-term striving to maintain a career in the housing market.

Meanwhile, Mary's snobbish, back-turning, middle-class neighbours only made her pine all the more for the family she had left behind a generation before. Never easily 'fitting in,' she now felt progressively disenfranchised, rootless in this manufactured environment where roots meant little. The inevitable, future loss of her only son to adulthood would be the final straw. So it was, by the summer of 1939, that John and Mary settled upon a small, inexpensive property in their old stamping ground of Beeston, Leeds, and packed their bags.

*Kenneth and Betty's wedding,
St. Peter's Church, Ealing, March 1942.*

7
Betty

Hilda Creak was born in the Gomm Road / Senegal Road, 'cockney' district of Bermondsey, SE1, on Christmas Eve, 1916. The eldest of four children, brothers' Jack and Kenneth followed with the youngest, a sister named Patricia, arriving in 1927. Although based mainly in the working-class district of South-East London, the Creaks' were really on call to their father's responsibilities at the Air Ministry. So it was, in 1930, the family moved to Newport, South Wales, where Hilda was expected to complete her education. As with most working-class girls, there was no expectation or encouragement from their elders that they should follow a career. This wasn't a point of view Hilda, in puberty, could relate to. On their return to London, three years later, Hilda got a job at Laurence's, the outfitters, in Charing Cross Road. This, to satisfy that 'expectation;' nothing more. As she had expected, this proved insufficient as future security.

While no careerist, she was determined to follow a course of self-improvement and not simply accept the status quo with life's duller inevitabilities. For a start, the name 'Hilda' had to go. Popular enough in 1916, by the late Thirties, the name was sounding unavoidably Edwardian. 'Betty' became the more acceptably modern standard for her friends. She began to hunger for books, harbouring a particular interest in literary novels and the more polemical pamphlets of her left-wing parents. In her mind, these opened aspirational doors, making the previous, modest expectations of their elders' anathema to both girls. Pat, her young sister, recalls;

'I knew that I didn't want to live the lives that my parents had led and I didn't want to marry somebody like my brothers, even though I'm very fond of them. But I knew that wasn't *my* life. In that sense, like Betty, I didn't want to be thought of as ordinary. So, I never went for boys who would've been just like my brothers…Not that it would've been like my parents because things just got better economically, but it would've been a dull life.'

Aged twenty, Betty had grown into a striking woman: handsome, rather than girlishy beautiful in the stereotypical mould. She was small, pale-skinned, with hazel eyes, Roman nose, cheekbones elongating to prominence, a firm chin and luxuriant, jet-black hair pinned up in the current style. At the very least, she was hard to ignore. The general look, best described as Italianate.

At a dance, in 1937, she met and fell in love with Jack Goodenough; a wine merchant at *Justerine and Brookes*, whose weekends were taken up in the Territorial Army. Jack stood well over six feet in height, long-boned and rangy in his frame. Within eighteen months the couple were engaged, but on 3rd September 1939, Goodenough was automatically conscripted into the Regulars. Pat recalls the following train of events:

'In May 1940, my mother and I joined my father in Oxfordshire. My father had been working for the Air Ministry at Brice Norton. I think Ken (Creak) stayed with my godmother in Bermondsey. Betty went to stay with Jack's widowed mother and his sister, Doris, in Vestry Road, Camberwell. In September, Jack was granted compassionate leave because of the heavy bombing in that area, and as his mother was a widow. He had a brother, Leslie, who lived in (Hayes) Kent. The family decided to go to (Hayes). I'm not sure why; whether it was to settle Mrs G. there, or just for the weekend, I don't know. The point was, the bombs weren't falling there; it was a neutral area. Normally, the woman next door slept with Leslie's family because of the war, but her husband was on leave so, of course, they slept in their own home. That night, Leslie and Jack slept in one ground floor room, and the women and children, plus Stocky the dog, slept in the other. A bomber, on the way home after beating up the East End, dropped...what must have been his last bomb on the Goodenough house. It fell on the room where Jack and Leslie slept. The women and children were more or less unharmed. Mrs. G., Doris, Betty and Stocky the dog turned up at our primitive, galvanised war bungalow still covered in plaster, dust, and bits of house.'

Understandably, Betty was too traumatised by this unexpected demise of her fiancee to stomach a return to London. Still grieving, she asked her current employers, at the G.P.O., for a posting outside the capital. By early 1941 she was working from Cheltenham.

8
Feb 1940 – March 1943: LAC 915084

Tom Wintringham was a middle-aged ex-Communist who, four years earlier, had led the British contingent of the International Brigade through the Spanish Civil War. Intent on contributing to this War effort on his own terms, he lobbied the wealthiest men he knew. His purpose was to open an independent training school, for the drilling of new recruits as Local Defence Volunteers. (Later, better known as the Home Guard).   His sights and his funding settled upon Osterley Park.

Wintringham comes over as a direct, uncompromising individualist, distrustful of an authority which no doubt viewed him as both an asset and a loose cannon. Described as 'a passionate advocate of guerrilla warfare,' he may, today, be perceived more as an eccentric but consistent advocate of direct action. There was no doubting his integrity or intent. Through the first half of 1940, he recruited three former miners, and comrades from Spain, as troop lecturers, chosen for their ability to disable tanks. Wintringham then blitzed a list of both local and national press (including, most notably, *Picture Post,*) with articles intended to promote a positive spirit of offence in the readership. Utilising and, to some extent, customising his own Army training, Wintringham and his Spanish colleagues initiated the local amateur volunteers in camouflage, decapitation of enemy motorcyclists by trip-wire and effective street-fighting. Such socialist entrepreneurism proved effective enough for some five thousand men – both amateur and regular army – to pass through his training school between July and October. George Orwell, himself a veteran of the Spanish campaign, attended at least one of the training sessions during this time. Later, the Government took it over as 'War Office No.1 School.'

Kenneth would have been blissfully unaware of all this when the call-up papers fell through his door, mid-February. He had chosen the RAF, swallowing the misguided consensus held between his colleagues at the paper that it was a cleaner, 'cushier,' and less brutal life than that in the Army. To be sure, he had applied to join a Miscellaneous Unit; a course in learning specific disciplines related to assisting the war effort. His role would be as trainee Teleprinter Operator. Typing, at least, came naturally, and Morse Code would be needlework practice compared to Army training. He surmised he could also write his own work, covertly, between duties, as if he were writing theirs. Surely, few would question the innocuous presence of a notebook? From such a position he felt he could gather material by observing and absorbing the atmosphere of Forces life during this Second World War. He seriously believed he could eventually offer an appraisal of this World War equivalent to what his hero, Williamson, offered for the last. The initial anger soon gave way to pondering such literary possibilities. Unfortunately for Kenneth, he knew few who would put him right.

Bolstered by Frank Lawrance's promise of his post being left open until war's end, it was on a bleak 16th February that he kissed 'Poppy' goodbye and reported, as instructed, to Unit No. 1, Radio College, Uxbridge, where he was, literally, submerged beneath his kit, an official number - '915084' - and rank of A.C.2. With him was a lugubrious-featured Londoner named Joe Molloy. Out went the casually stylish look he later referred to as representing 'the Chelsea set of Slough,' as off came the lank brown locks, yellow tie, snap-brimmed hat and suede shoes. Within six months, training would classify him as an L.A.C. (Leading Aircraftsman); a standard rank, equivalent to an Army Corporal. He passed the initial proficiency exam with a – for him – modest 81.2%. On 20th July, he and Molloy were moved to HQ Bomber Command at High Wycombe. Here, the bleakness continued. His billet was cramped, consisting of three iron beds, surrounded by walls of yellow plaster, and covered by magazine cut-outs' of partially naked girls. After duties one rainy November night, he returned and switched on the second-hand radio he was sharing with his roommates. In a brown-covered exercise book he was scribbling short story ideas in at the time, he wrote of the 'ack-ack, Beer-Beer' programme transmitting on the force's wavelength; a miscellany for the searchlight and anti-aircraft crews. One item featured an interview with a Fleet Street journalist:

'I sat down on the partly made bed as the interview went on, for what the journalist was saying struck forcibly across my thoughts. That day, a short story of mine had been returned yet again by yet another editor. Unable ever to take the advice so often repeated in "How-To-Write" books, - "never be disappointed," - I had been in a despondent mood all day. While the Sergeant instructor had been delving deeply into the types of generator used in aircraft, my mind was circling around this latest and past mishaps and disappointments in my literary efforts. Also, these thoughts (were) tinged with jealousy, for along with the rejected MS had come a letter from a reporter friend, now in the Army, recounting the success of a play he had written, which was being staged by a London Producer for a big show of troops. So, the journalist's words struck home. "After this war," he was saying, "new men will be wanted in Fleet Street. Today, newspapers are changing. They are crusaders and young men with vision and ideas for the peace will be needed to write the papers." He ended with "Who will be the writer of this war's *Journey's End*? Perhaps he is somewhere now, fighting or learning to fight, listening to this broadcast." I sat and wondered, and then wrote this for no reason at all.'

As was his nature, Kenneth was trying hard to turn the disappointment of this situation to his advantage. But it was proving difficult. As he had promised himself, he was writing copious, semi-fictional notes, as a basis for a projected novel 'of the "All Quiet" school.' But, the contrivance was proving hopelessly naive and self-serving.

'When this war is finished,' he wrote, 'I hope to make some money out of it. I hope it will provide plots and copy aplenty.' He had decided that his 'former position as a keyboard tapper,' was proving too sedentary and isolating. He felt himself in an administrative limbo not dissimilar to that of four years earlier. He pondered on how he could be expected to write like Remarque, Hemingway or Williamson, tapping out messages in a bomb-proof chamber fifty feet underground. Too late, Kenneth discovered that what was lacking was what he had gone out his way to avoid; experience at The Front. So, he applied for a post as wireless operator / aerial gunner: this, under a further misapprehension that, as part of the discipline, he might be accompanying the pilots.

Re-reading Kenneth's 1940 jottings, there is an uncomfortable sense of introspective pretension at work. While he was serious in his literary yearning, he was also writing self-consciously; ever hopeful of an eventual audience. To him, the setting of the text may be of little consequence, but the text itself is what mattered and what would ultimately count. An awareness dawned that words were important and never to be uttered unthinkingly or taken for granted.

Grudgingly settling in to his rota of duties – assault

coursing, bayonet practice, lessons, night watch and drill – Kenneth became an easily recognisable figure to the men, from his notebook scribbling alone. Few chanced an approach; this lean, stylish figure appearing intellectually superior and aloof. In July 1941, with national security the priority, and for the continuance of his study, he was on the move again; this time to the Air Ministry Unit, covertly based at the St. Regis Hotel, Cork Street, London W1. The 'plots and copy aplenty' that might have inspired a modicum of interest remained elusive. Not a site appropriate for launching Spitfires', it can only be assumed that the grounded wireless operating was the norm. Accompanying him, like a dubious omen, was the dependable Joe Molloy. Kenneth's second medical since joining up passed him as 'fit' for 'WO / AG' training. As did his third nine weeks later. But, so what? What mattered was his writing here, that one needful link to some literary future in the outside world, which so far remained pointedly ignored. It didn't help when Jack May, still yet to serve, inadvertently compounded his misery with this, written to him on 17th June from Harrow:

'Remember that article Stuart Campbell wanted me to write? You gave me some wonderful tips about it. Well, I slaved at it for a whole week. Took it to him. He liked it. So, instead of bearing the words, "Slo(ugh) Obs(erver) reporting staff," my card now says "Sunday Pictorial reporting staff." I've been lucky...incredibly, gloriously lucky. On my second day in the noo job I managed to write a story, which they liked, used in the first edition. For weeks after that I had a story in each paper. Then came the week when I had three stories in. Week before last I had an inspiration. I tied two stories together under a general intro. They used it as the page 5 lead.'

Pining for open air, Kenneth wrote in a melancholic frame of mind, perhaps to Poppy or to another weekend lover, such stuff as,

> 'THINGS REMEMBERED
> *A ferny place,*
> *A puckered pool,*
> *A dear-loved face,*
> *Fingers cool,*
>
> *A menthol gale,*
> *Trees' frosty lace,*
> *Winds' gentle wail*
> *Through star-spun space.*
>
> *Grass tracks*
> *Over sun-glossed downs.*
> *And we two, our backs*
> *To the dark octopus town.'*

*

On 31st October, Kenneth was sent for a further medical. During a recent assault course he had inadvertently hit his right knee upon a hurdle, mid-leap, leaving a throbbing, scarred bruise. Quietly hoping for a longer stretch off the more mundane duties to concentrate on his writing, the medical board passed him as otherwise 'fit' to continue. This mild disappointment may well have been heightened by the fact that he had yet to actually fly, even as a regular passenger. An enjoyable spin in a Tiger Moth at an air show during 1935 was his one cajoling memory; and looked like remaining so. He put the incident out of his mind.

Since arriving at the St. Regis with a growing pile of notebooks, he was at least getting noticed by his immediate circle. Christopher Bouchier, as equally handsome, perhaps taller and with a faint pencil moustache, began warming to him, as did one George Hilton. Already garnering an interest in the recent career of T.E. Lawrence, Hilton became sidetracked by, then schooled in, Kenneth's own fascination with Williamson. In return, Hilton awakened his dormant interest in Dixieland Jazz and American popular culture. Kenneth opened up, finally encountering a small group of servicemen with parallel interests. Hilton recalls how they spent their evenings off:

'We had great times in London. To a cafe first for a coffee and a sandwich, then a bus down to the Jazz Club at 100, Oxford Street to hear George Webb's Dixielanders. Many a time a service policeman pulled Ken up for not wearing his RAF hat. I remember one time – at Kingsway, I think – Ken responded with, 'While you're telling me off for not wearing a hat, there are thousands of people being killed in Europe!' Some of the NCOs' fell out with Mr. Allsop...He didn't want service life, you know.' But there was increasing room for irony; 'He was fond of pulling peoples' legs and feigning innocence. He was that sort of fellow.' Those with no special interest in books could become victim to the Allsop vocabulary. One such, a cockney WAAF girl from Poplar, East London, named Pat Witts, responded to a casually asked question with, "I dunno, mate!" Kenneth stopped in his tracks. "Mate?" he queried, with his clipped, tight-throated, Home Counties accent. "Mate! Only Tarzan had a mate." An early example of apposite, but undeniable, condescension he would utilise often.

The short stories and nature articles he was submitting to various papers were, in truth, half-hearted affairs. This and their lack of propaganda value, early in the War, might explain their being passed over. Certainly, Hilton confirms Kenneth's main priority was that 'he wanted to write a *real* novel,' he could remain proud of after this conflict had ended. Away from the Elysian fields of Osterley Park, factual inspiration betrayed him; human domesticity proving the obstacle.

Christmas 1941 ended with an invitation to an RAF dance in High Wycombe on New Years Eve. It is unlikely Kenneth felt any real enthusiasm, as most of the guests were his former, disinterested colleagues at Bomber Command. Accompanying Hilton, Bouchier and other servicemen from the Air Ministry Unit, Kenneth consoled himself with his expertise in using his dark, hunter eyes to search for skirt and a swift lay. On entering the dance hall, Bouchier appeared the lucky one. A small, narrow-shouldered, black-haired woman with good cheekbones and a flawless complexion was glancing at him. But, it was his 'rather thin and funny-looking' companion who soon asked her to dance, at which she duly obliged. Later, walking to the bar, Bouchier's companion took an inordinately long time to get the drinks, such was the elbow-shoving battle to pull before midnight. He looked back at her and winked a grin. Risking the cold but needing the space, he suggested they sit at a table on the balcony. They talked. He discovered her socialist background and dry wit - she, his intellect and idealism. Before they knew it, the crowd was converging to a circle, linking arms to sing *Auld Lang Syne*. In the wee small hours of 1942, they left together, stopped for a snack at a coffee stall, said 'goodnight,' Ken Allsop insisting to Betty Creak he would meet her again the following week.

Kenneth's sex life, between meeting Poppy in 1935 and Betty Creak in 1941, remains a blank. Jack May claimed that, on hearing of Ken's recent marriage, Poppy burst into incredulous laughter. Clearly, she had become used to his straying through the intervening years. We can only speculate. By the end of his sixteen-month stint at *The Slough Observer*, he had certainly gained a love 'em and leave 'em reputation. But, far from boasting about it to his colleagues, it swiftly palled, leaving him feeling empty and unfulfilled.

He had once confessed as much to May. A propensity to martyrdom in his more heartfelt writings suggests he poured out his heart, with dextrous verbal charm, to get what he wanted; passionate, short-term clinches for transient satisfaction. It is unlikely that he saw this as clinical or contrived. As with most young men in their teens, his heart ruled his head, manifesting a fiery, but ultimately fickle, intent to commitment. In other words, he meant it for as long as the feeling lasted. Unlike others, his habit of getting out quickly, once the physical engagement was made, avoided any long-winded, emotional fallout; at least for himself. He could not have handled the alternative.

For the first time in his life, he found himself intrigued enough by Betty Creak's idealistic socialism, allied to a certain honest vulnerability, to want only to position her, horizontally. After just the one meeting, he felt himself falling in love. They met again on the evening of the 8th or 9th January 1942, in Fitzroy Square, where Ken awkwardly, self-consciously, declared his heart. A third meeting, the following week, and the obvious didn't need stating in Ken's mind. "By the way, I've told Auntie Pattie...that we're getting married."

'She didn't know anything about this,' Pat Creak recalled.

Back at his billet, Ken was feeling vulnerable and pining for more;

'When we parted, I was engulfed in a ghastly feeling of utter desolation and loneliness, and for some strange reason felt *frightened*... I met Dan and had a dreary time. I was terribly depressed and tried not to let myself be; which is the worse thing to do. The only way to beat off depression is to admit it to oneself and examine the causes. At the time, I was feebly attempting to be cheerful and full of camaraderie, and felt like hell...' He insisted marriage was the only course for peace of mind. 'Betty, my own, my life, my heart, my whole existence and future is bound up in you. Without you

I can be nothing; with you, I feel I could snare a star. Until now I've been a half-person searching for his other part. Together we are completeness.' Ken, so far, had done little without good reason, practically and intellectually. But, there was no sly, ulterior motive here. He had simply got it bad; his frustrated, incarcerated, life-hungry heart bursting to the fore and pleading for attention. Between free weekends, from mid-January to mid-March, he bombarded Betty with telephone calls and letters on a daily basis:

'...an evening away from you is unbearable and painful... I am filled with a strange poignancy and longing, which has only been born within me once or twice in the past. Once, I remember, when I stood, one autumn afternoon, on the Hangar overlooking Selborne, where that practical romantic, Gilbert White, wrote his lovely nature book. Then, as dusk began to creep to the misty edges of the beech woods, I felt that that moment was everlasting. I was gazing on the shadowy vista of a dying world. It was the term I left school. Every rustle of a yellowed leaf in that pungent silence seemed to have a significance and omen all of its own. It was the end of an epoch in my personal life...'

The new epoch was set aside, beginning Friday March 16th. In the days leading up to this date, both had obtained compassionate leave; Ken staying with his parents in Leeds, and Betty with his Aunt Pattie at 86, Meadvale Road. Her intended was still impatient. He blitzed a brief series of 'announcement' letters to his Slough colleagues, now billeted for the Services, and one more for his future wife;

'I pray March 16th will be sent scurrying round,' he wrote. 'It's the gateway to a new life for us both, my own.' He hardly had long to wait. In the presence of Ken's mother, Mary, and Betty's mother, Mabel, they were married at St. Peter's Parish Church, Ealing, by its vicar, E.H. Loasby. Since the imposition of clothes-rationing the previous June, Ken, grudgingly, wore his grey-blue R.A.F. uniform; Betty, a second-hand wedding dress courtesy of his aunt, while her sister Pat, as bridesmaid, wore the dress she had only recently worn at her brother, Jack's, Boxing Day wedding. To the bridegroom's great relief, Aunt Pattie took charge of the reception.

Ken knew, instinctively, where they should honeymoon: in the region so many of Williamson's books were set. Around the north-west Devon coast they installed themselves at a guesthouse in the village of Croyde, run by a Mr and Mrs Staddon. This would be Betty's first taste of Williamson country and her new husband's boyish obsession. It is likely Ken talked of little else, so desperate was he to furnish and bounce-off a like-mind, after the claustrophobia of the air base. During their ten-week, whirlwind romance, he had given her a copy of Williamson's *The Flax of Dream*, written, close by, at Georgeham. Betty later stated she thought her new husband would have dropped her on the spot had she not shown her appreciation. To Ken, this would be her follow-up history lesson on his mentor. They consummated their love in Spraecombe Woods, situated, locally, in a small valley. Since it featured in the book, this was a twin coupe for Ken; a physical and a spiritual union in one, leaving each 'unaware of the cold, March day.' Of Williamson himself with his fascist sympathies, Betty returned to London, unnerved, and with a head full of questions.

Unable to afford a home of their own, Betty's parents offered the newlyweds accommodation below them, on the second floor of 100, Mount View Road, Hornsey, N4, in the district of Stroud Green. Since Mr. Creak was often away on Air Ministry affairs, and Ken regularly re-stationed by the RAF, the ageing Mrs. Creak could stay with Betty for mutual company, leaving 15-year-old Patricia some much needed independence on the third floor.

No sooner had Ken returned to his unit than, on the 28th, he was re-packing his kit for a further move; this time to G.H.Q.

at Leighton Buzzard. Hilton, Bouchier, and, of course, Joe Molloy, accompanied him. By now, and perhaps not surprisingly, Ken and Joe were beginning to get on, after an initial, mutual indifference felt since they first queued together at Uxbridge. This may have been a sign of Ken's more relaxed, more pragmatic, attitude to service since his recent marriage. Temporarily, War was keeping them apart, but only on weekdays. He and Betty were still together at weekends; spring allotting short but precious time for country walks and picnics, including a possible return visit to North Devon.

It was about this time that Ken returned to Mount View Road clutching to his chest a wounded crow. This was his first close encounter with these fascinating rascals in four years, since he last featured one in 'Country Log.' He and Pat made a recuperative nest for it in the tiny attic window and named it 'Rommel,' after Hitler's Field-Marshal. Ignorant of the bird's diet, they fed it lettuce and hoped for the best. 'Rommel' was released, flapping fit, just days later. Pat recalled; 'As a bird lover it was wrong to keep it, but this was typical of the many paradoxes in Ken's life.' Yet, such encounters were sustaining. Continuity was important to him.

These were comparatively sylvan days for Ken. It is remarkable, then, that a mannered, melancholic tone, still pervades his correspondence. The mannerism of the following letter, claiming a lack of self-worth from his past, transient relations with women, rings as hollow and pointless:

'...in all honesty, I cannot discover any logical reason for having been blessed with a wife such as you. If I had led a clean, saintly life...if I had endeavoured to direct my thoughts to one ideal only in a woman, if I had to fight like blazes for you, then winning through, I might have been worthy of you. Not that my life was any worse than the next fellow's; just a haphazard series of tawdry episodes through which I strolled – to you.' This is self-serving nonsense, and not what a new wife during wartime would find of paramount importance. If this seems harsh, then consider, 'if I had led a clean, saintly life,' and 'my life was...just a haphazard series of tawdry episodes through which I strolled – to you.' Here, he is self-regarding and not considering what Betty might actually want or need to hear. If he was admitting to past indiscretions, then why not make this plain, rather than couch them in a Byronic prose style? With more clarity, he adds: '...I feel such an utter worm, sometimes, when I've been surly and short with you, merely because I feel out of temper...I suppose it's the natural reaction of the guilty to be even more sullen when he encounters inexplicable kindness...'

The reason is to do with Ken's incorrigible vanity. Articulation of the heart had never before been on his agenda. The organ was an enigma to him. It was the intellect he could rely upon to both express what he needed to communicate and mask what he didn't. His was proving exceptional, but revealed its limitation when emotion obtruded. Betty loved him but not to the extent that this clouded her own judgement. 'Betty understands me, *absolutely*,' he confided to a friend, years later. She, in turn, could accept him as the 'vain bugger' he was, perhaps because she saw him as rarely, if ever, disingenuous. On 3rd September, he reviewed their first summer together with genuine fondness:

'I've been thinking you and I were in a score of different places – walking hand-in-hand across the moors at Dunkirk, with you, poor darling, limping with a lame leg and not complaining a bit, hiding your face fearfully while I climbed to a ridiculously easy magpie's nest in a lime tree growing above the stream, waiting patiently while I scoured a swamp for a snipes' nest, while the two birds circled around our heads... Then us both on all those wonderful days in Devon when the weather seemed to put on a special summer rehearsal especially for us... Then there was that burning Sunday in Tuesday Woods, when we ate our sandwiches with our feet nearly dangling in the lake – and that grey day in early spring when we came home with armfuls of sticky buds – and even that brief walk in the meadows at Caterton where we found that funny red fly and caught grasshoppers – every one is so vivid and clear, and so dear to me...

...up to my falling in love with you, I had no idea that there was anything emotionally lacking from my life, and would probably have resented the suggestion that there was...

...Providing you don't change and I change a little bit for the better, is there any reason why the rest of our life shouldn't be like these past nine months?'

A first for Ken with this letter, speaking truly from the heart. Already, experience as a husband was managing to inform and sideline his earlier pretence. The day before their first wedding anniversary, the once self-confessed romantic admitted to the 'deep and radical transition' that had occurred. Yet, with a certain determined pride, he fought to concede to mundane domesticity; 'Marriage almost invariably means "settling down," – and that in turn means an end to all the careless adventuring and philandering of youth. Well, perhaps in those two respects I have, quite willingly, I assure you Betty!, conformed. But, in no other way.' It was himself he was reassuring.

9
April 1943 – Feb 1944: 'Everything is forward'

Since his marriage to Betty, twelve months earlier, Ken's war maintained an unchallenging routine of modest progress, which managed never to test his distracted commitment. His work duties at GHQ, Leighton Buzzard, followed a standard pattern of written-theory and physical-practical that wouldn't have compromised the staunchest pacifist in peacetime. This allowed for evenings' home at Stroud Green, sharing with Betty country walks and film trips at weekends. The downside remained that such experiences were hardly conducive to the production of great, incisive works of fiction. Allied to this was the fact that he was now waiting for transference to another base, he knew not when or where. He simply had to make himself available when the call finally came.

So it was that, at Easter of 1943, Ken, his now ubiquitous notebook, and Betty, took a tedious, four-hour train journey West, from Paddington Station to the Wye Valley, for a week's rural walking. Betty, with her father, had arranged the stay at the local Plough Inn on the outskirts of Evesham. They were met by its proprietors, Mr & Mrs Morris, the husband, an employee of Betty's father. They made an oddly contrasting couple; he 'fat, jovial, talkative and shrewd,' she 'sophisticated in appearance, Oxford St. clothes and make-up. Her oddness...heightened by her deafness, which prevents her joining in conversation.' Ken was pleased to observe all this from the publican's side of the bar, 'with unlimited drink to hand.' The next morning, the

Allsops' awoke to a generous bacon and egg breakfast, followed by a bus journey across the Malverns' to Colwall, then a train to Ledbury, where they began their walk. Heading towards Rustall from Little Marcle they got lost, their map detailing footpaths recently ploughed up. Only the appearance of a farmhand with an Italian prisoner in tow, sitting on his cart, wearing a jersey with a large, ominous, black circle at its centre, betrays the world situation, as they ask directions. But these don't appear to matter as the couple spent much of the week, on foot, blithely following their noses, and getting wilfully lost. With no new Big Idea on the horizon, Ken can do nothing more but write, almost aimlessly, what he sees. Birds and flowers burst, in profusion, across the pages, like the ochre of the endless eggs he and Betty are served, wherever they bed down, for breakfast, dinner and tea. Blinded by love, this was direction enough.

From the start of their third day, Ken sounds more relaxed and content with his surroundings than he has for a long time; certainly, since the outbreak of War. Nowhere is this made clearer than when they reach the hamlet of Peneraig, just beyond the Wye:

'At the post office and gift shop, we enquired if there was anywhere we could find to room and the lady, a Mrs Roberts, offered to do so. (Sic). So, we left our bags in a spotlessly clean room and read in the meadow of a big estate, opposite, until teatime. After tea, we walked down the hillside towards the Wye, and while Betty rested on the banks, I strolled along, exploring. Saw nothing very much except the rooks mobbing a kestrel hawk, and a lesser black-backed gull flying aimlessly along the river. Later, we walked higher up the lane and read in a field, then returned to a magnificent supper, which included egg salad. (We've had eggs every day, so far!) and met the two Birmingham girls who are staying here and making it their headquarters for walks. We have been tremendously impressed by the kindness and friendliness of everyone we've met, from the people in the garage at Much Marcle, to the gamekeeper we encountered this evening. We had been led to expect just the opposite. We were told that the Hertfordshire people were taciturn and suspicious, but that is quite false.

We are both acquiring tans. The weather is glorious; never known such an April. Everything is forward and there are galaxies of flowers – violets, primroses, wild pansies, ladies smock,...cowslips and buttercups on every lane-side bank. We have seen a peacock butterfly and many others we could not identify.'

Fascinated by the smallness of great things, he becomes equally enamoured by the comparative cost of their daily meals. 'The bill for tea, bed and breakfast and coffee was 16/- ; very reasonable, we thought,' he wrote that evening from the lounge of Awnall's Farmhouse, just outside the village of Much Marcle. The following morning he'd experienced, 'the bill, which included breakfast of egg and bacon, came to 13/-! Ridiculously cheap, even according to peace-time standards.' On the fifth morning he recorded that, 'after leaving Symonds Yat (bill 18/6), we left the Wye behind us and headed down towards the Forest of Dean.' He opens the sixth day, announcing the bill to be '17/-, which included excellent supper and breakfast.' Such obsessive scrupulousness betrays an anorak tendency his long-held love of bird minutiae could only suggest. Poor Betty was certainly put through it on arrival at Symonds Yat two days before. Misreading their map, so disregarding the presence of interceding hills en route, Ken led the way, from a half-crouching posture, upwards and over through wild, hair clawing, woodland and ankle-threatening boulders. Directed to the appropriately named 'High View,' they stopped for a much-deserved rest before Ken encouraged a further climb up the rocks to sit and marvel at the surrounding view. His enjoyment was tempered only by the interrupting cluster of hotels and boarding houses. 'Commercialisation again,' he wrote disapprovingly.

On leaving Symonds Yat for the Forest of Dean, Ken was disconcerted to find the gauntlet he had to face and run. For approximately four miles, casually left along either side of the road, were salvaged 300 – 500-pounder bombs, he described as 'evil-looking brown cylinders with yellow noses.' Whether he liked it or not, his other responsibility was never too far to remind him. On Saturday 24th April, their last full day in the Wye before seeing the weekend out with Betty's father at Willersey, the dark clouds gathered and a wind rose up as they bussed on to Broadway. (This, naturally, after another egg-dominated breakfast). Though the commercialism in the village was evident once more, Ken found it quite subtle and tastefully achieved, repudiating the more blatant charges of contemporaries considered 'intellectual snobs' and 'the away-from-it-all haters of popularity.' He may have become the perennial outsider, but Ken was neither of these.

Back home, Ken completed and submitted a manuscript copy of a novel he had been working on these past few months, entitled 'The Ascending Circle.' It's subject matter is not known, other than it was a first attempt at a human issue story; unavoidable considering his experience of the previous three years. His first point of call, Frank Lawrance at *The Slough Observer*, seemed obvious. It appears Lawrance maintained a genuine enthusiasm for 'Allsop' as a writer, whatever their personal relationship may have been, and made it clear he'd give it priority and offer what advice he could in terms of useful contacts. He was also offered encouragement from a Mr. Hutchinson at Putnam's.

Around this time he received a long letter from his *Slough Observer* colleague, Mike Gardner. Now an RAF Sergeant based in Staffordshire, he too was training to become a pilot. This was the latest of several contacts Ken had received in the past year: the contents, as in previous letters, concerning Gardner's attempts to reconcile his less committed political views to Ken's own. In the midst of this latest, Ken read the following:

'I fully share your hope that I will not dive into the North Sea one dark night. Let it be known, however, that I do not intend to be in an aircraft that 'failed to return.' (German papers, please copy). I have too much to do after the present conflict in collaboration with cub reporters, Allsopp (sic) and May, and besides, my demise would leave the field clear for James Hadley Chase. Be assured, then, of my longevity and immunity, or else stick the above remarks in your 'Famous Last Words' volume.'

Ken replied, suggesting a time to meet.

If not tamed, Betty had calmed Ken's once romantic and insecure ego. Through this prolonged period away from the RAF, he was learning to settle and socialise into the role of the good husband. That Betty was already in her twenty-seventh year, with a tragically terminated long-term relationship behind her, gave her the necessary inner strength to maintain an independent and objective mind in her dealings with him. However, conspicuous by its absence is what the Wye Valley diary leaves out. Through Ken's introspective observations, Betty is reduced to the secondary role of companion, apparently following in his footsteps. Yet, the collective 'we,' regularly used, points (grudgingly, on Ken's part) to her sharing the decisions. The role of Betty's father, from the first entry, suggests the expedition itself to have been her idea, while – on returning to The Plough Inn on the last Friday evening – it was she who was the worse for drink: 'I felt pretty hazy, while Betty was definitely over!' She, handling it rather better than her younger, delicately constituted husband who, back at their rooms, threw-up into the toilet.

Another pointer to Ken's maturing nature was something his NCOs' would have found impossible twelve months before; his receipt, on Thursday 10th June, of a Good Conduct badge – and a 1st at Grade A, no less. With no accompanying notice of his next station, he and Betty visited Leeds on Saturday 19th, for a fortnight of visiting his parents, relations, a friend and – unavoidably – the surrounding countryside. The following Tuesday, he and John visited the historic country estate, Temple Newsam. While at this recently restored, 'vastly interesting house,' Ken headed straight for its refurbished library, perusing the ancient bird books and impressed by their hand-painted illustrations. Equally impressed by the surroundings, John produced his sketchpad.

Back at his and Mary's Beeston home, Ken received a letter from Frank Lawrance. Since they were more mutually respectful than good friends, it wasn't likely to be a social call. Curious, he opened the letter to read that Mike, his colleague at *The Slough Observer*, had just been killed on a test flight, soon after take-off. Ken broke down. He then tried to rationalise. He'd shared, with him and the others, this single-minded optimism for their futures, but was, perhaps, like him 'too convinced of his impregnability.' He recalled that, only in Mike's last letter, 'he assured me he had no intention of being shot down, as he'd too much to do.' Despite the correspondence, they hadn't met since joining up. Now stationed near by, Ken had been awaiting confirmation to meet. He pondered upon his own mortality:

'You feel so damned lonely – and begin to wonder if you're going to be the only one left when all this is over.'

In the evening he introduced Betty to Cousin Audrey and her husband, John. At dusk, they return, walking along Dewsbury Road, Ken noting, disconsolately, 'the depleted, bedraggled, Middleton Woods on one side, and the grass-tufted slag heaps on the other,' and an encampment of gypsies, huddled around a campfire.

The following day, he and Betty explore Beeston itself, Ken surprised to find the blacksmith's shop, 'worked by relatives of mother,' still open, returning through the fields of Cottingley, Old Wortley and Farnley, then catching a bus back at Gildersome. A day later, the Allsops' meet Audrey and her husband to visit the Bronte house at Haworth. Ken finds it even gloomier inside than out, while marvelling at the wealth of talent harboured in such poor and claustrophobic conditions, 'except Branwell, whose efforts at painting were pitifully amateurish.' He and Betty return (alone?), trudging across the windswept moorland, occasionally stooping to pick its abundant cotton-grass. On Saturday, they bussed to Otley, walking the rest of the way to Fewston, with the intention of exploring the natural reservoirs at Blubberhouse Moor. A closed footpath compels a detour to that at Farnley. Continuing the propensity to eat out, they picnicked on the side slope above the water, surrounded by 'tall, rich-coloured foxgloves.' Confounded by another closed footpath, they reach Lindley Bridge and its surrounding woodland. Via the wharf at Leithley, they return to Otley, Ken noting the bird life en route.

By the end of June, Ken's obsessive, on foot excursions, had finally taken their toll on his poor wife, who was left exhausted and with severe stomach cramps. A week later, after Haworth-inspired readings of *Wuthering Heights* and *Jane Eyre*, Ken could report that 'B. has recovered a great deal. She is brighter and much more energetic.' His new posting was also due: 'Two of the 16 go on the 14th.'

One week on and Ken was concerned that he had not heard from Frank Lawrance, to whom he'd first submitted 'The Ascending Circle.' With some irritation, he bussed to Slough to confront his former editor. He was not pacified. Entering his office, Ken saw a distracted Lawrance unearth it from beneath a pile of other papers and hand it back to him, unread. Of course, Ken was furious: 'Atrocious little blighter! After the fuss he made about having it.' Things were aggravated further when the subsequent conversation turned to politics. Lawrance voiced the prevailing mood of the time. Ken seethed:

'He spoke of the 'good' variety of Fascism! And assured me that the Russian peasants resented being bolsheviced (sic): they did not want the revolution, being ideally happy with their hovels and pigs; nor did they participate in the uprising. *Oh no,* it was the Thugs who took command of each village and forced the peasants into revolutionary action!!!!! I fell inarticulate.'

Despite these feelings, not helped since Lawrance delivered the recent sad news of Mike Gardner, it is unlikely Ken hit back too hard. He was *savvy* enough to bite his lip as possible insurance for any future work Lawrance may have been willing to offer. Indeed, Ken left this meeting to chaperone Lawrance's wife for lunch at The Adelphi. Grudgingly, he admitted to finding her 'dully bright.'

As if things couldn't have gotten worse for Ken's intentions as a serious writer, what followed took a turn almost blackly comedic. Just two days after the meeting with his former editor, the original MS turned up at his door 'battered and bedraggled,' after the Post Office at Mount Pleasant that housed it received a direct hit from a German plane the month before. With it was a covering note stating that it had been en route back to the agent's with its reader's report. Ken's access to this 'bald, untempered opinion of one's work,' deflated him still further. The reader, Eric Turrel, described it as 'indifferently written, dull (and) hackneyed.' Adding the admission that he was ill when he read it, Ken pondered on the resulting ambiguity of the statement. Was he saying the book was the cause of his illness? Ken then suffered the questioning self-torment all new writers endure from such rebuttals. Of its quality, 'How on earth can I tell? What guidance have I? And if it is so bad, why did Hutchinson of *Putnam's* concern himself about it so much?'

He had believed a little progress was being made but, ultimately, still had nothing to show. Betty received the full onslaught of his temper, not seeming able to do anything right. The smallest detail – a missing cufflink or skewed collar – set him off. Betty sensed her brilliant, demanding young husband was becoming dissatisfied with her and needed someone more on his level. She felt it was only a matter of time before he looked elsewhere. When she told him this, Ken panicked, appalled. That night, he left her a letter of apology, with the assurance,

'...you shouldn't entertain those silly ideas you voiced tonight – I mean about you boring me, and you being afraid that I shall suddenly become impervious to your charm...and vanish with some other girl...You allow yourself, too much, to be affected by my chameleon changes of mood. Of course, the fault is wholly mine for allowing myself to be swept about by my emotions.' He knew few other women – those with his intellectual drives - would put up with what Betty endured. This consideration ensured he always came back.

Disillusionment set in, and he wrote little, if anything, over the next ten weeks. The one, major piece of news he received was during the first week of August; to report to No. 2 Radio College, RAF Cardington in Bedford on the 11th for five weeks of physical endurance as part of his course. On an exploratory stroll through Bedford town centre with Joe, they found the place 'swarming' with newly arrived American troops. With little reassurance, he informed Betty that, 'Females, I judge, are in ratio of 3 – 1. All I need say is that if any lack of appreciation for you, my sweet, existed in my mind, all that would be necessary would be for me to be transported to Bedford for an evening. They're like vultures around carrion; and most of them seem to have an over-developed predatory instinct. A pretty shocking advertisement for the female of the species.' But, Ken was more tantalised than repelled.

From here, he would continue studying, leading to his final exam. If this is all he had expected, then his superiors made sure he would now pay for the last six months of civilian life. Already tired by the long journey up to Bedford, (which reminded Ken, forebodingly, of High Wycombe), he and Joe caught a waiting service bus to the camp. There, they were immediately read the riot act by Brown, their new Commanding Officer, informed of their next posting, to Oxford, and issued with a long list of responsibilities, ending with an order to scrub, spotless, the camp's toilets. Perhaps there had been a clerical error. This was more like the Army he had so carefully avoided. Finally escaping from their duties, later that evening, an exhausted Ken still managed to report back to Betty from the NAAFI's Instructional Wing:

'Cardington is vast, soulless, and terrifyingly sanitary. Little concrete roads run between rows of wooden huts – in one of which we were herded. Joe and I have beds together. Several trainees had arrived before us, but others are still lurching in with their mountains of kit... As yet, the full impact of being away from you has not hit me. These things usually have a delayed action. But, it feels very strange being on a camp again and far away from the peace of our eyrie. Is your mother coming home soon? I shall feel much more settled in my mind when I know there is someone with you...'

The following week, he rushes a response to Betty's request about how he spends his days with a tone of teeth-clenched resignation:

'...Every day we drag out of our beds at 6 am. A frantic toilet ensues, which includes a rapid run-over of our brass. Breakfast follows at 6:30, then back to the huts to do our room jobs...First parade is at 7:20. This is the flag-raising ceremony in which everyone on the camp takes part. Rest of the day is divided into periods. An hour at drill might follow; then, perhaps, rifle-training in battle order (overalls, ground sheet etc.); P.T. next, maybe, or over the assault course. Dinner is at 12:30. Next parade is 1:20. During the afternoon, we may have lectures with note-taking, or more drill, or musketry or grenades or... well, anything. Normally, we finish at 4:30. After tea, the first thing I do is to have a shower. The rest of the evening is spent polishing and cleaning in preparation for the following day, with a brief interval for supper in the NAAFI and, if humanly possible, an hour for writing to you. Lights out at 10 – and that, my sweet, is my day.'

That day, Ken also suffered a persistently aching throb in his left foot. It was a mystery to him, as he had not recalled hitting it during his most recent assault course; the only likely cause. The next morning, he visited the Medical Orderly. Dismissing it as 'practically nothing,' he, nevertheless, told Ken to report for twice-daily massage. He reported to Betty that 'at the same time, he informed me that I have flat feet – so, you <u>were</u> right, darling.' In the same letter, Ken responds to a comment by Betty that suggests his introspective, intellectually dominant personality was paying a price. 'Have I really been an oyster during these past eighteen months? I'm referring to your remarks about me never opening my heart to you, as I have done these past three weeks. I think you're probably justified. I'm a queer cove and often puzzle myself...' This evening, he reports back on 'a very hard day,' mainly taken up with further vaulting, P.T. and drill. It is clear that the theoretical discipline of his course was, by now, a distant memory, with the physical aspect now dominant. '...All the enthusiasm we had seems to have been knocked out of us,' he sighed. 'This course might be all right stretched over six months, but in 5 weeks it's a bit too concentrated and drastic.'

By the 31st August, the most tiring day since his arrival, a general fatigue, shared by the rest of the men, is compounded by the swelling around his still aching left ankle. He confides that he'll have to report sick tomorrow, and won't feel he has regained his freedom until he leaves for Oxford.

On Tuesday, 7th September, Ken sat the first of a three-day exam. (The following two days being further physical tests). Betty, due to visit him the following Sunday, wrote him in support:

'Your first day is over now, darling. I have been thinking of you and keeping my fingers crossed... At the library last night I got 'Death of a World' by Romain Rolland... The central character is a boy of 20, just after the last war, and of his struggle to see and to know and to be, and all the ideas that fight in his mind. I can imagine you in him, and I suppose I am more interested in him for that reason...

Last night I was fire-watching again, and there was a warning and I didn't wake up. I'll get the sack. I think I must be the world's worst fire-watcher... Dad rang this evening, and he is posted. Next Monday, he goes to that 'drome near Harlow. He'll be home for the weekend, I expect...'

That Monday morning, with four shillings and sixpence Betty had scraped together for him in his pocket, Ken experiences rare breathing space. If his NCO wanted him then he could find him. 'Policy for today is to lie low like Brer Rabbit and don't say nothing.' After the pain and effort of the previous four weeks, he was in a belligerent mood. 'Don't write, darling, until you hear from me at Oxford. By hook or by crook, I shall be seeing you next weekend...' By this time Ken's result came through. He had passed. 'I came 4th in our squad,' he was relieved to announce, adding that his Flight-Lieutenant thought his poise convincing enough for an NCO. A back-handed compliment, for he wrote his goodbye to 'all the muscle-bound, pea-brained hulks of men...the stupid, relentless discipline,' and the shouted, suggestive, macho phrases used to barrack non-conformists such as he; ' "standing like a WAAF in shame," or "like a ruptured frog," or marching "like a pregnant woman." '

On the 15th September – a day that must have reluctantly crawled around for him and Joe – they packed their kit once again and bussed to No. 5 Radio School at Oxford. He and Molloy spent their first billet at a bedsit in Old Marston, where Ken alleged they were 'starved by the ruthless landlady.' More likely, the two men were expected to make their own 'grub,' and so left to their own devices. A week later, they found digs at Headington, run by a Mr and Mrs Miles, 'Exceedingly nice people,' wrote Ken, 'being marvellously fed.' Life at the Oxford base was proving to be as leisurely as he had hoped. Conducive to the home stretch of swatting for his finals, while a further advantage proved to be its situation; south-eastern enough for he and Betty to meet *every* weekend.

For Betty, though, life at home with the ailing Mrs. Creak was proving increasingly stifling. Pat, her sister, felt their mother pointedly refused to accept this suave young Lothario in place of her eldest daughter's solid late fiancé, layering on the guilt for marrying him so soon. It is doubtful Ken ever felt at ease, seeing more of Betty's father on those few occasions their off-duty days coincided. With Frank Lawrance's offer of peace time work in mind, Ken wrote in his diary, 'We have been discussing moving – probably to Slo(ugh), after I've had a little talk with Lawrance over my post-war salary.' As if to dampen any rise in undue optimism, his attention is drawn to a painful swelling above his right knee, as though that of his rested left foot was seeking some form of revenge.

For the weekend of the 25th and 26th September, Ken acquired a forty-eight hour pass, which, for him, meant he could again sleep with his wife. The love he had felt for her in the intervening weeks had never been satisfactorily consummated, leaving an empty, pining tone in parts of the correspondence. Consequently, they felt they were still courting. A sense communicated through most wartime correspondence. So, the intimacy, when eventually expressed, was particularly intense. It was most likely during an early morning session of love-making that, at around 4 a.m. on the Sunday, Ken suddenly screamed in pain, shot out of bed, and vigorously rubbed his tender and throbbing right knee. After several minutes the pain died down. Later that day, an aching and occasional spasm caused him to walk slowly and with care. On Monday morning, a concerned Betty – herself unwell - kisses him goodbye, insisting he keeps in touch, as he journeys, apparently alone, back to Oxford. On Tuesday, he responded:

'It's got worse, and for the past few days I haven't been free of a constantly throbbing pain. I really think I must have wrenched a ligature or something, tho' heaven knows when and how. Tonight, I bought a bottle of embrication, (sic) and for the past quarter of an hour have been pummelling and kneading my knee. It definitely feels easier, and shall shortly give it another session... And, do you know, sweet, I too am breaking out in eruptions. I'm as spotty as a leopard, and have one rising just where I sit down! *Must be the eggs...*'

Ken made light of it, not wanting his wife fretting in his absence, but the lack of any explanation as to its cause left a nagging concern. 'I've no recollection of a bang or bruise...' he wrote.

He may have had no recent recollection, but his MO at Uxbridge - two years earlier - had no trouble identifying a scar over his right knee. Sixty years on, speculation after the fact is no more enlightening. In 1940, this may have been hairline enough to appear irrelevant, but a subsequent infection, dormant and quietly festering, is not unlikely. Medical theories still abound with no single, satisfactory reason. In Ken's case, his spoiled, childhood diet left, at least, something to be desired; perhaps the necessary iron and proteins required to fight such germs in later life were rarely on offer. Certainly, he preferred meat to greens and chocolate to just about everything else. And, as a boy, what Kenneth wanted, Kenneth got. His regular skiving from school was a consequence of his detesting the system, but also, most likely, genuine, semi-regular illness. That the latter was fallout from the former, is less convincing, as there is no evidence he was more scared of particular teachers than any other pupil, or that he was regularly targeted for bullying. Indeed, the 1934 diary suggests he felt some enthusiasm for his new school. Surviving medical documents from Uxbridge refer to his drained pallor. The lack of concern to follow this up, suggests this never interfered with his ability to carry out his duties. But he never made it to his final exam.

That Thursday, the 30th September, with a swelling above the knee now obvious, he finally reported sick. At the sickbay, the knee joint is brushed with Oil of Wintergreen and wrapped in a crepe bandage. For the next week, he winces through light duties. Each morning, he awakes, heavy-lidded, a little more tired than the day before, from the constant pain. By Wednesday 7th October, his leg is being X-rayed from various angles, and the general consensus is for him to be sent, immediately, to the nearest military hospital; the 107th General, situated in the grounds of Lincoln College on Oxford's High Street. Wheeled into its converted examination room, Ken looks up to the ceiling and down the walls, describing them as 'huge, beamed, friezed...with tall windows.' Eased onto his ward bed, he is quietly relieved by the presence of a radio at its side and the promise of a mobile library, by a reassuring doctor to whom he swiftly warms. Despite the pain, he is left feeling optimistic:

'I shall be in for about a week. The course is not worrying me. Before I left the School, I saw the chief instructor; he, too, was frightfully decent, and promised he'd fit me in for my final week when I reappeared...' His week pans out as a combination of applied poultices, daily check-ups interrupting his reading, (novels' such as S.P.B. Mais's *Education of a Philanderer*,) and pain-dominated nights tempered by Codeine, Nebutal and Aspirin. A picture is formed of the daily routine. During the day, at each check-up, two doctors would bend across his bed, feel and probe his already sensitive knee. Holding his right ankle, one of the doctors' then gently pulled the leg towards him. As Ken cried out, a painful spasm shooting up the inside of the leg, he just as carefully pushed it back to the preferred position of slight flexion. Ken would then be asked a line of questioning, apparently identical to the day before. No, he hadn't been to the tropics, he hadn't ever caught V.D. but, yes, his bladder often felt very weak. 'Mmm,' one would murmur to the other, 'it all ties up, doesn't it?' His colleague would nod slowly, leaving their patient, each day, in the dark. Ken resigned himself to the fact that, whatever was wrong with him, a week was not going to be long enough for treatment.

The results of his initial X-rays carried out on his last day at the School, pointed to the possible cause as Arthritis. But, those conducted here, now discounted this. The MO was at a loss on how to proceed. So far, all they knew was what it was not: 'No history of trauma. No recent cold or sore throat. Appetite good. No recent weight loss. No chills or fever.' This 'nil' response left the authorities little option but to transfer their patient to a hospital better equipped to handle a broader range of cases. On Tuesday 12th October, Ken found himself being wheeled out of the 107th General and into the American 2nd General, not far away. On inspection of their new patient, an H. Fisher reported:

'Localised general swelling medial to patella and above. Joint space. Maximum tenderness in this area. No joint space tenderness. No tenderness over patella or femoral condyles. Motion limited from 45 (d.) to 90 (d.) of flexion. No inflammatory area, leg or foot. Diag (nosis) undetermined. To be admitted for study. Csr. Blood counts. Tubercular X-Rays, suggest traction to leg for slow, full extension and immobilisation.' As far as they were concerned, it looked most like 'tuberculosis of right femur.' But, they weren't confident enough to tell him. 'No-one seems to know what's wrong with me,' he wrote. 'I've been probed all over. They concentrate on my stomach and glands.'

At about 2 a.m., Ken was uncomfortably awake to witness the exhausted arrival of a surviving US Army aircrew of a Fortress Bomber, who'd baled out after an aborted raid on the ball-bearing factory at Schweinfurt, Germany, from which sixty of their pilots were lost.

While his knee settled down, Ken must have felt something ominous in these surroundings. Here, he was being treated as some prize medical specimen. His bed felt 'luxuriously comfortable,' and the menu included items most British people could only dream about. It was all so strange to the new arrival: 'Spanish rice, chicken pie, sauerkraut, pancakes (with) syrup and bacon for breakfast. Most of the time I don't know what I'm eating, but I enjoy it.' His first taste of the real U.S.A. was tempered by his fellow patients; 'The Yanks have the radio on <u>all</u> the time and <u>never</u> listen to it.' So, afternoon naps – understandable after the sleepless nights - were out of the question.

This was just as well since, here, they were depriving him of blood for the, otherwise, usual run of tests. In the afternoon, a young woman reporter from the *Oxford Mail* arrived to interview men on the ward for their war experiences. Though pleased to see her, he could offer nothing of substance. On the morning of Sunday 17th, any suspicions he'd felt about the seriousness of his condition were compounded if not confirmed. Ken noted that,

'The L(ieutenan)t came to make an injection (just another move for which no explanation was offered) and I took the opportunity of asking him outright what was wrong with me. He said, they didn't know – but the leg trouble was caused by some disease which they are now trying to trace.'

He had acquired an enlarged spleen and glands in the groin area, and one of these would have to come out. The former self-assurance gave way to a new uncertainty when he was told yet more blood would be required the following day. 'The Lt. said this disorder may have been present years. I feel a little frightened. Should I tell Betty?' Ken continued to deny that anything in his past could have harboured the cause, as though consistently well. His appearance, to them, suggested otherwise. The report on the 19th stated that, 'He does...look chronically ill, and he is running a very slight fever.' The forty-five minute operation occurred this day, under a local anaesthetic of Novacain, followed, on the 21st, by yet another x-ray. There was a rumour, amongst the staff, that it might be Hodgkin's Disease. But, they were still lacking the confirmation to inform the patient. Betty's appearance on the Sunday was received with great relief. He broke to her what news he dared.

Thumbing through a Penguin soft-cover that evening, Ken fell upon the poem, 'Nothing is Enough,' by Lawrence Binyon. It ends:

> *'Will Divine Desire*
> *yet more excellent*
> *Precious cost require,*

> *Of this mortal stuff –*
> *Never be content*
> *Til ourselves be fire,*
> *Nothing is enough!'*

'Don't you think that's inspiring, darling?' wrote Ken the next morning. 'Especially those last three lines.' It was his last gasp as an untutored optimist.

Through the following week, Ken lost his appetite, the large American breakfasts daily turned away. Hot packs were applied to the knee. He asked for whisky to dull the raw nerves, a request they acceded to, in the form of one three ml. shot at 11 a.m. and one at 4 p.m. On the 28th, the report on the biopsy now stated that Ken had been suffering from a condition known as *Boeck's Sarcoid. (Sarcoidosis)*. He was informed the following day that his strain was harboured by the glands. Satisfied they'd lanced this boil, the staff could now proceed with longer-term treatment. By the 31st, a post-moulded, plaster splint was made, with his leg slightly flexed in the least painful position. Now more rested, Ken's sanctioned whisky, in the eyes of the M.O., was doing nothing to reinvigorate his appetite. This small pleasure was therefore denied him on 2nd November. It had been a very long and increasingly traumatic month.

Sixty years on from Ken's diagnosis, *Boeck's Sarcoid* remains extremely difficult to identify, instantly. The reason is not so much that it's hard to find; on the contrary, so many of the body's organs are so swiftly affected, along with its immune system that, at first, there appears no single, identifiable cause. The age group it most commonly afflicts are between twenty and forty. According the US-based Arthritis Foundation, *Sarcoidosis* is an inflammatory disease that can produce several differing symptoms, affecting the skin, lungs, joints, eyes and most other organs or tissue. The 'eruptions' Ken made light of - back on 28th September 1943 – point to an early physical manifestation, now referred to as 'granulomas.' Interestingly, one such type is known as *'erythema nodosum,'* that accompanies arthritis of the ankle, occasionally other joints, and a low-grade fever. The A.F. state that, 'it occurs in about 10 per cent of people with *Sarcoidosis*, and in about 50 per cent with the acute form, particularly those with swollen lymph nodes in the chest.' (Ken's medical records confirmed the presence of lymph nodes). So, the 2nd General Hospital's initial diagnosis of Arthritis was not incorrect. It occurs in 'about one-sixth' of those suffering with *Sarcoidosis*, the ankle and knee joints its main targets.

  Crucially, they add that the disease is also inconsistent in its effect, so near impossible to predict its duration for the victim. A single, clear-cut cause remains elusive although, suspected, are a viral/bacterial infection, a defect in the body's immune system, an unidentified toxic substance, an unknown environmental cause and an inherited or genetic factor. Unavoidably, Ken had become a victim of such uncertainty.

Ken's appetite remained poor into November, although his plaster splint alleviated the former exhaustion from the pain allowing for fitful periods of sleep. His right knee was now receiving ultra-violet radium treatment and local irradiation. By the 7th, feeling more stable, he read again, and voraciously, whipping through *Cover His Face*; Neil Bell's novel on the short-lived, eighteenth century poet, Thomas Chatterton, 'in which he disproves – to my satisfaction, anyway, - the popular theory that he committed suicide. Why should he have? He was a lusty, vigorous character – nothing of the aesthetical poet.' (sic). Finishing this, he immediately began Van Loon's *Lives*, lent him by 'another Van – Mrs Van Horn, the night nurse – Pennsylvania Dutch,' he observed. Being Sunday, Betty appeared. With typical self-interest, he reported; 'It's like a breath of fresh air to see her lovely face, and to talk rationally – about things that interest me.' Without even Tunks, May, or poor Gardner to argue politics with, or Hilton, books, Betty was becoming an ever more needed presence. From the Americans he gained little satisfaction, finding those here as shallow as the majority in the R.A.F. A possible exception was Ayres, whom he refers to as his 'first genuine American racketeer.'

Illustrated, here, in his diary, is Ken's growing ambivalence towards the country. Bordering forty, Ayres hails from Freemont, Ohio, and appears, to Ken, as a cross between Al Capone and Mussolini. A former gambling club owner, and likely anti-Prohibitionist, he then made his living in various ways, on the edge of legality. Ken sounds surprise at his casual openness:

'To Americans, making money is the most important thing in life – methods don't matter. Several have said to me, "I just can't see how anyone in England earns enough to keep alive." Ken was intrigued and, perhaps, a little envious. Yet, the bare-faced assumptions about the British, rankled:

'Most annoying trait of most of the Yanks I've met in here is the assumption that every Englishman is just dying to emigrate to the States. The few times I've tried to explain that, tho' I should love to visit (the) USA, nothing on Earth would compel me to live there, as I should be most unhappy amidst that swamp of automobiles, refrigerators and money-chasing, my listeners have been quite shocked. One said the other day, "You know, some of your English girls would make fine wives back in the States. "They make good wives here," I pointed out. "Oh, sure," he agreed hesitantly. It just hadn't occurred to him.'

During the second week of November, feeling flat, uninspired to even read, and with no deadline of escape to look forward to, Ken fell into depression. Even with the final diagnosis agreed upon, the authorities here still wanted a piece of him. He was, after all, proving a challenge. The endless routine of visits, tests and Americans boasting about him of their last sexual conquest, became amplified and suffocating. On the 13th, he picked up his pen:

'...I'm sick to death of being the guinea pig, and exhibited to various doctors and tribunals. I feel so awfully frustrated. God, how I want to get out of here and go home to Betty.' It didn't help that to his left were a new line of, allegedly, tough paratroopers, comparing operation scars and their degrees of pain. More out of boredom than improvement in his condition, he returned to stabbing food from plate to mouth in grim defiance.

A little relief came the following Sunday; accompanying Betty was Leslie Tunks, currently on leave from Northern Ireland. But, a further ten days passed before he could, again, pick up his pen:

'*No improvement at all*. Last night, I asked Captain Fisher, the Jew, how long I might be here. He'd "no idea." God, that might mean months more. I feel so fed-up, desperate, *impotent*.' On the 30th, his leg, quite swollen, was operated on. Re-set in plaster, the wound was left open for fluid drainage. 'They took some bone out, too.' His temperature returning to normal did nothing to dispel his misery; 'The days come and go and nothing much registers...I feel as if I'm shrivelling inside,' he scribbled at the start of December. A distraught Betty had to tell him that she couldn't visit again until just before Christmas. The next weekend she would be travelling up to Leeds to update and, hopefully, reassure his parents.

The next day, the gauze packs within his cast were removed and the leg reset. He yelled in pain during the procedure. On the evening of the 9th came the final straw: 'I was told...my leg is tubercular. I shall be in hospital for a long time to come.' As a result, 'I'm being transferred nearer home.' He was also told that the leg operation was performed under the assumption of a possibly present bone tumour, finding, instead, the T.B. He worried over how he could break this to Betty, on top of all the other alleged ailments. 'How can I put this on her shoulders? I was wishing, fervently, last night that I'd never met her. I love her so much and I feel so terrible, so wretched, that I should have given her this burden. It would have been better if she had never known me.' He also considered what he was missing beyond the ward window; '...Just to be able to walk across an open hill and feel the wind and see and hear the birds...'

On Friday 17th December, Ken was suddenly transferred back to the 107th General at Lincoln College. On arrival, he was told he was to be medically boarded for sanatorium treatment. The consequence of this was that his condition was deemed too serious to envisage a return to active service. Not wishing him to sound too pleased, this was never directly stated, though the rest of the ward made him swiftly aware. 'My feelings are mixed,' he wrote from there. 'How often and how fervently during the past three years have I wished I was out of the services. Yet, I cannot rejoice now with the knowledge of what has brought about my release.' Additionally, one big question mark hung over his future. The darkest option staring him in the face:

'Opposite me is a man who is plainly dying. There is death written in his face. All day long he lies languidly in bed and, occasionally, his great stricken eyes roll up and about like a wounded criminal. It may sound callous, but the sight of him sickens and angers me; he seems to be letting death take him without (a) fight.'

On Sunday, his Florence Nightingale ended her three-week absence as promised. From his parents, she brought him a new watch and, from herself, a wallet, Christmas cake and an illustrated book of Jefferies' selected writings. Too touched to reveal all, he gave her the most optimistic news; his eventual discharge. But, with no time limit pencilled in, he couldn't be sure when this would occur.

Despite the presence of family, Betty's Christmas was perfunctory. She was only half-heartedly hoping for his release, the bank holiday's passing confirming her fear. She felt a pang of guilt, that he couldn't even be spoiled back at the 2nd General.

'Have you smoked your five miserable Woodbines yet, darling?' she wrote. 'Honestly, though, it makes my blood boil to think of the indifference shown to military patients. The British authorities can have no conscience, otherwise they would feel ashamed at the difference in American hospitals...'

While awaiting news of his next transference, Ken is reduced to performing needlework-by-numbers from a pack of two naval scenes. His inspiration to write stalls at incomplete, imaginary nature sketches; impatience, pain and medical indecision over-riding the conception of a new novel. On Wednesday 29th, he feels resigned to reminding Betty of the imminent, second anniversary of their meeting. But she needed no prompting. The following day, almost certainly before its receipt, she wrote back her memories:

'I can remember you walking into the dance hall, dancing with you, our fight to get a drink, and our long talk sitting at that table on the balcony. We talked about everything under the sun, didn't we, dear? I think we knew quite a lot about one another after that first meeting, darling. Then the walk home, stopping at a coffee stall for a snack and then saying goodnight and promising to meet again and after you had gone feeling sure you would forget all about me in a day but, wonder of wonders, you didn't.'

On the 5th January 1944, feeling lighter than he had over the previous two months, he took stock and related to Betty what had sustained him since his admission:

'One of the things that makes me love you so much is that you have none of that strangling passiveness in you – that altho' you love me, your affection hasn't taken on that limpet character that is, I'm certain, responsible for the stultification of so many marriages. Appropriately, our love for each other is definitely Liberal in essence, not 'Tory and hidebound.' That Ken could lend - from their semi-regular contacts - a political perspective to the relationship, was typical of the naive heights his idealistic thought processes could attain at this time. It requires little translation to reinterpret how he really felt; that when she was with him she gave him what he needed but was wise enough never to overtly cling or hold him back. In this respect, Betty was successfully replacing his mother, Mary.

At 2 p.m. the next day, Ken is informed - in grave tones by two RAF Officers - that he is, unfortunately, to be 'invalided' out of the Services., While doing his best to sound disappointed, he can hardly contain his relief. Now under the care of the Ministry of Pensions, he enquires after the amount of due back pay. Betty would need it for him, after all. He hoped this would also speed his release from treatment as he couldn't take much more:

'I'm not in the frame of mind for reading. I'm on edge and inwardly seething...I've never before experienced this feeling of being imprisoned for all the world as tho' I'm behind bars with an iron ball chained to my ankle.' A series of transitory, bureaucratic blunders held up his discharge even longer than was necessary until the evening of Monday 17th January, when he was assured of two weeks home leave commencing the following Thursday. Ken's unquestioning relief suggests just how aware he now was of the permanence of his predicament, and that treatment would be ongoing and a very long haul.

Issued with a pair of crutches he would swiftly come to detest, it was a highly unsteady and irritable Ken who, mummified in blankets, was stretchered aboard the ambulance at the hospital entrance to alight at St. Pancras Station for a final ambulance journey to his home. He wrote in this year's journal:

'Getting me up to the flat was a problem, and after struggling with the stretcher up the first flight of stairs, it was abandoned and the orderly carried me up.' Betty had arranged for their bed to be brought down and into the front room. Not only would this facilitate convenience, but it also afforded a little privacy from Betty's live-in mother, who'd barely tolerated Ken's presence when he was fit. Frustratingly for the couple, Mrs. Creak and his right knee each conspired to enforce celibacy. All Betty could do was play him his favourite records and cook his preferred meals. A series of air-raids provided the only excitement and a chance for Ken to test his physical limitations as – gripping the banister with both hands - he hopped down the stairs on his left leg with his scaffold-supported right stuck, bazooka-like, straight out in front. On the 2nd, amongst mainly half-hearted replies to applications for work, he received one from Frank Lawrance. This, following-up his former editor's pre-war promise of a post-war job. Again, Lawrance managed to re-ignite Ken's ire; an unstoppable force meeting the immovable object:

'(He) has written in a typically objectionable, patronising style. Obviously, he is annoyed at my direct ultimatum, which left him little choice. He says he will be "happy to pay me union rates." I can imagine the extent of his happiness...'

But, he and Betty needed the work, now more than ever. Conviction alone would not pay the bills. Too quickly, on Friday 4th February, he was, with great reluctance, taken back to crisper, disinfected sheets, now situated in the Coleridge East Ward of the North Middlesex. On the 22nd, he is officially deemed 'physically unfit for active service,' receiving a war gratuity of £2, which he understandably viewed as a kick for already being down. He will not easily forget, or forgive, the R.A.F.

Ken and Betty in the back garden of 100, Mount View Road, c.1945. (Note Ken's crutches).

Ken convalescing on the same day.

10
May 1944 – August 1945:
Common Wealth

Even now, Ken was being messed around. The North Middlesex proved to be merely a holding station while the authorities continued searching for a more permanent home for his peculiar condition. The trouble was that civilian *as well as* military hospitals were responsible for prioritising the war wounded; a category Ken, strictly speaking, was not under. That every bed in southeast England was taken is highly questionable. More likely was the medical profession's fear of bad publicity should one bomb-scarred victim have to wait for his place. At least, as a casualty disconnected from the Forces, this is how he was treated. Fortunately, the authorities indecision allowed for an unexpected, indefinite break with Betty from mid-March.

Now sporting a trim moustache and a few extra pounds, Ken learned to tolerate his crutches to hobble, unaided, around the house. The last thing he needed to do, now he was out, was lie down. Relations between him and Mrs. Creak had not improved, though, and Betty, temporarily out of work, needed a new job for both their sakes. Moving out became an imperative. The further consideration was the continuing lack of sexual opportunity. Out of her mother's earshot, the main topics of conversation.

Seven weeks later, on Monday 8th May, he was accepted into St. Anthony's Hospital, North Cheam, Surrey. On the 10^{th,} Betty accompanied him to Ward 2; a pleasingly smaller, quieter and more intimate ward than he had been used to, with most of his fellow patients tubercular in various parts of their anatomies. Where previously, he had been helped out of his bed to the nearest 'Gents,' here he was expected to make his own way, as encouragement to befriend his hated crutches. But, this was fine by Ken, now so desperate for just a modicum of independence from the bed. The scene facing him at the window did not help:

'I'm still not allowed in the garden,' he moaned on the 11th, 'which makes me very restless after the freedom I enjoyed at home. It's so tantalising to see the trees and fields, with the sun burning down on them, and to be unable to get to them...'

The following day, Ken received a letter from Betty, enthused by an offer of a job as Constituency Agent at the Chelmsford branch of Common Wealth. Their candidate, readied for whenever Churchill cared to call a General Election, was Ernest Millington; a Wing Commander with the R.A.F. 'It has restored my confidence in the party,' Ken replied.

Common Wealth had been founded in July 1942 when the 1941 Committee of playwright and broadcaster, J.B. Priestley merged with Sir Richard Acland's Christian Socialist, Forward March Movement. This, as a continuing reaction against the Tory-Labour, 'anti-Hitler' coalition, that appeared just another excuse for the centre-left of the former and centre-right of the latter to complacently maintain a broad consensus on policy held since 1935. The void on the Left demanded to be filled. What linked both men was a middle-class libertarian zeal. After Priestley's early departure that autumn, the tall, thin-faced and bespectacled Acland took over, imparting the verbal absolutism of a Victorian pulpit preacher. Angus Calder, in his book, 'The People's War,' describes how Acland was generally received at this time:

'...his repeated calls for social revolution were a subject for laughter rather than admiration in the House of Commons. But, as a public orator, he could pack almost any hall in almost any town in Britain. In front of the very worried, very earnest, very idealistic wartime political audiences, his revivalist fervour was irresistible, as he painted on the one hand the Hell of the Old Order, on the other the Heaven of the New.'

Calder quotes one of his admirers: 'the burning sincerity of his enthusiasm' on discovering socialism allied with 'his acute insight...to moral and political problems' suggests his appeal paralleled those sensibilities of the aspiring middle classes. When it was perceived that the war was being won without a dire need for socialism, the publication of the Beveridge Report on the 1st December offered the party a new role. Despite the continuous lack of publicity from a suspicious, Government-backed Fleet Street, or broad base of support, Calder noted how, 'in by-election after by-election C(ommon) W(ealth) represented the refined essence of 'Beveridgism' – the revolutionary zeal, the millenarian dream, the unselfishness.'

It was inevitable that Betty should warm to this new party. Her parents were longstanding Labour voters, too often surrounded by fellow, white-collar Tories. But the stranglehold influence in the South the Tories had maintained since the last war, effectively stifled dissent. Of Labour at this time, Pat recalls:

'They were getting so unrealistic in their politics. They were terribly left-wing, except they did everything that right-wing people (did); the desire to acquire wealth and to be important and of some note in the country...' Rebellion was not in the younger Creaks' minds. They were far too 'proper' for that. They simply wanted a more representative voice. 'Common Wealth' offered this opportunity. Suspicious, himself, of Labour's old boy network, Ken warmed to Betty's enthusiasm, if not to the Party itself.

Party membership appeared to require a tolerance of administration and level of allegiance that wasn't in his freethinking nature. As representatives of this status quo, politicians were leaving him cold. But, Betty's alternative had possibilities. At least, when it came to the re-building of war-torn London, the Party was prepared to be radical.

At around 8 p.m. on the 26th October 1943, Betty invited Pat and their mother to accompany her to a local branch meeting. At 10.30 p.m. she reported back to Ken:

'The meeting was quite good. There was a speaker on the L.C.C. plan for London. It sounds awfully interesting. There are to be two circular roads within the present one: one north of Regents Park, the other through The Elephant and Castle, and then two arterial roads running through them North to South and East to West. Railway termini to be put outside the metropolis. i.e. Charing Cross to be moved South of the Thames: the South Bank to have an embankment and blocks of offices, Government buildings and theatres. The West End, (Kensington, etc.) to be flats for people working in the city. There is a lot more, but...we will have a long talk about it when we meet again, sweet. The Town and Country Planning Association criticise the plan because it is only proposed to disperse ½ million of the population, which means that a lot of people will have to live in flats, which said people don't want to do. The other alternative is to disperse more into satellite towns, but I wonder if the people will like that either if they are working in London. Anyway, I don't think it is wise to kill the plan because of one point of disagreement. There will be plenty of people only too anxious to kill it. People who won't want nationalisation of transport etc., which the plan will necessitate.'

A depressed Ken poured water on this, returning his own preference to what sounded to him like proletarian worker flats:

'(I) would hate to live in one myself, but the only

alternative seems to be these artificial dormitory towns, and that's a hideous prospect involving the blotting out of the pathetic remnants of countryside around London. What a wonderful thing (it) would be if, for one year, all business, commercial, and every other form of activity in London, could be suspended, every inhabitant except workmen necessary for the plan, shipped out, en bloc, to some remote place, and then the entire place knocked down, stripped and laid out afresh: then, when the priority work, the remodelling of the dwelling quarters of the city had been finished, the pop(ulation) could move back and the rest of the reconstruction...could continue at a more leisurely rate. Think it's worth putting forward?'

This last flippant note – out of character – only reflected both a fear and increasing lack of confidence in the staff and surroundings at the 107th. But, he knew of no other willing audience than Betty. Eight months on, resigned acceptance of his condition, allied to the easier going atmosphere of his ward at St. Anthony's, allowed for greater integration and even a little warmth for his fellow patients. From his last visit home he brought his typewriter, now a near-permanent feature across his lap.

On 19th June, he completed typing what he called 'The Ward Two Wire (incorporating the TB Times)'; a mock newspaper of fake articles, quizzes and poems, mainly by Ken for the amusement of the others. He was even corresponding with Betty's party through their Common Wealth Review, though this with the hopeful ulterior motive of getting his latest short stories published. As a second issue of the 'Ward Two Wire' went to press, Betty had some better news of her own. As part of the Party's own initiative for the war effort, she was to spend the summer as a Land Girl at an agricultural camp at Faringdon in Berkshire. Heavy rain threatened to turn her first few days into a mud-trudging ordeal that delayed consistent digging. But she and her comrades preferred to keep their knees dry. Replying to her report, Ken 'expected to hear gruelling tales of mountains of turnips, a sort of "Good Earth" saga in miniature. Still, perhaps that is to come...'

On the second Sunday in July, a tanned, fitter-looking Betty visited after Ken's knee had been exposed for a new operation two weeks earlier. As far he was concerned it had gone well. His main concern was her progress in finding a new flat. Clearly, her mother's demands were getting to her. He tried cheering her with the news of his renewed interest in writing. With Betty's guidance he had started contributing articles to *Common Wealth Review*. He would later attempt book reviews. Between issues of 'The Ward Two Wire,' he had conceived of two short, non-nature stories; 'The Man Who Could Float' and 'The Egotistical Dog.' The titles alone suggest he remained reliant upon humour to alleviate the depression. On the 2nd August, he submitted them to the Director of Talks at BBC Radio, signing off as 'K. Halliday Allsop'; adding his mother's maiden name in a desperate bid for cachet. Almost inevitably, these were also turned down.

The level of depression Ken experienced the previous Winter returned. In turn, his humour darkened. Utilising the rarely used skill inherited from his father, Ken produced a stylish series of blackly comedic pencil sketches, reflecting his current state of mind on the ward. In one, in ironic homage to Aubrey Beardsley, Ken's cigarette smoke curls exotically around him, his hair and moustache drooping, while he sits up in bed with a book on his lap as 'The Reader of The Picture of Dorian Grey.' Three others that survive are more disturbing. In one, he shivers beneath his bedclothes as spirits rise and crowd around his goggle-eyed, quivering form. In the second, he is still under the sheets, with a question mark over his head as nocturnal wildlife from outside his window invade the ward, as if beckoning him back to their habitats. While in the third, he sits up, types robotically, and stares a burning hole through the pillow at the foot of his bed. Beside him, he doesn't notice the failed suicide, weeping, face-down on the floor, holding up, accusingly, the length of broken rope. Both could be Ken. Either way, there is a ring in his laughter, bleak and disquieting.

High Summer, and Betty announced to Ken that she had found them a new home at 61, Claremont Road, in Highgate, N6. Relieved to move from her own mother, she paid a return visit to Ken's parents in Leeds, updating them on his condition and dispensing her own brand of reassurance. Her main purpose was to visit the Party's Central Committee Rooms at 49, Market Place, Malton, under a directive from Common Wealth's London Head Office at 4, Gower Street, Bedford Square. Here, Betty was asked to act as Party Agent for the lead-up to the forthcoming Thirsk & Malton by-election. The area's candidate was introduced to her as Edward Moeran; a 'young, good-looking and patently very sincere' Flight-Lieutenant and former solicitor who'd stood unsuccessfully for Newark in the by-election of 1943. The Party were in high spirits with the knowledge that the local Labour representatives were not putting forward their own candidate but throwing their support behind him in protest against the continuing Government coalition.

A further boost in fortune arrived, mid-September, with the offer of a new job at the counter of a central London bookstore. Previous to her labouring in Berkshire, Betty had been operating a switchboard in a windowless bunker-type room, of which Ken openly disapproved. She was earning only pennies but it was this or mutual penury. The first anniversary of Ken's incarceration saw him rallying to reassure her just how much he appreciated her continuing efforts:

'...the way you have helped me most during these lousy

months has been your moral support. Quite unconsciously perhaps you give me just what I need – strength. I know you don't realise how much I depend on you, my darling. Quite apart from your ability, re. forms and business matters, you are a bulwark for me.' Her 'ability' was proving invaluable to Party colleagues like Tom and Kitty Wintringham.

From mid-autumn '44 to late winter, a gap appears in the Allsops' correspondence. We can only speculate on what occurred considering the subsequent events. While his pain had never ceased through these months, his doctors' settled upon a course of treatment that was, at least, making life bearable. His wound remained sealed and he was looking brighter. For them, that appeared enough. Ken was finally allowed some limited autonomy from the ward. Reluctantly reliant upon his crutches, he learned to hobble, steadily, around the hospital grounds, reacquainting himself with the visiting birds. Almost inevitably, he rescued another crow with an injured wing. Hobbling back into Ward 2, Ken turned on the charm and persuaded the ward sister to allow him to keep it in a box by his bed until he could make 'other arrangements.' Surprisingly, the nurses tolerated the ugly black bird to the point of accepting it as a near permanent fixture, giving it its own temperature and diet charts. Its one bad habit was to regularly pinch any untended thermometers that took its fancy. When Betty stepped in to take the bird away to a more suitable home, a member of staff issued it with an official discharge certificate.

Ken's leave also stretched to accompanying Betty out of St. Anthony's once a week. The first stop was their new home at Claremont Road; Ken, no doubt, advising Betty on the rooms' layout and ambience. Often, they would catch a bus to watch a current Hollywood movie, or see a show. With Betty on Party business in Chelmsford, Pat would look after him. She recalls taking him on the bus for return visits to

Osterley and Nonesuch Park where 'it was the nearest he could get to the country and see the birds and just be out in the open air.' Best of all was a temporary release for Christmas. (It is unlikely the authorities would have deprived the couple for a second year running). A combination of painkillers, invention and mutual desperation succeeded in at least one awkward coupling.

Early in the New Year, Betty confirmed to him what he had been quietly dreading. She was pregnant. It was clear to Ken that they couldn't keep it. It pained him to tell her this on her next visit, but what choice had they? There was never any question of them starting a family under these conditions. Betty had enough to worry about on a sole, woman's wage, in a period when the differential with men was that much wider. Even with Ken's pension, only recently arranged, her commitment to Common Wealth left her unable to support a second dependent. And with the war threatening to enter a seventh debilitating year, uncertainty about their future was simply too great. Reluctantly, she accepted the situation. They discussed the unthinkable: abortion. A taboo subject in 1945, but the odds, so stacked against them, soon salved their consciences. Confiding to a close friend in the Party, this colleague offered to lend her the money. She felt she had to accept, as she wanted no one else to know, not even Pat.

Meantime, there were stirrings of an imminent General Election. The Conservative-Labour coalition that had held for the last ten years finally reached breaking point over Churchill's insistence on remaining Prime Minister to the end of the Pacific War, which may – or may not – prelude the end of war in Europe. To add to Labour's irritation, he unilaterally set the Election date for July 5th, with the results expected some three weeks later, after the services had their votes cast. This was out of the blue, and earlier than Labour had anticipated. Common Wealth saw their chance.

Betty's itinerary suddenly increased, as she found herself campaigning for funds and chaperoning colleagues at meetings across the constituency. A surviving sheet, dated Monday 9th April, highlights how Betty increased her commitment, despite the covert pregnancy. At 6.11 p.m. she meets Kitty Wintringham at Brentwood Station, followed by a meal at the local White Hart. At 7.15 the Party reps. convene at Hutton Parish Hall, booked for the occasion by Betty herself. David Mills, the chairman, introduces Wintringham who updates the assembled on how the campaign is faring in her part of the constituency. At 7.50 Mills introduces their own candidate, Ernest Millington, the R.A.F. Wing Commander currently holding the town of Chelmsford for the Party, who speaks for a further half an hour. After thirty minutes of questions, Betty explains the collection and Appeal for a further ten, after which Mills closes the meeting.

Ever outmanoeuvring what opposition there was, on the 7th May, Churchill broke the news that Germany had as good as surrendered to the Allies. The next day, VE Day, Betty accompanied her sister to Alexandra Palace, curious to witness the rushed, evening celebrations. Returning late, Pat offered Betty a side of her bed back at her room in Mount View Road. Betty accepted. During the night Pat's elder sister awoke with a start and cried at the sight of blood soaking the sheets. Pat recalled:

'I was amazed at first because I didn't know she was pregnant. You know, girls in those days weren't as knowing as they are now and it hadn't occurred to me...She then walked back to Highgate and I think I walked with *her, having just had a miscarriage*...but she called in at the doctors' on the way.'

The excursions beyond the hospital grounds increased in regularity and Ken was, more than ever, anxious for permanent liberty. Years after the event, he related how the offer of an eighth operation upon the right knee was to prove the final straw. The authorities may not have given up hope – he was, after all, an interesting case – but he certainly had. Just as he was getting used to the discomfort, it suddenly increased. He claims he demanded amputation. On the 14th May, his doctor, O' Neill, informed Ken that Dr. Fitzgerald – St. Anthony's surgeon – was operating on the 1st June. But, there was no guarantee that Ken could be fitted in. Testily, he wrote to Betty:

'He'll have to inspect the knee first, of course, but I myself don't see any reason why he should object as it has healed up marvellously.' This is disingenuous. He was now willing the requisite recovery through gritted teeth. Uncertainty over Fitzgerald's availability dragged on into the following week. So did Ken's grim determination to leave. The exertion drained what returning strength he had, leaving him sweating and tired with the knee throbbing its complaint. In one of these calmer moods he pondered over a second honeymoon:

'...I shan't be able to have that spring in the country that I'd hoped for but, if O'N(eill)'s estimation were right, I may still be able to go away in the Summer. And, my own dear heart, you and I are going away together. It will be North Devon all over again, even if we shan't be able to do all the walking that was so much a part of that week. Whether we do go to Croyde or somewhere else, I know it will be quite as wonderful: there is nothing I want more...'

On the 22nd May, the surgeon rang O'Neill, saying he would make the 8th June for his patient. Despair momentarily clouded Ken's hopes through the following day and into the night. That morning he was at the point of breaking down when an encouraging note from Betty, praising his courage, calmed him. 'Not much longer now,' he assured them both. 'A fortnight tomorrow.' On that fateful day, Betty sent a telegram from Yorkshire:

> 'ALLSOP ST.ANTHONY'S HOSPITAL NORTH CHEAM SURREY
> - DEAREST MY THOUGHTS ARE WITH YOU   NOW THAT THIS IS OVER YOU WILL SOON BE HOME LOVE YOU ALWAYS – BETTY.'
> -

No record survives detailing how Dr. Fitzgerald's amputation of Ken's right leg went. What is known is that the limb was sliced not just above the infected knee but mere inches below the thigh. One reason may have been a fear of upward spreading gangrene, and a growing consensus that the patient had suffered long and hard enough to warrant any possibility of a further operation. But his incarceration had not ended. As his prone form was wheeled out of the operating theatre he still had nine more weeks ahead of him. Tests upon the rest of his anatomy continued.

One morning, during the second week of July, as he sat himself up, the big toe on his 'good' leg began to swell and fester. Memories of his weak left ankle from two years earlier ominously resurfaced. But the wheels of his discharge had already been set in motion, just avoiding a further fall into depression. However, in its place festered a mounting impatience and anger.

To stay closer to hand for the final round of campaigning, Betty moved out of her digs at Ken's parents to live, temporarily closer to the canvassing, in Malton, West Yorkshire. Accompanying Edward Moeran on the last round of canvassing, he and Betty exchanged their hopes for the future with peace finally declared. They agreed the Election would be make or break for the Party. Betty hoped to start a family, her disabled husband her main priority. Moeran told her of his and his wife Nadine's intention to start a community of families, living and working with like-minded couples towards a mutual ideal for living. The one obstacle was purely practical; to find a large enough, cheap enough and available enough property. Betty voiced her interest in becoming involved and she left him with his promise that Nadine would call her once the right site had been secured.

In the town Betty found a hotel, The Oldfield, run by a couple supportive to the Communists' cause. Coincidentally, the wife's husband, on leave, was a reporter named Kenneth. The couple sympathised with Betty's situation, taking her out evenings for drinks. With the Election only a fortnight away, Betty took a week off from the campaign, tramping around the semi-rural district and noting sites for possible future holidays after Ken's release. Knowing of his eventual release, but not when, made his absence all the more felt. She couldn't understand why his side of the correspondence had suddenly stopped. Unaware of his anger, she wrote:

'I have had only one letter from you this week, and it has seemed such a long and lonely week. Please write to me, darling. I run to every post, and all I get is bills.'

For the last weekend before declaration of the Election results, Betty returned to Claremont Road to arrange Ken's final forty-eight hour pass. Now with just the one limb, his left trouser leg pinned up to his behind, he found himself even more reliant upon his loathed crutches. But, Ken's mind was elsewhere. Fleet Street's blatantly biased political correspondents had predicted, not only a Tory victory, but a likely increase in their majority. His wife remained stoically pragmatic in confirming that, whatever the outcome, CW's waning finances looked like their was no way back for the Party and their was talk of its folding. He grimly showed Betty the stump that remained after amputation. Far from gory, it appeared to have cleanly healed over. He assured her that he would be seeing O'Neill in a couple of days for the final okay on discharge.

The 26th July result confounded the critics. Labour had not only won their first General Election, but they had achieved it with a virtual landslide of 154; a swing of some 12 per cent. Common Wealth had, at least, managed to convincingly beat the Communists into fifth place while, disappointingly for the Party, sacrificing most of their star names in the process. Edward Moeran – in spite of sympathetic Labour turncoating – narrowly lost to the Tories, though garnered enough votes to save his deposit. Betty, of course, was deflated but she had no cause to feel personally responsible as Ernest Millington – her local candidate – took Chelmsford becoming the Party's sole victor. But as a victory it was definitely pyrrhic.

Ken wasn't overtly concerned by what would undoubtedly compound this little party's demise. To him, a far greater boil had been lanced with the coalition finally trounced by the minor partner. The exalted letter he wrote Betty from the hospital next morning, reflects a revitalised appetite and, for its detail and historical interest, is worth quoting in full:

'St. Anthony's. Friday.

Darling girl -

It's a great day for the English! Despite the shadow cast by CW's dismal fate I feel jubilant and excited. For darling in spite of our party allegiance, it is the establishment of socialism that matters and this is truly a Famous Victory.

Naturally, the first result I looked up in the evenings' last night was Thirsk. You may have lost, sweet, but you did magnificently. I went thru the whole list marking off CW contests – there were 13 in the edition I had – and except for Wintringham (what a damnable shame he didn't get in!) and, of course, Millington, you polled by far the highest figures.

Oh dear, those three-figure results which came after CW name after CW name – and poor old Dick Acland losing his deposit. But the whole thing was just a series of shocks, wasn't it? The most astounding outcome, I think, was the Liberal debacle. In ratio they did no better than CW.

But the most wonderful aspect, I consider, was the way the British people displayed a calm, firm, dispassionate attitude towards the issues involved and refused to be panicked by all the Tory stunts and sideshows. There's so much to be discussed about it all. How I wish you were here so we could rave to each other.

I was overjoyed to see that gang of toadies and sycophants – Belisha, Randolph Churchill, Sandys, Bracken, Amery, etc – were turfed out; and that Driberg, Michael Foot, Jennie Lee, Bevan, Maxton, McGovern, Levy, and dozens more of my pin-up boys got back. To my utter disgust I see Baxter and Gammans wriggled in again. . . . But, oh, it's a great day, a great day.

I had your letter sweetheart. In the afternoon I went with a fellow called Ken across to Sutton to see 'The Fifth Chair.' We went straight into the Granada and after sitting in there for about an hour suddenly realised that it wasn't showing there! We asked an usherette and she said it was showing at the County, so out we went – only to discover that the next showing was at 5 p.m., too late for us. So we went into a hot, crowded little tea shop and had a filthy cup of tea and a stale sponge cake. Altogether a calamitous afternoon. But on seeing the papers we were immensely cheered up and in the evening went down to the Nelson and drank to the falling of heads and a pox on the Tories.

O'Neill had just been round in a thoroughly bad humour. In fact the entire staff here look as if they'd been condemned to death. One or two of the nuns looked as if they were *going to be sick last night, and the idiot we have on this ward came in last night and said "Good night, everybody," and then, in a highly dramatic and perfectly serious voice, said "And good night Liberty!" They definitely think that any day now a band of armed Labour SS men will march in, rape them all and take over the place as a nationalised brothel.*

The past few days I've been making a nuisance of myself, and this morning O'Neill said he'd heard I was "getting impatient." Too damned right I am – but his tone was obviously churlish. Anyway, I don't give a hoot, and I'm seriously thinking, if no arrangements are made quick, of deliberately blackening my character with a maid (you wouldn't mind, would you darling, considering the Cause), as a means of getting out. Anyway, O'Neill said he had filled in "the forms" and sent them off, so I take it that is his sanction for me to be transferred.

I had an almost incoherent letter from Teddie, which indicated that he and Molly had managed to convince Wood they weren't after his sock of banknotes and stayed the night at the flat. I think he's coming down tonight.

I'm sending along last night's Evening News and am also keeping the Herald for you.

Write soon, my sweet. <u>All</u> my love,
*Your adoring
Ken.'*

The next day, an apprehensive Betty attended a CW meeting at the Committee Rooms. The agenda is not known, but a dissection of the result and discussion on the Party's future seemed inevitable. She was invited to the front to offer her own diagnosis, which was well received by all bar one John Wheatley, but 'he was immediately sat on and…didn't say any more.' It was already known that Betty was keen to continue, despite the lack of funding and a support base that hadn't really increased during the last two years. But, her Malton and Thirsk branch sent a resolution down to Head Office that they wished the Party to go on. It is testament to her loyalty that two days later she turned down a job offer for Labour's agent in the constituency. An attempt to persuade her, via letter, by the constituency secretary still failed. In retrospect, she may have regretted this.

On the 1st August CW's fate was sealed. A Mr. Barham, at Head Office, sent her an official letter, accompanied by a coolly guilty covering letter from Gower Street's National Agent, Carol Bunker:

'I am sure the Labour Party owes something of its success to the work our members and staff have put in during the last two years. However, the financial situation has been difficult for some time, and it is not likely to grow easier in the near future. The National Executive therefore decided that the whole of the Election team must be dispensed with, and drastic cuts have also been made in the indoor staff.'

Bunker added that the National Committee would have the final say at a meeting over the 11th and 12th August, but that 'it will not be possible for you to attend.' Her undoubted disappointment lasted less than a week. She was back at The Oldfield Hotel when, on the 7th August, he returned her the favour of a heart-stopping telegram. It was the news they had both waited twenty-two months to hear. It simply read: 'OK for Saturday, Betty.' Ken's War was – seemingly - over.

The Allsops' with first child, Andrew, c. 1947.

11
Aug 1945 – Sept 1948: Sanctuaries

'When I do start work again, I'm going to keep you in complete idleness for two years, in the same way you've kept me.'

Such was the hopeful promise Ken offered Betty from his hospital bed twelve months earlier. Now was his chance to prove it, although he couldn't have predicted the condition he would be in when finally released. On receiving his telegram, Betty excitedly gabbled back a breathless reply:

'Will we come back on Sunday? I have a meeting in Leeds on Monday and will be coming back here on Tuesday. Are you coming back with me, darling? And shall I book somewhere for us to stay the following week? I think I can only afford a week before I start looking for a job... Don't forget to answer all my questions, sweetheart...Am I to come to the hospital to fetch you or will you be coming home by car?' Months of dashed hopes had trapped this ever-growing list within her. In the event, she and Pat met him in the hospital foyer. There was no sense of relief. Finally released to liberty, Ken suddenly held back in the doorway:

'I can't do it,' he muttered through gritted teeth. 'I can't leave with these.' Feeling exposed, and angry with his crutches, the sisters did their best to coax him on. The emotional roller-coaster of the previous two weeks didn't help. For soon after the announcement of the Election result, Betty had two of her own. First, E.P. Millington – now a Labour candidate – had offered her the choice of being his agent in Chelmsford or for one of the other available, North

London constituencies. He flattered her with a financial sweetener, knowing she and Ken would now need all the help they could get. She may have felt compelled to accept; her GP confirmed that recent nausea and dizzy spells were the early stages of pregnancy. Initially, she appeared wary of broaching this to Ken, after the trauma of the recent miscarriage. 'Will you be pleased, sweetheart?' His release and a newly agreed pension settlement left them both in little doubt that it should proceed.

Finally installed in 61, Claremont Road, Ken unpacked his typewriter and set too, blitzing all the local and national dailies, enquiring after work, while Betty spent the first couple of days, tying up loose Party ends in Malton and updating his parents in Leeds. He pondered on chasing up Frank Lawrance's pre-War offer, but he was intent on moving ahead. 'Everything is forward.' The desire to be taken seriously as an author returned. He had left St. Anthony's with at least half-a-dozen complete short stories. Among these were 'The Stories of' Smirril, (a hawk), Whitestar, (stoat) King, (kingfisher) and Jasper, (the inevitable crow). All were set on those transcribed, semi-fictional landscapes of Devon, Yorkshire and the Wye Valley; the happiest days since meeting Betty.

On the 7th September, he began scribbling a short story, typically semi-autobiographical, about one 'Martin Chadwick,' discharged from service and hospital life, already equipped with an artificial leg. From the outset, there is no question as to Chadwick's identity. The recollections of service life and subsequent self-doubt the main character pursues remain fascinating and can only be Ken's. Not all the names were changed: ' "Face the truth, you sentimental, sloppy hypocrite," he told himself. "Apart from Joe, Babs, George Linton, Mike and a few others, they all bored you rigid, and just remember how often you've cleared out just in time to stop yourself screaming at their incessant, adolescent ramblings and stupid prejudices.'

Sitting opposite a WAAF reading a political novel, on the way home, he recalls a view of him by one of his few respected colleagues:

' "Chadwick, old boy, you're anti-social," Bendix had told him... "I wouldn't mind so much if you were a true-blue, die-hard Tory like some of the half-wits here... But you, my dear man, are living in a vaccuum... You have neither the "Every German is a Bastard" philosophy, nor do you believe that you are a crusader against Fascism. No, you drop your eggs with the cold-blooded dispassion of an automaton. You are emotionally sterile, you are negative. Now, have a beer." Outwardly, Martin remained unperturbed at Bendix's measured harangue. He was used to them, for the others in the firm belief that he had an "unawakened but definite political potential" frequently let fly at him.'

Ken's own conversations with the likes of Jack May and Leslie Tunks took not dissimilar turns. On a subsequent visit to his parents, Chadwick finds a gulf of understanding has arisen between them since 1939. 'To his mother he was still the same 19 year old boy he had been on that morning he reported to the recruiting depot at Blackpool.' His father offers him partnership in the tool factory, which a now irritated son declines. There is no suggestion that Ken, himself, had such a conversation with his own father. Ernest Chadwick is depicted as stern and remote, whereas John and Kenneth were quite close. But, there is a connection with Allsop Sr.'s own situation at that time that seems telling:

'...Always, at the last moment, Ernest Chadwick had withdrawn behind his barrier of aloofness, completely inaccessible and unassailable. Martin realised suddenly that his father no longer had the same effect upon him. Before the war, he had always felt awed and a little frightened in his presence; now his self-containment, his god-like isolation, seemed merely pathetic. "God, how terribly lonely he must be," Martin thought with a shock... He had an impulse to walk round the table and put his hand comfortingly on the other's shoulder, but even as the thought crossed his mind, he visualised his father's painful, embarrassed surprise and he compressed his lips to hide a smile.'

An exasperated Martin ambles out their front door, 'as fast as his leg would allow him.' Racked with guilt and uncertainty about his future, Chadwick stomps over the local heath, where chard patches of post-war, celebratory bonfires fizzle out and once blacked-out windows shine new light. Copulating couple after copulating couple are gradually illuminated. He bitterly implodes with anger at what he sees as the inevitability of their fate; mere fodder for the next holocaust. He cries with confusion and self-loathing, finding sanctuary in a pub, where he casually confesses to seeing the other side of the coin with a punter at the bar. An odd, anti-climactic ending, as though Ken himself were left hanging and hankering for some certainty; his head finally finding sanctuary with his heart.

It was soon after completing this untitled short story that Ken allied himself to a fund-raising cause recently formed in honour of Mrs. de Trafford's two R.A.F.-serving sons who were killed in action. As a 'creative memorial,' 'Windows & Ladders Ltd.' – based at 33, Moreton Street, SW1 - existed with the modest purpose of enabling disabled ex-servicemen and women to do varied, practical jobs for the community, including window-cleaning, plumbing, wireless mending and bomb-damage repairs. Listed on a surviving leaflet, they boasted the patronage of The Archbishop of Canterbury, Lady Violet Bonham-Carter and Mrs. Winston Churchill amongst their number. Interesting, since the set-up was openly socialist:

'The Company belongs to the workers,' it announced, 'they

have a living wage, plus various allowances on their takings and an annual share out of the profits. THEY HAVE DONE SO MUCH FOR US. WON'T YOU HELP YOURSELVES AND THEM AT THE SAME TIME, BY GIVING US YOUR ORDER?' True to his instinct for the ulterior motive, the persuasive tone has Ken's type-prints all over it. On the 23rd October, he used it in a letter to the BBC's Director of Talks:

'I feel that a few minutes on the air would not only be of invaluable help to the ex-Servicemen of this concern, who are now getting a fresh start, but would be of wide and general public interest.' Ken offered to present himself at a time convenient to him. While the secretary's acknowledgement was swift, so was the rejection. The admirable endeavour of 'Windows & Ladders' were of no further use.

The only positive response, so far, was from the Competitions Department of *John Bull* magazine. Ken was interviewed, on the 21st November, for the post of quiz and crossword setter by its editor, A..T. Mason, for the reasonable wage of £7 & 7s. per week. He knew, when applying, he could never become enamoured by a job, already a dead end, but it looked less boring than simple administration, and he saw at as, at least, a small step back into journalism. Two days later, Mason accepted him into the post. But, by Christmas, Ken's enthusiasm was already waning.

Either for Christmas or his twenty-sixth birthday, five weeks later, Ken received a pen as a gift by a woman named Dorothy. Accompanying it was a card bearing the legend, 'with love, Dotty.' Betty, noticeably pregnant, uncovered it while trying to tidy the house, alone, one afternoon. Distraught, she raced over to Pat's, wondering if she should leave him. Pat offered to put her up, but she returned later that evening before Ken knew there was anything seriously wrong. Dorothy proved to be a transient name in his life; never referred to again beyond the intimacy of Ken and Betty themselves. Too swiftly passing to be called an affair. But 'Dotty' was the first fling in a debilitating list for Betty that would strain, but never quite break, her will.

By the end of the year, Ken had finished reading a new book by a naturalist writer named Richard Fitter. Published as 'R.S.R. Fitter,' his *London's Natural History* studied and depicted – in, then, glorious colour – the bird-life habitats that encompassed the city's greener regions. Ken, so taken by Fitter's study, responded with his own detailed survey of observations.

On the 11th January 1946, he typed a dense, two-page summary of his nature notes, where he 'came to know all sections – public *and private* – intimately.' It reveals the growth of his stolen menagerie: the young owl 'pilfered' from a pair of tawnies in 1935, the young crow taken from the nest in 1937, the young hawk (or *eyas*) unearthed from an old oak and kept for several months through late '38 – early '39. Fitter replied on the 17th, asking for further details on the precise, annual number of nesting pochards while Ken was in Osterley, with wood-lark, stonechat and short-eared owl in Hounslow, 'partly on behalf of the London Natural History Society, who I know will be very interested in your records.' Fitter passed the word on to E.R. Parrinder; recorder for the Society's Ornithological Section. On the 24th February, Parrinder sent Ken some Society publicity along with a record form on past distribution of bird habitation on Hounslow Heath, he hoped he would complete to fill their dearth in historical facts for the area. Ken was willing to co-operate but two other contacts, received in quick succession, distracted him from his frenetic applications. He hurriedly responded without returning the form. One was from Nadine Moeran, inviting them to join eight family groupings at a disused mansion in Studham, Bedfordshire. This, a follow-up to an ad., placed in the left-wing *New Statesman*, enquiring after like-minded couples; the second, from Frank Lawrance, true to his pre-War promise of a post-war job. The features post at *The Slough Observer* was his if he wanted it. Under the current circumstances, it is extraordinary that Ken felt he had to choose. A subsequent Sunday meeting in the mansion with Edward Moeran, his wife, Nadine, and other hopeful applicants at the end of February, dashed any hope of them affording the rates. But the door was held open should any future couple decide to leave.

On their return, Ken picked up a card from Queen Mary's Hospital, Roehampton, which confirmed an appointment for the fitting of a new artificial limb. It had opened early during World War 1, in 1915, as a response to the unmanageable number of injured servicemen returning from France with arms and legs blown off by landmines. Over the next thirty years it also gained a considerable public reputation as a centre renowned for the amputee's rehabilitation; care for the mind as well as the body. A reputation heightened during the War just ended.

Ken's new right leg represented the limited technology of the time. A clip joint at the hip, held on by a leather strap harness, was clipped on to the socket and slung across his left shoulder and around the waist. After the fitting, the remainder of Ken's fortnight stay involved some practical counselling and tutoring on how best to use the new leg. This treatment may have been a little too successful. Impatient to regain independence, he quickly discarded the crutches and ambled awkwardly out the doors. As he alighted from the bus back to Highgate, his right heel gave way, slid forward and dropped him on his arse. Back home and calmer, Ken rolled-up his right trouser leg and showed the women his new appendage. 'It was tin. Cream-coloured.' Pat recalled.

'I suppose it was meant to be skin-coloured. Round the top

was a sort of a large cup-thing that fitted over the stump. That had a sponge edging to it that was supposed to make it more comfortable. But he was *never* comfortable.' The medical establishment's suspicion of a tubercular source was never finally settled. Almost immediately, Ken received appointments for more general physical check-ups, including one from Finchley's Chest Clinic in May. Reassurances would have been offered about the initial pain, that Ken's lack of experience could hardly counter.

Determined to get used to his appendage, he made exploratory visits out alone. Another fall occurred, later, on alighting a carriage at Kings Cross Station, where the leg completely detached itself. Under full, public gaze, Ken felt humiliated. Through subsequent weeks, the so-called 'initial' pain appeared reluctant to ease its grip. Still, he walked and he walked and he walked; with an almost grim determination. Ken had always been thin-skinned. Now, a permanently short temper established itself that, for the rest of his life, constantly bubbled beneath the surface of his reason.

Ken's disablement, allied to the imminent arrival of the baby, prioritised money as the main objective. Evoking his rush of blood a decade before, Ken then blitzed the national and regional dailies; over a dozen on the 20th May alone. Replies were coolly sympathetic but negative, most blaming the number of men returning from overseas in ratio to the current ration in paper. More out of desperation than want, Ken recalled again his former editor's offer and reluctantly gave him a call. Lawrance proved more than true to his word. For the inevitable salary increase, 'Allsop' would write the leaders, review the local Arts scene and pen a weekly sequel to his pre-War 'Country Log's. Stifled by the poor wage and working conditions at *John Bull*, Ken found it easy to hand in his notice. Belatedly, an earlier application to *The Sunday Express* came good, Ken suddenly answerable to two regular employers. He only pined all the more for a full-time post in Fleet Street.

During the 29th May, Betty went into labour and was rushed to University College Hospital. Overnight, she gave quite painful birth to a big headed boy, subsequently christened Andrew Lindley Allsop. Pat contrasted the occasion to today's routine:

'Ken and I went to see Betty. In those days husbands didn't stay with their wives...and I don't think we saw the baby...afterwards we both went to 100 Oxford Street, which was a jazz club at the time. I don't think we danced...maybe I did but he wouldn't have done. We spent the evening there, which was a bit of an odd thing to do when his wife had just given birth to their first child!' Like Ken at that age, little Andrew's broad cranium took after Mary.

No sooner was Betty discharged from the U.C.H. than she was joining the fray on behalf of her husband. In the first half of June she wrote a near begging letter to Tom Wintringham, pleading with him to put Ken in touch with any known Fleet Street contacts. He was hardly the most appropriate choice. On the 29th he admitted,

'I know practically no-one in Fleet Street, except editors who dislike me very much because I only write what I like; and journalists who dislike me even more because I earn unholy amounts by doing so.' He went on; 'I expect your husband will find things easier when paper is increased next month.' He ended, suggesting Gordon Schaffer at Reynolds News. Wintringham died just three years later, aged fifty-one.

Ken's renewed commitment to *The Slough Observer* posed a new problem. While he yearned to work full-time at *The Express*, they both realised that his leg would limit commuting in and out of the City. As Betty recuperated with friends, she perused the local press in search of an inexpensive flat just outside Slough. Back at Highgate, Ken caught the train to meet his first appointment in Fleet Street, for *The Express*'s news editor, Stanley Head. Coincidentally, this first assignment was to attend a meeting at University College, which he had seen only a few days earlier, to attend Betty. The following Sunday morning, he reported back his activities to Betty, well pleased:

'The students of London University were holding a meeting of protest in the Anatomy Theatre against the Government's housing policy, most of them having to live in waterlogged cellars, apparently. Also, had three other stories, which I could get my teeth into and WRITE. Had two stories in the first edition, but owing to the half-witted newsagent of ours, I got the People instead of the Express this morning, so I don't know what went into subsequent editions... What do you think --- when I got home last night I found a letter from Stanley Head, asking me to ring him on Friday, as he would probably want me that day, and also saying that he was going to pay me an additional three guineas for V-day, making it triple pay. It looks as though I might have wormed my way in before long, doesn't it?'

While things were looking up, financially, domestically, Ken was at a loose end. An abysmal cook, he did little more than scrape together cold collations learnt from the meals endured in the R.A.F. By the end of each day he had neither the patience nor energy left to prepare more. The continual, grinding pain from his own sliced joint ensured he would be reminded of that.

Situated just four miles south-east of Slough, the village of Langley had apparently gained some rural appeal for Ken, as he passed the area, each day, to and from work. Equidistant from the posh playing fields and well-mown lawns of Eton, Langley was mainly residential. It had been founded on the site of the original five woods and clearings from which it took its name. (*Lang-ley* meaning, literally, *'long wood'*). These were Middle Green, Horsemoor Green, George Green, Sawyers Green and Shredding Green. At this time, small enclaves of housing had been developed on the site and the areas where the woods once stood were still known by these names. Later, these 'estates' would merge into one town around Langley's church.

It was certainly a surprise to Betty for, with no recourse to her, Ken unilaterally placed a modest downpayment of rent on No.10 Marish Court. (So named after the de Marisco family, who acted as the manor's guardians' during the 13th century). No. 10 was the second-floor flat in a new low-rise block in a small square; built for those middle-class yearning for access to the country at bare minimum cost. The rooms were small, inexpensive and functionally equipped with basic provisions. What mattered most to Ken were its surroundings and accessibility to Slough, while Betty gleaned some snobbish delight from its seclusion.

Neither could account for the couple living beneath them. The Allsops' were left-wing, atheist, and social. Downstairs, the Youngs were Tory, church-going Christian and mainly private. After the September move, the Allsops' threw a combined housewarming – Christmas Day party. Around 12:45 am, Mrs. Young interrupted the jazz records and competitive, intellectual banter by yelling and pounding on their floor from below. The Youngs' Christmas had been spoiled by the husbands flaring duodenal ulcers. But, the new arrivals weren't informed of this until much later. Mr. Young wrote to the council to complain, but the lack of a polite approach from the wife infuriated Ken. 'That began a sustained vendetta.'

Cruelly, baby Andrew became the main target. With the lack of spare room, Betty was forced to keep his pram in the downstairs passage. On one side was the door leading to the Budds' flat and on the other, the Youngs'. On leaving No.10, the Allsops' were often appalled to find the pram pushed outside, in all weathers and at all times of day. In a heavy rainstorm, it would be there, with the hood down and filled like a child's bath on wheels. During this calm-winded winter, it was also found tipped over. The Allsops' wrote their own complaint to the council, and Ken was summoned before the Housing Manager. A subsequent lack of action ensured their feud would never be never resolved.

But, the Youngs' may have had a further reason for disliking their new tenants. On Friday, 20th September 1946, Ken's first *Slough Observer* leader appeared. The opening paragraph is sub-headed 'The Limitation of Liberty.' With tongue firmly in his left cheek, he claims letters had been received from 'Marish Court squatters,' complaining about the paper's criticism of their action the previous week. The leader emphasises its sympathy with their motive but not their conduct:

'Lawless and despotic actions can only bring about lawlessness and despotism. The fundamental meaning of democracy is that the liberty of the individual must end where another's liberty begins. To permit the present rule of 'grab' would mean a rapid descent to jungle conditions of the survival of the fittest.' In one leader piece, written on Boxing Day after the Christmas night party, Ken reports on Slough Borough Council's decision to build their first new, permanent houses, and a young boy's gift of his new cycle to his soon-to-be-hospitalised brother. He ended that it was,

'a pity the generosity and charity which manifest themselves at this season, cannot be perpetuated throughout the year!' Such heavy-handed references may not have been lost on the Youngs'.

'What is This Thing Called Jazz?' stands out, not only in its lack of context to local issues, but as a statement of intent. This aspect of Ken's life, recently neglected, was brought back into focus in reaction to his resentful neighbours. His first published piece of social history, it sketches the music's multi-cultural roots in America, where economic insecurity accompanied slavery's abolition and jazz, with autobiographical 'blues,' became the subsequent expression. The essay, like its subject, highlights his own brand of libertarianism, now guiltlessly, upwardly mobile:

'Fundamentally, (jazz) is the free expression of the human spirit,' adding it is 'the free-enterprise of music. Each player stands or falls by his own ability and ingenuity. He cannot, as in the modern thirty-piece swing orchestra, hide behind a barricade of team noises and fancy arrangements.' The text also reveals Ken's purist stance. The recent revival of 'basic' jazz, with bands travelling to pre-planned jam sessions, was
 'as far away from jazz as 'home-made' *factory* jam is from the real stuff.' His preference remains with those playing with the 'haphazard spontaneity' of its source, both in New Orleans and 'the turpentine and railroad construction camps of the mid-West.' Ken would never veer from this world-view, returning to both subject and setting at key points in his life. Others found the essay worthy of an encore, finding a re-print in the highbrow *Musical Digest* the following spring.

January 1947 couldn't arrive soon enough for Ken. Having sent in his copy for the first Saturday deadline of that Sunday's *Express*, he rang Stanley Head. Following this up with a letter, he lobbied for a further two weekdays' work.

'If this can be done, I intend giving up my job on the *Slough Observer* and devote the early part of the week to developing lineage in that area. But, as I am sure you will appreciate, domestic commitments make it necessary for me to ensure a basic income before taking this step.' It seems likely he had asked Frank Lawrance for a New Year pay rise and been turned down; to Ken, the final straw in their relationship. Head wrote back on the 7th that employment prospects in Fleet Street had not improved.

'This applies to Saturday staff as well as the permanent

people.'

Ken and Betty were barely keeping their heads above water; their growing child proving a bigger financial demand than anticipated. This, and the likelihood her beloved husband was having an affair, strained relations. Once positive sounds of conversation were now replaced by Andrew's demands and Ken's, irritable, barked responses.

For escape, he learned to drive and, as he couldn't afford anything decent, found the cheapest car on the market; a bone-shaking, decommissioned, military vehicle in flaking grey, still bearing its unit's markings. He had it sprayed a defiant, shining, deep red – with the pedals modified to take the false leg.

He needed to be accepted into Fleet Street as soon as possible, but his only option appeared a higher financial return from another local paper. In early February he was invited for an interview with Raymond Thompson - Director and General Manager of Swindon Press - for a post with the town's *Evening Advertiser*. When offered the job the following week, he immediately handed in his notice to Lawrance. With his confirmation letter, Ken enclosed two advertisements for the paper to print, enquiring after local accommodation. But he had no time for the responses. So, for the first thirteen days, he was forced to drive to the south-west and back under his own disabled steam. It was then he realised he had made a terrible mistake; an impetuous decision borne of desperation and domestic strife. On the 23rd March, barely two weeks after starting with the paper, he had to go cap in hand, first to Thompson who, understandingly, left open the door, and then back to Lawrance.

Just before Ken rejoined his old paper for the third time, a letter appeared in their office in-tray from a nineteen-year-old degree student in Botany at University College named

Peter Marler. Marler was canvassing support for a Natural History Society to be founded in the town. Betty Adamson, a committee-elect member living nearby, had simultaneously written a similar letter to *The Observer*'s sister paper, *The Windsor Express*. She claimed,

'the locality is rich in places of interest to the naturalist, and if we have enough keen and energetic people willing to run a society, there is no reason why valuable additions to the few existing records of local flora and fauna should not be made.'

Ken pondered on this on his return. He was totally unaware that his thirteen month-old letter to Richard Fitter, an author well-respected in the area, had helped fire an already ignited spark. He was equally unaware that the Slough community had anything to offer the amateur naturalist. Intrigued, Ken wrote to Marler, introducing himself and wishing to find out more. But his interest had to take a back seat.

Still desperate for extra money, he sounded-out an *Observer* colleague, Patrick Alexander. Alexander asked him if he had anything already complete he might show a prospective agent. When Ken mentioned the nature stories he had written in hospital, he told him he should try his own agent who had sold short stories 'for fantastic sums to *Colliers* and the *Saturday Evening Post*." The Strand address he gave him was of a failed novelist and editor of Gothic Horror anthologies.

Christine Campbell Thomson was a rare beast in the London of 1947; a woman, who ran her own thriving business, employing a second, Moira Curd, to act as her personal secretary. From half-Scot, upper-middle class stock, her late father had been physician to Queen Victoria's Private Secretary, Sir Henry Ponsonby, at Osborne House. Having initially proof-read authors' submissions for the publisher, Curtis Brown, during the Twenties, in 1930 she left to form her own literary agency, joining forces with D.C.Benson Ltd in the summer of '38.

When Ken Allsop made his initial approach on the 21st March '47, she had barely regained her voice, having suffered from what her GP dubiously diagnosed as 'post-war nervous exhaustion.' In contrast to her single-mindedness, she stood a tall, homely figure, with rounded shoulders, but a determined expression heightened by hooded, observant eyes, and a dry manner that didn't gladly suffer fools. To strangers, she appeared formidable but, with familiarity, enthusiastic, supportive and trusting.

Enclosed with Ken's introductory letter were the four nature stories he had managed to complete before leaving St. Anthony's, along with 'The Egotistical Dog':

'I am wondering if there might be a market for stories of this type in America.' On the same day, over a dozen, local, amateur naturalists were gathering in Betty Adamson's Slough home at 59, Wellington Street, to select a committee. The gathering included 'Messrs. Balfour, Barnard, Fraser and Bunce' and Peter Marler, already acting as secretary.

On the 26th, Christine Campbell Thomson returned her initial thoughts on Ken's manuscripts, finding them 'perfectly delightful,' particularly 'Smirril' and 'Whitestar.' His heart must have sank for the third time in as many months when she doubted their interest to most editors. However, she held out hope from an enquiring children's writer who'd recently visited, looking for contributions. Could he write more of the same? She then became the first to draw his attention to his literary Achilles Heel.

'You are apt to err on the side of over-writing – of giving every noun its descriptive adjective, so that the whole is a little top-heavy.' He should 'watch this trick.' The next day, conceding his weakness, he returned a longer example that Campbell Thomson promised to forward for the children's collection. But she and her secretary wanted to read it first:

'That you can so hold two townswomen must mean that you have "got something"!'

Living above the ever-eager broom of Mrs Young was festering violent intentions in Ken. He and Betty were becoming self-conscious, edgy and questioning over the sound level of every domestic chore. Andrew, now in at toddler stage, couldn't even play with his toys or call to his mother without the anticipated thudding, on cue, from below. Biting his bottom lip, Ken ambled downstairs to her door. Summoning what charm remained, he knocked. A short, squat Frenchwoman answered and glared up at him. His attempt at diplomacy fell on deaf ears as she shouted a line of Gallic-tinged abuse in his face. He could do nothing but walk away. Ken's impression of her was swift and disdainful:

'Typically French bourgeois. Smug, strait-laced, selfish, hard, are all the words that can be legitimately attached to her.' The feud continued.

An inaugural meeting of the Slough Natural History Society was arranged for the evening of Friday 11th April at the local Grammar School. The dozen attendees agreed on a mandate to foster interest in the surrounding area's flora and fauna, while exchanging information collected from field trips with both local naturalists and national societies. Marler invited Ken who, in turn, invited Bill Budd; his downstairs neighbour installed opposite the Youngs.' The new villager listened intently to the discussions, quietly surprised at the wealth of bird life already sighted and anticipated by the locals. By the end of the evening Balfour was voted in as President while Ken had somehow charmed his way onto the committee.

Over the following month of weekends, Ken was often in the county but rarely at home. The Society had given him a new excuse to observe and notate with a group of like-minds for the first time since leaving Osterley in 1940. He discovered the Buckinghamshire habitats in Langley Park, Hedgerley Park and the Fulmer Valley. Latterly, the nesting sites across the Hertfordshire border. Often in his company were Society members, Peter Marler and Bill Budd, or John Hunt and John Field. Around his neck, a camera to add to his old binoculars. With all these new diversions, Ken forgot his fifth wedding anniversary. Betty dropped the hint and, towards the end of April, he drove them westward for a few days in Cornwall, then back for a reunion with sites from their North Devon honeymoon.

Ken found exhilaration from the speed he could attain at the wheel. Like Henry Williamson, who often took corners too fast – paying the price on one occasion when his Silver Eagle tipped over on its side – Ken emoted at the element of present danger; a similar *frisson* he found obtainable by his extra-marital flings. At this time, Betty white-knuckled through the 'slow down, Ken' stage, which, as she would soon discover, fell on wilfully deaf ears.

But he wasn't just exhilarated. Ken found he could transcend his rocking gait and nerve-pressured pain by sitting within the controllable comfort of his own space and not have to consider the journey's intervening space. No more pain, only gain, his natural impatience found accommodation by this one ally. On May Day, they were speeding back through Cornwall, (the landscape of which Ken passed off as 'markedly uninteresting'), when they headed north across Dartmoor, through the familiar Barnstaple road to the even more welcome sight of coastal Croyde and a particular Guest House.

'We called at Mrs. Staddon's. She remembered us from five years ago and put us up gladly.' The wind and rain that had dogged them since the second day cleared before supper. They walked, hand-in-hand, along Croyde Sands. He looked up and could not help but notice:

'A party of six dunlin were feeding with two ringed plover.' Portentously, the smaller breed was about to oust the crow from his conscience.

'In one day – two urgent and longstanding desires fulfilled.' That evening saw Ken and Betty drive to Georgeham for a drink at The King's Arms: fictionalised, like most of North-West Devon, in at least one of Williamson's books. On entering the pub, Ken clocked the photograph on the wall, featuring 'Windles,' John and Margaret in the bar. The barman told Ken that Williamson himself had been around the previous week but offered only vague directions as to where he might be found. Frustrated, Ken drove Betty back to Croyde in angry silence. Once again, he had slipped through his fingers.

The next morning, following those directions he'd gleaned, they pulled up to Wind Whistle Cross and a farmhouse beyond a small field. The field gate was open and a Ford stood inside. Ken claims he sat motionless, undecided what to do, for nearly half an hour. A contrast to the bravado he showed in 1935, but that disappointment may have returned, here, with him, sapping his confidence. Betty suggested he might as well see who was in since they'd come this far. So, finally, he clambered out and ambled across the field.

He knocked at the door. 'At first I didn't recognise him.' As with his previous attempt at contact, this wasn't a good time. In fact, things were now far worse. Henry was, reluctantly, on the receiving end of divorce proceedings from Loetitia, after she uncovered his infidelity with Christine Duffield, his latest young 'Barleybright.' On top of this, the receivers had been called in to Old Hall Farm, and he had just returned from a one thousand-mile round trip in the Ford taking two of his sons back to school; 'Windles' now installed at an Agricultural College.

Henry was back in Georgeham, his daylight hours in the Writing Hut, bedding-down at friends close by. A melancholy had descended, sapping his energy and lending him a temporary stoop. With his hair almost white, Ken's initial impression was of a man much older than his fifty-one years. 'He was writing at a gate table in front of an open, brick fire,' (most likely the novel, *The Phasian Bird*, to be published the following year), and chewing some nuts from a dish. He recalled Ken's name from the holiday with 'Windles' and handed Ken some of the nuts. Interrupting himself as though on automatic pilot, Henry suddenly launched into how the Norfolk Farm was broken up and the effect this had on him.

'I felt every man's hand was against me,' he sighed at last. 'I was broken, neurotic.' Ken's own account gives an intriguing, post-war glimpse into this now unpopular man's reduced circumstance:

'He said he had seven completed books in MS in the drawer. He said he would not publish them, and was withdrawing 'The Sun in the Sands' and was going to work it into a several-volumed novel. He talked of his 'Barleybright' – "An unknown symbol. Like you, she came tapping at the door one day." We talked of politics and philosophy. Over the fireplace were two framed photographs of T.E. Lawrence. And Mosley and Hitler are still his idols.'

Ken went back out to call in a neglected Betty. Henry offered her some more of the nuts and encouraged the couple to make themselves at home on his bed while he read to them his recently completed, never to be published, sequel to 1941's *Story of a Norfolk Farm*.

'When he reached the end, where he is describing the dissolution of his own life and the breakdown of everything he had worked for, tears were running down his cheeks; he tried to hide them by raising his hand to his face. He brought out a bottle of rum and we drank it from aluminium tumblers, laced with lime juice cordial. We talked on about politics. He was locked up under (Section) 18b at the start of the war, and "beaten up and almost killed" by the Home Guard in Norfolk. "The villagers here, who almost lived on me, wanted to burn me in my hut." His name is banned on the BBC (and) he cannot get a passport. He is despairing, utterly disillusioned, nervously tuned up to a dangerously fine pitch. "He is like quicksilver," Betty said afterwards.'

The couple left, harbouring a deep impression of the author's profound loneliness. Ken had assured him there were others who understood and sympathised with his ideals. He tactfully failed to add that he wasn't one. Henry had hoped the younger generation might share them. This irritated the journalist. Ken's final verdict highlights the contrast in Henry's time-honoured, unquestioned mores in relation to Ken's: cynical, informed and new. Immovable positions that ensured a mutual misunderstanding they would take to their graves.

'His ideas are so twisted up and illogical,' grumbled Ken. 'The patriotism and single-mindedness he praises is to me a myth and a blind, unthinking acceptance of dogma; the thing that gives a cheerful fillip to any crazy war. "He is very like me," Henry remarked to Betty, and produced a photograph of himself wearing his new M.C.'

On the return journey after lunch, skirting areas still dormant with landmines, Ken, ever inquisitive, deviated down a narrow track at Saunton Sands and promptly stuck the car in a dense stretch of the stuff. Fruitless digging by the couple forced Betty to walk back to the Army camp stationed nearby to return with a truck that towed them out. Ken deviated again through the town of Putsborough and on to the Woolacombe Bay side of Baggy Point. The wind blew fierce as Ken got out and ambled over the hump of its promontory. Wincing up into his binoculars, he saw a peregrine falcon caught in a stationary hover. The wind, combined with his excitement, knocked the field-glasses from his eyes as 'it remained rock-steady, wings arched as in an heraldic design, head down.' Ken was ecstatic: not only from this being his first encounter with this majestic bird of prey, but as reassurance that the R.A.F.'s wartime extermination campaign of the beasts had failed. A red-letter day.

Henry divided his time between the Writing Hut at Georgeham, and sleeping over at the nearby cottage of his friends, Major Mike and Margery Mitchell. The day after their first proper meeting, Ken kept to an offer made by Henry to meet him there. Next morning, the Allsops' walked to the cliff edge of Baggy Point. Ken was hoping for an encore from the peregrine. But after a time of staring out to sea, he turned away.

At the Mitchells' that evening, Henry was in a lighter mood and insisted on playing a recording of 'Tristan and Isolde.' Lying stretched out upon his back in the middle of the room as he listened, he bellowed out how it was set in Lundy, and featured the story of an Irish prince and his love. Through pouring rain, Ken drove Betty the two hundred and fifty miles back to London, she having allowed for the fact that her husband's misguided hero was also quite mad.

The last day in May saw Ken accompany fellow society members to the seemingly disheartening setting of Ham Fields: Windsor's sewage farm at Wraysbury. But, again, his colleagues knew what they were doing. He found himself looking at a virtual lake.

'Large numbers of lapwing and three redshank, whose fluting cries cut clearly thru' the wailing of the plover,' he wrote excitedly. Plover? Here? As the more common drakes floated by, an Etonian boy, doing his own spying, casually announced he had just seen the much rarer *little* ringed plover in the next bay. With the rest of the group, Ken had read that its first sighting this century occurred at a reservoir in Tring – on the Bucks-Herts border – in 1938, when a pair nested and successfully hatched three or four young. Ornithological magazines had pounced upon the story. Six years on, a second pair nested on precisely that spot, with a third pair following soon after in a Middlesex gravel pit. By the end of this year, 1947, over a dozen pairs had been confirmed.

The group watched as a mate arrived. Excited, mutual whispers asked if they might actually be nesting before their eyes. After ten minutes of observation, the birds flew off and they walked over to the 'nest.' A member took a picture of the clutch of three brown speckled eggs sitting alone on, apparently, ploughed and unencumbered earth.

In the Society's company, Ken's usual sense of intellectual superiority was quietly deflating. And such events were revealing how, in a setting neither wholly urban nor wholly rural, he still had much to learn about birds and their favoured habitats. As Ken observed what the boy had found, it dawned on him that this tiny creature harboured a story. It was one *he* determined to tell.

Kenneth, in rustic gear, with eighteen-month-old Amanda and three-and-a-half-year-old Andrew, c. 1949.

Ken showing Andrew his shotgun as neighbour's son looks on.

12
Spying & Selling

Life at 10, Marish Court was not getting any easier. Not content with complaining about the Allsops' domestic noises, the Youngs' were now providing their own. Since they stayed in most of the time, they would argue, loudly, in French, and make up, by the husband falteringly playing Schubert's *Serenade* on a newly-delivered piano, accompanied by a dubious falsetto from his wife. On Sunday mornings, the radio would be turned to the religious services, prompting further communal singing. The floor and walls proving as thin as the skin of Ken's fraying nerves. He confided to his notes:

'The existence of such a state of affairs makes me unhappy. I'm conscious of it almost always, and I dislike the violent evil that their presence stirs up in me. It's not pleasant finding oneself willing death, destruction and disaster upon other people. Such a state sours ones life.'

Yet, it was in this disturbed atmosphere that Ken spent the next month researching and making notes on what was fast turning into the follow-up to 'The Ascending Circle.' An inspirational rush that could only have occurred with his local access to all the relevant sources.

Just three days after they had found the little ringed plovers' nest, Peter Marler revisited the scene only to discover a plough had casually scythed through the eggs, doing its day's work. But, a subsequent visit to a new reservoir at Staines found the pair already re-established, fighting for their survival. On the 18th June, Ken visited the reservoir with Marler and saw for himself one of the little birds circling around in 'flickering flight...revealing flashes of the white under tail coverts' and its scrape. Then, a third, lone bird appeared, pointing to a possible second nest. Ken returned with Bill Budd on the 22nd, bumping into E.R.Parrinder, who introduced himself.

'He told us that two pairs had brought off four young each in the reservoir and that, to his knowledge, eight pairs had nested in the Staines area this spring. They are spreading south into Surrey. He had just returned from Holland...and reported that the same cycle was in operation there.'

Ken was now buzzing and on a roll. On the 27th, he drove south to Burford at the invitation of John Cripps, the new editor of *The Countryman* magazine. Having unexpectedly made a name for himself in the county, he was now doing the same further afield. Cripps' intented to show Ken around the title's new location and gauge his interests as a possible future contributor. Lunching with them was none other than Richard Fitter, whose *London's Natural History* he had read eighteen months earlier. Inevitably, Ken brought the conversation round to the chances of a staff job. Cripps told him what he had gotten so used to hearing, adding, "but you never know when someone may drop dead." He kept dark his own, recent experiences of the little ringed plover. But he shook hands, departing with a further list of contacts.

The next day, Ken, on the Slough society's advice, continued behaving like some secret agent. At the reservoir, he rendezvoused with Parrinder and his London Branch chairman, Dick Holmes. Ken was disheartened to find the area 'seething with bird watchers.' A further London member appeared. It was clear the news had got out, and possibly through his companions. With the elements having washed away the most recent nest, Parrinder directed his three companions to a gravel pit, not far at Stanwell Moor. Raising his telescope he spied the object of their desire, and handed it to Ken. He noted that it was a fully-grown adult, unlike the ones found at Ham Fields.

'By next year, P.(arrinder) thinks there should be considerable spreading evident...In Holland he found them nesting in sandpiper positions near rivers, usually on dredged gravel, ...and even once on a cinder path. That sort of situation is available on Staines Moor.' Parrinder added that, as far as he knew, this small area was the only one in Britain where the little ringed plover were breeding. Ken returned to his car, thinking back over their two known appearances in 1938 and 1944 at the now abandoned Tring Reservoir. He pondered on the conundrum of those six missing years.

Armed with that day's field trip entries and related statistics, Ken spent all available summer evenings and weekends on compiling his own research. He pondered on a possible future story, making the little ringed plover its main character, but wanted to avoid the cutesy humanising approach to animals employed so successfully by the likes of Enid Blyton. He distrusted such characterisations, finding them irrelevant to the creatures' real lives. Consequently, he refused to read such stories to fourteen month-old Andrew, and advised Betty to maintain the embargo. While he stabbed impatiently at his typewriter, progress on finding a market for his nature stories was slow. Christine had submitted 'The Story of Smirril' to the children's publisher, but they returned it, agreeing with her that his style was 'too florid.' Ever willing to end such letters on a high, she added that the editor would have a better chance of placing it if tightly re-written. Ken preferred holding out for getting it and the remaining stories published as a collection.

On the 25th July, in desperation, Ken sent her a clutch of his own 'Countryman' cuttings to sell, re-worked, for the national press. Yet again, he was reminded of the paper shortage. It was just as well she was about to go on holiday.

The only other manuscript worth submitting was the story of Martin Chadwick he had written on leaving St. Anthony's. Hurriedly appending the title 'I Shall Never Return' for dramatic effect, he was asking for trouble. On her own return at the end of August, Christine had to inform him that

'it has been seen and declined by the most likely editors. I think it is too nostalgic for these difficult days.' Ken was deflated and, perhaps, too downhearted to dare discuss his work-in-progress, not wanting to tempt fate further. To cap it all, Betty returned from a check-up with her GP to announce she was expecting.

A re-galvanised Ken spent the last three months tapping out a new manuscript on a proposed satire with autobiographical overtones. Initially titled 'Pobbles,' then 'Pobbles Are Happier,' his indecision over the title alone pointed to a longer-term lack of focus. Misconceived from the outset, and more from desperation than inspiration, it became something of an albatross; three years later it was still unfinished. But by January 1948, an initial draft, a breathless rush achieved in the thin-walled hothouse of 10, Marish Court, was already complete. And he had listened to Christine, holding back on 'giving every noun its descriptive adjective.' But he thought twice about sending it to her, the recent string of rejections denting his confidence. So, he sent his partly autobiographical fiction to the one person he knew shared his perspective on country life: Henry Williamson.

Not for the first time in his life, Ken was forced into a change of plan. Relations with Frank Lawrance had not improved since his re-call, and the continued commitment to local issues was holding him back. Still, with a second child on the way, his sporadic income from freelancing demanded subsidy, so he embarked upon another round of job-hunts.

*

During January 1948, he shaved off the trim moustache he had worn for four years and bought himself a new 'town' suit and jacket. He was seriously considering falling back on estate agency work when, on the 23rd, he attended an interview for the post of publicist at The Travel Association. The job entailed writing upbeat publicity 'blurbs' for holiday brochures for British and American tourists; hardly taxing, but Ken may have hoped for a useful, literary discipline in writing to order. Again, he would not have the luxury of the ground floor, but at least the building had a lift. The T.A.'s was run by an attendant eager to make a little extra by producing for each entrant a cigarette case, lighter or fountain pen. Ken was made to wait until the morning of the 12th February to be offered the job, working under its Press Officer, Lyster Robinson. Later that day, he handed in his notice to Lawrence. He would not, this time, come crawling back.

On the 23rd, he received an enthusiastic card from Henry, suggesting he offer 'Pobbles' to his own publisher, Macdonalds. Two days later, Christine told him she had just heard from Latimer House who were quite keen on 'Smirril' and the other short stories, and wanted some other examples with his CV. On the 27th, Christine told him what he had waited six months to hear; Latimer House wanted to go ahead with the book of short stories 'as it stands, without any additional matter,' plus the usual ten per cent royalty for him as a first-timer. Gibbs, their editor, was also intrigued by the idea of a novel, Christine suggesting he sent it to her as soon as possible. Ken was jubilant. He phoned Henry who vaguely routed around for the draft he should have sent to Macdonalds. (Memories of Frank Lawrance with his first attempt).

'The position is a little awkward,' Ken admitted to Christine, 'as he has taken a personal interest in this book...' but Henry promised its immediate return. Alone, he toasted himself with a glass of beer.

On the 10th March, Ken drove to Reading Hospital to collect a re-fashioned leg. His pain had not eased as expected, the grinding of the joint exacerbated by his recent ramblings.

For a twelve-noon appointment the next day, Ken had an early chance to test it, negotiating the three flights of stairs to Campbell Thomson's office in The Strand to confirm terms. The pain still lingered but, now, was not his priority. His head was full of new projects and he marched with a spring in his gait. With him he brought the untitled novel and a proposal for his next. Unlike the finished work it would feature a bird as its main character; in this case, the little ringed plover he had spent the previous summer gathering so many notes on.

'I feel that this can be really something quite solid if I do it the right way,' he added. 'It's a matter of infinite pains, I feel, and I want to give it everything I've got. It's not going to be a carbon copy of *Tarka the Otter*, but I want to aim at that standard of subjectivity and fine accuracy.' But, it looked like Ken's bubble would burst again. A fortnight later, Christine returned Gibbs's cool critique on 'Pobbles.' It did not help that she concurred, suggesting Ken tried Henry's publisher after all as 'I like the book and will do my best to place it.'

During the third week of March, Ken set too on what was to become his second full-length novel. With at least six months research on the little ringed plover absorbed and still fresh in his mind, he could write swiftly and with insight without rushing headlong and unaided as he almost certainly had done with 'The Ascending Circle' and 'Pobbles.'

Much of April was spent negotiating the final appearance of the cover and illustrations accompanying the 'Smirril' collection now titled *The Sun Himself Must Die*. He knew what he wanted and heavily criticised the examples he had so far seen. He was also cool towards Gibbs, finding in him another staid, establishment figure like Lawrance. Gibbs then suggested he make his own approach to one David Wolfe Murray; a minor naturalist illustrator best known for signing himself 'Fish-hawk,' and currently working for the BBC.

Ted Jones was now also working at Broadcasting House, in a similar public relations role to Ken, and arranged the meeting at the BBC Club. On the 22nd he left the T.A. office carrying a draft of the collection for the 6 p.m. appointment at Broadcasting House. He had first lunched here with Teddy ten days earlier, but it was too swift a bite to take in his surroundings. His heart sank at the sight of so many middle-aged military types around the bar, all so similar and each calling the other 'old boy.' One who welcomed Murray was a walrus-moustached announcer about to make his name as the most recognisable face on radio: John Snagge. Murray appeared one these types himself but, over pints of beer and mild, Ken also found someone with 'a romantic interest in birds: particularly hawks.' Murray told him he would make his decision after reading the draft.

On the 21st May, Christine returned the proofs, adding that she thought it worth putting up for next year's 'John Llewelyn Rhys Memorial Prize.' Ken was unable to respond for another week. When he did, he could only return a vague acknowledgement, his attention diverted. Aware that Betty could go into labour at any moment, Ken had rushed to conclude an eighty thousand-word draft on the little ringed plover through the night of the 22nd May.

The next day, Betty was rushed to Slough Hospital where she underwent a second painful birth. She also left there emotionally hurt by her insensitive treatment. Years later, Amanda Allsop recalled how her mother later told her that if she had been her first, she would never have had another.

*

With a second noisy child to give fresh ammunition to Mr and Mrs Young, and space to write suddenly reduced, he and Betty realised the necessity of a further move. While they needed more room, Ken's expenses were also increasing at a rate far higher then his new income justified. T.A. lunch breaks and early evenings had become daily rounds of chasing up useful contacts, like Ted Jones at the BBC, or eating out with prospective London publishers. (Two days after Amanda was born, he was taxiing between appointments at Grosvenor House and The Ritz). As for his accounts, he rarely, if ever, saw the black again; but never reached so far into the red that he became bankrupt. Betty made sure of that.

On the last day in July he received a letter from Moira Curd at Campbell Thomson's, while her employer was away on holiday. It included a response from Gibbs to Ken's new novel, now titled *Adventure Lit Their Star*. Before leaving for a holiday of his own, he wanted Ken to know that, on his return, he intended to publish.

With this assurance of additional income, Ken found himself the excuse he needed to spring Betty and the children out of the flat's confines and away from their antagonistic neighbours. The month before Amanda's birth, the Allsops' were sitting, drinking outside at the local pub, when their eyes fell upon a Queen Anne style house opposite, 'white-painted with sunset-coloured roses clawing up the walls,' and, in unison, they cried 'Barwythe!' At least, this was Ken's story. Each had been quietly dreading returning to the nerve-racking claustrophobia of the flat. Now they were in a position to afford a little more. But, while Betty's exclamation was one of recognition, Ken's was of intent.

'On the way home, Bee was less sure than I. That was to be expected. My progression through life was a series of spurts, jumping from one impulse to another like a man leaping river boulders, a confused mixture of recklessness and hesitancy.' Nadine Moeran was called on their return. They were lucky. He and Betty could replace the family planning to leave later in the year, but would have to visit for a weekend to be 'looked over, you know. One of our few rules.' Ken brushed this off, casually convinced they would be accepted without question. He then took a gamble. Deeply reluctant to let the new baby suffer above the Youngs' as Andrew had, he immediately gave notice on their Marish Court flat. With no spring weekend available, Betty arranged the visit with Nadine for the 21st and 22nd August, leaving Amanda in the care of a babysitter. On arrival, they were taken to meet each couple, in turn, to be assessed on their social and political compatibility, and potential as contributors to the community. It isn't known if Ken made mention of his leg. To have broached the subject, himself, would have been unlikely. He wanted out of Marish Court a.s.a.p. Between the rounds of conversational drinks, strolls and communal work, he and Betty each demonstrated their personal qualities.

The day after their return, Ken spent his lunch break with Christine to finalise *Adventure*'s cover. He only really got to know her this day, as conversation deviated from the book. She could empathise with their bread-line struggles; the failed novels, ghosted books and 'anything to bring in a few shillings. But something always turned up.' In her school ma'am tone she added, 'if you yourself make the maximum effort, you will never be allowed to go hungry.' Before they parted, she confided to him an out-of-character, personal view of *Adventure*: 'You've written a masterpiece. I believe it's going to sweep the country.' He didn't quite believe this, but the praise boosted his flaccid ego.

By the following Thursday, a letter from Nadine, confirming the families 'general agreement,' sealed their fate.

Ken was just relieved to be out of that flat and in the English countryside. Betty's response was more pragmatic. Over that weekend she saw how liberated Andrew was, running in safety across the lawn and surrounding open fields with the other, often naked, children. Ken later wrote,

'If there had been no other reason, she would have gone there only to see Andrew given the chance to develop freely and happily. But there were other reasons also. "You've no idea, darling, how stimulating it was to be able to talk to other women about things besides rations and clothes and cooking," she said. "It's not so bad for you. You're out every day meeting new people and seeing new things. But since we left London I feel as if my brain has mummified." I knew how she felt.' For the first time since leaving St. Anthony's, Ken acknowledged how self-centred he'd been. To Betty, though grateful for the admission, this was hardly a revelation.

Barwythe.

Ken and Betty outside Barwythe, c. 1949.

13
Sept 1948 - Feb 1950: Barwythe

Each weekday morning, the eight families gathered in Barwythe Hall's large baronial dining room and served themselves breakfast.

'Everyone there shared an interest in vegetarianism, homeopathy, food reform,' recalled one of the women. 'All these things are mainstream now, but in those days it was very avant-garde and it was nice to find people who thought in the same way.'

After Max Martyn and the other men left for work, his wife Evelyn called on the other wives to round up their children and drop them off at the local school. The remainder of their day was divided between shopping, cooking, washing and, where necessary, fixing. 'There were rotas for absolutely everything, especially cooking.' By the Allsops' arrival, they were collecting to employ a housekeeper; a sign of the perfect mutuality already becoming compromised.

Shared responsibility in the upkeep of Barwythe Hall was the only house rule the Allsops' were required to adhere to as they moved into two largish rooms on the top floor. The £7 per week rent from each couple covered the mortgage and a separate fund for the maintenance of domestic appliances. The Moerans, with the Martyns, had been tenants from the outset, while other couples who'd answered that original call in *The New Statesman*, had since quit. The Martyns, independently, were about to leave. Reasons varied. Some found relations too easily divisive, with others called to better jobs.

While the husbands wore the same business suits and ties they'd used when living in the city, the wives dressed practically for home-based work in brown or dark blue dungarees, flat-soled shoes, their hair pinned up or back. Feminism wasn't yet a consideration for the women. Then its relevance would have been minor. The women felt themselves leading a privileged life, significantly more varied and democratic than that of the town-based, grafting housewife, trapped in a much narrower domestic routine. Shared responsibility afforded a mutual support system; a lot less work than that demanded of them as housewives. Evelyn Martyn later recalled every woman getting one weekday off-duty with free time at weekends.

As the Allsops' moved in, just before summer's end, they were offered to indulge in the custom of a regular sundowner scotch or sherry on the terrace overlooking the Hertfordshire fields. After dinner, Ken swiftly joined in with the political discussions, led by Edward Moeran, who, as Labour's South Bedfordshire candidate, was hoping to win the seat on his second attempt. At first, Betty tried jamming in her points between all too brief pauses. The competition proved too intense. But it was toward the end of such an evening when she had Moeran to herself, that he suggested she might like to act as his Political Secretary on the forthcoming campaigns.

As for Ken, it wasn't his political contributions in demand so much as his maroon-painted, decommissioned shell of a car. Passenger space was the premium, so he spent much of the first week ferrying Barwythe tenants and their late summer visitors to and from the local rail station. That Saturday, he drove to King's Cross to lunch with John Field, to discuss his final field trip with him, Bill Budd, and other Slough Society members on Blakeney Point - a nature reserve situated off the Norfolk coast. Ken had since handed in his membership to join the local Bedfordshire branch, but useful bird-watching allies in Slough were maintained. On the Sunday, Ken gave his old banger a much-needed rest, spending the day in its garage, while he assessed some internal wear and tear.

The weather chilled and the sky cast over as Ken took an annoyingly slow train en route to the Old Lifeboat House; a port used mainly as a study base-cum-hostel by London University's students of botany and run by its proprietor, Ted Eales. He'd hired the place from Eales for the Society's own studies at the cusp of the autumn equinox. Ken arrived carrying an outfit suitably English Bohemian:

'Gray flannels under cords, also gaiters, hunting shirt, skating pullover, scarf, fleece-lined flying leather jacket, and "cap" made up, pirate-fashion, of a stump sock." With his heavy binoculars, he felt their use along the damp, sole-sucking shoreline, while Field pointed out colonies of tern, gray plover, teal and sandpiper. Most of the birds co-operated long enough to be recorded and their habitats photographed, despite some distant target practice firing by the British Army, in place for the feared Cold War invasion. Ken was especially taken by the plight of its waning tern colony caused, in his eyes, by the sheer number of other visitors around him. A return visit, earlier in the year, was called for.

On his penultimate day, Ken notes his strangest encounter yet. During a tea break, a local, dripping wet in shorts and carrying a rifle, staggers, breathless, into the room from outside and asks for help to tow ashore a seal wounded by his shot. No one batted an eyelid or offered to help but, as one, got up and followed, too curious to remain seated. Ken's fascination is described in detail both sensually and medically precise. He is clearly aroused by the wet, beached carcass, the necrophilic tone evoking a surgeon too attached to his handiwork:

'Wonderfully streamlined. Reminded me of a 1948 American car, with all (the) mechanism sheathed by svelte molded metal: we could feel the 'knee' joints and elbows hooded by layers of flesh and skin. Fur close and tight, difficult to brush up. Mouth surprisingly small. Teeth yellow (old). Even penis conformed to torpedo taper by having only small cavity for protrusion. Nostrils flat and fluted. Shot with 256 *Metternich Soehnauer* dum-dum bullet. They got 6d. 1b for flesh, which is used for pig food and margarine (fat). This weighed 1 CWT or so. Good economics.'

As autumn cooled to winter, Ken became Barwythe's Van Helsing. Where a bat, rodent or other night creature invaded a tenant's room, Ken could be trusted to identify and deal with it. Where wives, home alone, were concerned, he was more like his nemesis, explanations often extending into unasked for reassurance.

'He tried to sleep with the women,' recalled Joy Scott who lived here with husband Herman. 'They wouldn't have anything to do with him... There was quite a bit of flirtation going on. Two couples swapped partners for a while. They tried to be discreet about it, but we all knew what was happening. Then when my baby was born, a very attractive midwife came to stay for a few days. All the men in the house were keen on her, and there were lots of secret meetings on the terrace.' But attraction wasn't all one-way. The young, good-looking village grocer was as welcomed by the wives as his deliveries, much to the concern of his wife and mother, according to Scott.

Ken's career had reached a junction at which he was at a loss to know where to turn. Somewhere over the last three years his intention of becoming a novelist had been sidetracked by the economic necessity of continuing journalism, itself then sabotaged by the paper shortage, forcing him into any job that maintained a living. His post-war commitment to support Betty as she had supported him had meant a greater level of personal sacrifice than he had anticipated. This to a man brought up on having his cake and eating it. So, here, in his ideal for living, he was as desperate and frustrated by his personal lack of progress as he had been at Highgate and Langley. Now, writing to order for the *Travel Association* was staunching the creative flow.

Too mentally tired to pen anything of significance, evenings and weekends were spent playing his part in the rota; clearing the garage, fixing faulty appliances or rebuilding the fireplace. Bolstered only by Christine's and Latimer House's praise for his first novel, Ken was prepared to set his sights on anything, whatsoever, so long as related to journalism. On the 19th October he penned a heartfelt plea to his agent:

'Very soon I am burning several boats. I'm throwing in this job. The reason is not merely that the job in itself is frustrating and dreary to a degree that baffles explanation -- but, much more important, under present conditions I am finding my own writing an impossibility. Lack of time is a factor, but the major obstacle is nervous exhaustion caused by having to endure for eight hours a day, five days a week, work that one loathes. So (with much trepidation, mark you) I've decided to take the only step that can give me the necessary freedom to get on with the things I want to do. As you already know, I haven't a pleasant little private income of about £1,000 a year to struggle along on, so this move involves providing by devious means the essential basic income.

Now, I'm working on one or two possibilities. One is Saturday work for one of the Sunday papers, which would bring in £4. 4s if I can get it. I have, too, several other things in mind, although none of them is by any means a concrete certainty. For instance, I've been wondering if there might be the hope of doing some reading for Latimer and am thinking of having a word with Gibbs on this point.

But any suggestions would be welcomed, and the reason I'm burdening you with all this is in the hope that you might be able to push something on the lines we discussed recently. What do you think?

I'm fully aware that you're probably saying at this moment "The young idiot!" and you're probably right at that. But circumstances have culminated in such a way – by producing an acute misery and an unsettled state of mind that makes creative writing impossible – that I'm convinced I must take a decisive step on this issue. Be tolerant, Christine, it's a bloody life, and my malnourished moral courage needs some support in this. Practically anything – including food parcels – will be a help.'

Christine's 'young idiot' was directed to write a similar plea to Aubrey Jones at Latimer House. Jones responded the following week:

'Your difficulties are common to many writers nowadays and I am not without experience of them myself. I only wish I could do something to help but I am not sure if I can make any very valuable suggestions.

If manuscripts come our way, which are in your line of country, and on which we should like your advice we should, by all means, be most pleased to turn to you, but I am not sure that this would be very frequent. As for the 'Sunday Times', I am afraid that there I could not help, for my own association with them was terminated some time ago.

I should have thought that the best thing was free-lancing for such papers as the 'Field', the 'Countryman', etc. Book writing should be fairly easy to combine with work as a natural history journalist, either free-lance or otherwise. I myself have no connections in this kind of thing but your name should be much better known after the publication of 'Adventure Lit Their Star' and we shall do our best to give you the maximum publicity...'

Jones was only repeating what Ken had long known, but he felt vindicated by such advice coming, directly, from his publisher. At their most recent meeting, Ken had handed Christine his latest short story: a drama on an adult's mental cruelty toward a child entitled *The Murder of David*. Its theme of stifled inspiration reflected his current disenchantment.

'The real theme is the murder of a boy in the physical sense, and the murder of the spirit of natural love, by the rigid minds of adult men.' Shortly after this correspondence, Christine wrote back approvingly of this little shocker, adding Aubrey Jones had felt the same, and that she'd try to place it. Momentarily, Ken's ego was reassured enough for him to broach a further idea.

A recent visit to nearby Whipsnade Zoo with the children had inspired the notion of an educational coffee-table-style book for older children on the Zoo and the daily duties of its staff. Accompanying his text would be professionally taken, high quality colour photographs. This soon sank without trace, but his close observation of Whipsnade's more exotic species planted an additional seed for his next work of fiction.

While following up Jones's leads, Ken approached the *Press Association*, enquiring after a possible reporter's post. As usual, he had not bothered scouring the papers for advertised vacancies, with competition already fierce enough. He was applying because he found 'publicity-propaganda too remote from the newspaper work for which I have been trained' adding he had 'a shorthand speed of 140 words a minute.'

For the next three weeks he was politely put off, though not definitively as he was clearly being checked out. After talking up his work rate while talking down his disability, he was invited for an interview at the Royal Courts of Justice. They capitulated with enough part-time hours to make it worth his while. On the 1st December, Henry Martin, the

P.A.'s Editor-in-Chief, wrote to invite him onto their Law Court staff at a starting salary of £11.11s. per week, rising to £12.12s., on completion of one year's service. Again, Ken felt relieved; even after Martin's proviso,

> 'I should like a written assurance that on the days you are in the courts, you will devote yourself, exclusively, to our interests and not undertake any form of work for an outside party, whether upon your own initiative or because you are approached.'

But, Ken was too concerned to get his own way to care.

He reported to his manager, F. Holmes, at 10 a.m. on Tuesday 11th January 1949. No enthusiasm accompanied him. At least, when he'd started with the *Travel Association*, he could kid himself with the idea of making the post his own. To bend the required text as much as he'd dare to exhale a whisper of his own voice. But, experience quickly dissolved that hope. Now, his sole wish was that he could emote, a little more, on his own terms by describing the cases he would be asked to cover. He'd brought with him his own notebook with this intention, using the jottings he made of witnesses, defendants and clerks in court as possible future material. In reality, he had merely exchanged one controlling and conforming discipline for another; replacing one 'association' for a second had virtually landed him in a parallel set-up, and no nearer journalism let alone creative writing on his own terms.

In a diary entry in early February, Ken reflects upon an article he's just read and the chord it strikes. Its author commiserates with those of Ken's age having to balance authorship with economic necessity. On reading this, Ken pines for a return to those 'fabulous days' when it was possible to make a living from writing alone. He does acknowledge a small but key improvement in his fortunes. With Betty back at work, campaigning for Moeran, and his wage at a level where he no longer feels the need to exhaust himself in a 9-to-5 routine, he has more time and energy to write. A fortnight away from *Adventure Lit Their Star*'s publication, Ken sounds a note of caution:

'How well will it go, I wonder. Max Martyn's calculation was that if all 3,000 copies sell – a by no means certain premise in these days of near-slump in publishing – my net return will be £150. Less the £50 advance, of course. On a strict financial plane, it is clear, writing is a waste of time. I would be much better employed in surging ambitiously forward into the jungle of Fleet Street: arriving for a job such as Pat Alexander has just landed, scribbling on *The Daily Graphic* at £18.18 per week. But I could not arouse interest in that.' He adds how present conditions at the P.A. afford little effort and enough free time to 'intensify production.' The voice accepts, in resignation, the sacrifice.

A week from publication he's in raptures over a letter from Henry; the first contact in two years. Like Ken, in the process of 'burning several boats,' he has transcended his earlier depression by repositioning himself. He is to marry his new 'Barleybright' – Christine Duffield – at Easter, honeymooning in France, then giving up his long-held position as Editor on *The Adelphi*. 'It uses up all my fuel.'

Now a divorcee, he has lived the last year in his Writing Hut and in the process of settling Christine in a caravan. His intended review of *Adventure* will be his last. The book itself he finds 'fresh and exciting,' though ticks Ken off for perceived cliché.

Ken is planning a third novel from his bed on the 21st March, when his first is released. His earlier anticipation had descended to a feeling of anti-climax, compounded by a recurrence of his trouble. Since Saturday night he has been consigned to bed, a tubercular abscess having erupted in his groin.

'The monstrous repetition of this...is too utterly depressing,' he confided to his diary. 'And there seems no way of tackling it at the root. The limb-fitting people have only talked vaguely about having the hard nodules of tissue cut out...' He rallied, with the help of drugs, to generally excellent reviews. The first Ken found was Edward Shanks's in *The Daily Graphic*. 'A fascinating picture. I read every word in it with excitement.' Norman Collins found it 'a miracle of exact observation, and if the little ringed plover could read, I doubt it could disagree with anything said about it.'

Belatedly, in May's *The Adelphi*, Williamson's review appeared. He'd written a brief outline of the setting, ending with a textual quote: 'There is a foreword and a prologue to Kenneth's exciting story – flip over them like a dotterel and come to Part One on page 21, and begin reading... and then go out and buy the book for yourself.' A sound advertisement, but Ken may well have expected more than this back-hander. Henry's attention really was elsewhere. That he picked on its foreword and prologue, though, is telling. Ken's fiction was the one area in which his home life, past and present, covertly obtruded. He is not fooling when, in the foreword, he states: 'The result is a combination of personal observation, recorded facts and imagination. Imagination was sparingly used, for I wanted the story to be truthful and factual, wild life as seen through the binoculars lenses.'

It is also remarkably unsubtle. Trapped within his literal perspective, Ken opens with a depiction of himself and Betty, named, here, Arthur and Mildred. As he begins trailing his first little ringed plover, Arthur unwittingly places his right foot upon an immovable nail that causes him constant pain. Limping, he returns home to face the wrath of his wife. Mildred had, 'remained baffled by his interest in ornithology. Resigned to his weekend expeditions, either alone or with the Society, she was still unable to restrain a simmering hatred for all birds and birdwatchers...'

The author's exasperation sounds personally held as he writes of the wife's response to his arrival:

"What enjoyment do you get out of it?' was the incredulous, bewildered question she asked fifty times a year... 'It's simply ridiculous, a man of your age wriggling about on his stomach and getting soaked to the skin to see a lot of birds...' Cunningly, he curbed his enthusiasm in the house, saving it for expression in the company of his Society friends, and finding in their response compensation for his suppressed domestic life.' He adds, 'Only once had he come close to striking his wife...' A safe distance of eighteen years is mentioned but that it concerned 'spending an October afternoon on the local sewage farm.' An ecstatic Arthur marches into their drawing room to announce he'd had a hen-harrier under observation for the past three hours. Mildred cuts across him to demand he take his 'disgusting boots' of the carpet or be thrown out. 'A white haze obscured his sight. For a flashing, intuitive moment he knew the sensations of a murderer. Just in time, his rage subsided and he slunk out to the kitchen with the muscles in his cheeks doing grasshopper jumps.'

Reading fact too far into fiction is fraught with hazards, yet the melodramatic nature of Mildred's reaction to Arthur's interest would jar, perversely, were it not based on personal experience. This foreword would be deleted from every subsequent edition.

E.R.Parrinder, as the London Society's ornithological expert, was aggrieved at this former Slough member turn-coating and taking their name in vain to promote his own work. He objected to what he saw as a direct reference to a London area 'Natural History Society' and the 'prose poetry' he perceived in the text, as well as questioning the validity of Ken's sources. When Latimer House sent this letter to Ken, he fumed. In his diary, he repudiated the 'sterile, humourless, purist attitude' of the school of Natural Science that took the physicists' view of the physical body over 'an automatic rejection of any sort of imaginative writing that sees the natural world in its colour tones and richly varied rhythms.' Quite why Parrinder took such issue is unclear. Certainly, Slough's covert, 1947 find and study of little ringed plover, circumvented the usual, unwritten rule of newly-discovered information being shared between other Societies. This may have fostered petty jealousies on publication. What is the case is that Ken was falling into the habit of reinterpreting fact rather too literally. The aforementioned 'local sewage farm' in the book's setting of 'outer-Outer London' is testament to that. This would not be his last such error of judgement.

During April, Charles Curran at the *Evening Standard* took on Ken as a freelancer. Impressed by the back copies he'd sent in of his 'Countryman' column from the *Slough Observer*, he offered him something – albeit now unchallenging to Ken – in a similar vein. The freedom he'd enjoyed to write about his choice of rural walk was, at least, transferred to Fleet Street, affording him that little extra cachet. From the start of May to the end of October, Ken contributed a regular column entitled 'Signpost.' But, with a tin foot now in the door, he stubbornly held out for features work. Through the aftermath of his regained confidence, Betty announced she was pregnant.

On the 4th June, Ken made a return journey to Blakeney Point. This time, he forsook the slow train and drove Betty, Andrew and Amanda for what was, ostensibly, the first family holiday. In reality, Ken intended to study the terns, who'd been predicted to return themselves this summer. Installed in a mainland guesthouse, he, Andrew and John Bean – the ten-year-old son of Ted Eales's partner – boated out to The Point to find the nests. John acted as scout having found them earlier and marked their positions with driftwood stakes and circular grooves in the shingle. Ken saw 'about 20 common terns and one little tern' flapping around the area and which settled as a brood on the nests the moment their back were turned. Ken noted the wide variation of markings and treatment of their eggs. The following day the crowds he'd witnessed the previous September were back, disturbing the birds and keeping them away from their young. An angry Ken chased off a large party of schoolboys inspecting the exposed eggs. It didn't seem to dawn on him that, at their age, he would have done the same.

Back on the mainland, while he and Betty spend the evening in the local 'Anchor' pub, he articulates his annoyance at the commercial draw of the place to her and the landlady, who sympathises at the overcrowding.

'Profit is the explanation,' he notes. 'The more people get across, the more teas Mrs Eales can sell, the more boat fares Teddie can charge. They're killing the golden tern...I think some action is overdue.' The terns subsequently showed themselves ungrateful for his support when, later, he was attacked by a disgruntled group for peering too closely at their eggs. Back at the local tea room (possibly the same one where he was shown the dead seal the previous September) he fell into conversation with Reg Gaze, the Norfolk bird photographer. Not on his own level, Ken soon turns away with a superior disdain. Later that week, falling into conversation with John Bean's mother proved more fruitful. Mention of Henry produced in her an admission. Her husband used to shoot rabbits on his land at Stiffkey.

'She said...HW used to watch from behind hedges to see if he was taking pheasants (and) when they were getting material for mending the roads, he used to stand by the lorry writing in a notebook.' Mrs. Bean was not left with a good impression. 'He was a proper old Blackshirt,' she sniffed.

Ken reports her adding that he was friendly with a Lady North, formerly of Stiffkey, but now resident in Blakeney, and that they held fascist meetings there. The Allsops' last day was fruitful for Ken. He reported discovering '40 more terns' nests' and '8 seals on a sandbank.' This time, all alive.

On the 16th June, Ken sent off his modified leg to Roehampton for additional improvements. For a day he was forced to rely upon his crutches and doing business, solely, by phone. On its return, he took a long weekend off from commuting getting used to it, while giving the usual assurances of there being 'pain at first' the benefit of the doubt. This didn't alter the fact that it was undermining his concentration. He was wincing over his typewriter as he hammered out 'The Terns' - a fictional essay from notes collected during the last two visits to Blakeney Point - and sent it off to Christine. The lymph nodes on his stump and the swollen growth by his groin still required attention. An appointment was agreed for August 2nd.

Ironically, only now were job offers accumulating at any significant rate. After his reunion with Ted Jones some fifteen months earlier, Ken had been keeping in touch on a monthly basis. During the spring, Jones informed him that the BBC's new Northern Region might be worth approaching with his knowledge of the rural area. On this advice, Ken wrote to their Talks Department Head. On the 13th May, R.V. 'Brian' Branston replied, communicating his knowledge and enjoyment of Ken's novel. Could he rush out a five-minute piece for an out-of-doors programme in July?

'The compere...will introduce, say, four or five separate items connected with outdoor country life...It would be pleasant if you could do a piece on bird-watching which could apply to this region, and I wonder whether you could centre it around the little ringed plover? I mention this, since you say the bird is nesting in the West Riding... Script length should be about 700 words, and payment will be £1.1.0 a minute plus expenses. The programme would be transmitted from our Leeds studios.' Also around this time Charles Curran called, offering him a trial in features: a travelogue report 'behind the Iron Curtain' in Hungary. Quite why Ken was deemed the appropriate choice as reporter isn't known, other than his singular tenacity allied with the brochure writings for the *Travel Association* which may have weighed in his favour.

Meanwhile, Betty's sister, Pat, now aged twenty-two, had fallen in love and become engaged to a Jewish degree student in Economics in his second year at Cambridge named Nat Solomon. Since Pat was also working in London, she and Ken met for lunch to discuss them both visiting Barwythe.

'I quite liked it because I found it quite fun, being single, going down and meeting very interesting people. I wanted them to meet him, naturally.' Her fiancée was much less convinced.

'I thought it was phoney,' Nat Solomon recalls. 'I thought it pretentious and unreal and couldn't see it standing the test of time. To me, they were kidding themselves they'd discovered a new way of living. I was totally out of sympathy with it. At the time, I was very left-wing anyway, but this seemed to me a way of opting out of society rather than trying to improve it.'

This came out in his first exchange with Ken who, not surprisingly, found him the typically jumped-up Oxbridge type he'd always loathed. Consequently, 'I was quite disparaging about Ken who, at the time, was a fairly junior journalist in the Law Courts. I thought that a pretty low form of journalism.' Far from alienating his future brother-in-law, this confrontation only served to spark the kind of combative talk in which Ken excelled. 'But, I think he respected people who stood up to him in argument: who didn't either slavishly follow whatever line he was advocating at the time or adopt an extreme and right wing point of view. So, my left-wing credentials stood me in good stead, even though I was a more earthy, prosaic and proletarian version of the ideology than he was.' They would remain friends until Ken's death.

On finishing 'The Terns' and his latest batch of 'Signpost's for *The Standard*, Ken hammered out the last few pages of a new novel; partly inspired by the family visits to Whipsnade and partly as a salvage job on the aborted photo-book project. Time was certainly at a premium. He hadn't the luxury of an unbroken stretch of summer. He required at least a couple of days to write the BBC North Region script, entraining from Kings Cross to Leeds to voice it, live, from their studio, and return to pen further 'Signposts.' He then wanted to keep his much-needed appointment at Roehampton, before heading back to Leeds to research Hungarian bird-life followed, perhaps, by a visit to his parents. Additionally, there was further work on 'Pobbles' and, only then, would he be in a position to put the finishing touches to the new novel, *Silver Flame*.

As a freelancer himself, Ted Jones was currently acting as a consultant editor for the publisher, Percival Marshall. Ken sent a copy to the publisher and, amid the haze of other priorities, let it slip from his mind.

'More time, more time needed,' he hurriedly noted, 'and I should be stepping up freelance output.' All of this before Curran's deadline of the 19th August, when he was expected to fly out to Eastern Europe. On the morning of the day before, Ken, accompanied by Betty and the children, was driving at his usual pace in the direction of Hemel Hempstead when, at a cross-roads at Great Gaddesden, a second car shot across his line of vision. Ken slammed on the brake, but skidded far enough on to hit the others boot and send it veering on up the road where it finally came to rest upon its side. Shocked but unharmed, the family returned in one piece. Ken, however, would be expected to appear at Hemel Hempstead Magistrates Court on his return. No one had either the gall or foreknowledge to tell him he was heading for a nervous breakdown.

Ken took Betty along on his first foreign assignment. Throughout their seven-year marriage, they had never been overseas as a couple. Now the chance arose and, with his usual visionary economy, he worked, vacationed and bird-watched as if one simultaneous discipline. Not for the first time, his single-minded distractions had drawn him away from her, only to return, in the nick of time, to restore her interest and affection.

The flight route from London's new Heathrow Airport to Budapest took them from Dieppe to Paris through to Basel on the Swiss frontier, to Buch in Austria. Hopes of witnessing bird-life peculiar to the Hungarian Plains or Danube Marshes were dealt a blow as the allocated time forced him to spend most of it in Budapest itself where 'the most evident bird was the ubiquitous house sparrow.' Then he'd been looking as a Brit. The object of his assignment proved more fruitful. He and his photographer were guided around the city by two, authority-assigned, boy guides. In the city zoo he found his 'huge collection of native birds' though 'many of them living under highly unsuitable conditions' in his view. '(Waders mournful in bleak concrete animal pens).'

Ken's second available week was spent, on the return journey, as the holiday with Betty and the children at the Paris stopover. But a further excuse to find more work beckoned. 'Plovers in Yorkshire' – the five-minute, spoken contribution to BBC North Region's 'Summer Scene' radio programme, had been broadcast 'live' on the 13th July. Now empowered to ascend in whatever he tried, on the 26th

August, from his and Betty's Paris hotel room one evening, Ken typed a letter to Broadcasting House's Director of Talks with an idea for *Woman's Hour*. The one aspect of his life he'd yet to exploit for payment had been his role as a father at Barwythe. In it, he put himself forward as the subject of a weekly series of talks on his progress understanding his children's needs and they, his.

'For Andrew and Amanda – and for the other ten children – it is a free and independent life...Then, there is the new baby, which will be born in the winter, and which is already meaning a readjustment in the family relationship, for Andrew is interestedly waiting for the arrival of his new brother or sister.'

The tone would be touching were it not for the motive. He returned, a fortnight after he left, on the 3rd September, with the article on Budapest already complete and wondering if all the research had been worth it. Percival Marshall's Editor, Peter Bayley, had scanned Ted Jones recent submission to him and been equally impressed. On his return, Ken found a contract waiting for him, with an option taken on *Silver Flame* and a possible further novel.

Ken appeared at Hemel Hempstead Magistrates Court not, this time, as a reporter but as a witness. The driver of that second car on the morning of the 18th August was announced as Godfrey Michael Turner, now of Nettleden House, Hemel Hempstead; and formerly of Barwythe! Ken felt no ill will anyway, but couldn't help suppressing a smile. He claimed that, on the day in question, he was driving a mere 35 m.p.h. and did all he could to avoid the collision. Turner then undercut him with the claim he was only doing 15 m.p.h. He added that he was in no hurry and that a hedge had suddenly obscured the view ahead. His next recollection was being asked if he could 'climb out of the car through the sun roof.' Turner was ordered to pay £5.5s costs and fined £10 for careless driving. A charge of dangerous driving was dismissed. What is missing from the above account is Ken's familiarity with court proceedings and his persuasive charm as the centre of attention. Ken was not pressed further in court, but simply accepted as the victim.

Nat Solomon's prophecy of Barwythe's dissolution was coming true. A 'why me?' tone had accompanied requests to adhere to the community's rota for some months.

'There had been some dissatisfaction with the housekeeping and the meals we were getting, and a few people, including me, felt it was a subject that should be dealt with at a family meeting.' He relates an argument he and Nadine had on the subject with one of the husbands. Ken asks him if he'd put the issue of the housekeeping on the agenda for the next meeting. Coolly, the husband says he won't as she (their housekeeper) is new and to question her authority would be premature and she should expect absolute loyalty. Ken fumed.

'I don't give absolute loyalty to anything if I consider it doesn't deserve it.' (He highlights the husband's 'catholic conscience' with distaste). A trivial excuse for dissent, but one Ken later admitted was a manifestation of a deeper problem. Couples were pairing off into select groups, defiantly following their own house rules as they saw them, so splitting the community into two grudging halves. The Scotts' may well have become distanced from the Allsops'. Joy has her own view:

'The trouble was that the sort of people who lived at Barwythe – intellectuals, or, rather, would-be intellectuals – didn't want to be bothered with all the drudgery that comes with a big house...The place could get very dirty, with food all over the floor. I found that quite depressing. Most of the people were nice but by no means all of them. Some of the men were remote and treated the place like a hotel.' She found Edward Moeran overbearing and occasionally dismissive of her children.

Ken's view of the bigger picture was typically intellectual. For him, the chasm that had polarised the group into two sets of couples was one of belief; radical Catholicism on one side, and the free-spirited Reichian approach on his. Any agenda there might have been for that evening's house meeting was discarded as emotions ran high between both sides. It plodded on into the small hours through ever-thickening smog of cigarette smoke. Eventually, tired and disillusioned, an agreement was mutually reached. They would take a vote on whether or not the community should close. The Allsops' and the Moerans' each argued that closure would be a positive move, opening an opportunity to re-start with a new mix of family groupings elsewhere and maintaining the ideals they'd all believed in. On the count of votes, they only just won the argument by 'a majority of three.' Ken was unforgiving and considered the alternative option with measured spite.

'Those who supported the proposal that the community should continue were the very people who all along had shown least enthusiasm for communal activity; who, in fact, had fairly well succeeded in transforming (Barwythe) from a community into a block of self-contained flats.'

As couples from both sides packed up to leave, the Allsops – on the 30th September, and with nowhere else lined up - struggled out of their rooms on the manor's top floor and into the nearby Lodge.

'Under some obscure legal clause, the rating authorities dealt more kindly with a house occupied only by caretakers...' Ken managed to ease the way by borrowing a canvas fire escape chute from one of the loft rooms, driving his car onto the lawn and placing one end in the back seat and the other up at the bathroom window. Items were then slid through the chute from there, back into his vehicle. The small Lodge's exterior evoked the Victorian folly. Inside, low-ceilinged, dark, but with an intimacy welcomed by the couple after the previous few months. The cooking range though was contemporaneous to the house, and had remained unused and *uncleaned* since that era. Betty found it a poor replacement to the three-oven *Aga* she'd been used to.

On the 24th October, Latimer House kept to their second promise to Ken by releasing his book of short nature stories as *The Sun Himself Must Die*. With reviews almost as uniformly positive as those for the novel, Ken was relieved but unusually pessimistic. He'd expected some tangible boost to his career, such as higher paid contracts, as a consequence of *Adventure*'s reception, but the disillusion and pain he'd felt up to its release continued, unabated. Now, he experienced no such hopes. His old friend, Ted Jones, maintained his support for the 'Pobbles' manuscript, but Peter Bayley could not yet commit to publication. He also feared the effect on his own writing. Seeking assurance from Pat Alexander over the phone, his friend could only warn him about what he might expect. Alexander told him he'd lost direction over the past two years, questioning his motives and suffering writer's block. As a result, he'd written nothing, in his view, of any consequence but "notes, scribblings and stray thoughts." Ken decided the best writing was intuitive; that it was 'better to pour it down on paper – never mind the infinitives split wide open...to get it down, fresh and fevered, is the first duty,' avoiding the original idea going stale through over-consideration. Ken needed such occasional reminders to be a little less intense about execution of ideas, to allow the ideas themselves to flow. The sheer number of jobs he'd committed to was not allowing for the time, necessary, to achieve this.

During November, Ken received a call from Bill Wade – an independent solicitor in Windsor – to say that it had been brought to his attention that, in his 'Pobbles' manuscript, various characters in the text were recognisable as certain individuals in Slough. Ken replaced the receiver, deflated. Consultations with Pat Alexander's choice of legal advisors followed but, throughout, Ken remained determined not to apply any re-writes. He couldn't, or wouldn't, compromise. In his eyes, he had only adhered to the same course as on *Adventure Lit Their Star* where 'imagination was sparingly used, for I wanted the story to be truthful and factual.' Stubbornly, he'd hardened this into a stand from which he wouldn't shift. An impasse ensued into December. Finally, a week before Christmas, he asked Percival Marshall to pull 'Pobbles' from their New Year schedules.

In 1940, Ken had approached his chosen career path, a cosseted and naive idealist. Inherently lazy in anything other than his pleasures, the War, his two years in hospital, the dubious decisions of town planners, and the economic demands of fatherhood, had all worn away such dreams, confusing his direction and cornering him into a far more portentous philosophy. He sums it up amongst his likes and dislikes for some prospective C.V., near the back of his 1949 diary:

'Politically, in recent years, his views have changed from Acland-ian optimism to Orwellian pessimism,' leaving only his desire to farm, that even he now saw as 'idealistic' and 'impractical.'

January 1950: Eric Blair lay in University College Hospital's ward for T.B. cases, slowly dying. In an adjoining room lay Betty Allsop, awaiting the imminent arrival of a new life: her third child and second son. Whether Ken ever sneaked a peak into the ward holding the patient he and everyone else would have recognised as George Orwell isn't known. But he later regretted this close shave to a meeting with his second idol. Having floundered in a mire of political ideologies during the War, Ken found in this one man an articulator of his new beliefs. He saw himself reflected in that 'rare and vanishing thing – the independent thinker,' while admiring 'his tremendous moral and physical courage.'

Come the 16th January, Betty gave birth to the boy - physically, at least, a less painful birth than the previous two, with his smaller head and narrower frame.

'He is long legged as a rabbit,' declared a grateful Ken. They christened him Fabian – after England's founding socialist society – and Halliday, after his grandmother's maiden name. (Ninety-four-year-old George Bernard Shaw, one of the Fabians' founders, was himself ailing towards death in March, which may also have been a factor in their choice).

By month's end, Christine Campbell Thomson had committed Percival Marshall to publishing *Silver Flame*, with the option still live on Ken's future works. Fortunately for Ken, his heel digging on 'Pobbles' had not irreparably damaged relations. Though pleased, he thought it too little security and too late for much celebration. His job at the *Press Association* now felt less like the diverse job of a freelance journalist and more like the pedantic, nine-to-five routine of a courtroom administrator. On top of this, he and Betty had been searching, in vain, for another property since last September. Frustrated, Ken's, by now raw, nerves, surfaced at regular intervals. Snapping at Betty over the most minor mishaps, against the background of balling Fabian, was now a daily ritual.

For the 23rd February, Clement Atlee, the Labour Prime Minister, called a snap General Election. With more family members than car-seat space at the site, Ken offered to ferry any intentional voters to the polling station at Leighton Buzzard. A water-tight excuse to refuse may not have been accepted as, for the second attempt of his career, Edward Moeran had put himself forward as the area's prospective Labour candidate. Ken returned to huddle, with Betty, through the night before a dead fire as the results came in on the radio. Although no party member, Ken reflected the general consensus that a Labour re-election would be the preferred result.

'Despite the weaknesses and shortcomings, despite one's criticisms and doubts, the alternative, a Tory Government, is unthinkable.' By the morning, Labour's margin of victory sounded secure. In fact, it was a close call, with the usual mixed messages of encouragement for both main parties. Turn-out was 10.5% up on the '45 election, but Labour gained only 2 ½% more of the vote than the Tories, with a mere seventeen more MPs'. The Liberals returned only nine, losing more deposits than they had ever lost before. (A decline compounded the next year, when they returned only six). The best news for Barwythe was Edward Moeran beating the sitting Conservative, Fearnley-Whittingstall, by around five thousand votes.

Ken and Betty's satisfaction was short-lived. The results were a much-needed diversion from their main problem, but this soon returned to haunt them. By the start of March, most of the original eight families had either left the big house or were waiting to move into new accommodation. And a Mr. Bagshaw, whom Ken described, contemptuously, as 'the wealthy and, it seems, permanently *liquored*, conveyor-belt manufacturer,' was eager to move in.

'I haven't written a word for six weeks or so,' he gloomily recorded. 'Can't. This nightmarish unknown is before my eyes all the time. It's an embittering situation. What a difference two or three hundred pounds capital would make. Without it, every door seems closed.' They had explored the possibility of moving back to London but prices, 'even at low rentals,' had shot up since the War.

On the 23rd March, he drove to the Maida Vale home of Mrs. Rhys, (who wrote under the pseudonym of Jane Oliver), to attend the Lewellyn Rhys Memorial Prize of 1949

Gala for *Adventure Lit Their Star*. The weight of the previous weeks suddenly lifted when he heard his name read out as that year's winner. Amongst the grudging applauders on his short-list were future names: Alex Comfort, Nigel Kneale, Brian Morgan and the previous year's winner, Richard Mason. Ken found him 'very Chelsea – velvet jacket (Paris model) and rust shirt; over-long blonde hair.' Mary Grieve, the editor of *Woman*, congratulated him with the suggestion he did an article for her. It was a fear he might have dried that goaded him to accept.

During the second week of April, Ken unexpectedly presented Betty with the keys to their new home. As was the case with Marish Court, this came as a total surprise as – to her knowledge - they had so far only seen the cottage from the outside. They saw that it needed some renovation but Ken harboured the notion that it had the potential to be the kind of home they could only have dreamed about on his modest income. So, unilaterally, he placed a successful bid. 'And on miraculous terms,' he exaggerated, relieved.

'£2,000 and 100% mortgage from vendor. Will need a lot of work doing, but it will finally look charming.' Despite his enthusiasm, Betty, nor anyone else, was ever informed of how he'd suddenly found the money.

Ken Allsop in Dirk Bogarde chic for author photo session, 1950.

Allsops' on holiday in Devon, 1950.

14
May 1950 - Aug 1955: 'Picture Post' Years

'Generically, he would be tall and slender: handsome but not shaved too well. Left in politics, but silkily public school in accent: slightly camp but instantaneous in response to girls. A man as adaptable to a poignantly brief affair in Berlin as to prolonged danger amid Malayan terrorists. His hair would be longish, his tie yellow and floppily knotted; his writing was vivid, idiosyncratic, wayward – but madly brilliant.' (Ibid.)

Ken later claimed that this was the indelible image he held of the *Picture Post* journalist before applying. He doesn't make the admission but, clearly, he is also describing himself. His ideal reporter was his ideal of a man: his ideal self.

In the second week of May, he wrote to the editor of *Picture Post* magazine inquiring after work. The reply, predictably, was negative but reassuring. He could come in for a chat. Grasping this straw, on the 17th, Ken arrived at the Shoe Lane offices adjoining Fleet Street clutching four story ideas. He saw the editor as 'a pleasant, easy, muddy-faced man, in shirt sleeves.' But Ken was told that he couldn't have picked a worse day. *The Leader* had just gone into liquidation with *Picture Post* absorbing most of its staff. Momentarily undeterred, Ken handed over the four ideas he'd brought with him. The Editor liked them but his hands were tied. Ken took the parting advice to write again nearer the summer as a possible start date. 'Payment: 30 guineas per article,' he hopefully recorded.

*

In 1950, *Picture Post*'s Editor, Tom Hopkinson, wasn't only the most respected man in Shoe Lane, but the most respected in the whole of Fleet Street; at least, an unarguable point amongst his journalists. Sir Edward Hulton, *Picture Post*'s proprietor, for whom Hopkinson had worked as Editor since succeeding its founder, Stefan Lorant, in 1940, had recently acquired a more jaundiced view. Sales of the weekly magazine had dipped sharply over the previous year: its net profits plummeting from that year's high of £209,097 to less than £50,000 this. The decline was from a two-pronged attack; first, from competition by its glossier, more shallow and populist sister papers such as *Everybody's* and *News Illustrated*. Here, the priority was on safe, showbiz orientated stories, accompanied by large, colour photographs of the new stars. *Picture Post*, directed more towards serious current affairs, had always included the occasional film-set report with a PR tone. But, it had never felt the need to compromise or go down-market. That is, until its advertisers began looking elsewhere.

Television's increasing popularity posed the second threat, supplying both types of story on a daily basis to anyone able to afford the gradually decreasing price of a set; often, ironically, advertised within *Picture Post*'s own pages. Hulton sensed the danger in their flagship title lagging behind the new medium. In a panic, knee-jerk reaction, Hulton, through his wife Nika, demanded that Hopkinson institute certain changes. To his editor, this was a first. While the two men were poles apart politically – Hulton, a right-wing Tory, and Hopkinson, a left-leaning Liberal – top-down intervention had never been an issue. Since 1938 Hulton's contributions on content had been mainly advisory: his employer, trusting him enough to leave well alone. If the magazine was to remain popular he believed it must become more populist and join the mainstream. Perhaps, in this subtle shift, Hulton couldn't see a problem. Either way, the

Hultons' determined to halt the decline in sales, whatever the cost. Unable to predict where the new medium of television was taking the Press, they could only experiment. The consequences would prove disastrous; but, also, perhaps, inevitable.

A new air of restless activity pervaded the offices in Shoe Lane. Amidst this, Hopkinson was in the process of interviewing for a new intake of photojournalists for the magazine. He found himself quietly acquiescing to the questioning, pragmatic and mildly cynical view most brought with them after the War. Previously, you were just grateful for the work, and performed your job with no great aspiration beyond its bounds. But its ending, jarring with the surprise re-election of Churchill that February, attracted recruits with an instinct for dissent and hunger for change. Journalists like James Cameron, Robert Kee and David Mitchell brought their own intellectual approaches to stories, while Fyfe Robertson, Denzil Batchelor, Cynthia Judah and Trevor Philpott each developed their own idiosyncratic styles.

Accompanying each on a report would be one of an even more independent band of freelance photographers: these included the droll, laconic Cockney, Charlie 'Slim' Hewitt, the ebullient, rotund Bert Hardy, the slight, moustachioed, Cypriot-looking figure of Thurston Hopkins, the tall, elegant Grace Robertson, or the lean, reserved and darkly handsome John Chillingworth, who'd risen above the confines as *Picture Post*'s tea-boy and dark room attendant after 1943.

The camera they all swore by was the new *Leica*. Hopkinson recalled how,

'With its small format, thirty-six pictures on a film, ease of operation and quiet mechanism (it) brought photography out of the studio and into the stream of everyday life...' Photographers could also click swiftly and inconspicuously as they 'could now steal pictures in places where photography was not permitted.' A considerable advance on the pre-War press camera, which, since it could not be hidden, demanded 'photography by consent.' By 1938, posed statesman or film star portraiture had descended to the moniker of the 'firing squad picture'; a cynical term coined through exasperation with its limitations. Liberated by the *Leica* – the first portable piece of technology - the cameraman could, literally, call the shots. This offered a certain kudos over the writer. John Chillingworth recalled:

'Tom Hopkinson's brief to journalists was "you're here to make sure the photographer gets his story. You can write it when you see the pictures we're going to use. By the way, don't write too much because there isn't enough paper!" Imagine that, these days...That was real journalism: not the crap you see today.' But Chillingworth maintained it was still 'a team situation' where, if the story lacked a visual immediacy, one would be created between them on the spot. He insisted it would be an obvious re-creation rather than a claim of documentary evidence.

But the *Leica* camera was about to become a victim of its own success in this very field. During June of 1950, a pair of *Picture Post*'s staffers named Haywood Magee and Stefan Schimanski flew to Japan on an innocuous mission to shoot its cultural highlights. En route, they stopped off in Malaya to refuel. Inadvertently, they found themselves in the midst of a burgeoning civil war with South Korea. They reported back to Hopkinson, who advised them to 'cut the cherry blossom' and act as British representative war correspondents. What they produced were graphic, large format photos depicting the retreat of the South Korean Army and their United Nations allies all the way down to Pusan on the southern coast.

Later, as Magee and Schimanski were resting in Tokyo, a local information officer told them that, if they were interested, there were two available seats on a plane going back to the North from where they had just escaped. Magee thought better of it but an impulsive Schimanski believed the situation was building and the opportunity too good to miss. It proved a fateful decision as a distraught Magee returned to England alone. The plane Schimanski was in had exploded over the Pacific en route to North Korea. But his final hunch had been correct. American reinforcements were about to be deployed into the country as the Korean War entered a heightened phase of terror. Back in Shoe Lane, alone at the end of the working day, a tired and mildly guilty Hopkinson pondered over where next to take the lead:

'Our two best men for the story were, undoubtedly, James Cameron and Bert Hardy,' he wrote, 'and I was making up my mind to send them, when there was a knock at the door. This surprised me, as I supposed the office long since empty. It was Hardy and Cameron...' Through August and September, the two men compiled three key picture stories from the various Korean battlefields. 'Inchon' – a report from the Allies landing force at Seoul's South Korean port – showed just what the *Leica* could achieve. With a sense of immediacy startling in its time, Hardy caught images of the U.S. Marines' seaborne arrival at the smoke covered port, the descent into the landing crafts and the scarred and tattered populace that greeted them, warily, with tired, raised arms. The third and final story proved controversial, concerning the treatment of prisoners, with perceived emphasis on what the South meted out on the North while the allies stood by. Hulton fumed when he read this, barring its publication.

'I knew it might cause difficulties,' Hopkinson admitted later, 'since any criticism of 'our side' could be regarded as anti-Western and therefore – in the climate of that time – pro-Eastern and hence, by another small stretch of meaning, as Communist propaganda.' Hopkinson waited until his men returned home then, to pacify his boss more than himself who was in sympathy, questioned Cameron on his intended angle. Cameron claimed he'd witnessed young, shaven-headed boys roped together and labelled 'political prisoners' by supporters of Synghman Rhee. Since the American allies overtly supported this regime as upholders of Christian democracy, Cameron felt that to report this contravention of human rights was simply his duty. Conscious of Hulton's anger, Hopkinson sat on the story for a week. As a sop to him, he spent much of this time scouring Eastern European magazines for an opposing view; of likely *North* Korean atrocity.

'To my surprise I actually found such a picture in a Czech magazine. It showed an American soldier dressed up by his captors in false nose and swastika, forced to march in procession, trailing the Stars and Stripes in the dust.' With Cameron's input, Hopkinson skewed the report as an appeal to the United Nations, posting copies to the Secretary General and the leader of the British Delegation. At week's end, he showed the proof to Hulton who acceded to him going to press the following Monday.

With his proprietor's approval, Hopkinson could have expected the heat being off. But, with no apparent rhyme or reason, what followed became a turning point for the magazine. Early next morning, Hulton called him from home, insisting that the Korean story be pulled. He gave no reason. An exasperated Hopkinson responded that since it was he who had originally ordered its inclusion, the issue would go ahead. Failing an adequate reason, he had no choice. Hulton silently replaced his receiver and refused to communicate, directly, with Hopkinson again. Subsequently, before Hulton Press's board of directors, Hopkinson put his case. In reply, a collective letter supporting Hulton's stance inevitably sealed his editor's fate. Fleet Street had already been informed of Hopkinson's 'offer' of resignation when the statement was pushed his way for signing. Hopkinson stood his ground, insisting he was being fired and would only sign a statement to this effect. Hulton concurred.

At the news of their esteemed editor's 'resignation,' his fellow journalists prepared to resign en masse in sympathy. Hopkinson claimed he was against this on the grounds of the magazine being more important than one individual. They needed some persuading but agreed with the proviso that his assistant, Ted Castle, take over. Castle was reluctant, being as willing to 'mutiny' as the rest. But, according to Hopkinson,

'he was given a guarantee of six months tenure, during which time he did his utmost to maintain the paper's continuity.'

There were intimations that Hulton was up to something, but no one was quite sure what. Meanwhile, Hopkinson couldn't have known that by falling upon his sword, he had done the Hultons' an early favour. By the last day in October, he was clearing his desk still wondering which of his U.N. recipients to whom he'd sent the copy had leaned on his boss. He took with him that final issue of *Picture Post*, which never saw the light of day.

White-walled Alder Cottage dates from around 1620 and, with no discernable front garden, fronted a wood at Digswell Water, Old Welwyn. This was ideally suited as an Osterley Park-type garden for the local children. Seven weeks after Ken's down-payment, the family moved in. Fifty years on, Andrew recalled what were his earliest memories as a four-year-old:

'The garden was still full of 'dragons' teeth,' – anti-tank defences – which was most bizarre...a hangover from the War. At about three feet in height they were as tall as me, so they looked huge. Why tanks would have been expected there is beyond me! But they were removed in pretty short order. The garden backed onto a wonderful adventure land of a wood, with no fence. I think, strictly, it was private property, but the children of the village were allowed to run wild through it. It had a tremendous variety of vegetation, of smell and feel...There was one area, down and to the left of our garden, going down towards the River Mimram, that was boggy and smelt very dank. Celandines and marsh grasses grew there, and you always came home muddy up to the ankles. At the back of the wood, the Mimram ran around two to three feet deep with trees that didn't quite cross it, but was an open invitation to us children to try bridging it. We fell in on a regular basis. Further down, where the B1000 motorway crossed the river, it became very shallow and sandy. A great place for catching sticklebacks, paddling and getting wet.'

He confirms Ken's limited resources at this time:

'He was always struggling to make ends meet, because he always spent the money he had. I think he was incapable of saving or planning for the future.'

But, the cottage's pretty exterior belied its interior state. On arrival, they found some of Ken's friends in the midst of sawing, planing and affecting basic repairs. In the garden, Nat Solomon and a neighbour, Geoffrey Hughes, set to on clearing and cutting back the overgrown greenery. Ken reassured Betty the short-term inconvenience would be worth enduring and produce the home they both so badly wanted. After all, the call from Tom Hopkinson was only a matter of time. Andrew also recalled the night terrors: from his parents' room, the pained screams of his father, as the nerves on his stump flared and throbbed on release from its ill-fitting tin limb.

Betty kept a half-hearted diary of her own between July and September. It reads as a brief but telling glimpse into the loneliness a wife was expected to endure in marrying such a brilliant but self-centred workaholic. It may have helped maintain her sanity, as Ken had slipped back into his raw-nerved state when home. He had begun to write again – an autobiographical satire on Fleet Street referred to as 'Mooney' after the main character – but this new enterprise bore few hopes. His award for the first novel had garnered positive reviews but not the expected higher profile. He had also recorded two further, brief essays on birds for BBC's North Region but, though competent, neither caught fire. On the 28th July she reports that,

'Ken is utterly depressed in his job. He wrote to *Picture Post* a couple of weeks ago but it seems very doubtful. Tonight, he is writing to (The) *Times, Observer, Illustrated*...' The following evening they attend a dinner party thrown by the Hughes'. John Knight and David Malbert are also there. Amidst the barrage of Fleet Street banter Ken clearly feels more at home in, Betty is excluded:

'(They) talked, or rather, *shouted* their heads off. Neither Geoffrey nor I had a chance to put in more than an occasional word. Talk mainly of books; the mediocrity of John Mortimer's (latest). Ken thoroughly enjoyed it but I'm afraid I didn't. Much of what was said seemed to me too clever-clever and rarefied, but my voice isn't strong enough to allow me to put any point.' A week later she reports approaches to *The Times, Observer* and *Illustrated* all failed and that he 'sent off 9 more ideas to 'PP.'' On the 16th August she admits that, 'K. and I have very few outings together. For special occasions Mum comes over. (We have been out only twice since we have been here)...This newsprint business is serious: K. has written to 'John Bull.'' Nine days later she can only summon disdain for a letter from Williamson. 'Rather pathetic. Now living in (a) caravan with new wife and baby. No money. Break with Faber's just completed after re-writing commissioned 'Madison' book.'

The 15th September finally sees the much-delayed publication of *Silver Flame*. Fearing a further anti-climax, she and Ken were apart through the reviews. 'I miss him terribly...' she confides. 'Ken badly needed this holiday. It has been a year of strain. The months of worrying over a house, the worry becoming, eventually, desperation. He works with hardly a rest, and was exhausted by 'Mooney.' He has lately been worn out emotionally and physically, unable to cope with the slightest upset.'

A few days before holidaying alone, Ken received news that Percival Marshall were provisionally willing to publish 'Mooney.' To celebrate, he took his agent to lunch at London's expensive Strand Palace, where she advised him to continue writing, undeterred, at his current pace. By the last week of November, Ken was trembling and on the point of a nervous breakdown, when he received a letter from Ted Castle, Tom Hopkinson's replacement at *Picture Post*. Ken was invited for a second chat. His interview was brief and history cruelly repeated as Castle prevaricated over a decisive offer. In his notes, Ken reported him as saying,

'My inclination...is to take you on for a six month trial,' adding, 'but I'm only thinking aloud.' Castle then sent him to Lionel Birch:

'a nice, shy, attractive, lanky, untidy man, who seemed a little embarrassed about it all.' They parted on good terms, with Birch promising a swift decision. But, by the end of that week, Ken had still heard nothing. The suspense was unbearable.

'If there's no letter tomorrow, I shall ring up...There's too much at stake...I feel there is no escape from my present predicament if *this* is shut in my face – but I so much want to work for 'PP.' There is no paper I'd rather work for. Since I have to do a daily job, it would at least be an enormous boost to my morale and sense of satisfaction to be working hard at responsible, vigorous and clean-cut journalism.' It was either his threatened letter or phone-call that finally persuaded Castle to go for the six-month trial, starting New

Year.

On the 2nd January 1951, Ken ambled into Ted Castle's Shoe Lane office with the impatience of one who'd been awaiting the inevitable for far too long. His initial, excited impression reflected the commitment and sense of urgency he'd last witnessed as a seventeen-year-old at the Iraq Legation. He told Grace Robertson that the relentless dark-suited comings and goings made him feel as if he'd joined a unit of crack troops. His new colleagues were struck, from the outset, by his own seasoned approach. Robert Kee recalled:

'He immediately fitted in, so easily and agreeably, with the very special, intimate, editorial atmosphere in which things were conducted...'

David Mitchell found him more conspicuous:

'What struck me - in contrast with the slightly self-conscious amateurism of the *Picture Post* ethos – was Ken's almost aggressive professionalism. Banging away on a typewriter with an air of glamorous toughness, somehow accentuated by his halting 'cripples' gait...' Up to now, he'd only been biding his time; wasting hours in dead-end admin work that had to be taken to keep his bed-ridden promise to Betty and support their children. Now, he could begin fulfilling a dream, the career harboured since reading Negley Farson's life story in 1937. His head full of half articulated ideas found solace in the Editor's demand for new stories each Monday morning from every journalist. With his increased wage, he bought dark suits, white cotton shirts and silk ties from the West End, taking late afternoon breaks, visiting the city's brothels. As usual, by week's end, he had little cash or energy left for Betty. Yet, as with all of Ken's desires, experience had a habit of grounding him.

As the 'new boy,' a closed office door was gloomily pointed out to him.

'I was told that if one looked inside, there was always to be found a glum huddle of transitory occupants, one or more deposed chieftains, each flipping in melancholy reverie over his old publication and tracing his downfall while he waited his pay-off.' Such was the darkly humorous insecurity amongst his new colleagues in Shoe Lane. Hulton's twitching wrists held aloft an axe that could fall at any time and in any direction.

With Hopkinson now gone, Ken was disappointed to learn that his first assignment for Castle was neither international nor jet-setting, but the parochial, shady topic of the Black Market trade in nylon, sold from pedlars' suitcases, in London's West End. He had a working week on this and also had to get used to taking his cues from the photographer that accompanied him; in this case, Ronald Startup. Despite the editorial demands on *Picture Post*'s employees to produce, enough material was submitted for the occasional report to be dropped or not completed at all. By the 18th March, Ken moaned,

'Farthest afield I've been was down to Eastleigh, Southampton, with Slim Hewitt, the photographer, in anticipation of the Rail Strike beginning. We were to do the Profile of a Strike, as it would hit a railway town. The strike didn't come off. Not too bad (for) a few days, except that we were staying in the dingiest, 'commercial' hotel next to the station... We arrived back on the Saturday, me just too late to see Nat and Pat who had their wedding reception at Alder Cottage.'

Ken heard rumblings amongst his colleagues that Castle's heart wasn't in the editorship. The ironic likelihood arose that he might not see out Ken's six-month trial. Castle himself could not be asked to constantly fight Hulton's cronies and justify his editorial decisions. Soon after taking up Hopkinson's reins, he discovered someone had been unilaterally inquiring into the European magazine field. With *Picture Post*'s circulation possibly dropping for a third successive year, Castle had his suspicions and rounded on John Pierce, the junior manager, whom he suspected of being in league with their employer. Distrustful of the editorial appointment that had been foisted upon him, it does appear that Hulton had advised one of his 'staffers' to keep an eye on Castle. Pierce denied going over his head. Then, on the 4th May, Castle was called in, coolly informed his post would be reverting to assistant editor, and that Frank Dowling – father of Brian, a *Post* journalist – had been appointed his replacement. Castle then realised he had only been a figurehead, reluctantly accepted by the Hultons' to stave off mutiny.

Soon after, Ken was on a job with Slim Hewitt in his birth county of Yorkshire. The phone rang where they were staying. On the other end of the line, a colleague breathlessly announced that Ted had resigned. On Ken and Hewitt's return to Shoe Lane, they discovered the identity of Hulton's private investigator: it was their new editor, Frank Dowling. Beneath a subsequent barrage of anger from his colleagues at the next meeting, Pierce insisted he'd heard of no directive to appoint Dowling. He seemed sincere. As the heat petered out, the assembled journalists agreed that Hulton was acting alone and may stop at nothing to reverse the magazine's fortunes.

The feeling of insecurity became tangible. Ken noted 'there's widespread gloom and apprehension in the office.' Castle had been the sixth Hulton editor to lose his job in the last two years: three from *The Leader*, which itself had recently folded, one from *Lilliput*, and now the second from here. With no antipathy toward Dowling personally, Ken remained disappointed by his arrival; a view coloured by him coming from the world of advertising.

'He is a woolly, bear-like man, pipe-smoking, slow of movement and speech, and he didn't display any great grasp of the situation.' Ken shook hands with his assistant: a tall, angular, ironic, middle-aged Scot, brows arched in world weary concern, named Fyfe Robertson, but known to all as Robbie. 'A man I like and admire,' he wrote, adding with a sigh, 'but even with him, it doesn't amount to a *Post* team.'

Ken saw the paper's integrity, and so his own, already being compromised by the new regime. Hulton's aim was clearly down market. That wasn't the *Picture Post* he'd waited seven months by the phone to join. He saw Hulton's intention as replacing all the progressive, instinctively socialist writers, with less committed figures who wouldn't rock his proprietorial boat. Against all instinct, Ken realised that, if he was to continue here, he must compromise. At a covert meeting with his colleagues, they sounded each other out as how best to continue. In advance of any confrontation, they agreed on their stand; one of mutually accepted division.

'One must naturally be loyal and support the new ed. The other is of strong disapproval at the management's dishonest handling of the situation.' But, from now on, this would be par for the course.

In mid-March 1952, Dowling announced he was leaving for New York to 'look at *Life*' and invited the staff to share a farewell drink. The following morning, John Pierce called a conference to dispel any rumour that he might have been pushed. Pierce told them that Dowling was going to America at their request, and that control of production would now be headed by himself with two named directors. There was immediate suspicion with one who, after business-like reassurances, left Ken feeling winded.

'(He) has the utmost contempt for writers – they can be bought at so much per head – and from now on, we have to model ourselves on *Life*.' Feature articles were to be dropped, separated from the news department, with a demoted Fyfe Robertson put in charge of only one. Ken saw his penchant for writing creatively was to be sidelined in favour of a more factual approach. In his view, this meant 'repeating in words what the photographs should already have said.' The journalists demanded to meet with their members, but only Pierce re-emerged, being 'consistently evasive and smooth.' Despite the strength in numbers on their side, a mutual feeling of impotence descended upon the writers. The journalists subsequently learned that Hulton, far from instigating the takeover, had initially contested it. A bigger and more faceless manipulation seemed to be at work. Ken and his colleagues felt helpless as to how best to respond. They had little choice but to bide their time and await future events.

By 1952, Ken and Betty had transformed Alder Cottage into a home recognisably their own. Friends seemed transient and few. Acquaintances were mainly minor celebrities from the nearby village: Frank Wells, son of the late H.G., and the family of the publisher, Frederick Dent. Six-year-old Andrew got on particularly well with a rather austere, elderly couple who lived in the low-set house 'with rather ornate swirls in the concrete rendering' next door. On one occasion, knocking on their door and asking the husband if he'd like to come out to play. He did.

At the dinner table - the only daily appointment that brought Ken out of his study - manners and correct language use were adhered to with libertarian zeal. When four-year-old Amanda used her natural baby-slang to ask to be excused, he made a point of correcting her.

'No, we don't say *can* I go wee-wee,' we ask *may* I take a piss?'

'Oh, Ken!' sighed an admonishing Betty.

This year, David Mitchell returned to *Picture Post* as its theatre and show business critic, after being sacked during one of Hulton's panic measures two years before. Relations were uneasy. He remembered a visit to Alder Cottage:

'At a party in his house, I recall jiving inexpertly with his wife and being struck by the incongruity of the half-timbered cottage with copper warming pans etc. on the walls with Little Richard records. As a Real Jazz fan...I enjoyed the evening. But I think Ken was irritated by my clumsy cavorting, which dislodged a brass ornament or two from the wall.' Each admired the other's writing but Mitchell's background rankled. Since refusing to contemplate university at seventeen, Ken had harboured a chip on his shoulder; especially toward those with the advantages of an Oxbridge education.

At London's St. James Theatre, the actor Michael Redgrave was about to appear in the Clifford Odets play, *Winter Journey*. Ken was keen to see it and asked Mitchell if he could procure tickets for himself and Betty. As a fellow journalist with his perceived connections, he had assumed it would have been easy.

'When I said I couldn't wangle this, he became quite angry,' recalled Mitchell, 'saying, "and Betty actually reads and admires your pieces!" He explained that he was suffering from writer's block and had a family to support, adding, "It's alright for you with a wealthy father and no family," etc. My slow Oxford drawl may also have irritated Ken.'

He could be petulant with even less cause. Thurston Hopkins remembers their last assignment together, across the Channel.

'Ken and I did 'a day on the continent with the Burwash Brass Band...' We came down to Newhaven and got on board the cross-channel steamer. We couldn't get coffee during the trip. Ken immediately goes and complains to the Captain. The Captain was up on the bridge and it was a very foggy day. You couldn't see where you were going. So, every ten seconds, this great foghorn blast came on. My memory is of him standing on the bridge arguing with the Captain while this noise blotted out half the conversation and accompanying expletives on a count of five. Ken certainly had a short fuse.'

Mary Allsop's health had been in steady decline for some months. Refusing John's continued advice to see her GP, by February it had taken a sudden turn for the worse. A final, exasperated imploring by her husband resigned her to her fate. Following the results of X-rays, she was delivered to the local hospital to await operation. Mid-March, John was told of the large, internal growth they'd discovered. Though removed, the cancerous tumour was found too late to ensure reversal of her condition. She rallied from the operation but recovery was not on the cards. On the 6th June, Ken's mother died, ten days from her sixty-third birthday.

Ken had intended to begin the family holiday he and Betty had arranged for France, but he temporarily stayed behind to help his father with the funeral arrangements. Four days later, in hot sunshine, Mary was cremated at Hendon Crematorium.

'I found the mechanical efficiency of the process somewhat repellent,' Ken grumbled later. In the stifling atmosphere of the car in the returning procession, made worse by the presence of unknown relatives from Leeds, he looked out at the town beyond the window and emphasised his theme; 'the raw inhumanity of their concrete roads, meaningless multiplication of trolley-bus wires and snack bars.'

Ken joined Betty and the children at Dinard, France, the following day. The droll and lugubrious Slim Hewitt was with them, ostensibly to work on a story with her husband. A few days were spent at a hotel nearby in the village of St. Jacut de la Mer, which Ken used as a base to socialise with David Malbert - a new Fleet Street friend soon to become a family acquaintance - installed at a local villa, with the Labour MPs', Tony Crosland and Roy Jenkins. (Ken arranging all this back in England with Betty, blissfully unaware). Midweek, the Allsops' made a bumpy, staccato car journey to Paris. Late that night, they arrived at their destination of the Boulevard Rochecourt, near Montmartre. The following passage from Ken's account of what greeted them, evokes the frustrated mixture of wheeler-dealer work and play he now took for granted:

'Very noisy, traffic and jazz from cabarets till early hours. On Thurs. spent morning collecting money telegraphed by 'PP' to Societe Generale on the strength of the pix we intended to get for the jazz feature I'm doing. Also, a frustrating period with Langelaan. He works in the office of Point de Vue, or at least occupies a desk there: a heavy jowly, (sic) phlegmatic man who grunts around a pipe. I'd asked him to make inquiries about jazz activities... and lay on something. He'd done nothing. After much prodding and urging, he made a telephone call and suggested we call on a girl connected with Le Hot Club de France. Also, he had no flash gear there, as he ought to have, and suggested that we tour Paris picking up the bits which were under repair. We went from there to find the girl; didn't. Back to him. At last, he contacted her, but without any visible consciousness of having bungled. For this, he gets £1,000 a year from "PP.'

In afternoon, took children to Eiffel Tower, which sent them crazy. In evening, we got baby-sitter; an oddish student, (sic) and took cab over to Left Bank, in search of jazz joints... We ate at The Two Assassins, near Aux Deux Magots; an excellent cheap meal. Then to The Cave, the cellar club under The Existentialists Club, where Claude Bolling's band was playing – very advanced 'cool' bop. Crowded and expensive – 10s. for a Pernod. Went on the the Club Vieux de Colombier, where there was a good French - New Orleans-style band led by clarinetist Claud (?) and starring ex-Ellington trumpeter, Nelson Williams. Good, but flashy and riffy. (sic). Second day, just loafed around Paris, shopped and spent evening eating an enormous and memorable meal. Left Paris 6 a.m. next day for Bologne, where we hurriedly bought some Martini, Dubonnet and brandy and rushed aboard. Got home midnight – 18 hours solid travelling.'

The recent intake of food and drink was having a proportionate effect upon Ken's waistline. Boyishly slender until recently, he had put on at least a stone in weight since joining the magazine. This lent him a burlier physique, but still slim enough to maintain his current expenditure of energy after an overhaul on his new tin leg. His annual salary had now increased, significantly, from £1,000 to £1,500. Between assignments abroad, eating out on duty consisted of large, cheap meals provided by the Newspaper Workers' Club in Gunpowder Alley, off nearby Fetter Lane, ('the best place for food in this area') followed by a conspiratorial scotch or two in 'The Two Brewers' with colleagues straight after work. Less salubrious surroundings than those of The Ritz, but Ken's main priority was the quality of both food and company. He had no interest in being 'seen' with anyone, in particular. But he often protested too much; to such an extent that, conversely, he could inadvertently appear the greatest snob of all.

In July, he and Betty considered building a house at the new Home Counties project of Welwyn's Garden City. She'd had serious trouble trying to converse with the Digswell locals who kept themselves, very much, to themselves, based upon the social barriers built around their various jobs. Ken saw how isolated Betty was feeling, with no-one she could confide in while he was away. But, the rootless base of his own, broadly middle-class, upbringing threw him into a crisis of conscience. He saw the Garden City new town as a victim of the type of intellectual scorn he himself often directed at such places, and felt a sense of guilt at sharing this view. Not for the first time, he and Betty found they could ally themselves to nothing but their own instincts.

A second motive to move was the local school Andrew and Amanda had been attending this past year. Aware it was a church school, he may have been hoping they weren't following through with the Christian ethic. But, he found the curriculum 'stiflingly religious' and 'steeped in Bible lore.' As a devout atheist, he was horrified by what he witnessed as a parent before the summer recess. One teacher admonished four-year-old Amanda with 'God knows when our souls are clean or dirty.'

He and Betty shared doubts over its vicar who ran the school. One evening she took Andrew to see *The Adventures of Robin Hood* at the cinema. They found themselves sitting next to the Reverend. Before the main feature, the *Pathe* newsreel featured the Aga Kahn leading in his latest Derby winner. The man of God was furious. Betty concurred that a man with such wealth already should add to it in this way.

'I don't care about his money,' the Reverend growled. 'It's his filthy colour I object to!' Driving back to the village, they passed a film poster advertising the adaptation of Rumer Godden's *The River*.

'I would like to see that,' said Betty.

'It's about India,' grumbled the Reverend. 'Disgusting place, disgusting people.'

'Then what's the point of your Christianity,' she responded, adding, at one of his further remarks, 'That's like saying the unemployed in the Thirties didn't want work.'

'But they didn't!' he insisted. A third consideration was that, since Mary's death, his father had been living alone at the bungalow of their final address in Bushey. (Little did his son know that his long sexually frustrated father was already making positive plays to a German au pair). Again, money was the deciding factor that dashed his worthy dreams after Betty had poured over the accounts. She made it known to Ken that a large percentage of his monthly expenditure was not being replaced. Living from wage packet to wage packet meant that – despite their increased status - there were still no savings to draw upon.

Once again in dire need of sterling, Ken responded to an offer made by Peter Bayley at Percival Marshall. How much he was offered isn't recorded, but certainly a sum above his status as a novelist, and enough of an advance to pay for the recent family holiday to France. He had never before written a novel for any reason other than as a labour of love. Even 'Mooney,' the Fleet Street satire – released as *The Daybreak Edition* the previous year – found support from some of its targets. Now, for the first time, he resigned himself to producing a book at his publisher's initiative. The *John C. Winston Company* of Philadelphia, U.S.A., described their Winston Adventures as 'a series of tales based on the little known incidents and nearly forgotten lives of unsung heroes that helped shape history.' They also claimed each story as being 'authentic in every detail.' Though enjoyable and worthy children's fare, Ken may have afforded this a cynical chuckle. A month on from the advance, no progress had been made on the text. It was not through want of trying. Amongst the publisher's publicity, the only direction he'd received from Winstons' was the title – *Last Voyages of the Mayflower* – and the central character of a twelve-year-old boy. A feverish run of phone calls to his American agent and their reps. had produced nothing, whatsoever, for him to build on. Turning his flailing attention from his task, he typed,

'I sit in a mood of bitter regret at ever having agreed – out of pure avarice – to do it. If I had £70 in the bank, I'd send them a cheque to nullify the whole thing.'

As Ken walked toward Shoe Lane on the morning of the 16th July, he was intercepted by colleague, Gordon Watkins.

'I'm afraid I have shattering news for you,' said Watkins. 'Robbie and Frank are sacked and Pierce is taking over as editor.' Robertson called Ken into his office and confirmed the whole story. Pierce was to take over Dowling's post, hiring Jack Hargreaves – of *Lilliput* and *Housewife* magazines – as Ideas Man, effectively replacing himself. Dowling later informed Ken that, on confronting Pierce on the subject in his office the previous week, the latter swore he had no intention of becoming editor.

Intending to pre-empt the board meeting pencilled in for the following day, a High Noon crisis meeting was convened for the forty-strong staff. When pressed, only a handful of the attendees were in favour of condemning Pierce, outright. The inevitable suspicion arose amongst the others that they were on a promise of future promotion. To avoid division, a compromise motion was agreed, expressing 'grave alarm' at the threatened changes. Finding themselves, for once, on Hulton's side, half a dozen of the journalists, with Ken in tow, taxied to the Hultons' home to hand in the vote from the meeting and demonstrate their support. Having finally negotiated past the mildly obstructive butler, they found Nika Hulton's elderly mother, alone and startled by the intrusion. She called her daughter who, minutes later, entered the room:

'She listened to our declaration of loyalty to her husband, and distrust of the new rule, and then said – not noticeably moved by this spontaneous show of faithfulness by the minions, we thought – that she would let Mr. Hulton know we had called.' She took the letter, peeved that the directors weren't informed of their meeting. Anyway, her husband 'could not personally see us. He was at his club. We trooped out, back to the short-lived, *Life*-style version of our pet and sustenance, but, in the long term, back to the game of snakes and ladders, back to further permutations of editors and staff.' It is unlikely that it was their idea to mirror *Life*, but that of their faceless financiers intent on recouping recent losses. The Hultons lacked the influence they'd long taken for granted as proprietors. According to John Chillingworth, this left his old boss little more than a figurehead.

By September, Pierce's policy of hiring hands from other papers had effectively made impotent the core of the magazine's staff. David Mitchell viewed them as 'a mass intake of dead-beats' and was promptly sacked. In truth, they were experienced Fleet Street hacks, but with little time or sensibility for the magazine's long-held principles. The tall, droll, stripe-suited and bespectacled Macdonald Hastings, who'd freelanced for everyone from the old-boy BBC to *Woman*, Ken dismissed as 'that high-powered spiv,' though kept this view to himself. Warwick Charlton, another experienced recruit, appeared an even less relevant choice. To Ken, Pierce had taken him on 'apparently on the strength of his ability to get free air-travel!' He added, 'this is cut-price journalism at its lowest.' Against his contract, but not his conscience, Ken searched for more up-market publications to write for that would fill the intellectual void wilfully left by Pierce.

With no significant savings in his bank account by which to afford a move for his family, Ken sought a more solitary refuge. Trevor Philpott was renting a flat from *Picture Post* news-editor Sylvain Mangeot, but having trouble maintaining the monthly payments. (The Frenchman, Mangeot, was often spied in the Shoe Lane office, asleep over his typewriter). Grace Robertson recalled his former role as one of the journalists.

'Sylvain suffered from a form of sleeping sickness. It was rather off-putting if you were in a foreign country with him because you didn't quite know what to do, exactly. I was told to leave him alone.' On the lookout for a central *pied-a-terre* himself, Ken discovered this and, through mutual agreement with Philpott, moved in with him at the end of month. On this occasion, his ulterior motive, like Philpott's, was sexual. After hours visits to call girls were no longer sustainable to one becoming quite a well-known name. The inevitable bad publicity he could do without, so a flat-share with one in his position had become the obvious option. When advancing on a target, Ken always maintained his natural charm, never descending to unsubtle suggestion or lasciviousness. Ideally, he preferred curvaceous, dark-eyed brunettes – not dissimilar to Betty - over pale, slender blondes, though the drive was totally undiscerning with prostitutes, where his need for release was blind. Anyone available would do, if the time since his last sex session had been more than a few days.

The Coronation summer of 1953 compounded Ken's worst fears. The build-up to the crowning of Her Majesty dominated *Picture Post*'s pages in glorious, and expensive, colour. The day itself was covered in detail as was the Windsor's first, overseas visit. Ken bit his lip and pressed ahead with his own.

On the 20th July, he flew to Cairo, Egypt with Ronald Startup for a whole week to cover celebrations for the National Day of Liberation on the first anniversary of Neguib's presidential coup. Considering his outspoken nature, it is likely the board was actively encouraging him to take his time on such assignments! This was just as well as his most recent leg-fitting at Roehampton had not succeeded in abating the ongoing pain. Consequently, he took with him his prescription of Dexedrine amphetamine tablets. By the end of the week he'd (unilaterally?) increased his intake from two to three a day.

As the heightened pain tried his patience for meatier fare still further, early in August Ken called Michael Foot at *Tribune* – the left-wing monthly. He rattled off various ideas for stories, all previously tried on, and rejected by, his new bosses, and admitted he was still under contract to *Picture*

Post. Foot then put him on to his own recent replacement in the editor's chair, Robert Edwards. Edwards confirmed he'd be happy for Ken to contribute as a freelancer but couldn't give long-term assurances over available space, at a premium as always. He also agreed that a pseudonym was advisable. Ken would have to be published at his own risk. He chose a *non-de-plume* first used as a one-off, back in 1947, after his two most treasured possessions: his penis and scarlet-painted automobile. Thus, 'Percy Redcar' was born.

Dishearteningly, his first submission – a post-war reflection on Belsen concentration camp – was not placed, so Ken followed this with a modified, personally angled piece on his recent visit to Cairo, the original of which having just been rejected by Dowling. The first of a years contributions Edwards would take of 'Percy's.

He'd been planning a lunch appointment with the editor to discuss further ideas when the ongoing struggle for power at Shoe Lane suddenly intervened. Hulton – via the board – had just brought in another new face to overrule and undermine his editor, named Jock Drummond. Over Dowling's head, Drummond appointed the writer, Hilde Marchant, to join Slim Hewitt on a job in Spain. An angry Dowling then decided Ken should replace Marchant; not as any reflection on her – well respected by her colleagues at Shoe Lane – but as a simple snub to Drummond. Though sympathetic, Ken admitted feeling awkward 'having hi-jacked the story' from Marchant. In the confusion, Ken departed unaware of the story – if there ever was one – he'd been expected to procure.

With only hours' notice, Ken's head was off his pillow at 4.15 next morning and heading for Waterloo to meet Hewitt, their guide, a London rep. from the sherry company, Gonzalez Byaz, named Harry Grierson and an elderly freelancer, 'Shep' Shepherd, who'd subsidized Grierson to join the assignment. The element of alcohol was an ominous portent. A disdainful Ken claimed Grierson and Shepherd began drinking on the flight over to Madrid from the Bordeaux stopover. This didn't avoid him downing three brandies and a Pernod up to 'Shep's collapse later that evening. At Madrid, the quartet headed for the airport bar to continue where they left off, so missing the bus they'd planned to board to their hotel. Ken found Grierson and 'Shep' 'intently tanking up' on cognac poured, blindly, into their glasses. The following evening the quartet continued their drinking with Ken 'in considerable doubt about the whole enterprise.' While no teetotaler, Ken had always made a point of not drinking excessively on assignments. Here, he was undoubtedly influenced by Grierson's intake, if to a lesser extent than Shepherd. But Grierson had a reputation for making important journalistic contacts with an approach both direct and persuasive. The bargain was in taking the whole man as you found him.

'Shep' later told Ken that Grierson had assured him traveller's cheques' would not be necessary since he'd be paying for everything on arrival.

'Result: 'Shep' was almost picking up cigar stubs from the gutter most of the trip.' Just then, Grierson strolled into the bar, his pockets bulging with pesetas and ordered the drink-weary 'Shep' to bed, pulling the cigar stub from his mouth and calling for a taxi to the Capital Bar. Ken left with him, in grudging admiration at his ability to obtain cash. With the original point of the assignment a scotch-obliterated memory, Ken spent the remainder of the stay a victim of other's circumstances.

One evening in Jerez, as Shepherd strolled uncertainly off to the nearest bar, Grierson took Ken and Slim to his favourite nightclub. Between numbers, the dancing women sashayed over to where Ken sat and eyed him suggestively. Not an unusual occurrence, which Ken took in his cynical, journalistic stride.

'Most very attractive,' he noted, 'but, one suspected, mostly unproductive – probably earning their dowry with fiancées approval.' A day or two later, Ken attended his first bullfight. Only the pageant and coloured costumes of the matadors left any real impression, the fights themselves too amateurish to avoid the callous picadors. Back at the hotel, he related the experience to one of the guests, a psychiatrist at Guy's Hospital, Oxford, who'd known David Mitchell.

'He drew Freudian significance from amputation of the bull's ears and tail and their presentation to (the) matador (as) substitution for balls and penis, manhood etc.'

By now, though often inebriated, the journalist in him was getting desperate to produce a story. He found he had little choice but to sound out Grierson who at least had broad experience of the culture. He painted a picture of life under General Franco from his own wheeler-dealing perspective. That you could stand on your soapbox, call Franco a shit, and get away with it, while the only capital offence was to carry a gun.

'Even an aristocrat always addresses a workman as *senor*,'' Ken noted. All this time, Slim Hewitt had been quietly performing his job of taking miscellaneous shots of Spanish life. Both men returned to Shoe Lane with the semblance of an article, though Dowling was past the point of anticipating veto. Again, it was *Tribune* Ken could turn to, to print the politically slanted article – 'Franco's Secret Weapon' - his own paper no longer desired.

The pain from Ken's stump was not easing. He'd learnt to live with it as best he could in recent years – its constancy forming a numb cushion – but the inflamed nodules from the late Forties had returned, negating the efficacy of his Dexedrine. The temptation to grit his teeth and down a whole bottle with kamikaze abandon was intense. To an extent, this blurred his focus on the magazine, already compromised by the continuing, cynical manoeuvrings of the board. To compensate, he was drinking more; never an unlimited quantity beyond his control, but enough to numb the tension after work; a scotch or two in the afternoon followed by several more, after work, into the evening.

But, his continued self-discipline regarding alcohol and women was remarkable under the circumstances, a clear head for writing his single-minded priority. Godfrey Thurston Hopkins recalls the look of disappointment on a woman's face when Ken prioritised a job over her available time. It maintained his sanity if not his good ideas. A modern-day, socialist parable of Jonathan Swift's *Pilgrim's Progress*, was one of his worst at this time though, surprisingly, accepted by Dowling. John Chillingworth was with him for this project that followed a twin demonstration of his other pastimes. He recalls:

'I went to the Shetland Islands with him. We did a story about an island wedding and then went to Fair Isle. It was when we were on our way back from there, on a train, in the middle of the night. I can remember Ken saying, 'Well, we've only got a half a bottle of whisky left. Let's go and see what we can find.' Off down the corridor he stomped, looking in all the compartments. In one of them he found two young ladies. Without hesitation, he pulled the door back and said, 'I've got some whisky! Would you care for some?' And, for some reason, they said 'yes.' (Laughs) With that, the next four hours were really quite bizarre. I was terribly green, I suppose, at the time, but I got the hang of what it was all about. He absolutely needed female attention or contact. It didn't matter how it was or where it was, it was the feeling that one was responded to...sexually. Something, I suppose, all of us – looking back – would be highly embarrassed about.'

But Ken required such small justifications to himself that he was still sexually attractive. The ugly and painful inflammations on his stump only added to his insecurity. He had little choice on the 6th April but to hand in his doctor's certificate to Shoe Lane and report back to Roehampton. He was installed in Ward E – a forty bed ward sixty yards in length and under the care of a Portugese doctor, Mirek Vitali – a specialist in limb replacement – a sister, and two nurses; Fleming, a male, and Pugh, a woman.

Supplies demanded of Betty hadn't changed since his last long-term internment of 1943-45, except he now brought his own typewriter. He was still an employee of *Picture Post*, with a contractual Sword of Damacles over the staff for his prompt discharge. On Tuesday 13th, the stump was operated on. Three days later he was discharged for the Easter weekend. He was returned on Bank Holiday Monday, taking his binoculars, anticipating a little idle 'twitching' in the hospital grounds. Ward life was predictably dull, but little continuous peace was possible with the post-operative cries of his fellow amputee patients: a condition too familiar to Ken, experiencing this on a semi-regular basis at home. On the 24th he was discharged, again, temporarily legless, to allow his stump to heal and for Roehampton to search for a suitable replacement.

During this time he was researching an article on the history of the RAF. One of his contacts had been the limbless Battle of Britain veteran, Group Captain Douglas Bader, who had also lost his right leg as a result of the conflict. Politically poles apart, he and Ken found a shared interest in country matters, with botany Bader's speciality. On the 1st May, Ken received a hollyhock from the war hero and former Roehampton patient, which sparked off a correspondence and further exchange of plants through the summer.

For the rest of the month, Ken was expected to report to Roehampton once, sometimes twice, a week, first for a measurement then, after several aborted attempts, a fitting for a pylon. (i.e. a support or modified brace to hold the new leg). The rest of the time was his own but, once more reliant upon crutches, he bored easily.

On dry days he'd be sitting out at the back of Alder Cottage, noting down descriptions of passing birds. When bored even with this, he obtained an air-pistol and resorted to shooting at passing rabbits, as he had in his teens. Through June he received visits from his father, his father's older brother, Tom, Pat Alexander, John Chillingworth, with at least one letter from Henry. The biggest surprise was one from the Hultons', which may have felt particularly awkward. On the 2nd July, a fortnight after a successful fitting, Ken took possession of his new leg. No records survive as to its improvement on earlier models, but it felt secure enough for him to resume duties on Monday 5th.

During June, Robert Edwards unexpectedly decided to publish Ken's piece on Belsen. On the 17th July, Michael Foot, through Edwards, invited 'Percy Redcar and wife' to a *Tribune* party the following night, set in the grounds of High Elms; a tall white house facing Hampton Court's green and owned by J.P.W. Mallalieu, the former Labour MP for Herts. during the Attlee years and a friend of Foot's. With insinuating charm, Ken used the occasion, with Betty, to lobby for work in Fleet Street, finally making public his intention to leave *Picture Post*.

Despite the charm, they weren't subtle in approach. Hearing of a contingent from *The Observer*, Ken needed an eventual audience with its owner, David Astor, and may have been disappointed by his absence. However, Betty ascertained from Michael Peto – its Hungarian-born photographer – that Kenneth Obank, whom Ken knew but also absent on holiday, had Astor's ear. Michael Foot, whose brother Dingle was Chairman of *The Observer* board - told Betty he'd have a word with Sydney Elliot, the editor of *The Daily Herald*. Ken found the conviction politician much warmer and less belligerent than he appeared on the TV his family pressured him into buying. Neither approach gained a result. But one surprising source did. Ken was pleasantly surprised to find the trumpet player, Humphrey Lyttleton, performing close by on a riverboat down on the Thames. He had just handed in his positive review on the jazzman's autobiography that morning. Before the night was out, he made an approach for an interview, so easing the way to a future beyond the Hultons, the board, and conveniently situated right next door.

In December, Ken was horrified to learn that, on his second assignment to Spain in fifteen months, he'd once more be reliant upon the services of Harry Grierson. On the morning of the 1st January 1955, coldly awaiting their man at Waterloo Station, Ken communicated his agitation to Godfrey Thurston Hopkins, his photographer for the occasion.

'He's a sponger,' he told him. 'We must watch him. He'll drink his way through the expenses if we're not careful. I neither like nor trust him.'

Hopkins has left a previously unpublished account of the assignment, which was to suffer a fate similar to the first. Having boarded the train and made for the restaurant, seemingly without him,

'Harry Grierson staggers into the compartment. He swayed over the introductions and directed a blast of alcohol fumes into my face. He looked dirty, half-drunk, beaten-up, as if he had just emerged from an all-night brawl in a brothel. He spoke with an insolent, condescending drawl, like Trevor Howard – whom he resembled physically – badly overacting as a deadbeat drunk. This was the man who claimed he could introduce us into the Royal household of the ex-King of Spain.' Previous experience had told Ken not to doubt this. On this occasion he and Hopkins travelled via Portugal, the capital already known to Hopkins.

'On the plane to Lisbon we contrive to get seats well away

from Grierson. Ken tells me about the air hostess who claimed she was a member of the Twenty Thousand Club, membership of which is confined to those who have fucked at over twenty thousand feet – in this instance, with the captain of the aircraft.'

At a local Lisbon fish bar over a snack of seafood and lager, Grierson casually announces that the letter 'upon which the success of this trip hinges' has yet be received by the British Embassy. Suggesting they take a cab there, it mistakenly arrives at the Ambassador's residence some metres away, forcing the unlikely trio to climb a steep hill, on full stomachs, the rest of the way. From here, Ken only speaks to Grierson when he absolutely has to. Three days of constantly phoning the Embassy for the vital letter concludes when they're told its posting was purposely held back until the day of their arrival. They have little choice but to remain in the city for its receipt, before heading on to Madrid.

Inevitably, being a port, they first take in the darker side of Lisbon's nightlife. What followed, possibly at The Texas Bar, is blunt in tone but worth fully transcribing, since it offers a rare glimpse into Ken's sexual proclivities. Still intent on pumping Grierson on the current whereabouts of the letter, he and Hopkins find their man, unwashed, bloodshot-eyed and dissolute on brandy, in the early hours, at a table surrounded by several dubious and dangerous-looking women. Hopkins continues:

'We drank several brandies, abused Grierson from time to time, but stayed on in the ripe atmosphere of the bar, which was large, with a comfortable dance floor and a reasonably efficient band playing (beneath) the varnished hull of a fishing boat suspended above the tables. Because the heat and cigarette smoke was getting at my eyes, I longed to go back to the hotel. By this time, Ken had begun to examine the faces of the numerous women seated alone, and found one which interested him. Presently, various women began to encircle our table. Ken had settled down to a sentimental flirtation with one of the least repellent of the whores, and I found myself landed with a blonde who kept slipping her hand onto my thigh and digging her fingers into the flesh. Grierson was driving a bargain with his..., then came across and borrowed two hundred *escudos* from Ken. At this point, I told Ken I was getting out and left him fondling the hand of his girl. I was awakened by the light being switched on in our bedroom. Ken entered looking sore-eyed and exhausted. 'How was it?' I asked him. 'Awful,' he replied. 'I was glad to get away. Not worth it, even as an experience. The whole thing was pretty squalid. Never had such an amateurish fuck. Not the slightest attempt on her part to *do* anything. And the extraordinary coyness of insisting on wearing a nightgown!' I laughed at his expression of disgust. 'Oh well, that's my first and last prostitute,' he said as he undressed, and flung himself wearily on the bed.'

To sleep off the previous night, he and Hopkins turned in early the next day. After ignoring the nearby ringing phone, an impatient thudding on their door confirmed what they'd most feared. Angrily, Ken got out of bed and opened the door.

'Clear off, Grierson, you bastard!' he shouted, slamming it and hobbling back to bed. The thudding continued and Hopkins took over. 'I need five *escudos*!' said Grierson. 'Don't give it to him!' Ken shouted. 'Let the bastard rot!' Drained of drinking money, he'd nothing left to pay either the cab driver for bringing him there or, according to the porter that followed him, The Texas Bar owner who'd been unwisely talked into accepting credit. Ken was adamant the police should deal with him, even if it landed him in jail, but Hopkins – fearing yet more aggravation - paid off the ninety-four escudos owed. There is still no sign of the letter when Ken and Hopkins agree to make the move across to Estoril and told Grierson, naked and smoking in bed, a ubiquitous brandy bottle at his side, to prepare the way with the authorities.

Later that day, Grierson re-appeared saying it was all fixed and that 'the boy' – as he referred to the young Prince Juan Carlos – would see them that afternoon. But after having been allowed to drive their hired car up to the royal residence it appeared that Grierson had mucked up again. As Grierson alighted from the passenger seat, an aide of the Prince reminded him he'd been told not to come until he'd received a confirmation call that morning. In the event, the Prince was unavailable. With unerring confidence, Grierson then asked for an audience with the King. The aide informed him that he held no personal audiences with the press. Grierson calmly insisted and the aide left to make a second attempt. 'Another last, desperate bluff,' sighed Ken as they waited. When the aide returned to confirm the King's refusal, Grierson asked for a pen, was led into an anteroom, and wrote a personal letter. By now, 'Ken was beyond speaking: I was both furious and ashamed.' The letter also failed to change the King's mind.

On the car journey back to Lisbon, Hopkins heard Ken take out his long-held loathing on their guide.

'I want you to know, Grierson, that you're a cheap crook, not even a clever one, but a failure of a crook. You're the cheapest skate it has ever been my misfortune to deal with. Everything about you is dirty, and rotten and bogus. It's all I can do to keep my hands off you and, if you give me just one more excuse, I'll beat you up so that even your own mother wouldn't recognise you...' Apparently, Grierson took this in silence, suggesting he'd heard it from others, quite often, before. Back at the fish bar, Ken and Hopkins agreed they would formerly sack Grierson before flying on to Madrid. This they did, which somewhat placated Ken. But, for the remainder of the assignment, they were stuck with him. There were only four of the eleven allocated days left and, with Grierson's notorious knowledge of the city, - the one thing he could be relied upon to deliver - time was of the essence.

They checked in to the Mayorazgo Hotel, just outside the city centre. Ken and Hopkins' brief, to update readers on the cultural influence of the Franco regime. On one of their three nights here, Grierson took them to the old part of the city; significantly less troubled by tourists than today. Hopkins recalled how swiftly drink passed through Ken, a possible consequence of his medication. He takes up the story:

'We were going down this narrow street and Ken said, 'I've got to go *somewhere!*' In old Madrid there were no convenient places to pee. We passed a wall and he said he'd have to go against there. Our contact said, 'No no, I know just the place.' We happened to be passing a large studded door. He went up, banged on it, and it was opened and a woman looked out and he said something to her in Spanish. She said, 'come in, come in,' and we found ourselves in a magnificent businessman's' brothel. As Ken was excused and our contact walked off, I was left alone. I sat down on a large *chez-lounge* with my camera equipment. Suddenly, a half a dozen flimsily-dressed girls appeared and were draping themselves around me. They were making fun of me, to an extent, but also had their eyes on business. Ken came back, saw me sitting there with these girls, burst out laughing and asked for my camera. He took several pictures of me sitting there.

After that little incident, I realised that Ken had been talking to our contact. Ken had obviously said to him that he'd like to see more, an exhibition. So, a deal was made with the madam. I saw Ken hand over some money. Then, we were taken up a long, winding flight of stairs. And the thing I remember about that place was its very large rooms with very low ceilings.' (Grace Robertson later reminded us that it wasn't an establishment for *standing* in). 'Then the girls were brought in and Ken and myself were asked to choose one of them. I chose a reasonable-looking girl. Ken, for some reason, chose a very fat girl; almost gross. So then, they did their little lesbian exhibition on this vast, ornate bed while I photographed it. Our contact couldn't believe that we were *not* going to screw any of the girls, considering the cash he'd handed over. But neither Ken nor I were the least bit attracted...everything was wrong about it. But, I shot all this stuff on one roll on my *Leica* – including the pictures Ken had taken of me downstairs. We went out, had a meal, rewound the film and forgot all about it.

Several days elapsed and during that time there was an Australian filmmaker in Madrid who'd been caught taking pornographic films. The films were taken from him, processed, and he'd been put in jail. But, anyway, it was enough to startle both of us. It was enough to get Ken very jittery and he was worried about us taking that roll of film back and if we were held up at customs, and it was processed, then it would get back... It seems so far-fetched. Looking back now, I think how absurd we were! We were a couple of innocents... of course, I should've just stuck my film in my back pocket and gone through as we did.

Anyway, in the hotel the night before we were due to leave Madrid, I was sitting on the side of the bed with the ribbon of stills and I said to Ken, 'Let's have a decision on this. What are we going to do about this film?' Ken said, 'I don't want to risk it. Get rid of it.' I did and wiped it in an instant. It's something I've always regretted.'

By 1955, loyal, company man Pierce had, himself, proven expendable with former 'PP' writer Lionel 'Bobby' Birch now holding the editor's chair. At a subsequent staff meeting, the Board announced the magazine's most radical change yet in policy. The future was presented in a positive light. There was acknowledgement that the magazine had lost its common touch and needed reconnection to the market. There was a moment's silence. Cynthia Judah recalls what followed. Evoking Orwell,

'Ken said in his sardonic voice, 'Are we all going to be turned into *Prole Feed*, then?' I wasn't sure what he meant, but I knew it was something a bit daring. There was silence and then Bobby laughed one of his great, shoulder shrugging laughs, which set-off everyone else. I think *they* knew what he meant.' The comment deflated the atmosphere and, momentarily, the announcement's significance.

Len Spooner, the editor of *Illustrated*, was presented as the latest recruit to reverse their fortunes, along with one of his photographers. The irony was not lost on the departing journalists that their once great sales rival had effectively made them the new *Illustrated*. The metamorphosis complete, staff journalists resigned *en masse*. Most photographers remained, long used to their wider brief and comparatively free hand. Ken had been portentously vowing to leave for the past two and a half years. The generous annual salary, promise of further news coverage overseas and covert freelancing elsewhere helped stay his hand. He'd later sound regret, committing so long to 'the kind of lightweight variety show that had always been eyed with distant disdain.' One of his last assignments on home turf harked back to cub reporter days: a bitter sweet encounter, at a dance class, canvassing three sixteen-year-old ballerinas on their voting intentions in the forthcoming General Election. It was *The Slough Observer* all over again.

Ken only had to sneak next door, en route to or back from lunch, to hand in his pseudonymous reviews of new books and jazz recordings to the *Evening Standard*'s deputy editor, Charles Wintour. An action encouraged by Dan Farson, who'd been freelancing, regularly, for Wintour for the past year. To avoid verbally blowing his cover too to the hounds of Fleet Street, Ken, with Dan, forsook the popular El Vino's for the relative anonymity of The Cock Tavern across the way. Since April, 'Percy Redcar' had alternated between 'Peter Carson' and 'Richard (as in 'Dick') Evans' but they were merely diverting variants on the theme of the motor as phallic symbol. Assurances of a contract from Wintour, and an offer of work at the new ITN building, each allowed him to drop the monikers for good and, on Friday 19th August, he finally cleared his desk at *Picture Post*.

15
Henry and The Grey House

On the 27th June 1953, Ken drove the family to Devon for a fortnight's holiday with Henry. Again, he was alone with only three-year-old Harry for company, his son with Christine, but at the caravan in Georgeham he'd bought for her before she became estranged. As usual, Ken planned his own bird-watching itinerary. With the typewriter, camera and binoculars, he also took a walking stick and supply of *Dexedrine*. The constant assignments had recently exacerbated the ubiquitous, nerve-grinding pain, making further, unbroken treks impossible.

For the first couple of days, Ken seemed to make the effort to play with and involve his three children, hobbling with pace as they ran through a humid storm, picking heather and pointing out to them their first buzzards. On the 30th, the Allsops found Henry, alone again, at the Higher House bar in Georgeham. Dressed in khaki hunting jacket and matching shorts, and clearly the worse for drink, he'd just produced the MS of the latest installment on Philip Maddison from a canvas fisherman's bag at his feet, and balled out whole paragraphs to the locals. The smile of recognition that greeted Ken, stopping him mid-flow, avoided any trouble.

'Said he'd lost his nerve when I last saw him,' he reported. As Henry took off his coat, Ken noted he bore 'a fine, knotty, bronzed body for a man over 50.' Henry was due to record a talk for the BBC: his first for some years and a sign of slowly returning acceptance. Together, they remained within a ten-mile radius of Williamson country, staying long afternoons with the children on Croyde Beach and Woolacombe Bay, with sight-seeing car convoys of mutual friends in between. Betty remained, mainly, with them and the children, preferring the kind of distance which, with Christine, she could only sympathise. The next day was spent bird watching with the family on Baggy Point until well into evening when the children drifted asleep on the rock.

The following evening, Ken met Negley Farson. His twenty-six year old son, Dan, had been a colleague of Ken's since joining *Picture Post* as a photographer in October 1951. Blonde, pale but freckle-featured and mildly corpulent – a bestowal from his father – with the small, innocent mouth and voice of an Edwardian clergymen, Dan was 'out' and content with his homosexuality. As were his parents, who never really understood how to bring up their only child. Like Ken, this was his first staff job. Unlike Ken, a former Cambridge graduate, though they shared enough interests for Ken to overlook this. Discovering they'd independently planned to take their summer breaks here, an ideal opportunity arose to introduce Ken to his father at The Grey House, his parents' home. He noted his first impressions of the now aging journalist.

'Negley, big, red-faced, showy U.S. accent, drinking tomato juice and only allowed so many cig(arettes) by Eve – on diet.'

Informing him that he and Betty were staying with Henry, Negley darkened to purple. The name was taboo here, neither Negley nor Eve prepared to forgive him his fascist sympathising past or related, continuing friendship with Oswald Mosley. There was also, in the eyes of Negley's son, the contrast in character: his father, a hard-bitten extrovert, with Henry, a romantic introvert. For years they'd known each other as fellow members of The Savage Club back in London.

An opportunity to watch them spar inadvertently arose late the following morning. Dropping the children off with the elusive Christine at Ox Cross, the Allsops' collected Henry's Aston and drove to the local Three Tuns pub for a ploughman-style lunch. Installed in its 'snug,' Negley suddenly appeared by their table, sweating and drunk. Dropping down in the seat next to Henry, the broader man leered lasciviously at Betty, then launched into a diatribe against the taller man's alleged Devon heritage and the past relationships he'd supposedly betrayed. Betty later related that they discovered such attacks to be a semi-regular occurrence, with him telling Henry 'he was bogus and all balled up about sex.' Ken tactfully excused himself, saying he'd an appointment for a haircut, while Betty followed a distressed Henry out of the pub.

For the first time, she felt some sympathy for the man. She spent almost two hours with him, trying to get him to relax. He threatened to throw himself into the nearby river, then changed his mind, Betty 'repeating over and over again that I wouldn't allow it because I loved him, Christine loved him, Ken loved him and we all loved him.' He then suggested a more heroic end, trying to save someone else until Betty pointed out the receding tide would only land him in the mud. He finally resolved to sue Negley for slander but, on returning to the pub, his nemesis had been collected by taxi.

Ken spent the next night with Henry in his Hut. A brave vigil, since it was around this time Henry confided to Eve Farson that he thought he really was going mad, experiencing fits of shouting and banging his head against the Hut's walls. But Henry's radio discussion at BBC Bristol, in his honour, was due the following day, and he thought he'd never make the planned 5.30 a.m. departure without a close to hand alarm call from his friend. Ken later recounted the subsequent events to the author, Colin Wilson, who'd make his first visit to The Grey House three years later.

'He'd shaken Ken out of bed at about five in the morning, and Ken had said, 'Henry, it's only an hour's drive to

Bristol.' But Henry insisted on leaving instantly. When they arrived, nobody was around but the cleaner who let them in. Up they went to the canteen, whereupon Henry took off his coat, his shirt <u>and</u> under-vest and sat there with a great pile of papers before him, frowning and writing merrily away, being the great genius preparing for the programme on his life. In due course they went to the studio for a run-through, Henry watching from behind the glass partition at the side while Ken sat down with the other guests, the poets Ronald Duncan and Charles Causley. As they discussed Henry's novels, Ken said he'd like to move on to talk about *Tarka the Otter*, *Salar the Salmon* and his other animal books. Then it was suggested they discuss his ongoing series, *The Chronicle of Ancient Sunlight*. Duncan said, 'Well, I don't want to. I think it's shit.' Causley concurred, 'Yes. I think it's shit, too.' At that moment, they looked up at the soundproofed screen and saw Henry glaring at them through the glass, his face contorted in agony. Afterwards, Ken rushed behind the screen and found Henry lying face down and beating the floor with his fists. Somebody had left the microphones switched on. That kind of thing was always happening to Henry.'

In July 1956, Colin Wilson was the twenty five-year-old, self-taught Existentialist philosophy student who'd convincingly channeled his middle European literary influences into their first public voice, *The Outsider*. Since its release in May, a certain mystique had been growing around this thin, floppy-fringed young man in roll-neck sweater and National Health glasses on aquiline features not unlike those of the English actor, Michael York – bolstered by two highbrow previews from Cyril Connolly and Philip Toynbee. The mystique, in retrospect, was superficial, with Fleet Street, to a man, consigning him to the same stable as this year's model Angry Young Man, Jimmy Porter. (Playwright, John

Osborne's *Look Back in Anger* opened at the West End's Royal Court Theatre just two weeks before. Its publicist must have rued the day he first used it, although that dubious honour should really rest with the pro-communist writer, Leslie Paul, whose 1951 autobiography bore the title).

Farson read the work and recommended him to Ken. On reading his copy, Ken was instantly caught. What almost certainly affected him were the passages highlighting the dilemma constantly raging within and the subsequent questions he'd asked of himself. The theme is control. The subject in this case, Van Gogh:

'If there is an order in the universe, if he (the artist) can sometimes perceive that order and feel himself completely in accord with it, then it must be seeable, touchable, so that it could be regained by some discipline. Art is only one form of such a discipline.

Unfortunately, the problem is complicated by quite irrelevant human needs that claim the attention: for companionship and understanding, for a feeling of participation in the social life of humanity. And, of course, for a roof over one's head, and food and drink. The artist tries to give attention to these, but it is difficult when there are so much more important things to think about; and it is all made more difficult by the hostility of other people who every day arouse the question, Could it be that I'm wrong? Sometimes the strain makes the Outsider-artist think of suicide, but before he gets to that point, the universe is suddenly making sense again, and he has a glimpse of purpose.' (p. 89, 1997 edition).

'His last words to Theo are the words of a man who feels that defeat is inevitable, that life is a baited trap; *who kills himself to escape the necessity of taking the bait again.*' (p.90, ibid.).

'...Van Gogh's painting has the Outsider's characteristic: it is laboratory refuse of *a man who treated his own life as an experiment in living.*' (p.92, ibid.).

He saw in Wilson's book a young iconoclast too rootless to be affected by the structure or strictures of class; a man on the cusp of making it without the bestowal of social advantage. In other words, he was poor but intelligent. Ken saw a purity of spirit worthy of respect, and one whose route he might, himself, have followed had he been less advantaged.

Wilson met Dan Farson, in his role of *Standard* journalist, who showed the young writer his first – and glowing – review, at the Romilly Street bookshop run by Soho regular, David Archer, whom Wilson recalls as 'a nice queer who gave away most of his stock.' Farson, in *Never A Normal Man*, recalled his woeful lack of salesmanship.

'The bookshop was doomed because Archer loved his books so dearly that he hated to part with them. Once, I heard him tell a potential customer to try Better Books in Charing Cross Road. 'But you have a copy on the shelf,' I reminded him as the disconsolate man wandered off. 'Well, yes, but it's the only one.'

Six weeks later, on the 6th July, Farson introduced Wilson to Ken there, the author inviting them back to his rooms in Notting Hill where he lived with his fiancee, Joy Stewart. Expectation mixed with disdain turned Ken to write 'squalid' in his diary. The following day being a rare, free Saturday, the three met again to visit a photographic exhibition by John Deakin: a seedy, pernicious, Soho homosexual and staple of Farson's drinking haunts. By the evening, Ken invited Farson to accompany him in his car to Devon for what was becoming an annual pilgrimage. This was fortuitous, as Wilson had been planning a cycling expedition through to Cornwall.

'Then Dan said, 'Why don't you come down with me and

Ken? You can start your holiday from our place.' So, we sent our bicycles down to Plymouth to be collected at the station and we drove down with him.' Arrival at the Grey House afforded Wilson his first striking view of Farson's aging father. 'As we walked down the little slope to the front door, we saw Negley sitting outside in the sunlight, trouser leg rolled up to his knee from a war wound which had taken a huge chunk out of his shin and periodically began to suppurate. This great, broad-shouldered figure with his grey hair looked a bit like Tolstoy. Gorky described Tolstoy – the first time he saw him – as sitting under a tree, looking like some nature god. Negley struck me the same way.'

Negley emoted with the young men's combative conversation, forging 'an instant rapport.' Dan, so used to his father's condition, was equally taken by Ken's mobility across the rocks and sand. So, he was surprised when, at Woolacombe Bay a day or two later, Ken suddenly held back from joining his three friends for a swim. Negley sensed what was wrong, understanding his apprehension. Ken had avoided swimming since the amputation in 1945. Ambling over to him, Negley, with firm intent, offered his support as Ken nervously unclipped his false limb. Placing his left arm around Negley's neck for support, he braced himself, hopped a few feet into the waves...and relaxed. He later told Dan that the experience had most likely been 'a psychological breakthrough' waiting to happen. Never again would he feel quite so vain and self-conscious about his disability in public. He made a phone call to one of the team at Roehampton with a similar admission.

Back at the Grey House, Negley enthusiastically related his globetrotting experiences to the three men, who lapped it up. Dan recalls the laughter as so infectious that even his father had to leave the room. Later, Ken realised he'd somehow have to make a point of seeing Henry: but how to achieve this without tipping off Negley? The last three years had done little to cool the men's mutual hostility. Ken confided in Eve, who agreed that he should go. On the Monday afternoon, he drove to Ox's Cross. He found Henry typing in his Writing Hut with the door ajar.

'I was thinking of you this morning,' said the older man, his usual greeting. Ken noted the moustache he'd grown back, now snowy white:

'Looked well and brown, green-shirt buttoned up to neck. He seemed in good spirits. Henry said about the Amis school of new writers: 'I wouldn't want to sell a million books, I'd feel there was something wrong, but I would like a bit more appreciation.' That evening Dan and I drove to Georgeham and met Henry in the pub and had some drinks. He has his *Tales* and *Life of a Devon Village* exhibited in there at 3s. 6d. each – the pub is now tarted up like a coffee bar with fancy wallpaper. 'Subtopia,' HW said.' It could have been here that Ken mooted the idea of doing a rehabilitative article on Henry, as viewed today, and with his participation, which its subject vaguely misconstrued would be 'Kenneth Allsop's eulogy.'

The next morning, Ken found Negley in a dark mood. Farson figured they'd been rumbled and that his father might, consequently, drink away his anger. They drove back to London with the car's hood down. Farson later revised his view:

'I am sure my father did go off on his 'binge,' but I doubt if this had much to do with Henry. For this was the pattern by then, a rage of frustration at seeing friends leave for London and Fleet Street and the mental excitement he longed for – a natural reaction.'

Six months on, Colin Wilson had his own experience of Grey House life, and one that inadvertently did him a big favour. During a dinner party at their Notting Hill flat, on the eve of publication of his second release, *Religion and the Rebel,* Joy's angered father burst in wielding a horse-whip and cried, 'Wilson! The game is up. You're a homosexual with six mistresses!' The precise wording sounds unlikely, though it's supported by his fiancée and Dan Farson. Mr. Stewart had suddenly panicked for his daughter's welfare after her bed-ridden sister, Fay, read Wilson's jottings for the, until then, unpublished novel *Ritual in the Dark*,' featuring a sexual psychopath. Misinterpreting them as entries from their future son-in-law's private diary, Stewart and his wife had duly rushed to their daughter's side.

Farson recalls that,

'while Colin rolled on the floor with hysterical laughter, a fellow guest, the infamous Gerald Hamilton – who was the original Mr. Norris for Isherwood's novel *Mr. Norris Changes Trains* - crept out and phoned *The Express*, receiving a small fee.' Mr. Stewart was distraught, almost certainly with embarrassment. 'I wanted to teach Colin a lesson,' he was reported to have said. '(Joy) thinks he's a genius.'

More from awareness of the adverse publicity than fear of Stewart Senior, Farson smoothed the way for Colin and Joy to flee to North Devon and sanctuary at The Grey House. Forty years on, Wilson recalls,

'When we got there we decided Joy had better leave just in case her parents tried another attempt at kidnap. So, she stayed at a little inn in the middle of Dartmoor while I stayed on with Negley and Eve. Then, my friend, the author, Bill Hopkins, rang from London to say that *The Daily Mail* had gotten hold of my journals...I'd originally handed them to Mr. Stewart with the assurance there was nothing in them that would raise anyone's eyebrows.' But, *The Mail* published large extracts while *The Express* was willing to pay to publish even more. 'Negley said, 'Don't sell it to them. Never sell your private life to a newspaper.' So, I said they could print it for free provided Bill Hopkins edited what they used.' A large cartoon double-spread, featuring Wilson running away from Joy's furious, whip-brandishing father followed. On reading this, Ken's prominent brows furrowed.

'He was so concerned at this kind of stupid publicity. It had nothing to do with being a writer, or about the kinds of things I was writing.'

Wilson stayed three days. After collecting Joy, Dan decided, like Ken the year before, that they couldn't leave without seeing Henry. He took it for granted that Negley shouldn't know, telling Wilson that he wasn't popular in Georgeham either, alienating the locals with his 'neurotic egotism.' On arrival, Henry flourished his latest manuscript and read, not the usual novel chapter awaiting release, but a stoic defence of his alignment to Oswald Mosley's British Union of Fascists. Wilson adds,

'I had met Mosley, and found him brilliant and enormously likeable; so this was a matter on which we immediately established a bond of sympathy.'

Joy was particularly taken by him, though their admiration gradually strained to the unending intonation that seemed to stretch to afternoon's end. On leaving, Dan asked Wilson what he made of him. He said he'd found him impressive if rather too talkative.

'He intended to be,' grinned Farson. 'That's typical Henry. He knows we're not supposed to see him, so he wants us to be late for dinner, just to stir things up.' During the next two years - Negley's last - the feud tired into jaded acceptance. Wilson related what followed in a letter to Ken. On a further weekend at The Grey House, Wilson still felt anxious about broaching the taboo name. During a drawn-out excuse to absent himself from their company, Negley sighed and said,

'Do go and see him, for God's sake! I wouldn't want you to feel I objected.'

Ken interviewed Louis Armstrong on three occasions; first for 'Picture Post,' then for the 'Evening Standard,' and BBC TV's 'Panorama.'

16
Sept 1955 – Sept 1960: 'This is Kenneth Allsop...'

'I possess a TV set. I spend a great deal of time watching the programmes with an amalgam of fascination and anger.'
                                    (Diary entry, Tues. 7th Sept. 1954).

Such ambiguous fascination for BBC Television was widespread among Britain's viewers up to the mid-Fifties. Ken didn't share the attitude of blind condescension regularly heaped upon it by colleagues who should have known better, equally suspicious of its motives. His own view was more accommodating and proactive. He conceded the dominant triviality in the programming: fine as light relief, but so much of a willful underachievement as to be asking for others contempt. He also knew that, as a tool, it could offer a great deal more than the weekly diet of *Quick and Easy Dressmaking*, *Television Dancing Club* and *Picture Parade*. On a typical weekday's schedule in the mid-Fifites, the ratio of entertainment to information was around 3 – 1: on a par with that month's issue of *Picture Post*. *Panorama*, the new current affairs 'window on the World,' alone checked this imbalance. The eyes and ears of the journalist's children were more readily accepting; the *Watch with Mother* puppet series' fast becoming a staple for the junior Allsops after school, especially *The Woodentops* for six-year-old Amanda.

Ken's ulterior motive in owning a set was to angle an idea for a TV column to Kenneth Obank who'd returned to *The Observer* from holiday in September 1954; a means to an end in eventually reaching David Astor himself. In the meantime, he attended a voice test at Broadcasting House for the role of News Analyst. The post entailed joining a regular panel of journalists the BBC could rely upon to hire as sharp reactors to current events. A stock, mock-up script was thrust in front of Ken, inhibiting his usual self-assurance. On the back of his reading, Peter Donne – the recording producer – sent a memo to the departmental Head on the 13th:

'Having regard to the fact that this was not his own script, Mr. Allsop read well and with intelligence. He has a voice of somewhat light calibre, but it is clear and resonant, and his speech is well articulated. With an increase in confidence he might well make a successful news analyst.' This tactful, but undeniable, snub was compounded after three months' silence with a written admission to him that, soon after his audition, the News Talks panel had been discontinued. A contributing factor to this administrative change was the imminent advent of *Independent Television News*. The aged Churchill's last gasp as Conservative leader was to see through the bill proposing a commercial service, which the BBC received with a panic not dissimilar to that felt by Edward Hulton over them.

Undeterred, twelve months later Ken was recalled to attend a second audition for the post of newscaster at a closed-circuit studio in Highbury for *Independent Television News*, due to broadcast in five weeks. Dan Farson had applied and reached the final ten. (No further call came for him, but within six months he was reporting for *This Week*: ITV's new challenge to *Panorama*). In the waiting room this day, Ken met two other short-listed finalists: a shorter, stockier figure beneath a butter-coloured cowlick, already known as the athlete, Christopher Chataway, and a bespectacled figure with a severe expression named Robin Day. Waiting to test them in a side sound booth with their 'dummy' scripts based on the previous day's news was Assistant Editor, Geoffrey Cox, and his boss, Aidan Crawley. With the network of regional stations requiring a unifying structure for their news, Crawley – a one-time Labour MP - had founded the company earlier this year after a time as a BBC Presenter. Day recalled the filmed test itself a few years later:

'We had been asked to memorize our material so that we would not have to look down during the audition. They wanted us looking full-face into the camera as continuously as we could. I took a final look at my notes. The phrases which last night seemed crisp and bright were limp and dull, but it was too late to make any more changes.

'Are you ready?' called the floor manager, listening to the director's orders on his headphones. I nodded.

'Stand by.' He stood to one side of the camera, and raised his arm above his shoulder. 'Thirty seconds to go...Fifteen seconds.'

Suddenly, the floor manager jabbed his hand down towards me. A red light glowed on top of the camera. This was it... I ended dead on time. I flopped back against the chair. Though at this moment nothing was further from my mind, that working up second by second to the tense climax of transmission was to be part of my daily life during the next few years. Lights, cameras, clocks, signals, were to form the ritual setting for the culmination of a day's work.

'Mr. Crawley says 'thank you very much.''

Ken experienced the same, although Day's declared relief at the finish would, for him, have been rather less. He had little riding on the result. Television remained secondary to *The Standard* contract he'd only postponed signing. The lack of expectation went in his favour. Day and Chataway were offered a three-month trial, becoming the first two newscasters seen on ITV. Crawley and Cox, without Peter Donne's qualms, made Ken the third. He was to report to Television House – on the corner of Kingsway and Aldwych

- at 10 a.m. on Monday the 12th September in readiness for the station's official opening ten days later.

On arrival, Ken discovered how markedly similar, structurally, the routine of editorial meetings, news gathering, travelling, interviewing and recording events was to what he'd been accustomed. The one major difference was the time factor. It quickly became apparent there was little, if any, room for mistakes, retakes or rewrites. Such obstacles were unaffordable luxuries. He was expected to live and work by the clock to a degree he'd never thought feasible. One of his first pieces to camera - interviewing Donald Campbell as he prepared to leave for America and a forthcoming attempt to break the world water speed record - was cut to all of twenty-one seconds. Quizzing future Labour Prime Minister, Harold Wilson, on his views regarding a report on the state of the Labour Party, was clipped a slightly more generous ten seconds later. 'Immigration to Britain from the West Indies' was longer again, though still laughably fleeting. The level of *gravitas* attributed to this weighty topic is best summed-up by *ITN*'s surviving paperwork on the item:

'Black woman and a little girl and little boy. Shot of interior at Paddington. Kenneth Allsop asks two men what sort of work they are going to do and they reply, hotel work. Allsop then speaks to their future employer, who says that these migrants solve a present problem with staff in hotel business. Allsop also asks a woman if she is joining her railway worker husband. She replies, yes.'

Ken stayed with ITN only four more weeks. A note in his diary for the 2nd November reminds him to hand in his resignation. Why remains unclear. What is known is that the ITN board was totally unprepared for the full financial cost of worldwide coverage and, with ITV already enduring a painful birth ripe for cuts, Crawley himself was considering his position. Ken may then have lost confidence in his own performance as well as that of the company. The first ITN board had little experience of news, coming mainly from Entertainment. Ken had had his fill of boards. It was *Picture Post* all over again.

A fortnight earlier, he'd interviewed Chataway for a (short) profile and may have subsequently sounded him out on his imminent debunking to the BBC. Chataway was soon to be seen tackling the treatment of West Indian immigrants for *Panorama* in far greater depth, perhaps in cautionary response to Ken's straitjacketed effort. He'd temporarily delayed Wintour at *The Standard* for this work but, in retrospect, the on-screen results hardly justified it. A better deal than he'd been waiting for manifested in the interim, offering him the twin posts of Book and Jazz Critic.

We will never know just how long his original, expensively filmed, recordings lasted with their quick consignment to the cutting room floor. Today's freelance reporter videotapes and records his own choice piece, and is equally responsible for its editing en route. But not, as then, the final broadcast cut. To Ken, this would be tantamount to creative interference; hardly what commercial television existed to fight against. Such ideals were fine but he also knew the value of his looks on the open market. The screen test he'd believed discarded had since been passed to the company's advertising department. Within days he'd be before the cameras again, shooting ITV's first toothpaste commercial.

But the mixed feelings about television remained as he left the station on Friday the 18th, returning to the more familiar surroundings of Shoe Lane the following Monday. But the process and its demand for quick, unilateral decisions had excited him. If only he could have fought for more airtime.

Ken signed for a year under Charles Wintour's deputy-editorship. What the time would lack in challenging new discoveries, it more than made up for in sheer, enjoyable self-indulgence. He caught the sweat-ridden performances of deaf singer, Johnny Rae, a young Johnny Dankworth and Cleo Laine at Ronnie Scott's, and Louis Armstrong blowing in Paris. Rock n' Roll's invasion from the States he captured amidst the debris of discarded seats and mass arrests around British cinemas as, of all rebels, the staid-looking Bill Haley slapped his strings with The Comets. Ken wrote one of the first Fleet Street pieces on Tommy Steele, whose *Rock the Caveman* entered the very middle-of-the-road 'hit parade' early in 1956. Generally, Ken liked and understood the new pop music, seeing no problem with offering the same critical discernment usually reserved for the jazz.

Four long-lasting friendships formed here in the Editorial Department. The burly and dependable Peter Black reviewed the box. Alan Brien worked as film critic having just finished a year reviewing TV programmes for *The Observer*. A dark, balding, hawk-featured Jewish émigré, liked and feared in equal measure for his plain-speaking, Brien was then being pursued by a beautiful, Nordic blonde American named Nancy Ryan. Quentin Crewe had been a leader writer for two years. Suffering muscular dystrophy since childhood, this ebullient, bow-tied figure ambled between the office desks, an inverted left leg supported by a ubiquitous cane: an inevitable point of recognition for the new boy. In his autobiography, Crewe evokes the paper at this time:

'The editorial department was on the second floor in a huge, crowded room filled with ugly desks in jumbled rows. There were windows on two sides of the room, but they were not for looking out. One side faced a blackened brick building thirty feet away; the other a murky street. They let in a filtered, fuzzy gray light. Telephone wires trailed from the ceiling on to the desks, where the telephones sat next to typewriters that looked ancient even then; sturdy relics from before the war. There were only two enclosed offices – the editor's, which had rippled glass so that one could not see into it, and John Junor's.

The news desk occupied a far corner: the Features desk, the centre. The critics and leader writers ran parallel with them, and the 'Londoner's Diary' had a cluster of desks to one side. The noise was prodigious, the clatter of typewriters, the cries of 'boy' to summon a youth to take copy to the printers' chute, reporters yelling down telephones to distant countries.'

Assigned to Ken in Features was a recent graduate from Girton College, Cambridge, named 'Kay Tinniswood.' Ken found this slim, brown-eyed brunette, cool, intelligent, with an artistic temperament and - for someone precisely half his age – already well travelled. They began an affair. For Ken, this wasn't the usual excuse for quick sexual relief, now conveniently to hand, but something much more profound. The danger of a husband and wife working together can be heard in loud, short-tempered exchanges. Several of their colleagues have since accounted for such arguments becoming a regular occurrence from 1956. No doubt alive to Betty's welcome, regular use of his diaries, the name 'Kay Tinniswood' appears conspicuously absent. (Frustrating for this researcher, if understandable at the time). But the liaison swiftly became Shoe Lane's and, later, Fleet Street's biggest open secret, remembered by many today. The relationship proving durable enough to threaten even Betty's stoic tolerance.

In early April, Ken looked over a prospective love-nest in Stephen Court, Talbot Square, W2, conveniently situated next to Paddington Station. On Monday 16th he moved in, making arrangements with a like-minded male colleague from *The Standard* to share the flat as cover. This allowed Ken to make no secret of the address in his diary, or face-to-face with Betty who'd naturally assumed the set-up was as it appeared.

On the 24th May, Ken and a *Standard* photographer flew to Paris for six days for a series of articles on the forms of jazz popular and flourishing across the Left Bank. Torch singers such as Charles Bechet and Edith Piaf were experiencing competition from younger, hungrier and more pretentious performers like Juliette Greco. Ken contrasted the two women, seeing Greco as representative of the new cynicism. For him, her message was "you too can have a depression like mine." Ken was told how "Piaf's fans like her to look hungry. Greco's like her to look disillusioned." He puts it down to a purely monetary motive: one new to him.

All the while Ken was making his own inquiries in a bid to return to television. Dan Farson, whom Ken was regularly drinking with for lunch or after work in Soho, had just been offered a reporting role on *This Week*: ITV's shamelessly obvious, six-month old challenge to *Panorama*. (Its initial take-off subtitle, 'a window on the world behind the headlines' had been grudgingly replaced by 'looks at the world of people and places in the news'). Tom Hopkinson – now at *The News Chronicle* – was also there advising on features as was Geoffrey Hughes, a director and a Fleet Street colleague of them both. Aware of Ken's continuing interest in television, Farson encouraged him to apply. A direct approach to Hopkinson may have seemed ideal, but Ken experienced a sudden attack of self-consciousness toward his former, idolised employer. Instead, with a list of programme ideas before him, he phoned Hughes from *The Standard*. To no avail: Dan's presence had marked the completion of the team.

The move to Fleet Street in October 1956 can be viewed, not as merely another, impatient change of scene, but a genuine promotion within his field. A.C. Wareham, Editor at *The Daily Mail*, had been headhunting him for the post of

Literary Editor; more than a new, highbrow term, Ken would effectively be running his own department. Early on he received a call from Rae Jeffs, the Publicity Manager at Hutchinson the publishers. It was her responsibility to wine and dine Fleet Street's literary editors as shameless insurance against negative reviews. New to the job herself, a bond was sealed on their first meeting. She met Ken at Euston Station, sharing a brief drink before he continued on to an interview. She was surprised at his appearance, in a black and white checked suit - reflecting the live jazz scene absorbed this past year – and a *Brylcreem* cowlick hanging by his right temple. The false leg wasn't obvious by his otherwise stiff gait. The topic still hadn't been raised when, on a subsequent evening, they visited The Gargoyle Club, for him to soak up some atmosphere for another job. With couples jiving around them, she'd been trying to drop an encouraging hint.

'We sat there all evening, drinking, and he wouldn't dance. I said, 'Why don't you have a go with me? I can fall with your help as well as without.' 'No, no,' he insisted. He was a very polished performer in every way and didn't want to make an exhibition of himself.' His clothes, at least, he had control over.

During December, Hutchinson sought out the rights to *Borstal Boy*. The memoir was currently being written by Brendan Behan; a new and already notorious Dublin-born playwright who, despite the intellectual plaudits layered upon the London opening of his first play, had just mumbled and sworn drunkenly through his first TV interview, to Malcolm Muggeridge, live on *Panorama*. They put Jeffs on to him. Despite her Home Counties, middle-class formalities, and his working-class abandon, the Dubliner, in a soberer mood next morning, warmed to Jeffs. From her Irish roots she was, at least, 'a Gael.' Acting as intermediary between him and Ken, she smoothed the way for a *Mail* 'exclusive.'

On 6th January 1957, Ken flew to Dublin for a three-day stay, ostensibly to review *The Hostage* – the new play - and interview the wayward, hard-drinking and belligerent son of the city responsible for both. In a way, the play was to Ireland's theatre what *Look Back In Anger* had been to England's eight months earlier. A direct, pro-Republican rebuke to Establishment mores, an English soldier is kidnapped and held at gunpoint in a Dublin lodge for the continued imprisonment of an IRA plotter sentenced to hang. Only the latter's release will ensure the same for the soldier. Radically for its time, the play's characters offer Brechtian asides to the audience. Also due to his influence are its songs; carousing numbers penned, among others, by Behan himself. Having already scored a hit with *The Quare Fellow* in 1954, the playwright was verging upon celebrity as the national dailies queued with sudden interest in the follow-up.

Ken's interest was more personal. Since Colin Wilson's novel offered a certain justification for his own *Outsider*-ish feelings, he now actively sought out figures living parallel, hobo-like lives.

'I don't argue the issues,' Behan told Ken after a large lunch. 'I mirror what happens to the people involved. This play is about the ordinariness of people – which is an extraordinary thing at such times... The only solution I suggest is for the people not to allow themselves to be fooled by the Establishments of any side...

Some people say they've got friends on both sides. I'm proud to have enemies on both sides.' For once, by this dishevelled, unshaven and uncompromisingly honest Irishman, Ken sits enraptured.

'He hose-pipes his conversation around him,' he notes, 'quenching opposition into silence.' They'd meet, professionally and personally, at least three more times over the next six years.

His next article featured another of his new *Outsider* discoveries, again through the efforts of Rae Jeffs. With gypsy-raven hair, eyebrows and cheekbones, twenty-six-year-old Rowena Farre was proving a literary mystery. His first review of *Seal Morning* – her debut 'novel' – was based upon the assumption that its fiction was autobiographically based. Not having yet met her, Ken concluded that she had fallen in with people of the road, had 'continued to lead a sharply individual life, enviably invulnerable to Jet Age conditions' and – according to a friend – had packed a rucksack and headed for Tibet.

'I think she is looking for something that she feels she may find there,' was the ambiguous advice. On the 19th February he asked, 'Where is Rowena Farre?' fired by intervening sales of 30,000 copies, serialization rights in both the UK and America, and an absent presence that may or may not have headed East. Neither Jeffs nor Raymond Anderson, a Hutchinson editor and her last witness, could track her down. The next day Ken declared he believed in her and that he didn't buy the idea that the book is a fake or the disappearance, a publicity stunt. Now Mrs. Rae Sebley, his former Hutchinson publicist recalled that heady month in 1957:

'One or two of the reporters got wind of some little thing she'd slipped up on, and they started looking into it. They rushed off to the Orkney Isles and other places, and one journalist actually got killed in a car crash... Ken was then dispatched to find out exactly what did happen. And, of course, we couldn't find her...(Later) somebody had written a review saying she was very homespun, made all her own clothes and things. And this incensed her! This brought her forward. She came marching into the publicity department, saying "I've never even made a pocket handkerchief!"... I arranged to meet her at The Savoy with the idea of tipping Ken off. She said, "Yes, alright."... She would meet me there for coffee at 11 o'clock. So, we (met as arranged). Ken turned up and I said, "Oh, fancy seeing you!" She realised she'd been tricked. He pinned her down. He said, "Now, tell me...I want to know about this." He was like a dog with a bone. She realised she was cornered, suddenly became hysterical and rushed out. We rushed after her to stop her but she'd disappeared. But Ken had got an awful lot of material, realising it was he who'd been hoodwinked. And the whole thing turned out to be a hoax...

She never forgave me, of course, for tricking her... She was schizoid, there's no doubt about that, because nobody could've behaved in that way. And I felt we'd both been wrong – Ken and myself – to actually pin her down, to get her in a corner. I thought she was going to throw herself over the Bridge. She really was beside herself...

It's interesting that she fell into the trap simply because somebody had said she'd made her own clothes! She then wrote another book that wasn't a success. It didn't do terribly well. Then I'd heard that she'd died. We did discover that her real name was Lois Parr. A most extraordinary woman... Had I realised then what I realise now - that she'd had a medical problem - I would never have tricked her like that. Later, Ken agreed with me that we shouldn't have done it. He felt he'd stressed her more than he should.'

The piece from their encounter appeared at the end of March. An example from their bizarre and vague conversation does little to counter what became her mythic status:

Ken: 'Naturalists say that, let alone teaching a common seal to play musical instruments, it is flatly impossible to rear one – they always die.'

Farre: 'I did it. I have never actually met anyone else who

has reared a seal, but I am sure it can be done. I've never been to a circus, but they train dolphins to do tricks, don't they?'

Ken: 'How long were you in Iceland?'

Farre: 'Three weeks.'

Ken: 'Wasn't that long enough to discover that there aren't any Eskimos in Iceland?' etc.

*

Over lunch with his deputy editor, Bill Hardcastle, Ken negotiated spending a long weekend with Williamson. The ruse was as a preliminary visit to arrange a profile on Henry as an exclusive to tie-in with his forthcoming release, *The Golden Virgin*, later this year. Richard Williamson, Henry's fourth son, was nineteen and on leave from the RAF, when he experienced, at first hand, Ken's restless energy as he accompanied him to the field at Ox's Cross.

'Fortunately,' Richard remembers four decades on, 'the roads in April 1957 were deserted compared to those of today, partly because petrol rationing following the '56 Suez Crisis was still in force.' At 6 pm, on Friday the 26th, he agreed to meet Ken in his office at *The Mail*. On arrival, Ken's secretary was instructed to show him a stack of articles, reviews and books on the Angry Young Man, the topic currently holding most of his attention, while he finished up. Richard was surprised by the concentrated wealth of research on show, smothered in scribbles and amendments.

'Though used to my father's chronic work appetite, this was all at an even more frenzied pace.' Richard recalls their waiting car as an open Three-Litre Ford Zephyr in scarlet and black. As they sped in the direction of the Digswell cottage for a night's stopover with Betty and the children, he felt the contrast between Ken's and his father's handling of the car. 'It was not treated with any sort of reverence or respect...it just had to go fast. That was what it was for.'

He also discovered that Andrew, Ken's eldest, was to be addressed under a new name. Now in his eleventh year, the boy had this new name down to start at the local Grammar School that autumn. Having been constantly teased by school chums for the alliterative variations inherent in 'Andy Allsop,' (not helped by the new BBC TV children's programme, *Andy Pandy*) the boy had haggled his parents for a change. A list was drawn up. With no swift, mutual decision imminent, it was Henry that settled the choice. Evenings away from The Hut often induced him to the gramophone to play, relentlessly, an adored soundtrack to Richard Wagner's *Tristan and Isolde* to whoever happened to visit. Lying on his back in the centre of the sitting room, he'd close his eyes and blissfully conduct while probing for anticipated praise. (Inevitably, Christine's and the family's own views on the recording were more openly expressed). So, 'Tristan' it was.

Ken awoke first on Saturday.

'Allsop was fussing about at dawn: on the telephone, scribbling notes, finally stuffing weekend gear into a hold-all.' Back in the Ford, they cruised at a reasonable pace until they reached the outskirts of the countryside when Ken suddenly put his foot down.

'Over Salisbury Plain we flew, the driver pointing out the skylarks which vanished behind in a split second. Around every bend on the wrong side of the road we swept, I being on the outside with the most information of what was surely to be a collision, at closing speeds of 90 miles per hour. At one point, Allsop shouted at a woman who walked across the road a hundred yards ahead, but I was used to that with father. Allsop remained otherwise calm and relaxed, pointing out that "that hedge always reminds me of an eyebrow."' The stay, according to Richard, was 'as relaxed a weekend as either of these two tetchy, impatient writers could have without the nagging guilt of time-wasting spoiling everything.'

Henry was more at peace than he'd been for some months. Ken laughed a lot as Henry embroidered past literary scenes over bottles of cheap Beaujolais. 'They spoke as close a language as father ever allowed with any of his friends when, as always, the schisms could quickly develop.' Henry was still essentially guarded with any mutual friends of the offending Negley. The trio spent Saturday afternoon on Exmoor. Between conversations, Ken wandered off alone to observe a buzzards nest in the nearby wood. Such short walks were all he could manage now, these snatched visits representing his only opportunities to bird-watch.

'There's a plate glass window between me and the natural world compared to youth,' he moaned at the time. To help fill the void, he'd begun a bird novel - *Rare Bird* – the first since *Adventure*, on which he updated Henry. Sunday was spent up on Baggy Point, probably at Ken's goading. The exertion exacerbated the nerves in his stump. Par for the course by now. Back at the house, Henry tightened the nagging knee-joint area with a length of hard twine.

Ken drove himself and Richard back to London that Monday morning. Richard claims he was already outlining the story of the bootleggers in prohibition-ridden Chicago on their return. A book he wouldn't begin writing for another eighteen months.

'He seemed quite unaware of any danger on the road... I was really glad I never had to travel with him again, especially in the two-seat E-Type, Jaguar XK, and Aston Martin he later owned. He had tremendous confidence on the open road but I for one preferred father's driving: and that's saying something!'

*

The BBC's light current-affairs *Tonight* programme had been broadcast from Studio M at St. Mary Abbott's Place in a modest Kensington cul-de-sac since Monday 18th February. Hardly ideal, but they were wedged between a rock and hard place for the anticipated three month trial. *Tonight*'s Producer had hoped for room at the regular accommodation of Lime Grove Studios. With the unfurnished Television Centre still three years from opening, making do would be the shape of things to come. Lime Grove consisted of a series of Victorian, red-brick terraced houses, themselves, too small and ill-equipped for the purposes of modern television production. Up to 1949, the site housed Gainsborough Film Studios; notable for producing star actors like Stewart Granger, and James Mason and Margaret Lockwood in brooding, noirish costume dramas such as *Fanny By Gaslight* and *The Wicked Lady*. Comedy vehicles and contemporary thrillers, like Hitchcock's *The 39 Steps* with Robert Donat, (a friend of Henry's), were also made there.

Lime Grove began broadcasting for much smaller screens the following year. Present there were two contrasting figures sharing the same goal: an inspirational Welsh Producer of twenty-six named Donald Baverstock, described in a B.F.I Dossier on the programme as gaining 'the reputation of...a blustering and rumbustious Celt. He was short and dark; with his broken, squashed nose...he might have been a rugby player. He nibbled his thumbnail when he was thinking, he thumped tables and he called everybody "boy"... He had shrewdness and a driving energy that unnerved a lot of his broadcasting contemporaries.' His ability to intimidate with the belief that anything was possible was infectious enough to make the barely adequate surroundings appear bearable to his staff. From the outset, he instilled a belief that somehow overcame the lack of facilities. His iconoclastic approach certainly divided opinion within the BBC as Derek Bond – a film reporter on the first night edition - recalls:

'(In 1957) I was working for the very popular, but staid, *Picture Parade* programme which was very <u>Establishment</u> BBC, and I almost became schizophrenic working for both programmes at the same time. The divisions within the Corporation can best be described by the following; I had been recording material for *Picture Parade* one evening and went into the Club at Lime Grove afterwards for a drink. As I was leaving, Donald grabbed my arm and said "Derek – not a good idea to be seen drinking with those old farts!"'

Bond regularly attended morning staff meetings where Baverstock – like a younger Lloyd George at a union meeting – would impress, "Remember boyos,' it's the *question* that does the damage!" 'This was a reference to the technique of putting a strong criticism followed by a soft question,' said Bond. 'A nervous and inexperienced interviewee would hasten to answer the easy question, leaving the smear of the criticism unchallenged.'

That attitude broke the hold of the gentlemen's club elite that had hardened after the war, witnessed, and sneered at, by Ken. At his side was a subdued, Scots-born, Oxford graduate in classics and modern languages with straight, oil-black hair and the bearing of an Air Force lieutenant, named Alasdair Milne. Each had arrived from *Highlight* – a ten-minute, early evening filler of light reports and interviews, the blueprint of which they'd brought with them to build on.

For now there was a half-articulated sense around that anything was possible. But the content of the first *Tonight* – while succeeding in its modest intention to inform and entertain without patronising – hardly appeared groundbreaking. The first in a five-nightly, forty-minute slot after 6 p.m., consisted of a light 'What the Papers Say' review - a soon-to-be regular topical calypso from Jamaican actor Cy Grant - (written by Bernard Levin) - Derek Bond on the 'offensive' statue of Aphrodite in Richmond Park - the diminutive Derek Hart interviewing American broadcaster Ed Murrow - and an 'impression of shops on Charing Cross Road' by a tall, beaky-nosed and curly-headed performer from the Cambridge Footlights Revue named Jonathan Miller. The headline from the following morning's *Daily Express* neatly set the tone of Fleet Street's intrigued support: 'BBC FIGHTS ITV FROM KENSINGTON CUL-DE-SAC.'

In the studio, the regular team comprised its tall, avuncular, bespectacled Presenter, Cliff Michelmore, the bow-tied Hart and the tall, blonde, leonine-featured Geoffrey Johnson-Smith. Baverstock recruited an array of individualists for the film reportage over the following weeks: Alan Whicker, the 'dapper, sprightly agency man from *Exchange Telegraph*,' was often witnessed, wrapped in an overcoat, cycling to Kensington. Tony Essex - who'd had a creative but inevitably edgy relationship with Baverstock prior to *Tonight* – was hired for the editing, alongside three former staffers from *Picture Post*: Mac Hastings, Fyfe Robertson and Ken's former flat mate, Trevor Philpott. An early sign that the trickle of staff departing the magazine might become a torrent, since Cynthia Judah and Gordon Watkins were already lieutenants in Baverstock's production team. Still searching for a television vehicle, Watkins advised an increasingly restless Ken to watch the show's progress.

By May, with the programme about to surpass its three-month trial, and space bestowed at Lime Grove, its paper equivalent in Shoe Lane was folding; a victim of *Tonight*'s success and its own coffin's inevitable nail. History records that – true to form - *Picture Post*'s staff only learned they'd be made redundant, *en masse*, when a message from Reuters tapped across the office tape-machine hours before. Sheer irony ensued when – possibly in place of a Hulton refusal - *Illustrated*'s current editor accepted an invitation from Baverstock to explain, live on-air, *Picture Post*'s demise. In the last issue, Sir Edward Hulton had signed off:

'I would be extremely insensitive if I did not feel strong emotion as I write this...Actually, by the very nature of the case, it is difficult to choose the right metaphors.' After reading this, Ken was later assured there were plenty flying around the magazine's office from which Hulton could have chosen. But the *Post*'s loss proved *Tonight*'s gain, its format seeming a natural haven for all its newly redundant employees to be welcomed by former colleagues already there.

On Sunday 5th January 1958, a new, occasional, afternoon book programme was broadcast from the ABC Studios to ITV's Midlands and northern regions only. *The Book Man* involved four or five authors presenting and then discussing, in turn, their latest publications with the 'Book Man' himself, Simon Kester; a tall, bony, bald and bespectacled figure with the demeanor of an Oxford don. As Literary Editor of the country's most popular paper, its director, Guy Verney, invited Ken to edit the programme. Verney related what he was aiming for:

'We hope to achieve the same result as a well-written review; that is, to give an idea of what the books are about, and whether the author has succeeded in his intention.' This greatly appealed to Ken's journalistic zeal as well as his vanity. It was also a logical progression to a man who lived by ulterior motives, with *The Angry Decade* pencilled in for a May release. Inviting Verney for drinks at The French Pub, the director found himself charmed by Ken into featuring his companion with his own new release on the very next edition. It was Colin Wilson.

Christopher Lucas was darkly handsome, Spanish-born, and employed as *The Mail*'s New York Correspondent. Like Ken, he harboured a penchant for jazz. In early April he suggested Ken visit himself and his wife, Jean, at their apartment there, for a tour of the city's clubs while on his own assignment for the paper. He couldn't wait. Ken had been a full-time journalist for seven years now, but had yet to engineer a convincing enough excuse to work in the country that, since childhood, held him in such awe. One was all he needed, having managed to negotiate a week for the paper and one for a contact-making holiday to run concurrently. On the premise of delivering three uninspiring interviews for *The Mail*, he set to maximizing publicity for *The Angry Decade*'s American release. 'Beat' was a slang term referring to the methodically rhythmic delivery of the pot-smokers, angst-ridden street poetry then gaining public credence.

Stepping down from the plane on the morning of the 9th, his diary records the fascination of an Anglo-Saxon in Ancient Rome. On arrival at his room in the Taft Hotel, he marvels at its 'air-conditioning, central heating . . . water on tap, TV, radio, shower.' He interviews Beat poet, Jack Kerouac, for the British release of *On the Road*. With a group of city socialites, he accompanies Kerouac to The Bowery district and 'The Fine Spot' where Donald Byrd is playing with the Peter Adams Quintet. Over the next few weeks with the Lucas's, he sees Buddy Greco swing for singer Marion McPortland at The Embers Club, the new theatre of social commentary – the musical *West Side Story* and the play, *Jamaica* – Coleman Hawkins at the Metropole, and the Stan Getz Quartet at the Village Vanguard. After hearing a reading from Kerouac's contemporary Kenneth Rexroth back at The Fine Spot, Ken travels via San Francisco to Los Angeles. Here he spends a day at Fox Film Studios and a day at Warner's meeting a host of contract-players from each. On through New Orleans for sightseeing, on the 26th he is back in New York, staying with the Lucas's after arranging the return home flight.

Late afternoon on the $30^{th,}$ he arrives at the playwright

Arthur Miller's East 57th Street apartment to keep a 4:30 appointment for *Encounter*. He is instantly hit by the contrasting display of the intellectual with the sensual. Marilyn Munroe – Mrs. Miller - enters 'like a twirl of spun sugar in matador pants and fisherman's jersey,' to mix the drinks, curl up on the sofa to discuss Russia for a few minutes, and swiftly leave the remaining 'isolated pocket of workmanlike maleness.' The star-struck Brit finds Miller pragmatically jaded with his society. 'Before the Second World War millions of people lived beyond their means – but they felt guilty about it. Now it has become normal and accepted to live on credit. Hedonism has dulled our sense of social responsibility... America was always in a state of becoming. Now we've got there and we are uncertain whether it was the right destination.'

On the 2nd May, after Ken and Lucas exchange a selection of jazz records from their personal collections, the former styles himself a New Yorker, buying a suit that would become his trademark look back home. After taking in Mort Sahl's new satirical discursion, *The Future Lies Ahead*, they go on to a production of Miller's *Crucible* and more gigs at Cafe Bohemia, including Ken's first live encounter of Miles Davis.

Jetting back to London on Monday 5th May, Ken ambled down the steps of the plane, high on, and profoundly influenced by, what he'd witnessed the previous month. Comparing Ken's diary entries with his published articles, it is hard to know how much was work and how much play. The encounters with Kerouac and Rexroth represented the sum total of his 'Beat' research, while the party tours drew out evenings committed to publicity.

The following week Huw Wheldon responded to the American copy of *The Angry Decade* Ken sent him from New York. He couldn't see a window for a feature in his new BBC arts series, *Monitor*, as he'd just covered the Angry Young Man phenomenon while Ken was away. Yet, so taken was he by the quality of the prose that he confessed a reluctance to dropping the matter entirely.

'The thing goes on haunting me and, if anything occurs, I will get in touch with you.' The book was causing a stir elsewhere within the BBC. The day before its British release he finally received an invitation to Lime Grove to guest on *Tonight*. Geoffrey Johnson-Smith grilled him on his impressions of America, the interview with Jack Kerouac, and any parallels he saw in their Beat Poets with the England's so-called Angry Young Men as portrayed in the book. With no chance of a repeat, Ken was fortunate that Kenneth Adam – the Controller of Programmes – had witnessed that evening's edition and been impressed by the performance. He memoed the Head of TV Talks the next day: 'I had not seen him on television before. He is a distinct find, easy to look at, relaxed in manner and talks fluently and well.' When Baverstock informed him of the response, Ken upped-the-anti. With typical bloody-mindedness he dug his heals in and refused to let go. While there may be work for him, Baverstock advised caution. With no permanent position on the team available, he'd have to wait his chance. Johnson-Smith – his interviewer – was suggesting he might not renew his current contract.

By the end of August, Wheldon stood true to his promise and contacted Ken on the verge of *Monitor*'s second series. The result of their meeting survives in the BBC Archives. Dated the 14th September, Wheldon introduces Ken's interview with Leonide Massine: the straight-backed, Teutonic choreographer of ballet and ex-student of Diaghilev. What Ken knew of the form was based upon only two sleep-interrupted visits made with Betty during the previous five years. Here, he sits dark-suited but, wearing beneath, a blue-striped, American shirt and skinny tie: a New York influence and a look he'd foster over the next two years. He is calm, polite and conversational and, perhaps, slightly nervous. He sits back for most of the ten minutes, alternating folded arms with fingers clasping around the good left knee. A total contrast to Massine, who is lean, formally erect, vocally vociferous and protective. (Particularly when Ken voices doubt over Massine's claim that he has founded a new, accessible form of teaching, intimating how – on demonstration - it looked just like the old).

From Friday 19th September, Ken took one whole week off from all journalistic duties. There was now no ulterior motive to sideline him from the amount of sheer physical graft needed to transform what he'd unilaterally settled on as the new family home. Betty subsequently involved herself in the acquisition of a property in the rural region of Holwell, near Hitchin in Hertfordshire. Semi-regular summer visits to the farmhouse and land surrounding it had fostered new friendships; in this case with the Benensons and Tennysons – 'Gurneys' joint-residents. Owning the adjoining land were the Muckle brothers.
'Their reputation locally was of ferocious cussedness and fathomless wile,' wrote Ken in a personal note: 'The Muckles father, a local butcher, acquired the farm in the agricultural depression before the First World War, and he lived there with his two sons and daughter (none of whom married) until the 1920s.' They were never good farmers. A combination of a reluctance to spend money and an inability to make it, caused the property to slither from neglect into decrepitude. After a few years they moved to a village three miles away and sold off the house and adjacent buildings, standing in half an acre of land, retaining a right of way from the cart trail that bisected the back garden, a Polish corridor, later to be the cause of bitter dispute, through to their meadows and buildings. The sale was the apparently simple act at the end of a secret theory of cunning complexity. The

house was falling to bits, without electricity or piped water, and in urgent need of costly maintenance work. Their belief was, as one of them told me towards the end of his life, that they would gain some capital, that the purchaser would put it in sound shape, that property values would fall and that in five years they would be able to buy it back, rejuvenated, at a depressed price. Part of their theory worked. It was bought by a rich banking family (the Tennysons') who did all the structural repairs, installed central heating, put in electricity, plumbing and damp course, tore down partitions and walls to restore the great drawing room to its original size, crossed by the massive 50 feet central beam...' But the family's subsequent resale meant the mercenary Muckles' died before being able to buy back the property and make the intended killing.

On discovering the property, Ken immediately harboured dreams of renovation of his own. By 1958, Hallam Tennyson – a descendant of the Victorian poet – was due to fulfill a long-term commitment in London, leaving vacant his family's half of Gurneys. The Benensons' were also preparing to move back to the City, though keeping its converted barn, in their name, as a base from which the politically inspired Peter could fight for a prospective Labour candidacy in the forthcoming autumn General Election. The arrangement was that should Peter win the seat then the barn would be kept. If lost, ownership would revert to the Allsops'. Ken could not wait a year to stamp his own preferences upon the land. Dubiously, at the age of thirty-eight, he considered himself rich enough to start modernising the property throughout. Tristan and Fabian – now twelve and eight respectively – needed little encouragement to join in with the clear-up operation and planting of shrubs and trees. Benenson's wife, Margaret, recalls that,

'when the farmers, who had originally lived in the house,

died, Ken was able to buy extra land, and demolish the wall between the front garden and pig sties, giving a wonderful view. They also changed the front garden and cleared the pond...' As if enough hadn't been spent in purchasing the property, the gardens – to Ken – lacked a public show of expense he'd soon have to display.

By Christmas 1958, *The Book Man* was no longer regional but transmitted across Britain. What better time, then, to conceive of a programme to provoke with a jolt the cosy, early Sunday afternoon complacency of the casual viewer. Brendan Behan's autobiography was due for release. With Rae Jeffs, Ken devised an invitation. Jeffs herself relates what followed:
'(Brendan Behan) had been booked for television interviews with Dan Farson on *This Week* and Kenneth Allsop on *The Book Man* while *Tonight* had also expressed an interest in him... We were due at the studio almost at once so we grabbed a taxi and instructed the driver to take us to the ABC Television Theatre at Aston on the outskirts of the city. As soon as the rehearsals began, Brendan began to show the strain he was feeling. Red-faced and tousle-headed, he muttered to himself, argued with the producer, abused Ken Allsop, and dismissed the list of questions Ken had prepared as utter rubbish, and each coherent sentence he spoke contained at least one obscene word... The programme was being transmitted 'live' and a repeat performance of the Malcolm Muggeridge interview seemed an odds-on certainty.* Nor were Brendan's opening remarks on-the-air likely to give encouragement that it would be otherwise. "I'll start talking," he thundered, "when I know which camera I'm supposed to be looking at." It was Ken's unruffled, but assertive, reply, "Forget the cameras; just look at me," that produced a remarkable change in Brendan, and sitting straight up in his chair, he proceeded to give ten

minutes of first-class entertainment to confound and relieve the studio audience. He appeared to be completely sober, and after making one or two unfavourable comments about the British, he settled down to talk seriously and sensibly about *Borstal Boy* and Borstal institutions. He concluded the interview with a selection of songs from *The Hostage* to be faded out singing, 'Don't muck abaht with the moon'...'

*Behan allegedly returned 'foul-mouthed' responses to questions from the staunchly Christian Muggeridge on the BBC in December 1958.

Still intent on using the Mondays' he was meant to keep free, from the 23rd February 1959, he began recording for a current affairs programme for ITV's own 'northern region' studios at Granada Television in Manchester. As a sop to Betty to snatch what rest he could, he took the return overnight sleeper train from Paddington. With the early scripts written by freelancers (boasting the former Labour MP J.P.W. Mallalieu among their number) Ken's own experience soon encroached. From *Searchlight*'s debut at 10:30 p.m. on Monday 13th April, the programme took less than six months to go from being a team effort of youngish, hungry hopefuls to a vehicle for Ken alone. So, as well as presenting the programme, he was conceiving each subject to feature in the fortnightly editions while writing all the scripts.

The first, 'Children in Fear,' – *not* written by Ken – was on the then, highly controversial subject of parental child beating; something which, despite a notoriously sharp temper, he never indulged in with his own. Subsequent editions betrayed his ideological fingerprints. Typically close to his heart was the current state of the city, hospitals, and the railways: each topic reported on and each connected by the course of environmental social policy and where it might be heading. Its future preyed, increasingly, on his mind.

The Christmas '59 edition touched on the ambivalent

relationship with his late mother. That weeks *TV Times* asked 'How well looked after are the aged members of the family? How many of them are lonely because their families have forgotten them? Tonight's *Searchlight* turns its beam on... 'The Lonely."

By Easter this year, Ken's expensive finishing touches to 'Gurneys' gardens were being installed. Joining the pairs of geese and peafowl already keeping Betty and the children awake at nights with their screeching calls, were two pairs of fan-tails 'imprisoned in the dovecote until they have integrated.' Fabian showed most enthusiasm for his father's latest 'pets,' looking as if he might grow to share it. A recent fall while attending one of his birds had wrenched a tendon and put the Allsops' youngest in hospital for two weeks. With only a hand plaster to show for his exertions, the boy was back in the barn loft, feeding and watering the new acquisitions. But if there were hopes from the others that Ken's menagerie was complete, he had other ideas.

In September, the Benensons laid plans for Peter's campaign to be the prospective Labour MP for Hitchin in the forthcoming General Election. Ken offered what limited public support he could, leaving the inevitable administration to the women. But his ambivalence to Labour itself continued intact from the previous three elections. Betty, meanwhile, remained a party animal, embarking on daily rounds of door-to-door canvassing with Margaret. At one glance of their red rosettes, the majority slammed them in their faces: by now, an occupational hazard for Betty, to which she had hardened herself.

She made it her business to lobby for backing by the few left-wingers remaining in the village. The Nottingham-born author, Alan Sillitoe, still riding the crest of a public wave for *The Loneliness of the Long Distance Runner*, (due to be filmed by Tony Richardson) lived close by at a white-walled cottage in Whitwell, with his fiancee, the poet Ruth Fainlight. From this initial meeting, Sillitoe made further contacts on their behalf and a larger, mixed contingent arrived, including the artist, Terry Hajula. The cottage soon felt like the sole hub of dissent in an otherwise Government-supporting stronghold. A *frisson* of excitement swelled in the tranquil surroundings. Sillitoe was called on to give a more public speech in support of Benenson. But, while caught up in the private enthusiasm of the others, he blinked:

'Though our house was plastered with Labour posters, my heart wasn't in it because Labour used the Suez campaign as something with which to berate the Conservatives.' His newfound success may also have loosened his working class ties. It represented a more general lack of focus. Much later, he recalled the speech he gave as 'an embarrassing peroration that went on far too long.' A final burst of publicity was called for. On Polling Day in October, Ken appeared in his Jaguar, leading a slow procession of horn-beeping vehicles through the village bearing *VOTE BENENSON* placards. This may have swung a few amused undecided villagers in their favour. But the previous lack of focus sealed the candidate's fate. Benenson lost to the sitting Conservative by just a handful of votes.

Ken turned forty with great reluctance. The former concern for his image sharply increased after watching the playbacks of interviews recorded by the BBC's new, recently purchased, videotape machines. One way he dealt with what he perceived a threat to his good looks was to lose weight. The stone or two he'd put on after the lean years prior to *Picture Post* was ebbing away, through a reduction in snacks aided, less controllably, by the TB ever present in his blood. The effect of the latter now afforded him a burnished, slightly wasted complexion, maturing but not spoiling his good looks. In tune with the new decade, he also radically restyled his hair. Replacing the thick, hair-creamed side-parting and drooping cowlick was an American-style long crop, brushed across the top and forward at the sides revealing, at either temple, a baby wisp of silver. Complemented by the mauve-striped shirts, dark, skinny ties and narrow-lapel suits discovered in Chicago in the spring of '58, the new dress code was economically sharp, smart and cosmopolitan. No British journalist had ever dressed like this. But increasing with his vanity was the almost disgusted tone of a staid reactionary.

The literary voice of British jazz suddenly found himself manhandled to the sidelines by a new, proactive audience. He couldn't handle it. Two of his *Daily Mail* pieces, the first from July, the second from September, reveal how swiftly he was acting his age. (And pandering to the lower-middle class of his readership). During the last weekend in July, Lord Montagu put on the Beaulieu Jazz Festival in the grounds of his home in the New Forest. Attending were 'barefoot beatniks, leather-jacketed tearaways, boys in Castro beards and tropical khaki, girl art students with hair as long as their pullovers.' There is a sneer in his description of those now regularly in attendance at such festivals, but his severest tone is saved for those teenage 'ravers' who pulled down the bandstand after climbing upon it, en masse, for a better view of the performers they'd come to see. While the effects of excess alcohol in a humid climate may have influenced their disruptive action, Ken proceeds to sound-off about 'the frightening scenes of venom and violence I saw explode...in that tranquil New Forest village,' as though physical violence ensued. None is mentioned, only that against property, including the light stands for the BBC cameras transmitting the event, cutting it before its ending. Ken is rightly angry, but the voice of this anger has become both disproportionate and disconnected:

'Whacky dress and wild fun do not, necessarily, spell

delinquency. Yet, for a certain product of our Affluent Society this seems to have become a rebel's uniform of viciousness – and the degree is fine between beating up a jazz festival and beating up negroes in Notting Hill and Jews in Germany.'

In contrast, eight weeks later, Ken reviewed Miles Davis's first night of his British tour. He finds his coolness 'too cool' to sideline in his piece. Well aware of his 'boorishness...rooted in the race stigma of being a negro in America,' Ken highlights what he sees as the contempt with which Davis treats his audience: turning his back on finishing a number and playing the next through their applause.

On reading this, Kenneth Tynan – a devout disciple - wrote an open letter to the 'Mailbag' section, printed two days later. He accused Ken of devoting '12 paragraphs to complaining about Mr. Davis's platform demeanour and only one to the music itself.' Personally, he was 'delighted he let us concentrate on the music,' ending, 'would Mr. Allsop upbraid the members of a string quartet for failing to joke with the audience or introduce their numbers?' Beneath this, Ken replied that far from *missing* the usual stage antics expected from other performers, he felt *relieved* at their exclusion, adding with characteristic earnestness that, 'an audience might reasonably expect civility and good manners from a public entertainer. Even string quartet members manage to bend their stiff shirtfronts into a final bow.'

Such a misunderstanding highlights the main difference between Ken and his America-admiring, jazz-digging namesake. Where the left-liberal Tynan was awed by Davis's aloofness and ambiguity – welcoming the covert display of egotism – the more traditionally libertarian Allsop sees the display as simply 'ill-mannered' and as such best excluded. Two years later, in America's *Playboy*, Davis recalled and railed against this argument. 'Some critic that didn't have nothing else to do started this crap about how I don't announce numbers, I don't look at the audience, I don't bow or talk to people, I walk off the stage and all that... *I ain't no entertainer, and ain't trying to be one. I am one thing: a musician.* Most of what's said about me is lies in the first place. Everything I do, I got a reason.' Over the next twelve years, the press would regularly refer to Ken as 'the television personality'; a term he'd grow to loathe. But, in refuting it, he'd use precisely the same argument.

October 1960: a new man joins 'Tonight.' (BBC)

17
Sept 1960 – Oct 1964: 'Tonight'

On the day Tynan posted his rebuttal of the Miles Davis review to *The Daily Mail*, Ken was at Lime Grove keeping an appointment with Donald Baverstock. Accompanying the Welshman was the BBC's Assistant Head of Programme Contracts, F. L. Hetley. Ken had been lobbying Baverstock for regular work on *Tonight* for the past two and a half years, but only now were its makers in a position to discuss terms. He may not have been flattered by the real reason for their capitulation: that they were desperate. But, thanks to his friendship with, and encouragement from, Gordon Watkins, he'd already been tipped off.

The reliable Geoffrey Johnson-Smith had been gone a year since his election to Parliament as a Tory MP and the team still hadn't settled on a permanent replacement which, by now, they badly needed. Alasdair Milne recalled that,

'Cliff and Derek Hart had to cope with what was, quite often, a chaotic and uncertain studio situation. Cynthia and Gordon both pushed Donald and me quite hard to get him.'

Thanks to Watkins, Ken was also aware of this, lending him knowledge to his advantage but not the BBC's. This put him in a position to drive a hard bargain. He told them he could commit from Tuesday to Friday each week, but needed Mondays' to complete his regular *Mail* columns. They agreed to this. He then cornered them into pursuing a minimum guaranteed salary of £3,500: five hundred more than the going rate. Baverstock accepted on principle but Hetley shot him a doubtful look on departing. On the positive side, the result of their discussions produced a deal of 168 studio appearances and 15 filmed stories over Ken's first contractual year. Baverstock braced himself and memoed the Assistant Head of Television with the bid for the extra £500:

'If approval for this contract could be obtained fairly quickly, there is a chance that we may be able to start using his services early next week.' The Board took a predictably dim view, fearing acceptance would set a precedent among the other broadcasters.

But Ken had already made his first regular appearance - on the 4th October, interviewing Brigadier General Herbert Vogel, on the aims and achievements of the Tennesse Valley Authority and his role as Chairman. Grace Wyndham Goldie agreed to persuade the Controller, by memo, three days later:

'(The Editor) can manage this on his existing budget. I am sure a contributor of this experience would be extremely valuable to *Tonight*. I understand...that you would have to give formal approval to a contract of this kind, since it is over £3,000. I very much hope that you will find this possible.' Ken knew that with the formidable Wyndham Goldie on their side, he'd got them. With smug self-assurance he scrawled underneath, 'Very good idea, KA / 10/10.' But the Corporation noted this successful regulatory challenge and vowed not to be swayed again. Since he felt it his duty to the family to maintain his cost of living and, for himself, increase his personal status, neither would Ken. Inevitably, this proved to be the first of several such confrontations.

On reflection, Ken's demands weren't arrogantly based. At least, not in substance. None of the studio interviewers, from Cliff Michelmore down, had significant experience in print journalism. Former *Picture Post* colleagues such as Trevor Philpott, Mac Hastings and Fyfe Robertson had but, on

Tonight, specialised solely in filmed outside broadcasts. Also the case was Ken's previous TV experience: not vast, but at least on a par with Michelmore's.

Relations between the two men were quickly established; established as tolerant, but no more. As studio colleagues, they formed and maintained a credible partnership, but friendship would never be on the cards. Ken was considered too full of himself and remotely intellectual for the avuncular, practical front-man. There may also have been a petty, mutual jealousy. Although Ken decried the shallow, fatuous nature of celebrity, Michelmore's high profile within the BBC and popularity without was a mystery to him. He considered Cliff's comparative work rate as presenter and link-man a sinecure of a post that hardly justified his status. On Michelmore's side, the new team member posed a demanding, rung-ascending threat he'd never felt from his long-standing studio partner, Derek Hart. But their mutual professionalism was noted by each and bonded them in the studio.

Less accepting of the new appointment was Fyfe Robertson. Since leaving *Picture Post*, Ken's relentless cheating on Betty – compounded by his current affair with 'Kay Tinniswood' – had become a major *cause celebre*. The aging Robertson, disgusted by his behaviour, vowed he'd never work with Ken again. Fortunately for him, *Tonight*'s production itinerary ensured he'd never have to.

In October 1960, the plush White City studios of Television Centre had been open three months. But a transfer there for the *Tonight* team was not on the cards. Resigned to the makeshift surroundings, Ken encountered, at first hand, Studio H: the smallest of four in the building. (D, E and G the others). Directing proceedings on the floor at this time was Kenneth Corden, who remembers the haphazard set-up:

'It was reached by lift or staircase from reception to the first floor. The office accommodation was something else. So limited was it that the *Tonight* team had to be squeezed into neighbouring, semi-detached houses that the BBC had acquired and adapted. Without much sensible planning, those whose job it was created an incredibly difficult first-floor access, via narrow corridors over the scenery entrance. Along these corridors, which snaked up and down through the different houses, passed producers, film crews, artists, presenters, secretaries loaded with scripts...and maintenance staff. Okay if you were fit – but Ken with his one leg had a hard time of it. He would stumble, carefully, down the last flight of stairs to arrive, often breathless, in Donald Baverstock's or Alasdair Milne's office, not complaining but with a wry smile that indicated things could be better. Sometimes he would be greeted with the cry "Hello boyo! Your item's with..." X or Y in another office on another floor. This is what he really hated. With great dignity, he would scramble, with books and half-written scripts, up and down the loathed corridors to other offices.

On occasions it was to visit me in my office, which just happened to be in one of a collection of caravans parked in the old back garden area of the semis.' I remember one wintry day, with howling wind and rain, when he beat on the door with his stick. "Why don't you move into one of these old semis'? The stairs may be steep but I need a forklift truck to get into your fucking caravan!" Later, an office was arranged especially for journalist/presenters to write and discuss their scripts, much to Ken's relief.'

In a written retrospective on the programme, Deirdre Macdonald suggested that the team's ability to compensate for the lack of facilities may have been a contributing factor in its success. 'They did whatever they felt they had to do and counted the cost afterwards. They worked at fever pitch for, literally, years. There was gloom, despair, exhaustion, exhilaration, stress, euphoria, pressure and triumph. They were an arrogant bunch, believing that what they were doing was the only worthwhile job in television...that they were set apart from their colleagues.' With Cynthia Judah unmarried but engaged (to Robert Kee - quietly brilliant at *Panorama*) and Liz Cowley wed but career-minded, this suited the mainly male team. The home-making wives invariably suffered. When Gordon Watkins effused upon his time here his wife, June, shot back that this only showed he'd had no idea how difficult it was at home.

To me, she drily added that,

'by the nature...and intensity of their work on this daily programme, one did not see much of one's own husband, nor of anybody else's.'

Once again, Betty found herself resigned to the inevitable.

Liz Cowley had joined the programme in March 1958 – first as a reporter, then film director. A Canadian-born, former reporter for *Reveille*, Cowley was sharp, dry-witted and brash. She was also a voluptuous brunette with a barefaced sexual bluntness, magnified before the stuffy, buttoned down, English, Fleet Street hacks. By October 1960, she'd transferred to lobbying for interviews with the famous, infamous or just plain interesting in the arts. When Ken joined they were teamed to share responsibilities researching and finalising the on-screen questions. If Ken was anticipating another conquest then he found himself second-guessed. According to Cowley:

'The game of sexual dominoes I was...prone to play with my *Tonight* godlings – dominoes in the sense that I leaned and others (but not all others) collapsed – was, of course, tried in the early days with Ken. The diary rather petulantly records his response: 'Me: "How far do you see me as your type?" Ken: "Do you really think that is a proper question?" So, and I'm glad of it, any sexual side to the relationship was firmly *acidised* before it could start.' (Can he be pictured with a slightly embarrassed half-smile, looking down at his shoes?) He was, anyway, too embroiled with 'Kay Tinniswood' to contemplate a second affair.

The two earliest surviving examples of Ken on *Tonight* reveal the contrasts within the programme that made it so popular with viewers. The first is a personally directed send-up. He is presented as one of 'The Michelmore Sisters,' jigging in line ahead of Cliff and Derek Hart, each dressed in matching striped blazer and straw boater and miming to The Andrews Sisters number, *Hold Tight, Hold Tight*. Just eight weeks on from his first regular appearance, he looks self-consciously stiff, the eyebrows' earnestly arched. The second is an interview with George Bernard Shaw's friend and biographer, Hesketh Pearson. (Ken knew of Pearson from his biography on Shakespeare, read in hospital during the war).

Ken can be seen to have perfected his technique. The diction is clipped but insinuating. He leans forward, challenging, the steady hunter's gaze on his subject that Henry first noticed in him as a fifteen-year-old. His questioning is faster-paced than of his earlier effort on *Monitor*, lending a breathless urgency of the type actively encouraged by Baverstock. He is also noticeably slimmer than before, with his hair in the new shorter style. Pearson is a wry-eyed, avuncular old pro, clearly putting on a performance for the cameras, and one a quietly amused Ken is clearly restraining himself from succumbing to. His subject is particularly good on a postcard correspondence, maintained with Shaw after a note Pearson had written and forgotten for a production of *Heartbreak House*, that consisted, solely, of one - two word exclamations:

(Shaw) 'Why?'

(Pearson) 'What?'

'The note!'

'Oh, that!'

'Yes!'

'God knows!'

'He doesn't!'

At the interview's end, there is a pause and Pearson, thinking himself off-camera, leans toward Ken and asks, 'That fill it up alright?'

After each interview, Ken would amble over to Cowley, clutching his post-programme notes, intent on a post-mortem. He sounded highly critical of chances barely explored or missed completely, taking as much of the blame as accusing. His short-temper, notorious to Betty and his closest friends, came to the fore, his flattened nerve-ending flaring to make him 'tetchy and difficult' for the rest of the night. Readied for work next morning, the old charm resurfaced.

Whatever his apparent feelings, his public and private views of himself were drifting, increasingly, further apart. All the while, the unending, nerve-numbing pain in his right leg stump compelled him to face, constantly, his own mortality. But, right now, he was enjoying the fruits of his labours and needed no grounding. At least, not that he was aware.

In January 1961, the actor and author Peter Ustinov was invited to Lime Grove, ostensibly to talk about his new film, *The Sundowners*. He arrived almost in disguise, sporting spectacles and a Slavic beard. Ken was assigned to the interview. During the conversation, Ustinov reduced most of the BBC staff and crew to audible hysterics with his well-observed, satirical impersonations of recognisably bureaucratic types. In Ken, he found someone – rare in a journalist – of a similar intellectual capacity. But with the usual limit on time, Ustinov's report - on his attempts at making his fictitious country of Concordia recognised by the U.N. - had to be curtailed.

Recognising the additional mileage to be had from him, he was invited back in March during the publicity tour for *The Loser* – his first novel - on a promise of supper (presumably in addition to the fee) in exchange for a more in-depth update on his travels. This would be televised as a late-night conversation between himself, Michelmore, Derek Hart and Ken. On the night, Ken initially appeared quite relaxed, until he produced a personally engraved lighter that consistently clicked open at the end of a new cigarette at ten-minute intervals. In under the scheduled hour, five were to be found stubbed out on the set's ashtray.

In May, the young comedy team that had taken the previous year's Edinburgh Festival Fringe by storm and were due to perform their set at London's Fortune Theatre, appeared on the programme. Of the team of Peter Cook, Dudley Moore and former *Tonight* mimic Jonathan Miller, it was the unassuming, bookish, bespectacled figure of Leeds-born Alan Bennett who caused the furore. The sketch, 'Aftermyth of War,' featured Bennett, in character, ambling around the set with a stiffened leg and speaking in a clipped, military brogue. The astonished gasps from the studio crew were lost on the performer, whose satirising of Douglas Bader had previously gone down well. It was only after the interview that he was taken aside and informed that his questioner suffered the same disability as his target. Years later, Bennett offered me a reflection:

'I hadn't noticed that Allsop walked with a stiff leg and so didn't know, when he was interviewing me, about his disability. If this wasn't made plain, I'm sure my colleagues gleefully advised me of what was, in almost a literal sense, a *faux pas*. Had I known at the time, I'd perhaps have been less embarrassed, though age and experience has taught me that, generally, the person least offended is, in any case, the one who occasions the embarrassment.' Ken's own response remains lost with the broadcast though, twelve months later, they were invited back for a reprise.

With the promise of a second year *Tonight* contract to add to that ongoing with *The Mail*, Ken could afford to spend more weekends at home. Further compensation was due: mainly to his children who'd endured years of him having to absent himself in search of the next fee. Amanda, then thirteen, believed he felt 'very keenly' his exclusion, making his return to the fold all the harder for one who'd never found intimacy easy in the first place. Along with the physical bar to play, she feels his mother would have insisted upon restraining any show of affection of his own. The physical bar to play distanced him still further.

'Added to that was his inwardly directed – perhaps self-absorbed – mind, and the two working together caused his basic difficulties in communicating, especially with small children, who obviously hadn't learnt to converse intellectually, nor to follow accepted codes and rules of superficial social conversation.' His way of handling it was, quite literally, to resort to type.

For the past two years he'd gradually acquired research material on the Chicago of the 1920s' and the gangland involvement in prohibition. A valiant if misguided attempt to divide his attentions between this and his family sorely tested his easily snapping nerves. He still could not comprehend why the self-discipline he adhered to in his studies would not transfer to domestic life. Betty had seen it all before, of course, but his three children, now grown-up, were no less victims. Feeling guilt from the previous night, on the morning of the 6th May, he left a note for his daughter:

'My dear Mandy,

I'm so sorry I upset you at our midnight tea. I think the reason was that, after sweating at the book for about 8 hours, I was as tired as you were and edgy and sore-headed. But I didn't want to get at you. Please accept my apology – and also...my thanks for all the work in the garden today... I hope you feel revived and refilled with energy tomorrow.

Your always loving (but too often rude and irritable)

Daddy.'

In August, Ken received an inquiring letter from his old R.A.F. colleague, George Hilton, whom he hadn't seen for some seven years, since his time at *Picture Post*. In his reply of the 24th, Ken responds positively to Hilton's expressed interest in T.E.Lawrence, mentioning that he'd visited the grave while staying with David and Jean Malbert in Kimmeridge, Dorset the previous year. He offers his views on the man:

'Have you read Williamson's Genius of Friendship, his very moving account of his rather strange relationship with TE? Actually, I've never much admired Lawrence's writings – too much self-conscious 'greatness' in his prose, and *The Mint* seems to me a very contrived piece of artificiality, but nevertheless he was a fascinating person. I think the Rattigan play is a very superficial and shallow piece of observation on him.' He recalls their time, before his hospitalisation:

'It's odd how those now very distant years of ghastliness in the R.A.F. still remain very vivid in one's memory – I suppose etched deep by the frustration and loathsomeness of them. I now have contact with no one except yourself.'

He recalls, just once, bumping into Bourchier and,

inevitably, Joe Molloy:

'Do you remember him? A rather lugubrious man with a permanently anxious expression, but whom I seemed destined to be with all my R.A.F. days, from induction at Uxbridge (Christ, it brings upon me a wave of nausea just to write those words) onward.'

Ken talks of the 'crazed impossibility' in getting *Tonight* on the air, right up to transmission, and that, though 'gruelling,' is a 'quite exciting operation.' So, meeting in town now would be even harder than before. Instead, he invites Hilton to 'Gurneys,' as,

'my routine is in *The Mail* in the mornings, a snatched drink and sausage in a pub, down to the BBC for film-viewing at 2 pm, and there until one reels out of the place at about 8 pm.'

Ken emphasises his desire to return to more domesticated living, but sounds less than convinced of its attainment:

'Life hurtles on too hectically, really, for comfort. One's rather pathetic urges are still toward living a sane, settled life and quietly writing books, but somehow the rat race seems inescapable. As a kind of compensation to myself, I still spend most weekends book-writing, the latest result of which is *The Bootleggers*, ...published here (it came out in America last week) on October 2$^{nd.}$ (It is) a kind of social history of the Prohibition gang era in Chicago, a time and place that have always fascinated me...'

That day Ken attended the Hutchinson launch party for *The Bootleggers* at 'Foyles' bookshop in Charing Cross Road. On a high of anticipation, he'd somehow succeeded in featuring his own book for that evening's programme: the relative indifference to previous publishing days now banished to the experience of semi-obscurity. Bristling with the attention, he handed round persuasive drams of his favourite scotch to waiting, fellow critics.

Under Rae Jeffs supervision was a turnout of the London

literati that also featured two of Ken's new American admirers, deep in an increasingly animated conversation: the beat poet, Gregory Corso, and author and critic, Norman Mailer. As their voices rose, Corso took offence to a typically machine-gun peppered aside by the writer of *The Naked and the Dead* and suddenly let loose a left hook. A rugby-scrum clinch followed with Mailer's head ramming into the small of the back of John Moynihan, now assistant Literary Editor at *The Sunday Telegraph*.

'Corso yelled, clutching Mailer round the stomach and heaving with wild arms,' Moynihan recalled. 'Mailer wheezed, pushing the author of *Gasoline* on the carpet and sitting on him like an Alaskan bear.' The sudden scuffle panicked the Hutchinson staff, and Frank Norman, the scar-faced, perennially black clad ex-convict playwright of *Fings Ain't Wot They Used To Be*, was called upon to aid in separating the writers. Shouldering his way through the party, he looked down. Gripping Corso's arm behind his back, Norman raised him up, frog-marched him out of the room and onto the street.

'Ken was amused by the incident and wrote in my copy of *The Bootleggers*: "For John Moynihan – 2/10/61. For this Chicago-style occurrence – K.A...."' Ken's well honed instinct for publicity was such that, by the time he'd collected himself, Mailer had received an invite from him to appear on *Tonight*'s next available window to discuss his current thesis on 'The Hipster and The Square.' Quite possibly, the topic that caused the fight. The emerging immediacy of British television was serving Ken well...

..and wasn't doing his ego any harm. In anticipation of *Tonight*'s one thousand and first edition, Ken was invited to air his views on the new single releases on the BBC's primetime, weekly pop single review panel, *Juke Box Jury*, along with Michelmore, Hart and, unfortunately for him, the bizarre addition of the sixty-year-old Fyfe Robertson.

Meanwhile, another chance arose to reconnect with his family. On the 8th September, he, Betty and the children took a smooth boat crossing over the Irish Channel and a tour of Dublin and the rural Republic with Henry. There, possibly, for a meeting of the PEN Society (Poets, Essayists, Novelists) and a lengthy stay with members who'd shown him the country years before. Ken could still not escape his commitments, though, as he was expected to return bearing an interview with Brendan Behan for *The Mail*.

The second week of September saw the three studio anchors grace the cover of that week's *Radio Times*, anticipating *Tonight*'s one-thousandth edition. Tellingly, each were photographed separately. Michelmore himself dominates, full-length, self-consciously casual on the left of the cover, Hart beams warmly at him from the right, while Ken appears, smaller still, pig-in-the-middle, directing at Michelmore his hard, hunters gaze. Their professional relationship is unintentionally summed up in this tableau with a telling irony.

Views on Ken were set from his second year on the programme. Most accepted at face value the image he'd cultivated since returning from his first visit to America. Dorothy Snoxell had been Baverstock's assistant before answering to Alasdair Milne, now the programme's editor. She recalls 'a very charming, intelligent man, with a most attractive voice,' who 'perhaps viewed the onset of middle-age unhappily.' Jan Fairer, a Production Associate from day one, remembers the boyish enthusiasms. Inspired by its portentous command to journey, *Hit the Road, Jack* – the new single by gospel-blues singer Ray Charles – was played relentlessly. He impressed upon Fairer J. D. Salinger's ambiguous novel, *The Catcher in the Rye*, as a must read. Pulling into the Lime Grove car park most afternoons was his latest toy: the newly launched, revolutionary E-Type Jaguar: 'very impressive to a young girl.' To jump the queue he'd lobbied the company's Chairman, Sir William Lyons, through a series of persuasive phone-calls from Lime Grove and Fleet Street, much to the amusement of his colleagues. Rae Jeffs was disdainful of the purchase.

'I told him: "A two-seater? That's a very selfish car to run with a family." He was nineteen going on twenty in his behaviour.' Rather, it was more a final, open admission to Betty of his ongoing relationship with 'Kay Tinniswood,' whom both Jeffs and Cynthia Judah recall seeing at Lime Grove after the evening's broadcast.

Judah had known Ken from his last two years on *Picture Post* and been partially responsible, with Baverstock and Milne, for *Tonight*'s founding when it folded. Here, she was 'arts producer' and so in regular contact with Liz Cowley and him. The charm wasn't fooling her. She saw it as a cover: for what, she could never quite pin down.

'I remember talking about it with Derek Hart. There was something a bit sentimental about him. I'm not quite sure what it was. Perhaps he felt sorry for himself. There was something a little bit false there, so that when he was telling a story or being gregarious there was a slight feeling it was an act. He wasn't quite sincere in his feelings or social relations. A bit of a poseur, maybe. Picking up how to behave from others...' Dorothy Snoxell adds:

'He was always beautifully turned out, even dapper, with never a hair out of place (and) rather *aware* of his appearance.'

Whatever his ascendancy in broadcasting, it was for the *Daily Mail* literary reviews that Ken was nominated by *The Bookseller* trade journal 'the most popular writer of the year.' His disdain for the current, cool, posturing in jazz, first articulated against Miles Davis, had been well received by the broadsheet reader. Just as Ken sang George Gershwin's praises as a classical composer against the music snobs -

who'd deemed him too populist - so he wriggled in irritation at the popular, eccentric performances of Thelonius Monk – prowling the stage between piano solos – and comedian Lenny Bruce, dismissed as 'a stunted, creepy, defensive neurotic.' This, against the 'minority, egg-head' effusions of friend Alan Brien, George Melly and, of course, Kenneth Tynan.

Movements Ken could relate to. Cults, as he saw them, were something else entirely. These prioritised 'free decision and free action' over wider concerns that are the 'antiquated...stale, robot-thinking of...statesmen and their policies that need scouring through with winds of change – a change that must come from the willingness of us ordinary citizens to think and accept new thoughts at larger levels.'

Ken is not arguing against the Establishment - he is too much a part - rather, those types too often promoted to run it. There are great minds amongst them whom we – as citizens – should listen to and support. A view the idealist he once was would have ridiculed. But his professionalism was never questioned; even by his literary agent who'd frowned upon his extra-marital pretences.

Easter 1963, they flew to New York's Chelsea Hotel and another *Mail* interview Jeffs had arranged for Behan. Despite being absolute opposites in dress and bearing, she saw them as mutual outsiders.

'Ken was on Brendan's wavelength...he understood this tormented soul.' His imminent autobiography, *Confessions of an Irish Rebel*, was being mumbled into a tape-recorder, the task for which its alcoholic author had fled the country. The rest of Fleet Street assumed the Irish playwright to be drying out, secretly, at a clinic in London, but Ken was offered the scoop for the dishevelled guest, installed there beneath a pseudonym.

'Ken knew but never betrayed him,' recalls Jeffs. 'He could've made a fortune. Those sorts of journalists don't exist today.' She takes a dimmer view of the black, American dancer, Katharine Dunham, also at the Chelsea, who almost charmed away Ken's undivided attention. At Behan's side, she was in the pay of Bernard Geis - his American publisher - to act as his companion and so afford a public veneer of respectability. But Dunham was tiring of her role by his belligerent behaviour. Jeffs claims that, for her efforts, Dunham casually admitted to withholding Behan's royalties. Incensed, Jeffs called Geis to complain before telling Behan who reacted as though ignorant of the fact. The argument continued that evening in the downstairs restaurant where Behan shouted his abuse at Dunham. Not even Ken's disarming charm had any effect this time.

'He said, "Brendan, you can't use that sort of language, whatever she's done." He told Ken to "fuck off!" and that he'd "knock his block off" etc. - very abusive. I kept quiet because I knew that, in some ways, Brendan was desperately hurt. He thought she liked him... and he was quite suspicious of me for a little while after that.'

Next morning, a penitent Behan accepted Ken into his room to play back the sought after tapes and respond to a few follow-up questions. His mood was wryly cynical, and he admitted to tax problems. The voracious press was bearing down, demanding a piece of him, while he saw his allies as ignorant.

During the winter of 1962, a major but ill-defined structural overhaul was put into operation at Lime Grove. With the departure of Baverstock, (promoted to operations at the new Television Centre), one new outside-broadcast reporter and one new studio interviewer were recruited to start the post-Christmas season. Julian Pettifer had previously roamed his microphone around the shores of Hampshire for Southern TV. Tall, blonde, and with an aquiline profile, he could easily pass as the departed Johnson-Smith's younger brother.

Young Pettifer was well liked, respectful to his elders, and methodically unobtrusive in his approach. The same could not be said for the new studio face, Brian Redhead. Physically, Pettifer's opposite – stout, moon-faced and bookish – he also adhered to Catholicism. Not a feature to endear him to the agnostic, sceptical *Tonight* team.

Previously features editor at *The Manchester Guardian*, and a local television presenter, he perceived the post he'd been lumbered with to be little more than a fill-in sinecure. Liz Cowley recalled that on his first night, in January 1963, he threw away the pink card - from which interviewers' read their cues - with a dramatic flourish. Frustrated, he made known his next target.

'There are only two posts worth doing here,' he'd announce more than once in conversation, 'the editor's and Michelmore's.' His tone of superiority around the set was entirely stonewalled by Derek Hart, who avoided him with silent contempt. Ken utilised his black humour to wind him up. Cutting remarks scribbled across the back of used pink cards for the new recruit's attention would be left, strewn about. On the most memorable occasion, a sensational headline on a strawberry blonde's murder - found in that day's *Evening News* - was clipped out and pinned to the office notice-board bearing the legend, 'REDHEAD STABBED TO DEATH IN SOHO.'

Peter Batty joined *Tonight* the same year as Liz Cowley, and was now, temporarily, film editor. He remembers Redhead as 'more or less sent to Coventry' for his attitude.

'I was a small cog again,' grumbled Redhead a few years later. 'And they didn't seem to want to accept ideas from newcomers. I really fairly rapidly reached the conclusion that I'd moved downstairs... there was, by that stage, a very definite feeling that the programme was *theirs*, and they didn't want interlopers like me trying to change things.'

There is some truth in this. By the show's seventh year, a

general feeling prevailed that not only new blood but also new ideas were needed to justify its continuance. Alan Whicker had left Lime Grove – no longer on his bike but with the first in a long line of expensive estates - to go freelance with *Whicker's World*: an occasional series of globetrotting interviews with the rich and famous that would run, in various guises, for the next thirty years. Derek Hart, suffering an unworkable relationship with Redhead, followed his course and handed Milne his notice.

As with *Picture Post* a decade before, attempts at revamping followed, in quick succession, and with varying degrees of success. Antony Jay, a sketch-writer since the intake of 1958, and future conspirator – with Jonathan Lynn – of the sitcom *Yes, Minister*, was promoted to editor from the associate post. Not desperate for the job, he suddenly found himself out of his depth.

'It was...the unhappiest time of my life, apart from a term at boarding school,' he recalled. 'I kept feeling I was failing to take the programme ahead, or feeling that somehow I was letting down the concept of producer-control.' He adds that he was well aware of Cliff's, Ken's and Derek Hart's high status and credibility with the public by then, and too many creative errors on his part could compromise these. A lack of direction was felt all round.

'They weren't disloyal, but I could sense they were very unhappy... It's a very difficult position for an established presenter. The public automatically assumes that he's responsible for everything that happens on screen. It must have been horrid for Cliff, having to keep saying, "It's nothing to do with me..."' When Jay moved – upwards – as Head of Talks Features, Milne then appointed Gordon Watkins 'for sentimental reasons.' After only one month, Peter Batty replaced him. Through no fault of his, the timing of his appointment represented the nadir in the show's life.

Morale was low and nervousness increased as contracts

came up for renewal. At first, Milne offered Batty a relatively free hand to attempt his suggested changes. These included theme nights, guest singers in place of the calypsos, and two of the studio team both presenting and reporting on the one item, dispensing with the long held routine of repeating on film what had just been introduced 'live.' Michelmore felt his anchorman role compromised by this last experiment and voiced his objection. Ken and the departing Derek Hart were more encouraging but did not have Cliff's influence with the Corporation outside the corridors of Lime Grove. Between two camps, Batty was left on shakier ground.

'I went off sick for a short time,' he recalled. 'Partly through worry and partly because I hadn't had a holiday in eighteen months and was very run down.' Milne took over in his absence realising he'd have to reverse several of Batty's changes to stave off the programme's demise. A call from a headhunting Lew Grade at ATV sealed his fate. In his favour, Batty's one surviving legacy to the programme was *Tonight Productions*: a unit formed to deal exclusively with filmed specials that proved marketable overseas as products, and popular with the waning home audience. The most enduring of these remains *The Great War* series, featuring moving new accounts from, amongst others, Henry.

With Ken's profile elevated, he was offered a vehicle. ITV's *Searchlight* first echoed then expressed his growing concern for the environment and its effects on people by the Establishment. *This Nation Tomorrow* looked at similar issues but from the wider, political perspective. Also fortnightly, the programme mixed extended film reports with reflected studio discussions directed by Ken. Subjects covered over its four-month life included 'The Church of England,' 'The Impact of Personality in Politics,' 'Sex and Family Life' and 'Trade Unions.' These were serious studies demonstrating to critical doubters the *Tonight* team's willingness to not only delve beneath the veneer of celebrity, but accepted social taboo. The resulting public reaction to the more serious approach vindicated the clumsy course of changes the team had endured.

On *Tonight* itself, gone were the shallow *vox pops* on the eccentric habits of passers by and the knowing, comedic, studio links. In their place, filmed reports were extended, along with the more serious interviews. With fewer changes of set and mood during a single edition, the programme felt slicker, more seamless and self-assured. But the usual technical errors – 'live' on air - still occurred, from which Ken wasn't immune. Kenneth Corden recalls directing him on such an occasion:

'Ken had a rapid literary flow but, like a lot of journalists, couldn't remember it on camera. Those were the days before autocue had been invented and, instead, jumbo 'idiot cards' with enormous lettering were pinned to the camera under the lens. Once he'd got through the jumbo introduction, he could turn to the interviewee and play it by ear. One of the worst (dramas) was when Ken was entering the studio with Cliff already live on-air with his first introduction. But the first item wasn't there so I rang Cliff at his desk to say "go to Ken" instead. While Cliff filled in, Ken was hurried with his interviewee to the nearest available seats with a camera and its jumbo card already pinned up. Ken set off but the look on his face when he realised in the first sentence he was reading someone else's words will forever be with me.

Worse was to follow. The floor manager saw the missing jumbo card pinned to another camera far away, across the other side of the studio. The cameraman helpfully panned to Ken, locking on the telescopic lens so that he, at least, looked the right size. Ken set off again but the jumbo words were now not near enough for him to read. In close-up, live on-air, he faded into bewildered silence. With a hesitant cough he finally launched in, and brilliantly, making it up as he went. Afterwards, he was congratulated on his ease and fluency.

"Shows you what you can do, boyo," (said Baverstock) "without those idiot cards..."'

The 'rapid literary flow' was well used from 1963; a reflection not so much from his long-running editorship at *The Mail*, as from his new BBC Radio series, *World of Books*, regularly exchanging guests with the *Tonight* team. As well as the grandees of English literature, Ken now taxed the newer, younger voices on television, having acquired the position of elder himself. Tables began turning. But this new level of authority brought with it greater challenges to him and heights from which to fall. The BBC Governors, still smarting from his all too favourable terms negotiated in October 1960, waited below. They hadn't long to go. Potential black marks were gradually presenting themselves.

On the 13th March this year, Ken had filed a report for *Tonight* on life at Durham Prison. The staff arranged for one of their more trustworthy prisoners to be interviewed by Ken, with a view to presenting the institute in the most positive light manageable. No apologist to circumstance, Ken arrived with the intention of treating the prisoner as he would any interviewee. However, on his return to Lime Grove and the report's subsequent broadcast, Milne called his reporter into his office to relay a response from Durham: the Governor had been in contact with his solicitor. The Governor's complaint – extant in the BBC Archives – was based upon Ken's apparently provocative line of questioning, leading to honest responses from the prisoner that suggested mismanagement by the prison authorities and by the Governor in particular; for them, a public relations disaster. The Governor claimed Ken "invited (the prisoner) to divide his allegations into two parts; those concerned with 'brutality' and those concerned with 'the inadequacy of the Prison...Medical Service." The prisoner then offered a specific example whereby another prisoner, 'suffering an obsession with execution, barricaded himself into his cell,.' As punishment he was placed, 'immediately next door to the condemned cell' instead of the punishment wing 'as would be normal.'

A further six months of exchanged calls and letters followed between the Governor and the *Tonight* offices, a concession finally being made, on screen, with an apology from Michelmore between items. But Durham's Governor considered this too little, too late. By April 1964, his assistant solicitor, speaking on the Governor's behalf, pressed home that Ken's report had presented 'a plain and grossly defamatory allegation against our client' that was 'completely false, as was fully demonstrated by the Report of the Visiting Committee.' They demanded approval of a much fuller apology on screen, along with payment to their client of costs and damages to his reputation. A tired Milne expressed exasperation to Grace Wyndham-Goldie that the controversy remained ongoing.

Time, as always, was the luxury so rarely afforded on the programme. In the following instance it's deficit only highlighted a growing perception, oddly among the more conservative viewers, of a presumptuous arrogance in the journalist. A display of his ambivalence towards women presented itself when he interviewed Helen Gurley-Brown - the American author of *Sex and the Single Girl* – on the release of its sequel, *Sex and the Office*, via a link to the BBC's Manchester studios. Flanked by three single girls from the *Tonight* offices, Ken opens with his stall already set, based on what he sees as just a cynical cash-in. He announces to the viewers that Gurley-Brown has 'hastened out' another 'predictable' bestseller. Facing her, he opens well enough:

Ken: 'Can I just get one point clear; are you in fact *recommending* a shift in public morality so that it becomes openly permissible for a single girl to have sexual affairs?'

(Guards go up).

HGB: 'I'm not *promoting* anything, lest of all promiscuity. I think there has been a change in morality for single women. I don't have to promote it. It already exists.'

Ken: 'Yes, your book is a little... Errm...' (off-screen, the studio director catches Ken's attention. He hurries on). 'It titillates but it doesn't explain a great deal. I'm looking at one particular place where you say "the unexpected guest," you say "as sometimes happens... you didn't know, the night before, you were going to have a guest for breakfast but there he is, *ravenous*." Is this promiscuous or not? I don't know.'

HGB: 'I don't think it's *promoting* promiscuity. It may be promiscuous. But you asked me whether or not I were...'

Ken: '*Recommending* was my word. Not *promoting* anything...'

HGB: 'Well, I'm not recommending it. I just say that sometimes a man does spend the night. I don't think it's sensible to say these things don't go on. I know they do go on. If they do, I think it's best to handle them with some tact and delicacy.'

One of the *Tonight* women, Mary, is then asked to offer her prepared question and expresses distaste at what she'd read as the outdated supplicant role of her sex in the book. Gurley-Brown repudiates her perception that women were depicted as dependents, insisting she is representing the single woman's life as it stands and not as it should be. Off-camera, Kenneth Corden motions to Ken to wind things up.

Ken: 'Well, Mrs. Gurley-Brown, my impression is that you've made a girl sound like *a cross between a tart and a Playboy bunny*, but thank you very much indeed.' (He turns from the monitor and the link is cut).

In hindsight, Ken querying her concept of the single girl as being predatory (as any equivalent male) sounds comic and - considering his own behaviour - perverse. Otherwise, his valid opening question is swiftly sidetracked with the misunderstanding over 'promoting' and 'recommending.' Without his pre-interview assumptions, time may have been available for clarity. But with only one of the *Tonight* women able to put a question to Gurley-Brown, their dissent is left equally unchallenged. Gurley-Brown would have the last laugh: *Cosmopolitan* magazine debuted in America the following year, for a wide readership entirely suited to her view as its founding editor. As four years with *The Daily Mail* saw a reactionary middle-aged tone set in to some of Ken's observations, so four years with *Tonight* was eliciting similar prejudices. He was becoming jaded.

His natural reaction was to branch out. A freelancer since his teens, Ken saw no conflict of interest in sharing his allegiances with other, broadly related media. He'd begun exploring the possibility of advertising *The Mail* on ITV while still under contract and put it to Grace Wyndham-Goldie. From discussions with Kenneth Adam, they agreed his request was unrealistic, fearing the precedent it might set among the other journalists should they also demand it as a right. In any case, he'd had a nerve in even mooting what was, in her eyes, 'an embarrassing request.' Wyndham Goldie added that the fear of compromised allegiance might be soothed if Adam, personally, called Mike Randall at *The Mail* to assure him that their decision had no bearing on their cordial relations with his paper. The head of Television Administration concurred that they should adhere to the principle of long-term contract holders staying within their remit.

'I am sure this policy has been to the Corporation's advantage.'

Unable to reach Randall, Adam sent a pacifying note. His instinct had first been to agree to Ken's request but Wyndham Goldie's notorious 'iron whim' impressed upon him the consequences as 'too daunting.' Once again, Ken had soured employee/employer relations. But further distancing between them was imminent.

A final change in the studio set-up helped maintain interest enough to fulfill his, and the programme's, final year. The departed Peter Batty's discarded idea of two interviewers reporting the one item became a virtual necessity when Michelmore expressed the desire to spend less time at Lime Grove and more with his family. Replacing Hart in the studio and Whicker on film was now unavoidable for Milne.

Still instinctively as eager for change as Baverstock had been, he searched outside Fleet Street for less parochial voices. He found a fellow Edinburgh-born Scot, of Icelandic parentage, formerly from *The Scotsman* and now assistant editing *The Scottish Daily Express*. Wearing heavy horn-rims and a carnation in his lapel, Magnus Magnusson – the future presenter of documentaries on Nordic history and question master on the long-running quiz show, *Mastermind* – cut a more stylized business-like figure in 1964. On location, Cathal O'Shannon appeared with his wiry frame and skeptical, Republican-Irish wit, inviting as well as dividing audience affections with the best of *Tonight*'s reporters. A refreshing find and radical, for the time, amongst the long, taken for granted, line of affected Home Counties accents.

In September, yet another contact was received in the

interminable case of the Durham Prison Governor V. *Tonight*; in this case from the Governor's personal solicitor, Leslie Newcombe. While there was an acceptance that the demanded apology had been broadcast, Newcombe had now served a writ on the Corporation claiming he'd been defamed in the original broadcast and, oddly, in the subsequent apology. This, apparently, because the apology didn't mention him, directly, by name. With fingers collectively crossed another was mutually agreed to and broadcast. There would be no further contact. If not personally responsible for his interviewee's responses, Ken, by association, received a dent to his reputation: now questioned by those envious of it. His response to this protracted affair is left unrecorded.

The Adam / Wyndham Goldie restrictions on where he could work still rankled. At the end of the month his annual contract was once more up for renewal. He decided he wanted out of its full-time demands but not the programme.

He also pondered his future with *The Mail*. Should he resign, he needed certain assurances; mainly that he'd be offered additional work at Lime Grove to compensate for the financial loss. Sounding out Baverstock, to whom he still deferred, he was advised to go back to Milne and ask for fewer appearances with an increase rate of pay but an additional contractual commitment of two years. Ken put in writing his bid for a minimum guarantee of £4,250 for just three studio appearances a week and four on film per year, with an option on additional filming once free of *The Mail*.

'Third,' he ended, 'could I be offered other television work – either appearances before camera for other programmes, or other *Tonight* productions, or script-writing assignments?' Milne provisionally accepted his bid on contract clearance from the Head. Their acceptance allowed him to hand in his resignation to Randall. That Ken desired more TV and not a wholehearted return to Fleet Street was a sign of the adrenal rush he thrived on. He explained the reason for his preference and what he saw as the still unfulfilled possibilities of TV the following year:

'Peculiarly often, a magnesium intimacy flares between interviewer and interviewee, particularly in the studio. There is a kind of unspoken compact sworn: they are blood brothers under the strobe lights. For there, even if the encounter is a hostile one, even if the interviewee knows he is going to be brought into severe question, there almost always springs into being...a feverish empathy in the bleak glare of the execution shed where television confrontations take place... Both are conscious of going over the top together, of being two dice shaken in a crucible, and there is a curious alliance to come out of the flames: a double-six.'

So, despite – or perhaps because of – his jadedness the previous year, Ken was pursuing a course of perfection that covered every aspect of his craft. The intensity with which he applied himself was becoming obsessive. To Alan Brien he'd fallen into a routine where he rarely appeared 'off camera.' During one conversation Brien could take no more. He'd asked Ken his view on a pressing news item of the day.

'Well,' returned Ken, with lecturing *gravitas*, 'there are *four* points to be made about this. One...'

'For God's sake, Ken!' exploded Brien. 'There aren't four points at all. *Just answer the fucking question!*' Ken withdrew, understandably hurt by Brien's impatience.

The obsessional frame of mind remained with him on returning to Gurneys. Amanda recalls, on more than one occasion, she'd return home from college to find their housekeeper upset at the treatment her father had given her. Each mantelpiece ornament - removed for cleaning - had to be replaced in *exactly* the same position it had been found, facing *precisely* the same way. He'd miss nothing. A five-degree misalignment could darken his mood. This also applied to each table and chair in every room. Their housekeeper decided that the only way to avoid Ken's wrath was to chalk around every item. This proved useful for the shelf items but particularly useless for the furniture, where she'd mistakenly vacuum the chalk marks off the carpets before repositioning, so inciting further anger.

18
1964 – 1965:
Betty, Again

Ken's finishing touch for his land around 'Gurneys' was in full cry. The pair of peafowl often led the screeching, night-long chorus by the rest of the menagerie, keeping up the disgruntled trilling of the recently installed white doves. Through the day, 'Pyewacket' - a Siamese cat – and 'Sherlock' - a bloodhound 'neurotic...with no sense of smell' - roamed the grounds blithely causing minor accidents.

Tristan was now eighteen and away, as often as possible, from the stifling responsibility of being a famous father's eldest son. Sixteen-year-old Amanda, much against her will, was staying with a family in Heidelberg, Germany, on a 'paying guest-tutorial scheme' in a bid to dash her German grammar teacher's belief that she couldn't pass her intended 'O' level exam. So, pubescent Fabian was left in the care of Betty; a quietly determined, if increasingly isolated, centre.

The house and grounds stood within the constituency of East Hertfordshire, but just the other side of the boundary encompassing Royston and Hitchin itself. In the absence of Benenson who'd failed, by a margin, to take the seat for Labour in '59, Betty looked next door, in North Herts., for political inspiration. Hitchin's new Labour candidate – up from Southampton - was 31-year-old Shirley Williams, another daughter with a famous mother in Vera Brittain – author of *Testament Of Youth*. One afternoon, Betty phoned the constituency office number printed on a Party flyer and volunteered her services to the candidate for the upcoming General Election of 1964. Subsequently better known as

Liberal Democrat Baroness Shirley Williams, she recalled:

'Although I wasn't her MP, I was her nearest *Labour* MP. It was a seat absolutely on the margins of whether Labour would or wouldn't have a majority – of three - in Government.' As in the '59 Election she, and, later, Ken, seemed to emote at the idea of being, as Williams put it, a 'Labour enclave in this Conservative, rural hinterland.' But between the energising, combative doorstep arguments during canvassing, life for Betty as her own door closed at dusk continued as before.

After Williams was invited back to meet her well-known husband, she saw the problem. In his company Betty appeared,

'intelligent but very repressed; self-repressed, if you like. She did not leap into conversations and say, "I don't agree with that." And he didn't treat her well. He was a bit of a bully...' She unwittingly reflects Cynthia Judah's observation. 'People almost always show you parts of themselves they expect you to like, and he *wanted* us to like him. He wasn't about to reveal bits of himself to us we probably wouldn't have liked very much... I only learnt of her qualities from canvassing, without Ken leaning over her shoulder.'

The following year, Betty received a letter from a student at Edinburgh University. Angus Calder was researching a doctoral thesis on the history of *Common Wealth* and inquired after a possible interview. Betty was glad to accede to both the visit and the accompanying attention. On arriving at 'Gurneys,' Calder recalls,

'I was then both naive and impressionable. I remember a house in good taste, and a woman who seemed lonely and very unhappy. Since I admired and liked Kenneth Allsop as a TV presence, I found this rather upsetting.'

Betty appeared more than a little vague, in manner, mildly absent-minded. She recognised these traits in herself, later feeling the need to write a guilt-induced letter, apologising for the absence of a meal and sufficient recall, but offering some relevant papers unearthed after his departure.

Yet, as ever, the symptom of her isolation also held the cure. One evening, soon after, Ken entered the house and announced his intention to drive across nine thousand miles worth of America's northern states: and he needed her with him.

19
Apr – Aug 1965:
On the Road

On Friday 23rd April, his Temple Chambers tenancy up for renewal within forty-eight hours, Ken moved into rooms at 8, Hill Road, off Abbey Road NW8, in St. John's Wood. One of his first phone-callers was the Broadway composer and producer, Buddy Bregman. *The Bootleggers* had attained the status of a classic in America and Bregman was keen to adapt it into a musical. Ken was amazed by the idea and suggested they met at Television Centre.

It only seems a logical move in retrospect. The subsequent productions of *Thoroughly Modern Millie, Bonnie & Clyde, Sweet Charity* and *Cabaret* cashed in on what was a new, modish interest in the Roaring Twenties and Thirties inspired by the book. Ken promised him an outline of a script within the week.

On the 14th May, Henry was midway through a yearlong celebration in honour of his seventieth birthday, due on the 1st December. Devon's Rougemont Hotel was the setting for the annual West Country Writers Association conference. As President, Henry's role on the agenda was to submit a second batch of his original manuscripts in a presentation ceremony at The Clarence, nearby, to the Head Librarian of Exeter University, the first having been interned there two years earlier.

Henry, fired with anticipation, took it upon himself to invite and install his own list of thirty-six sanctioned attendees, which quickly rose to sixty on the day. These included his first wife, Loetitia, (with whom he was back on speaking terms) and most of his children. Six guest speakers were also booked featuring the poet, Ted Hughes, and Ken. But Henry soon realised that the day itself was out of his hands.

Outside, the hot and sunny weather ensured a baking humidity within the main hall, filled to capacity with University officials, celebrities and a core of aged Association members. One such was the playwright of *The Lady's Not For Burning*, Christopher Fry.

'The guests were issued with lapel name-badges, but Henry refused to write his in, leaving it blank. When questioned about this he said, "I'm waiting for my personality to return." A strange man.' Henry's anticipation thus drained away as cumbersome BBC cameras – there to film the occasion for a timely documentary – obscured views and rights of way. Meanwhile, the speeches, while idolatrous, were dragging on far too long for comfort. The other attendees became uneasy when they clocked their long-limbed, snowy-haired Guest of Honour sitting back, hunched in his chair, the dark, baleful eyes fixedly gazing into the distance as he methodically lobbed sugar lumps from his seat at targeted sitters. At the end of the sixth speech he wearily rose, ambled to the rostrum and declared,

'It is said that speech is golden but silence is divine,' before sitting back down. Afterwards, he departed hot, bothered and frustrated that the day seemed stolen from him. According to Anne Williamson,

'Henry was a little hurt that the University did not show their appreciation. He...felt that the conferment of an honorary degree might have been appropriate for the occasion.' His past could never be totally shaken, though, particularly from the younger, liberal-educated faculty whom she claims repeatedly blocked his conferment. As a riposte he resigned his five-year presidency of the

Association though, accepting their lack of culpability, agreed to continue as its number two to Christopher Fry, named as his replacement. Ken spent the rest of the weekend with Henry at Ox's Cross, calming his ego while mooting further ideas.

Tonight's final edition went out on Friday 18th June. An uncharacteristic atmosphere of calm descended upon the studio for, perhaps, the first time in its eight-and-a-half-year run. The feeling of anti-climax was tangible. Hardly surprising since the team had been bracing themselves for this inevitability since the near-fatal revamps of 1963. Consequently, plans for long summer diversions were well in advance by its broadcast.

Between an extended item with Fyfe Robertson, rocking in a boat before the incomplete Avon Suspension Bridge, and a fascinating, if macabre, interview by Magnus Magnusson on the history of Auschwitz's corpse incinerator, Ken's second with Beatle, John Lennon, was an afterthought. His first (no longer in the BBC Archives) occurred in March the previous year with the release of his first collection of nonsense verse, *In His Own Write*. Then, Ken revealed how the same literary discipline long used for jazz could be equally relevant for pop. Having quoted 'Good Dog Nigel' to camera, he turned to Lennon with,

'Several critics have been suggesting that you were under the influence when you wrote it – the influence of James Joyce, Edward Lear, Lewis Carroll, James Thurber and Paul Klee. Would you reject all of these or have any of them influenced you?' Lennon was initially guarded and pleaded ignorance. 'Spymill,' Liz Cowley records him saying from her diary. 'Do I know the others?' But a later question registered something the Beatle was then pondering:

'When you write a song for the group,' asked Ken, 'is your approach completely different, or do you look on Beatle lyrics as really another form of pleasant nonsense rhyming?'

While Lennon's answer wasn't recorded, Liz Cowley, at least, was disappointed, generally, by the laconic responses, hoping for some scoop. But, off-camera, Ken had pressed Lennon further at the Lime Grove bar, suggesting – on this evidence – that he could afford a broader and more ambiguous range in his song lyrics than those on teenage love currently in vogue. Lennon, in return, was taken by Ken's level of interest; a contrast to the other middle-aged, Fleet Street 'squares' whose ignorance he'd long taken for granted.

The publication of his follow-up, *A Spaniard in the Works*, heralded a return visit to the *Tonight* studio. Chubbier and longer-haired, Lennon remained his characteristically casual self, but was now more familiar with, and amused by, Ken's own clipped use of language:

Ken: 'Living in *the butterfly world of pop as a Beatle*...

(Lennon quietly laughs and Ken acknowledges)

...do you find this undermines peoples' serious acceptance of you as a writer?'

Lennon: 'It does, but I didn't really expect them to take me seriously... They do take *it* more seriously than I thought, so that's good enough for me.'

As advised the previous year, Lennon was chaperoned out the back to avoid the ubiquitous screaming fans.

Tonight ended with no fanfare. But later, in the bar, a small reunion had gathered for the farewell that included Alan Whicker. Over drinks, Ken communicated his enthusiasm at the planned drive through the States. Whicker recalled the surprise he'd felt at the bravado.

'He was quite confident that he could come back and pick up from where he'd left off, at a time when competition to get into television from Fleet Street was so intense. He wasn't worried about that...'

But Ken had been advised to keep quiet about the offer just made – most likely by a former *Tonight* editor named Derrick Amoore - to front his own, more heavyweight, late-night current affairs programme. Still in the planning stages as *Tonight II*, one thing assumed early on was Michelmore's lack of interest in this direction. Yet, when Cliff got to hear of this, he fumed, arguing that his pivotal, maintaining role throughout the life of *Tonight* deserved him greater consideration. The production team soon capitulated before ensuring, for the time being, Ken's continued role as lieutenant. This must have exasperated the more impatient man. It is as well that the mutual, professional respect between both held, since this decision did Ken no favours in his own pursuit for greater recognition and recompense within the Corporation.

Extended pay negotiations with the Talks Manager at *World of Books* – the first of two new radio series - had produced, in percentage terms, a reasonable enough increase in her eyes. But Ken spent most of this time pressing for an ever-higher rate on the grounds that the base-rate to begin with was unreasonably low. Compared to his escalating scale from *Tonight*, this was undeniable. But he pursued with a wounded petulance:

'It bears no relation to the economic rates standard in journalism today, no relation to the value put upon one's work in every other field, and no relation to the amount of research and preparation – apart from the physical undertaking and time taken in getting to Broadcasting House and doing the interview – required if one is going to fulfil one's undertaking to one's professional capacity.' He had no problem offering his services where needed, since he found the programme 'personally satisfying...but this is precisely the situation the BBC too often trades upon to get cheap labour.' The accusation would echo down the years.

With the new, late-night, current affairs programme not pencilled in to debut until that autumn, Ken was handed a window in which to research his next book. The first stage to commence with the drive across the United States. As with all such sojourns away from the desk, his decision was last minute and a complete surprise to Betty. He needed no excuse. Ken must have sensed the endless run of ill-fitting tin legs from Roehampton could only match his still pulsing adrenaline for so much longer. *The Bootleggers* had quickly turned into his most critically acclaimed book, particularly in the United States, where it broke him as a serious author.

Eager to take advantage of his heightened status and pen a follow-up with related themes, on his second favourite country, Ken pored over a land-map of the continent in his weekend study at 'Gurneys.' True to the spirit of his new subject – the under-class of train-jumping travellers known as 'hoboes' – there would be no pre-emptive list of interviewees. How could there be with such transients? All he could do was take in the car for a full MOT, bring a supply of pens, pencils and notebooks, Betty to help with the itinerary, and see what, and who, transpired en route.

The drive would last two-months. For the first four weeks she would accompany him as navigator and second opinion, after which he would leave her at La Crescenta, California, with John and Marjorie Edwards: another couple with three grown-up children Ken had fallen in with at an airport lounge in Copenhagen on returning from an assignment. Any romantic notions he may have harboured about the journey – *his* journey – were soon jolted out of him and Betty on board the DC6 to New York on the 22nd June. 'Terrible...flight, terrible service, terrible food.'

Installed at the Winslow Hotel, a rush of phone calls to confirm contacts ensued while they resorted to public transport until the delivery of their hired car (a Ford, registered 'BHN 160') four days later. With it they drove to Washington via New Jersey, Pennsylvania, Delaware and Baltimore, arriving at the Statler Hilton Hotel after 7 p.m. As they spent the following day researching at the Dept. of Labour and the Library of Congress, a break entailed a visit to John F. Kennedy's grave at Arlington Cemetary. Two days on they headed for Palaski, then the Appellations, where they spent the night at the secluded Paluski Motel. They reached Nashville two days later, where Ken negotiated with two (prospective?) publishers, followed by a visit to the RCA recording studio where Wesley Rose was concluding a mix on Roy Orbison's next release.

Crossing the Mississippi, they then spent five days in Little Rock, Arkansas, ostensibly for Ken to write up his notes. Here they stayed with the family of Jack Smith: manager at the Alamo Plaza Motel and uncle to Arkansas Democrat George Armstrong. On to Springdale, Ken interviewed the local Reverend and a number of his migrant workers based at the town's Labour Camp. 'Hottest yet = 99 d. en route,' he noted as they zoomed out towards Oklahoma and another contact on the 10th July, and the appositely named Liberal, Kansas, and a trailer park for some unplanned encounters, note-taking and supper at its local Holiday Inn.

Back through Oklahoma, through New Mexico, and a rest – for the car – at Capulin, he interviewed an 'old cowboy' who took them to see its volcano. Three days later, they'd passed through Colorado, Utah, Arizona, The Grand Canyon and The Hoover Dam at Boulder City to the relative civilisation of Las Vegas. Next morning – the 16th July - they reached Los Angeles and the Edwards at La Crescenta.

On the evening of the 20th, they drove into the city to catch the new James Bond movie *Goldfinger* - at which Ken beamed and marvelled at the Aston Martin. From here they drove for dinner at Sunset Boulevard's La Provence, the Whisky-A-Go-Go, and a discotheque, where Ken favourably observed The Enemies: a 'Beat-ish' group doing Beatles covers. At least one of his companions derides the new cultural scene.

'John Edwards takes it for granted that anyone with long hair is a delinquent shit-carrier.'

Ken was back on the streets of LA the next day for more interviews at the City Mission. It was during this stopover that an incident occurred which Ken would point to as symbolic of the USA's double standard in the matter of personal morality. John Edwards was regaling Ken with his own experiences of the country from the driver's seat of his own car. In the back sat the Edwards' youngest. Whatever else they shared, a disregard for the speed limit was a given. A motorcycle cop sped in front of them, waving Edwards to pull in. As he swaggered over, they were unnerved to see this armour shielded warrior openly carrying a holstered gun. Casually, Edwards produced a ten-dollar bill, pulled out his driver's licence, put the note inside, closed the cover, and handed it over. The cop took the licence, clocked Edward's son, and demanded both men get out of the car. He motioned Edwards to follow him about twenty yards back. Putting his face close to his quarry, he removed the folded bill from his licence, handed it back and earnestly whispered, 'Whaddya tryin' to do? *Corrupt the kid*?'

Ken suffered a not dissimilar encounter, later that week, when he was caught doing 80 mph in a 65 mph zone. Hearing the suave English accent, he asked Ken what he was doing in the country. Ken told him. The cop responded saying he'd let him off if he consented to giving him a free copy of the book on publication. Seeing how likely it would be for them never to meet again, Ken readily agreed.

On their return to the house, Betty was left in the Edwards care as she readied for a return to England while Ken headed, initially north, to Davis, for the remainder of the journey east. From here, on the 24th, he wrote a longish joint update to Tristan, Amanda and Fabian:

'I'm now 500 miles away from Mummy and the Edwards, and north of San Francisco, and having finished my business here, move on up into Oregon to look at some lumber camps, and then I shall begin the rather daunting-looking return journey through the northern states. I've just come up the San Joaquin Valley... I think it's all going satisfactorily; I'm certainly amassing a good deal of material but I find it a bit difficult to be sure, until I draw back from it and try to assess how it'll all jigsaw in, just how relevant it all is.

One thing I've discovered: the hobo may be officially extinct, but actually is alive in large numbers, still riding the freight trains, still down on the railroad tracks, still drifting on from hobo 'jungle' to hobo 'jungle.' I've talked with quite a few of them, the spoil of a society that still very wastefully mines its human material, the kind of by-product of a nation still very much in transition between settlement and stability.' He understates just how gruelling his itinerary has proven, 'then the finding of people and situations, the interviewing and note-making, the transcription in the motel room in the evening.' He admits to missing their mother, but for her practical help as much as her 'good companionship.'

He tells them he has notched up 4,442 miles so far. 'The Ford has up to now run in a very stalwart fashion: no breakdowns at all, touch piles and piles of wood.' And ends in an odd tone that sounds happily detached. 'I get a tremendous amount of interest out of travelling, especially out of America, but it never fails to strengthen my gladness that I live in England and that I have 'Gurneys' and my children to return to.'

As Betty left the Edwards on the 26th to fly from New York back to London, Ken headed for Klamath Falls, Oregon, and the rangers of the U.S. Forest Service. By now – with the spaces between stopovers seeming to widen - he'd run out of substantial provisions, scrounging what sandwiches and snacks he could from the few roadside cafes he saw and the appointments he kept. On he drove, to Montana – and his first substantial meal in days – Harlowton, South Dakota and Iowa.

By the 2nd August he reached the welcoming and familiar skyline of Chicago where, unsurprisingly, he opted to stay for three days. (His diary notes that Fabian arrived in L.A. that day for a holiday). He headed for the nearest restaurant: the Berghoff, 17, West Adams Street. 'First *real* meal since Saturday,' he noted, relieved by the rich cuisine.

Next morning - en route to the City Mission and an interview with a homeless black and his guardian Superintendent - he wired his arrival to Nelson Algren. The fifty-six-year-old, Chicago-born, writer of *The Man With the Golden Arm* had befriended him after a *Daily Mail* interview during that first visit in 1958. Algren returned an offer of dinner in the company of Betty – his new wife – for the following day. Ken's excitement soon became tempered by a drained feeling when he awoke which, as was often the case, he kept to himself. For his diary, he expressed distaste at what he was shown:

'First to drinks at 1958 Evergreen, then to what (Nelson) called "a nice, beat-up Italian joint," which it was, but good grub. N. knew all the hookers (pros) in there. On to a very roughneck dive called The Shamrock (where he'd also taken Natalie Sarrault and Joan Littlewood). A wino bar, with low-grade (blacks), poor whites and Indians, mostly all stoned, dancing to juke. One (black) with a face like a roadmap from stitched-up razor slashes, had been a Sugar Ray Robinson sparring partner. Finished up about 1.30 (a.m.) at Jazz Ltd., (a) club run by half Jap. and half Irish, with good N(ew) O(rleans) band with banjos and sousaphone.'

Of course, he was revelling in it all. This was the world at which he saw himself an honorary member. Algren left him with an invite to a party thrown by Putnams, his new publisher, for his next book – *Notes from A Sea Diary* - on the 11th. Having secured his flights back to England from New York, Ken drove out of Chicago on the 5th, looking for a motel at Ann Arbour, Michigan, that proved non-existent. After an hour of aimless driving, he stumbled across the small town of Ypsilanti and the ambivalently named Your Motel on the eastside. Collapsing onto its one available bed, he wrote back to Tristan and Amanda:

'I'm deeply thankful it's nearly over: these long, endless days of hurling along are pretty killing, and after hunting up material in South Dakota, I virtually abandoned Nebraska and Iowa, for time was short and I felt pretty used up. I just got across as quickly as possible those vast and rather dull land-distances... I feel, at the moment, I've had a bellyful of migrant workers. I thought I'd try to talk to some trucking companies in New York, and the drivers, and get some dope on internal flying. I do hope that things are organised at 'Gurneys' and that by now Mummy's home and settled. Take care of her and yourselves.'

On the 6th he left Ann Arbour for the University of Illinois then drove through Toledo, Cleveland 'through violent lightening and rain storms' reaching Newton Falls, Ohio, mid-evening. The following evening he celebrated his relief by booking into New York's Waldorf Astoria, and noted that he'd just completed 8,419 miles through 27 states.

With his return flight not due out until the 13th, (a Friday, which must have filled him with foreboding considering the flight here) he rested awhile, then soaked up some the city's ambience. It was while dining in the city's skyscraper restaurants and ascending/descending between their floors that he made a mental note of the incessant, soporific 'music' emanating from the hidden speakers. Finding the company that copyrighted the banal covers, nearby, he arranged for himself an on-spec article – 'Music by Muzak' – and aimed it at Mel Lasky; co-editor of *Encounter*. On the 11th he made Algren's publisher's party for his new book before arriving back in London, two days later, miraculously in one piece.

Feeling the pressure, Ken pores over an early script for the new series named '24 Hours.' (BBC) 1965.

20
Sept 1965 – Jan 1968: '24 Hours'

Back from America to edit a growing mountain of reports and observational quotes, Ken threw himself into work at his Hill Road study. The whereabouts of 'Kay Tinniswood' at this time is unknown as she didn't join him here. Never alone for long, he'd soon engage the time and attention of Cliff Michelmore's new secretary. Along with the manuscript, his new BBC TV series demanded equally urgent consideration: less for artistic reasons than those of the usual monetary necessity. But it was this very necessity by which he thrived.

A re-energised Ken brimmed with new, unsolicited ideas and impatient resolve. He tried selling an idea to John Montgomery at A.D. Peters – his new agents - of a weekly pop show that took a serious, critical approach to the medium, 'from a purely personal angle,' as he'd so often done from Fleet Street. Montgomery returned an ill-informed reply that programmes such as *Newly Pressed* and *Pick of the Pops* already treated the medium in this way and that public interest was waning. (Oddly, a view prevalent at the time, by those professionals who had little liking or understanding of popular music. Its downfall was also predicted in a *vox pop* sequence in the first edition of the groundbreaking, Liz Cowley-produced youth programme, *Whole Scene Going*, in January 1966. In the first edition, a nineteen-year-old Tristan Allsop made his TV debut as the only sombre-suited member of the audience, unsuccessfully quizzing a dismissive Pete Townsend of The Who about his current income. (He recalls his own brief performance as 'terrified and tongue-tied')). But Ken's idea would prove prophetic, with the analysis offered on such weekly BBC programmes as the album-orientated *Old Grey Whistle Test* on TV and industry opinion on the radio singles review, *Round Table*:

'I confess I had considerable doubts about whether *Tonight* should have been strangled,' he told the *Radio Times*. 'But in the first week of *24 Hours* there was a new kind of urgency and impact that made for a more exciting show. The shift of emphasis jacked me up.' He added that he hoped the new team would continue 'the sardonic approach, the touch of acidity where desirable. We're trying to employ it better than on interviews with movie stars.' (A comment that, one-day, would return to haunt him).

The main shift was to a much larger studio and increased budget. Derrick Amoore had risen through the ranks of *Tonight* as production assistant, film producer and recent editor, so was the natural choice. Recalling the abortive trials of 1962/3, flexibility was 'the keynote of *24 Hours*' as the new programme would be named. The *Radio Times* boasted how 'the studio itself is flexible to the point of being revolutionary.' While interviewed by them, Amoore describes the set as featuring,

'a magic box smack in the centre, made mainly of curved glass. If we want to interview someone, for example, and not be bothered with what's going on in the rest of the studio, we can set (it) up in front of this glass and simply light it so that it becomes a reflecting surface. On the other hand, if we want to see right across the studio, we just light it in a different way so that it becomes transparent.'

Allied to an increase in budget was a more serious, analytical approach comparable to that of *Panorama*: the team's former rival. But *24 Hours* benefited from immediacy of reporting, with their journalists on call at key posts around the world. Poles apart in age and experience, Fyfe Robertson and Julian Pettifer were still *Tonight* veterans and out on permanent location, while Michael Barratt – tempted away from their rival – joined them before a longer studio stint. Here, Presenter Michelmore found himself sitting - as static as any newsreader - before the 'magic box.' On *Tonight* he could perch upon its side and exercise some freedom of movement. By comparison, this was a desk job and would have remained so had the larger budget not stretched to regular 'specials' from overseas.

Joining Ken for his studio reports was the political analyst, Ian Trethowan. If politically sympathetic, they proved a volatile match, Trethowan far more staid than Ken. As a reluctant rocker of boats, he frowned upon Ken's open libertarianism. Shirley Williams, knowing them both, suspects there may also have been some competitive jealousy on Trethowan's part. Ken's new attire of navy-blue, pinstriped suit, pink shirt and flower-patterned tie only magnifying the contrasts with his more soberly dressed colleague.

But as with the later *Tonight* encounters, his callous ego could often act as an obstacle to his usually persuasive interaction. On an early edition, the ongoing issue of doctors' pay prompted an invite to a Dr. R. A. Cooper to appear, to offer what was hoped would be a dissenting view. Cooper takes up the story:

'I arrived at the studio to be met by Kenneth Allsop who gave me a list of five questions to consider, which would be the basis of what he was going to ask me. I asked if I could meet my opponent, but was told 'no' as otherwise we might collude. I duly studied the questions, was ushered into the studio where, *en passant*, I introduced myself to Lord Cooper (then President of the White Collar Union) and asked him if he knew my father, Andrew Cooper, who was a member of the Central Electricity Generating Board. Not only did he know him; they were great friends. The interview started and Allsop turned to me and asked a question completely unrelated to the points he had left me considering. I had done just enough media work to ignore his question and say what I had come up to say. To his surprise, he found that Lord Cooper was completely on my side. On that occasion we won the day. Allsop was one of those presenters / interviewers who was not interested in what his guests had to say. *He* was the most important person there and the only thing that mattered was *his* view of situations...'

On the 26th November, John Chillingworth - his old *Picture Post* photographer and friend – threw a house party to which were invited all his former Shoe Lane colleagues. Also present were Chillingworth's girlfriend and future wife, Roslyn. Years later, it would be Ken's presence that sustained her memory of this party: it wasn't pleasant. Amongst a memorable turnout of friends, Ken stood out with his vocal bravado, perceived by her as arrogance. Chillingworth concurred that he'd found him altered from the idealist charmer he'd known in the Fifties.

Ken's wilful independence was also alienating members of staff. As Derrick Amoore planned the coverage for the swiftly called General Election, his employees found themselves fielding premature attention from Fleet Street's television reviewers. With the medium going through a period of technical expansion and popularity not witnessed since the start of ITV, someone capitulated and a supposedly confidential directive escaped. Early in 1966, while scanning that day's papers at Lime Grove for future items, Ken exploded at seeing – with no warning - the role he and the team were expected to perform. He hurriedly typed a private letter to the Controller, Paul Fox:

'Yet again, as is customary in this ill-mannered organisation, I

have had to read in the press the announcements of the function and personnel of '24 Hours' during the election campaign. I don't know who it is who prepares and issues these statements to the newspapers, and who sees fit to regard me as the invisible man in this operation. But, even apart from the public line-up, no one here has had the courtesy or candour to consult or discuss with me what role it is proposed that I should perform in this period. But this continues to reflect an attitude that has obtained from the beginning of this programme. I know perfectly well that a section of editorial opinion – not the editor himself – prefers to place reliance upon others than myself; and frankly I am by no means certain where your support lies.'

He ends with the flourish of threatened resignation:

'I see little reason to continue the arduous duties of 24 Hours in this atmosphere. If I am to continue, I suggest that my position is, once and for all, clarified.'

As he awaited Fox's reassurance, he received one, unexpectedly, from Dorothy Williams at *World of Books*, on an interview broadcast the previous evening with the American author, Truman Capote, on the British release of *In Cold Blood*. 'It was a marvellously sensitive revelation of a most strange person,' she wrote. Still inwardly seething, he replied how 'it is so rare to be complimented from within this ruthlessly professional organisation, so I do especially value your note.'

His impetuous spirit pulled him up sharp soon after the New Year celebrations. At 12:30 am, on the morning of Tuesday 4th January, he was on his way back to his rooms after a long day at Lime Grove when his E-Type Jaguar collided with a Ford van along the Barnet bypass. Suffering mild shock and concussion, an ambulance took him and the van driver to Barnet Hospital for tests. X-rays revealed he'd also suffered a worrying knock to his 'good' left knee from the collision. But, with no internal wounding apparent, Ken was discharged three hours later. He spent the next two weeks recuperating back at Gurneys, doing little writing and thinking about the *real* patient. He quickly bored. With his beloved E-Type in the nearest garage for repairs, he considered himself recovered enough to borrow the new S-model – courtesy of Jaguar's chairman - as a temporary replacement.

En route back to *24 Hours* on the 17th, Ken stopped off at Roehampton to deliver his leg for its regular testing. On its collection next day, his first item for the programme was in the company of two doctors on the salient subject of the causes of migraines.

Michelmore also endured the demands of the programme in a way he'd rarely experienced through the *Tonight* years. Apart from the uncertainties of early 1963, his absences from the studio were often through family commitments or holidays that his profile, and stamina, could maintain. Here, his own health was suffering, along with his enthusiasm for the subject matter, as predicted by Amoore. With an agreed decrease Michelmore's hours, Ken now regularly presented the programme and often on consecutive nights. With the national spring council elections around the corner, his number two on these occasions was the Canadian-born political analyst, Bob Mackenzie. (Balding, bespectacled and avuncular, he looked, ironically, not unlike Michelmore himself).

Ken's profile was at its highest when journalist Charles Fox visited him at his Lime Grove office for the *Radio Times*. But, in the midst of internal bickering, a new disenchantment revealed itself in candid admissions:

"'I still feel nervous. I still get tense. It's partly because there are so many things that can go wrong. *24 Hours* is much more gruelling than *Tonight* ever was, because it aims at being more up-to-the-minute. We often re-jig the programme twenty minutes before it goes out. And the studio set-up is complex. So, you're not just interviewing people, you're also keeping an eye on all sorts of things that are happening just round the corner. It's a bit like a juggler trying to keep five balls in the air at once.'

Kenneth Allsop, looking rather like an amiable eagle, wearing – inevitably – a flowered tie, sat in his tiny office at the BBC's Lime Grove studios. There were still three hours before *24 Hours* was due to go on the air. Meanwhile he toyed with a plateful of jam-roll and custard.

'It's midnight by the time the programme is over and we've had a drink and talked about the evening's disasters. I've got a farmhouse on the Bedfordshire border, about forty miles out of London, but I can't face commuting in the early hours. So I don't see as much of my wife and three children as I'd like to. It's usually about 2 a.m. before I get to sleep. I surface around nine or ten, and theoretically there's a full working day ahead for me to write in. In fact, it gets swallowed up, so the only time I get down to my book is on Saturdays and Sundays.'

The book is a study of the American migrant worker, the hobo. And just like Allsop's last book, *The Bootleggers*, it reflects his obsession with the United States.

'It's the mixture of violence and rootlessness, and the meretricious glitter of the place that gets me,' he says... 'I'm a neurotic worker,' he confesses sadly. 'I've lost the capacity for leisure. And that's something I mourn and feel miserable about. But I have this terrible, compulsive need to produce something – a book, or a script, or an article. I suppose you could say that I'm hooked on work.'"

But the 'amiable eagle's real and instinctive love rarely failed to distract. From the eighth floor of Broadcasting House, in the office of a colleague after lunch, his eye was caught by a 'peregrine circling and gliding high above (the) area between (the) new Post Office Tower and new office blocks, in bright sunlight for (a) couple of minutes.' The time for serious contemplation was long gone, and seemed likely never to return.

By the summer, Ken's inability to live within his means was finally brought home by Betty when she'd presented him with Gurney's latest quarterly bills. Ken's appetites, those for his cars, his menagerie, the maintenance of the farmhouse and London *pied-a-terre* had each contributed to backing the couple out to the brink of bankruptcy. Extremely reluctant to leave what had been his dream home, Betty soberly advised that they could at least remain in Hertfordshire. By September, they'd found a compact but smart, white-faced detached house in the semi-rural village of Braughing, near the town of Ware and, reassured over intended modifications by a local architect, made a welcomed offer on Fleece House.

Ken wanted contracts exchanged as soon as humanly possible as he was committed to an eight week stretch of reporting encompassing not only *24 Hours* but also his new radio review programmes: *The Critics* and *World of Books*. For these he must travel across Montreal, Toronto, Banff, Vancouver, Seattle, Los Angeles, La Crescenta, (the LA home of the Edwards), San Diego, Mexico City, Acapulco, Boston, Augusta, Poughkeepsie and New York; a schedule almost as gruelling as the previous year's hobo trek. But, for once, he couldn't get his own way as he'd also insisted upon structural changes ahead of any move, which only served to protract the sale.

The early diary entries for the trip don't suggest any new urgency to economise. While the BBC paid the usual expenses for accommodation, he dined with his French-Canadian guide at an exclusive 'skyscraper rooftop rest,' moved on to a strip club, coffee shop and 'existentialist bar in Rue St Catherine' on the first evening alone. On his first Friday, in L.A., he joined the Edwards for drinks then spent the rest of the weekend as their guests, sunbathing, eating, watching TV and, occasionally, writing. Experiencing loneliness in the time put aside for working, in Mexico City he complains of feeling 'very tired and dispirited' and, despite the expenditure on restaurant meals, missed those offered by Betty. Dissolution threatened as he 'killed time at the Hotel Pan Americana;' most likely with the Argentine girl who'd accompanied him and his guides that day.

The next morning he flies to Boston via Chicago, his recent car accident returning to haunt him:

'Left knee in poorish state: constantly aching and worse; steps become increasingly painful to negotiate.' Waiting at the Statler Hilton Hotel is a note from Betty, keeping him informed of negotiations on the sale of 'Gurneys' and purchase of Fleece House. 'Didn't go out,' he wrote. A sum of $783 from the BBC ($776 in traveller's cheques) is drawn the following morning, which ensures the aimlessness of the trip and pointlessness of its expense continues.

It isn't until he reaches New York on the 8th October – to begin work at the BBC's office there on Monday 10th – that what he was being paid for began in earnest. On arrival, he checked into the Algonquin. His hotel bill was seriously questioned after he found his room's skirting boards layered with dirt and passing cockroaches. Having rowed with the staff about the conditions, he was offered another room, dined alone, and turned in early. But he still wasn't well.

'Didn't eat all day,' he wrote on the 13th October. 'Dysentery, my condition still bad, feel groggy.' But this may have as much to do with his constant late nights and inconsistent dietary mix of rich and junk food as his ongoing TB. Stories related to the equally interminable Vietnam War dominated Ken's itinerary over the next four weeks: from British Foreign Secretary George Brown's peace proposals addressed to the General Assembly to the induction of boys into the U.S. Army at Poughkeepsie Draft Office. It was from here that Ken drove thirty-five miles north for his next assignment; to the 'atomic proof complex' set in a mountain of iron ore. His environmental sensibilities instantly bridled at its tasteless majesty.

'Whole concept of this 'Motel in the Mountain' (is) deeply deranged – the safe shelter for 200 picked men of Standard Oil New Jersey, with Ford, Kleenex and TV for 30 days, while the world outside simmers down to a radioactive ash-pile.' An intimation of what would become Ken's chief *cause celebre* at home. Interviewing, viewing of uncut rushes and writing commentary was consuming most of his work time, squeezing out what was left for the radio. He wrote a guilty response to an enquiry from Jocelyn Ferguson at *World of Books*, who'd booked a replacement host in his absence:

'The trouble is that new commitments keep developing from London... (You've) probably written me off as a hazardous risk... My apologies for being so undependable.'

A sudden influx of local contacts and BBC TV colleagues alleviated some of the weight. These more cultural stories of a personal interest were welcome, affording him much-needed observations on the burgeoning psychedelic movement. At the Museum of Modern Art he witnessed David Smith's metal sculptures; he followed this with a visit to East Village to witness Andy Warhol's *Exploding Plastic Inevitable* exhibition at The Balloon Farm. The next day he interviewed the author Tom Wolfe, whose *Kandy-Kolored, Tangerine Flake Streamline Baby* had, unsurprisingly, just put the daffodil-tied, striped-suited southerner under the literary spotlight. That evening Ken watched a series of uncensored art-house movies with friends and on to The Brown Jug, 'a fake English pub' into the small hours.

Later, a short, nervous afternoon in the Bowery district was calmed by a further contact with Betty on the sale and purchase and a visit to the Stairway to Stardom studio at West 53rd Street. Here, he witnessed a class of novice belly dancers in action. Ken was encouraged to join in with the beginners which, momentarily, *he did*. (Sadly, not caught on camera). With a week still to go on his American assignments, he was seriously flagging. Predictably, his $776 was already running out and he was reduced to going cap in hand back to the BBC offices. As their comparative pittance ran out he borrowed from his English contacts. In addition, the nerve-endings on his stump were flaring again, causing unwanted but unavoidable interruptions of bed rest back at the Algonquin.

It was a penniless and exhausted journalist who ambled carefully down the aircraft steps at London Airport on the evening of Thursday 10th November. Betty, Amanda and Fabian were there to meet him, driving him back to a half-empty 'Gurneys' for four days of complete rest, Ken lacking the strength to argue. He must have known he was weaker during this American trip than the last. But perhaps all his expense had been worth it.

On the 25th, he was tipped off that *24 Hours* had won a BAFTA for Best Factual Programme. By the following week he had completed the manuscript on the American hobo, researched during last year's freeway drive across the States. He named it *Hard Travellin'*.

By 1967, *24 Hours* had settled into a distinctive style never before witnessed on British television. Its iconoclastic mix of hard-hitting reportage and revelatory set-tos' with those usually lauded, swiftly made *Tonight*'s previous attempts seem an irredeemably cosy memory by comparison. Now, bolstered by *Panorama*'s decade-long run and that of ITV's *This Week*, *24 Hours* could wear its social conscience unashamedly upon its sleeve.

In January, on the back of the first of several subsequent

repeats of Ken Loache's controversial TV film *Cathy Come Home*, there featured a follow-up, half-hour studio discussion featuring the views and experiences of five homeless families. Critiques of South African Apartheid and the U.S. bombing campaign in Vietnam were highlights in February.

Mid-afternoon on Monday 27th, Ken met the great Welsh actor of stage and screen, Richard Burton, and the Italian director of his new film, Franco Zefferelli. An adaptation of Shakespeare's *The Taming of the Shrew* pitted Burton both with, and against, Elizabeth Taylor; the tempestuous love of his life since 1960's *Cleopatra* and cast, inspirationally, as the Shrew of the play's title. Pre-publicity ensured interest well beyond the range of the red-topped tabloids, as the volatility of the actors' relationship and the demands of the press was taking its toll on them both. Burton had, by all accounts, been hitting the bottle the previous night, so was in no mood, by morning, for quizzing by a sardonic intellectual. During the course of his probing, Ken asked the actor if he thought his wife's higher public profile was, in any way, detrimental to his own career. Hearing this as a slight against her, Burton roared an expletive and swung a clenched fist at Ken's head, which swayed – just in time – to one side. While Burton may have missed his target, the incident had shaken the normally unflappable Ken, who returned to his flat 'unwell' that evening, an hour before transmission. March highlighted a studio discussion on abortion, in the light of David Steel's 'pro' bill, while, in April, only the former *Tonight* team members could follow an item on racial discrimination with one on the vogue for topless waitressing.

While staying in London with his daughter, Sarah, Henry visited Lime Grove for after-broadcast drinks. With no available window on the programme, in May Ken invited him onto *World of Books* to speak on Joseph Conrad. After the morning recording, he drove Henry and his Producer, Jocelyn Ferguson, to a French restaurant in Charlotte Street. Ken recorded how Henry,

'looked older. He'd (been) blind in his left eye, he said, for 48 hours. Doctor said, "refraction would begin." He talked about dying several times – just wants to get the last novel finished.' (He was working on *Lucifer Before Sunrise* – Volume Fourteen of the Fifteen *Chronicles*). Once more the man was in a depressed state: this time from Christine who, after rambling incoherently and going AWOL the previous summer, had been diagnosed with a mental breakdown and resided in a hospital near Exeter. Divorce proceedings were once more in the offing: this time from Henry.

Now more than ever, the old man felt publicly shunned. Those contemporaries who remained his friends – often found amid the claret and cigar smoke of London's Savage Club - were well used to his eccentricities and unquestionably loyal. While Betty remained somewhat doubting, Ken's view of the man never wavered from his first judgement twenty years before. For each, an opportunity was arising for their mutual but contrasting affections to be publicly aired.

*

Meantime, on the one thousand-acre island set on the St. Lawrence River, Montreal's *Expo '67* was being heralded as the largest international fair of its kind and the highlight of Canada's centenary. As with London's Greenwich Dome thirty years later, the initial bias toward shallow entertainment was criticised enough for a re-think and a swerve toward one for science, culture and the pretentious sloganeering of 'Man and His World.'

The *24 Hours* team's contribution was Utopian: to beam, live, three of its forty-minute editions back to Britain. Thus far, the longest transmissions of their kind. Michelmore and

Ken were posted there on Saturday 27th May for the first of the three on the 30th. While Michelmore enjoyed the technological spectacle of it all, and the shuttling between each country-represented pavilion in the mini, futuristic taxis, his lieutenant was left cold. One guilty perpetrator, *Habitat '67* - a scale model proposed as 'a new concept in urban dwelling'- appeared as a series of light, caravan-shaped boxes atop each other in a pyramidal heap akin to the ultimate Spanish coastal resort conurbation. Meanwhile, the minimalist, agoraphobia-inducing stretches of space between sites simply served to turn his mind more to the work at hand.

There were no distractions worth losing his fee over this time, and no opinion was deemed worthy for the diary. Summer was more typically family focused. On the 18th June, Amanda was accepted into the National Youth Theatre. 'She's very pleased. We're delighted.'

Having secured a further pay rise, he sold the E-Type Jaguar. The replacement treat was a dark green Aston Martin; an equally indulgent purchase inspired by the two most recent James Bond films. On its release from garage modifications, he swung it into the space set aside by the lawn at Braughing's Summer Fete, which he'd agreed to open on Saturday 22nd July. Awaiting him amongst the gathering of local, middle-aged stall holding couples were two, quiet, Luton-based girls in their late teens: one brown-haired, the other blonde and busily snapping colour *Polaroids*' around their new hero. Janet and Jenny 'James' were close, childhood friends who'd become quite enamoured by the handsome co-presenter of *24 Hours*.

'We did not present ourselves as sisters,' recalls Jenny, now Jennifer Godfrey, 'but distant cousins. (I am sure - if we delved far enough back into history - it may have been so). Janet had a terrible home life with both parents hitting the bottle... Consequently, she spent a lot of time with my family who came to look on her as one of us.' Such attention had become par for the course for Ken, who was rarely seen in public without a girl, often of their generation or even younger. If sex still mattered to Ken, it was no longer the priority. Conversation mattered more, even with casual flings, and its absence quickly bored him. Quiet or embarrassed 'fans' were politely indulged but not encouraged. Before he ambled back into the Aston, he exchanged a few self-conscious words with the 'James' girls along with their offer to send him copies of the colour shots just taken. These have survived. In them, Ken looks as distinct and alone as the shot of his privately parked Aston. Silver-haired now, in a tie and tweed jacket and with his hands clasped behind his back, he looks more like a visiting dignitary than one of the community. He has become not just a figure well known but something else; something he'd swiftly tire of refuting - a television personality.

Colour was also under experimentation at Lime Grove, tests for which Ken sat in on the morning of the 4th August. While it wouldn't be utilised on the programme for another two years, it heralded other changes planned for the autumn season.

Two days later, Ken left a luncheon attended by overseas royalty, an unnamed princess, the chairwoman of Sotheby's and an amorous Barbara Cartland with a suddenly disabling viral attack. 'Violent stump pains,' he monotonously recorded, 'and temp. of 103.' While visiting Roehampton, Mirek Vitali insisted he take an extended, month-long holiday with no work commitments whatsoever; inviting Ken to join him and his wife for the first fortnight at his Lisbon villa just to make sure. Meantime, a further week off sick meant sudden but unavoidable changes to the Lime Grove production schedule and being forced into doing little more than making phone calls of apology, updating Vitali on his condition, and promises to contacts for the immediate future.

He wondered how much more he could take. With Michelmore now a virtual elder statesman at the BBC and planning to covet his own TV vehicles next season, Ken returned, still unwell, to front the programme on consecutive nights along with interchanging lieutenants Bob Mackenzie, Michael Barratt and a lean, slender-faced young Yorkshireman named Michael Parkinson. On the 17th, Ken finally submitted the final draft script for the *Bootleggers* musical, sealing the deal with Buddy Bregman.

The same day he received a briefing on a court case at which he'd just been approached as a prospective witness for the defence. For the past twelve months the subject of censorship had been a recurring theme in his work, the abolition for which he was becoming closely identified. Publicly, it had begun twelve months earlier when he and Robert Pitman – his old *Tribune* colleague – issued a 'pro' and 'con', two-part pamphlet on *A Question of Obscenity*. In his half, Ken conjures a memory from 1940 when he and his fellow RAF recruits 'gathered in a hangar' to receive a lecture and watch a film with 'gruesome close-ups' on the horrors of irresponsible sexual activity and its consequences. 'I can't stop you doing it,' warned their medical officer, 'but by God I'll stop you enjoying it.'

Pitman argued against a 'bored and sophisticated apathy for tolerance.' He also queries his 'opponent's apparent ambivalence toward the strip-club phenomenon in an earlier *Spectator* article. 'The motive for all (his) reluctant research is not made entirely clear...' In fact, Ken used the same cool, statistical approach for the subject of sex as for his bootleggers and hoboes: screening the fact that he was enjoying their seedy ambience on a regular basis.

A year on, the BBC broadcast a town hall debate on the subject, featuring both 'adversaries' and chaired by the writer and critic, Al Alvarez. At the same time, Hubert Selby's American novel *Last Exit to Brooklyn* was inciting a howl of hyperbole in the British press that hadn't been exercised since the *Lady Chatterley* case three years earlier. No lover of hyperbolic literature himself, Ken nevertheless saw a chance to make his most telling stand yet on the topic of obscenity. With the abolition of the Lord Chamberlain still a year away, (holding sway over every pronounceable word in the performing arts), Ken agreed to refute what he saw as the ill-considered, one-way yell of press hostility on his return from Portugal. The novel's Soho-based publisher – *Calder & Boyars* – had been accused of publishing an obscene work purely for profit under the 1959 Act. The called accusers – mainly aged university professors – were united in the view that the book was indeed a 'great money maker' which featured no redeeming condemnation of the violent acts portrayed. As a subsequent defence witness, midway through the trial, Ken gave it greater intellectual credence, claiming that, unlike the current crop of 'cheap pop novels...written to give cheap thrills,' it had a literary merit that 'impressed by the truth.' But the accusers had their day. The case was lost – to Ken's disgust – and it took a re-trial and the persuasive wit of John Mortimer, as defending counsel, to reverse the decision six months later. By this time, most of Europe was experiencing a new, darker mood of dissent.

In return for Mirek Vitali's Portugese hospitality, Ken asked Hodder & Stoughton - *Hard Travellin*'s publisher – to include a dedication. As if in answer to the question *what inspired you to choose this subject?* Ken follows this with an explanatory prefatory note. While sketching the train-jumping hobo, he looks within, harking back to his idealised, *Outsider* status at 'Gurneys':

'He often...squandered the money he had sweated for. He

was a wild and recalcitrant wayfarer, bothersome to the settled citizen who disapproved of him and, perhaps, secretly envied him. Out there in the offing, he developed his own distinct life and philosophy: tough, reckless, radical, sardonic.'

And, he is present in the subtly defiant, hopeful last paragraph:

'His habitat has changed but his habits have not, not all that much. For he is still there, a sundry part of the tidal restlessness of American life; and the hobo idea, or impulse, is even more widely present, the eagerly seized inheritance of the young of an urbanised society in which the hobo is theoretically obsolete.'

On Sunday 19th November Henry and Sue Scott – wife of journalist Gavin Scott (called away at the last minute by *Time* over the devaluation crisis) – visited Fleece House for a night's stay. Ostensibly, his guests were there to witness – first hand – the notices for *Hard Travellin'*, due out next morning. 'Good reviews in *Sunday Telegraph* and *Observer*,' were already noted by a hopeful, if flu-ridden, Ken. However, he also used the occasion to broach to his oldest friend a new series BBC1 intended screening in the New Year entitled *Personal Choice*. Interviewers from *24 Hours* and their rival, *Panorama*, had been offered the chance to choose their ideal interviewees for a run of cosy Sunday half-hours. Henry agreed to Ken's request, anticipating an easy, idolatrous ride of the kind intended by the BBC themselves. He trusted his old friend would be kind.

Like a Fairy Godmother bestowing favours, the *Radio Times* announced that 'as long as the people chosen are accessible and willing to be interviewed, the interviewers can ask for whom they wish.' Predictably, Michelmore fronted the queue, opening the series with his choice, Mary Wilson – wife of British Prime Minister, Harold. After, at Lime Grove around 3 p.m. on Thursday 7th December, Ken sat with

Henry before the cameras. We are taken back to the start of 1935:

Ken: 'Henry, one of the most significant moments in my life was when I was fourteen and I discovered in a library your book *The Lone Swallows* and the revelation in this was that there was someone else on earth who felt as I did about the countryside – about nature. I can only suppose a religious revelation to be of this bliss and intensity, so for all my teens you were my, sort of, personal *Maharishi*. And, eventually, I forced my attentions upon you. I suspect that a good many of your admirers had this sort of introduction to you.'

HW: 'I understand the feeling so well because when I was a young man, I discovered Richard Jefferies who wrote about the English countryside with such beauty and truth that it inspired me and set me on the same path.'

Having settled Henry into the talk, Ken posits 'a single purpose' he sees running through the books; that characters such as Willy Madison in the *Chronicle* series and others are all prophet-type figures intent on resolving the emotional paradoxes of love and war that causes man to war with himself. He asks Henry to explain the philosophy. Initially, Henry recounts the truce with the Germans he was a part of as an English Private in Flanders in 1914 and the shock at finding the unity in their plight and how neither side had the moral advantage. He is then asked if he ever doubted himself being regarded as a prophet or whether this was ever a conscious intent. He replies that he saw few of his 'acts' up to such a standard. Henry's subsequent responses have been polite and measured if, perhaps, a little distracted by Ken's hunter's glare until the latter hints at his prepared theme.

Ken: 'Have you always been absolutely certain of your own

motives – I mean by this that you're a very powerful man in your writing, you're powerful in your magnetism and in the intense emotionalism of your writing. Does it give you satisfaction to influence people, even to dominate them?'

Henry replies that he used to try and correct people, but that experience has shown that such action only antagonises. Ken presses him on such doubts as he has felt, adding that he has always appeared to him to be one of those writers' whose life is bound up totally in his writing. 'This doesn't really make simple happiness very easy, does it?' Henry concurs, referring to 'freeing one's devil,' which he explains as harmony created from beauty; an evolutionary process that frees him from the animal instinct.

True, at least, to the programme's title, Ken then starts to personalise the conversation. Picking up on Henry's admission of bearing bad habits, he asks what these are, 'because...you and I have had some pretty jolly times together, including some memorable booze-ups in Ireland and London and Devon...' Infuriatingly for Ken, Henry calmly diverts his subtle coaxing with an unrelated response: one on ever-delayed promises to himself to start writing. His friend tries again.

Ken: 'Henry, you're a contradictory and complicated man, and your dedication to the ideal of a new man in tune with himself and with nature and with his own family, has in fact resulted in a fairly disrupted personal life. Your marriages haven't worked, and now you live alone, and you seldom see your children, I think. Do you ever feel that the cost of your sense of mission has been too great upon yourself and upon the people close to you?'

HW: 'No, I think the mistake I made was taking on other peoples' troubles, instead of getting on with my own work.

But I must say we're a fairly harmonious family now. I see all my children... And my wife, Gypsy,...thinks I've done very well.'

Ken: 'But, looking back...'

HW: 'So, she's... *she's brilliant*. She's lovely.'

Ken then asks him to recall his time at the Norfolk Farm and how his hope of future inheritance by his children failed. Henry, by now, is not happy and tires of this further reminder.

HW: 'Well, I've told all this in my last novel – *Lucifer Before Sunrise* – where Philip, who is myself, has a tremendous gap between his ideals and what is. In other words, he is a phoenix, he comes out of the battlefield, to make a perfect world, as Hitler did and other people, and if you do that and insist on perfection, if you become a perfectionist, you go wrong...'

Henry then recalls the 'terrible time in England' in the Thirties, of the unemployment and that you could purchase Norfolk land for £2 per acre.

'And the arable tradition had largely gone down after twenty years of dereliction. I tried to put it on its feet and I said I'm going to do it. I hadn't any money but I wrote articles in the newspapers and broadcast and I was going to help England and, in association with other people, were going to create a land fit for heroes... (Pause) But it doesn't work out like that.'

Ken then offers him the chance to lance a thirty-year-old boil.

Ken: 'The central contradiction in you, or so it appears, to many of your friends and your admirers is your fascism, your loyalty to Mosley and your defence of Hitler which you still make. When you were active in the fascist movement in the Thirties, did you ever think it through, to consider what sort of life this might have meant for the average person, living under the system, living under the fascist state?'

Henry looks momentarily vague but his reply suggests he'd been waiting for Ken to bring his position up to date and attempts a hurried defence on what he maintains as their shared values.

HW: 'Well, I'm awfully sorry, I don't agree with that at all. I don't think Mosley, who is still my great friend... (Changing tack). He was an ex-soldier, he was even younger than I was in 1914 and, as A.J.P. Taylor has shown in his *Oxford History*, he had the only idea for the welfare state two generations ahead. He cared for three million unemployed. He wanted to make the motor roads. He was told he couldn't get the money because the City of London would not allow the second Labour Government to have the loan. So he said, who rules? The City of London or the Parliament that's elected? Then he went into the streets and his reputation, of course, went down like that. Of course, every kind of oddment got into his party. I saw the same thing in Hitler's men – there were awful crooks in it – and you must have a democracy. You must have it in Parliament. Although it's slow, it wins in the end. It must do, as Churchill said.'

Ken concedes that Henry's beliefs appear modified from what he'd formerly assumed. But, for him, the contradiction remained of his belief in strong leadership and his own bohemian lifestyle. Henry replies that Ken is assuming rather a lot. '*I know all about you, Henry...*' Ken interrupts with further familiarity. His interviewee is again put on the defensive. 'Well, it was probably true in the past, when I was running the farm...' He relates how his life in Norfolk forced him to improvise a training regime to overcome a lack of skills by a number of his workers. '*Why is that being a dictator?*' he asks. 'I treated them as my equals.' Ken pushes him on his earlier accusation of failing in his personal relations, at which Henry, again, is cornered into conceding.

Ken moves on to yet another contradiction he sees in need of explanation. He holds that Henry has written about the horror of battlefield life with a power that is unequalled, yet still sounds like an apologist for Field-Marshal Haig and his Generals, 'though you're certainly not a pacifist.' Henry proffers a weak, unconvincing response that he knows 'the tremendous strains' a General must put up with, and Haig, especially, was 'a most sensitive man... The German historians, who know their stuff, called him the master of the field. And he was because he saw them off.' Yet, a Eureka is revealed: that what unites Henry's defensive replies is the immovable belief in his ability to put himself in the position of his fellow being – man and beast - however naive its articulation.

After a brief reference to his first published journalism and Ken's first cycle visit of '35, the exchange is drawn to a conclusion.

Ken: 'You now spend almost all your time in that hut on the hilltop in Devon that I've known for many years, but rather isolated and alone now. Do you feel to be isolated and alone in the artistic sense that your beliefs and your ideals which you've worked for all your life have been rejected as they were at the start?'

HW: 'Well, I rather feel out on a limb, but then it may be that my writing's no good. On the other hand, it may mean that I'm in *the tradition* and that the faithful few will keep me alive... you know, the small minority which keeps all artists alive. Which kept Jefferies alive, and Hardy.'

Henry ends the programme suggesting the likes of *Tarka the Otter* and *Salar the Salmon* wrote themselves from an inspiration detached and spiritual: the only explanation when he now flips through the pages. He ends, clinging to a new concept, so far, ill thought through:

'I believe that the collection of genes in my blood...the super-sensory perception and racial memory, which the scientists are beginning to show that the genes carry... I am a trustee of the gift that was inborn with me...that's my feeling.'

At the end – as the closing titles rolled and music swelled – it was clear both men had arrived with different agendas. Ken's intention was of an air-clearing exercise, where long-held bones of contention – now used against Henry by a new generation of detractors – could be honestly exposed and explained. Yet many of Henry's responses frustrated Ken in a way not dissimilar to his reactions of 1947. It appeared little had changed for Henry, while Ken had advanced beyond reach. Ken's attempt at objective distance ultimately jarred against Henry's more myopic, pre-war Utopianism, leaving the former sounding like some hectoring youngest son. But, Ken's attempt to come to terms with Henry's former fascist sympathies had not been in vain. Henry's final comment about the genetic 'racial memory' remained with him long after they'd left the studio festering, half-formed in his mind, for the rest of his life.

According to Anne Williamson, after the programme's broadcast on the 7th January 1968, Ken's 'aggressive questioning' upset several of Henry's friends,' who'd found him 'too rough and thrusting.' Henry bemoaned in his diary the fact that he hadn't been able to see the questions beforehand, which, of course, was precisely Ken's intention.

'I thought he was just a little "near the knuckle" when he mentioned my "two marriages that hadn't worked out," and also a slightly snide remark about my (apparent) approval of squires.' Anne Williamson adds that, from then on, he was 'a little wary' of Ken.

With two weeks off from *24 Hours* for the Christmas recess, Ken had a chance to air his half-formed, scientific views to Martin Gilbert, who'd remained an acquaintance since discussing his first work of social history – *The Appeasers* – with him on *Tonight* in 1963. (An interview that ended with Gilbert demonstrating Hitler's typical courtesy to women guests. Leaning forward, he'd lifted Ken's arm and planted three kisses along its length. 'We were friends from that day.').

Ken was in need of more space and time to write his own work. It didn't help that his Braughing home - with no front garden, and its entrance opening directly onto a busy main road – was affording little of either. On hearing this, Gilbert invited Ken down for an overnight stay at Oxford's Merton College. With him he took copies of *The Bootleggers* and his latest. Having just completed the biography of the late Winston Churchill, authorised by his son Randolph, Gilbert was now in the second of a three-year fellowship. The elegant surroundings, crystal decanters dispensing port and brandy, and a long evening's discussion - Gilbert developing a suggestion of supporting Ken should he wish to apply for a fellowship of his own - began softening the latter's long held antipathy. At the end of the week, Ken sent his letter of application, again with both books, to strengthen the bid.

A hopeful Henry Williamson meets a challenging gaze from Ken for 'Personal Choice.' (BBC), 1967.

Ken being enrobed as Rector of Edinburgh University by His Royal Highness, Prince Phillip. February, 1969.

Amanda, Tristan, Betty and Fabian gather around Ken at the post-inauguration reception.

21
Feb 1968 – Jul 1969: The Merton Term Retreat

Dr. Desmond Morris had already made his name as an animal behaviourist in print and zoologist on television, presenting *Life* – a natural history series – for the past two years on the BBC's new, second channel. Surprisingly, in mid-Sixties Britain, and the Home Counties in particular, there existed a still vocal minority of churchgoing viewers who found his pro-Darwinian narratives blasphemous. Their problem – mystifying in retrospect – was that his evolutionary stance was accepted as historical fact from the outset, rather than objective conjecture as was often presented. Even in these supposedly liberal times, the century-old theory could still rankle enough to divide popular opinion. Yet, Morris, almost single-handedly, won around a majority of the less vociferous with his tweed-jacketed, country practitioner charm and easy, reassuring manner.

By the end of 1967 *The Naked Ape* – his accessible and well publicised book on the subject – had polarised those God-fearing few enough for Ken to have accepted one of his latest programme ideas: BBC Radio 4's *Wildlife Review*. A weekly panel of current biological thinking composed of naturalists and environmentalists discussing the latest developments in the field. On the edition of the 31st December, Morris was one of his guests. After the broadcast, the doctor offered to return the favour on what would be his final edition of *Life*. Another presenter was needed, anyway, since its topic was his soon-to-be best selling book and, according to Morris,

'I could not very well interview myself... Ken had an excellent voice, a natural elegance and sharpness of mind, which made him an ideal broadcaster. I had done the first fifty-two programmes in the series and then, early in 1968, I left England to live abroad.'

On obtaining the programme, Ken admitted to no formal training in any of the related sciences, but that his interest was that of 'a lifelong amateur.' With unconscious condescension he adds that, while 'much maligned,' he finds most scientists 'quite good' at communication. Again, Ken feels the need to wear his restless heart on his sleeve when comparing his past life to the present.

'I live in a permanently desperate state of which I theoretically disapprove; it's absurd, but there's always something more I want to do; can't help living at full tilt.'

Publicly, Ken's profile was once more on the ascendance. Privately, at least, this was quelling an ongoing argument with Paul Fox over billing and related gratuities. Michelmore, committed but much less driven than Ken, was tiring of commuting during hours he'd wanted with his family. On top of this, a continued police presence outside his house – called on after a death threat he'd received from a friend of one of his recent interviewees – was taking its toll. A re-think of his future was on the cards while he convalesced.

In the studio, Bob Mackenzie and Michael Barratt were now Ken's permanent lieutenants. Barratt recalls Ken, at this time, breezing into the studio each night carrying a large tumbler of scotch that he'd place beneath his desk moments before going on-air. He also recorded a second *Personal Choice*, with his friend and former *Evening Standard* colleague, Quentin Crewe. He explained his reasoning to the *Radio Times*:

'He has had to cope with a complexity of physical disability that reduces mine to a sprained thumb – yet this has, hitherto, never been known to the millions who read of his activities and travels. Quentin has increasingly seemed to me – increasingly as his difficulties have multiplied with the years – the most impressive and courageous man I know...

...I hesitated to invite him on to *Personal Choice* with me, and he hesitated before accepting, because both of us have, I think, an equal distaste for sentimentality...and both of us share the view that, in the field of professionalism, there should be no special allowances made.'

But the result proved a touching and moving conversation with the now permanently wheelchair-bound traveller and critic. On its broadcast, both public and press were almost unanimous in their praise. But Ken's TB – dormant until now - ensured he'd be in no position to appreciate it.

On Monday 5th February, he experienced stabbing pains in his bladder while passing water. Urinary trouble he'd dismissed the previous November was diagnosed a second time. His GP at Braughing was concerned enough to refer him to a Portland Place specialist: Sir Eric Riches. En route, that Friday morning, he stopped off at Roehampton for the regular stump check, from where the additional test results were passed on. At Portland Place, a change in his medication would allow for several daily hours of functional mobility, but his condition was such that he was then referred to Middlesex Hospital for X-rays. Results on his specimen confirmed that the TB in his body was sating its appetite on at least one of his kidneys. Removal was mooted. In the short term he had no choice but to endure treatment and an extended stay in hospital.

This bombshell was tempered by the news that his application for literary study at Oxford's Merton College – endorsed by the newly renowned Martin Gilbert - had been accepted; the one term fellowship to commence from April the following year. Ken was quietly thrilled at this prospect of establishment recognition by those he'd once envied and sneered at. In response, he stubbornly continued to work - on another edition of *Life* and other, more short-term, freelance commitments. With Betty for support, parties of friends were still entertained - and visited - for drinks and conversation.

But, even by his own expectations, he was a weak man. Then what occurred on the 17th - a Saturday night - put his condition into some perspective. Fabian Allsop had just turned eighteen when, returning late from a party with friends in a loaned van on the A507 passed the Hertfordshire town of Baldock, he suddenly lost control, skidding off the motorway and crashing, at speed, into a telegraph pole. Fabian suffered a severe concussion. His friend in the passenger seat, a seventeen-year-old American student, was killed outright. Receiving the news in the small hours, Ken and Betty rushed to Hitchin's Lister Hospital to find their youngest son comatose in the emergency ward. Assured by the staff that his situation was not critical, the couple spent the Sunday in Braughing, telling what they knew of the incident and offering their condolences to the dead boy's parents. Ken himself was interned next day for an indefinite stay at St. Andrew's in Cricklewood, North West London.

All this time their twenty-year-old daughter Amanda had been staying in Rome as an *au pair*. On receiving the double-blow from her mother, she rushed home to lend support. She found her father on a daily injection of streptomycin and a double dose of mixture to be taken orally. He was 'desperately depressed – he found physical imperfection intolerable, and the thought of his body giving out on him angered and frustrated him.' It didn't help that he was given no end date for discharge. It must have felt like 1943-45 all over again. Perhaps this was communicated as, five weeks later, he was allowed out for extended treatment at home, the doctors having decided against his kidney's removal.

'He was ill for the whole summer,' recorded Amanda, 'and

in a state of intense, withdrawn depression.' Bed-ridden at Fleece House, he was offered no choice but to cancel *all* appointments and work commitments at Lime Grove. So, for the first time since the War, Ken was forced into submitting to the dictates of the condition.

After several uncharacteristically blank diary pages, the 23rd March records that Tristan came home from the University of Kent for a three-week stay while Shirley Williams and her Cambridge philosopher husband Bernard called round. All the while he slept on through a drug-induced haze. In April, Ken rallied enough to respond to concerned enquirers, detractors, and belatedly finish an article for *Nova*. Enough to leave him breathless and force him back horizontally. From here, at least, with all the internal renovations complete, he could observe the landscape gardeners laying and seeding the new lawn and note the extreme changes in the weather occurring this year. On the 9th, Betty helped him dress and drove him to Portland Place and a regular check-up with Sir Eric. Before they left, Riches informed Ken that, with no obvious remission in sight, surgery might still be necessary.

Later that month, Fabian, out of hospital but suffering post-traumatic migraines, was received in court with sympathy and fined a moderate sum for what was deemed 'careless driving.'

A further X-ray by Riches on the 22nd subsequently revealed a more noticeable improvement in the staunch of blood to the kidney. The *streptomycin* shots, at least, could be discontinued from May, allowing for an indefinite postponement of the threatened surgery. Over the course of the month he was functioning comparatively normally, while the TB maintained its dormant, gallows-like, shadow. He helped Tristan complete work on the garden to his specifications and noticed the birds again; now nesting in *their* new home.

With his return to *24 Hours* confirmed for Tuesday 4th June, he gave an interview to a journalist from the *Sunday Times*, eager for an update on his health. Looking drawn and clearly suffering weight loss in the article's accompanying shot, Ken sounds the slightly defeatist, martyred tone of 1966:

'From childhood I wanted to be a novelist,' (he casually fibbed). 'But the novels I've published I can barely open without cringing. My abilities are journalistic. I can write documentary stuff...crystallising things, which are not apparent. I don't see myself as an author. I am an old-fashioned journalist who writes everything down because while other people have total recall, I have total forget.'

He admits to pining for the immediacy of 'live' television: 'It leaves scar tissue. It's obligatory to be in it.'

His impatience to return to *24 Hours* confirms the limit of his aspirations. On the surface, his profile was higher now than it had ever been. During a drug-induced afternoon in March, he was told he'd garnered most votes in the bitterly contested poll to replace Edinburgh University's current Rector, Malcolm Muggeridge, who'd left mid-term, disgusted by the students' liberal, pot-smoking morality. Ken bid an unsparing good riddance to his predecessor:

'I can't stand his anti-sensuality thing,' he said. 'Anything one can do to mend the damage he did must be to the good.' Sentiments that struck a chord with the young, liberal generation. But the level of publicity surrounding the infighting between the candidates' supporters made the victory appear somewhat pyrrhic. Dissent over the selection process was matched only by that over the age, political persuasion, and ultimate use of the potential winner. For some years the post had been little more than a sinecure and its holder, a mascot for Edinburgh. The links to the student union and student welfare generally, progressively disregarded. Paul Routledge, in his biography of Gordon

Brown – the future Labour Chancellor of the Exchequer and a student there at the time – states how,

'in recent times, the poll was invariably regarded as an occasion for campus merriment. The candidates were usually drawn from showbiz or the media, and the winner did not take the job too seriously. This absentee-rector situation suited the authorities admirably. The Principal presided over a group of establishment yes-men who simply rubber-stamped his wishes.' The student union itself was after a *student* rector – one of their own – who, in their eyes, would restore those links and best represent current student concerns. As with the other short-listed finalists – comic actor Alistair Sim, journalist and writer, Claud Cockburn, and educationalist, A.S. Neill, - Ken was not perceived as one of them either. Only Steve Morrison, studying Politics there, seemed to bear the correct credentials. But the broadness of the field – splitting the vote – went against him and it was Ken who rose up through the centre, collecting the 'undecided' votes. Sullen-faced Brown, in line for the editorship of *Student*, the University's magazine, was not happy at the choice of this English establishment figure. His principal, Michael Swann, a right-winger who'd come unstuck for holding shares in South African companies while supportive of the University's Anti-Apartheid Movement, was relieved by the outcome. Each would reverse their opinions in time.

*

Ken was poised to permanently replace Cliff Michelmore on *24 Hours* who he'd heard wouldn't be renewing his contract that summer. On top of this, Buddy Bregman's production of *The Bootleggers* was about to go into rehearsal for its Broadway opening in the autumn. But, jadedness was setting in. His continuing thirst for new knowledge and experience could no longer be reconciled with what he felt was his obviously failing physique. The TB would never leave him. He knew it. He'd always known. The lifelong pain from his stump and endless, ill-fitting false limbs he'd learnt to bear, but was he seriously expected to drag around the rest of his body while age gradually robbed what strength remained?

Before the 4th June return to Lime Grove, he began scribbling half-articulated notes for a projected autobiography. Amongst a list of one-word memory joggers was a term that might offer the one hope for ultimate control: 'suicide.'

It was the mortality of others that faced him on his return to Lime Grove. On his first day back he reported on the assassination attempt upon Andy Warhol by Valerie Solanis – the sole, unhinged member of S.C.U.M. (Society for Cutting Up Men) - followed, the next night, by the fatal gunning down of Robert Kennedy during the Democrat election campaign. But his disenchantment remained intact which, on arrival, he was compelled to direct at his employers. For no sooner had he returned than he found it necessary to defend his interviewing technique.

The charge was of arrogance and – worse - bias. An 18th June discussion on the issue of germ warfare, with a Dr. Rose and Mr. Gadsby of Porton Down, highlighted Ken's preferences all too clearly in the view of John Grist – the new Head of Current Affairs. Nine days later they met with a mutual hope of clearing the air, but Ken received a reprimand. In Grist's view, he'd felt too strongly about the subject to be impartial, suggesting Michael Barratt might have been a wiser choice. The journalist, Philip Purser, was in the studio, observing on the night. Grist told Ken that Purser's subsequent review backed up his concerns. He'd accused Ken of 'breezing into' the studio, faking an attitude of indignation, then 'breezing out.' The next day Ken wrote to Grist, the slant borne of his growing interest in biological science:

'I deliberately sought to raise the moral and ethical criteria which seem to me implicit in preparation for bacteriological warfare – the question of where, when and whether scientists take a stand and proclaim their duty as being wider than to individual nations but to the human race at large. There was no concealment about the questions or the question-line: this was discussed beforehand in the editorial office.' Again, he is accused of promising one set of questions and delivering another. On them, he claims he purposely avoided the 'pretence of indifference' in favour challenging his own, and presumably most others, assumptions on the morality of chemical warfare. But his starting point was the assumption that it was *wrong*. His goal, he claimed, was for both Rose and Gadsby to 'declare themselves, and explain how they squared such work with the Hippocratic oath of medicine.' He ends questioning just how far the BBC's impartiality should extend when dealing with 'incitement to violence, racialism, child cruelty...to war itself?' Grist, in his capacity as Current Affairs head at least, bought the arguments, though a new generation were seeing at first hand Ken's intransigent independence.

July was spent in argument over the BBC's sickness insurance policy that was on the point of, or was already, running out. Ken indignantly stated neither he nor Betty was ever offered the chance to apply for a second ongoing policy that didn't require annual renewal.

On the 11th August, an apparently innocent article on *24 Hours* by Kenneth Pearson in the *Sunday Times* managed to ignite further dissent. Friday 21st June had witnessed Michelmore's final edition, with Ken attending the subsequent party. A second autumn 'shake-up' in its format was deemed necessary from the ratings war with *News At Ten* on ITV. In the article, John Grist was quoted as saying that Michelmore's departure six weeks earlier, '"means that we have lacked a senior, experienced man for some time." In the next three weeks, three new interviewers will sign contracts for the programme and be fed before the cameras after September.' Crucially, Pearson adds that 'the opinions of professional critics...have begun to deplore the programme's lack of objectivity.' Still quietly seething from his dressing down in June, Ken read this in apoplectic rage. How could it be read as anything other than a personal snub? On the 13th he opened a memo back to Grist, characteristically sardonic:

'How heartening and morale-building it was to read in the *Sunday Times* – along with several million of the public – one's chief's denigration of the quality of his staff...' (adding) 'this very pointedly and directly discredits me, and is seriously diminishing and damaging professionally.' He adds that he has spoken to his solicitor, who agreed that the piece was 'gravely defamatory' within the law, compounded by a *Wanted*-type photo, that week, in the *Radio Times*. He demanded redress and would take his grievance to Paul Fox personally. Yet, with the article's accused unnamed, the inference pointed also to Ken's colleague, Michael Barratt, who'd just verbally committed to two more years with Current Affairs. He also memoed Grist believing,

'I was regarded as a senior and experienced member of the team. It seems, however, that you no longer regard me (or indeed any of my colleagues) in that light.' Grist, though, was away on holiday through the debacle. It was left to Paul Fox - now promoted to Controller of BBC1 - to deal with what threatened to become a deluge of internal complaints. Phone calls were made between he and Grist and, on the 15th, Ken spoke personally to Pearson with the BBC solicitor's knowledge. The solicitor recited denials Grist made regarding the inaccuracy of his quotes. Pearson, however, insisted to Ken that what he'd reported were Grist's precise words. Ken decided that, since what was stated was printed in quotes, he tended to side with the journalist who offered to 'present a fairer picture of the work done by Mike Barratt and myself' in a follow-up article.

All this, of course, left the absent Head of Current Affairs at a certain disadvantage painting him, inadvertently, the villain of the piece. He hadn't reappeared on the 13th September when Ken advised the BBC solicitor to tell Grist to return a 'prompt letter' on his return. The following week, with the new series back on air, Grist found himself the target of a mutinous army of employees. He wrote immediately to the *Sunday Times* new editor, Harold Evans, refuting entirely the content of the two controversial quotes.

'The fact that Cliff Michelmore was to leave *24 Hours* had been discussed within the BBC for several months. The public announcement was made several weeks after the decision. At the same time as Cliff's departure was arranged, it was decided that those who were presenting the programme were more than adequate and although we regretted Cliff going, we would make no major changes.'

With an apology returned, redress was made in a follow-up article. Such was the turnover of work that, by the time Grist returned, Ken had been sent off to America for a fortnight of filmed assignments.

It was while he was packing to leave that *The Spectator* – that, like *Nova*, had been featuring a *Personal Column*, semi-regularly, for the last couple of years - published his latest, 'On Living With Pain.' The most public declaration on his state of health thus far, the article has also become a seminal statement on his maxim for life. It shows him, for once, vulnerably human. Typically, though, still he observes – detached - far more than he personally judges. Written over the summer, soon after his return to Lime Grove, he contrasted his own views on how best to deal with pain with those of his various friends. Some 'proffered help, concern, a bundle of books, a note of commiseration, a word of support.' Others just as close, if not more, in spirit 'remained silent and absent.' Disappointed but accepting, he puts it down to 'part of the social machinery of mutual comfort.' He concedes that while anaesthetised on his back at St. Andrews Hospital, he had time to reflect.

The confession is peppered with a personally directed distaste.

'There were the crude emotions that swilled in at high tide during the mournful hours of being sorry for myself. *Hadn't one bloody well paid one's dues already...* Agnosticism didn't prevent indignant rancour that one had been sorted out again by some malignant cosmic bullyboy. Wasn't there a rationing system for doling out retribution and suffering? Had the computer got jammed on the Allsop programme? How about moving the finger on to some of the bastards of the world, indestructible with rude health and virility?' He reflects further on what has been an endurance of twenty-five years. 'Since I was twenty-three, on morphia (sic) and the danger list with a smashed and gangrenous knee, I don't think there has been a waking hour when I have not consciously been in discomfort at best or agony at worst. This derives from wearing an artificial leg... No matter how snug and streamlined it is, abrasions, bruisings, achings and nippings continue, and one seldom dismantles oneself for bed without feeling to have been stretched on the rack for the past sixteen hours.'

He talks of experiencing the 'invisible limb' syndrome, where nerve pains can seemingly be felt running up and down the false leg. They vary from 'mild tremors' to flaring 'attacks of horrible violence, when electric shocks stab through the stump as if live, high-voltage wires are being jabbed at the tip in some esoteric, Bond-ish torture...' He doesn't believe pain can or should be borne continuously, without periods of relief. He recalls the nun who told him, while bed-ridden and screaming for a painkilling injection in one of the military hospitals in 1943-4, that 'our lot on earth was to suffer.' Justification, in his view, not only for his agnosticism but also for his future intellectual path. Mind consistently over matter. To deviate would concede, perhaps fatally, to the pain's dominance. 'Incessant, grinding pain, he ends, 'interferes with the preferable condition, that of the medieval aspiration to *virtu*, the shaping of an educated mind that can reason with elegance, order and profundity.' Unavoidably, on his terms. The article shows a more intimate side to him that the bravura of the later *Mail* articles and more heated *Tonight* and *24 Hours* interviews had threatened to banish for good. It would be a turning point for Ken, and one positively received. Meantime he was nearing fifty, the tubercular attack on his kidney had taken its toll, and he knew the pain was just waiting to gain the upper hand. The waning adrenaline, in tow, would force him to attend to it indefinitely.

The writing of, and subsequent reaction to, his *Spectator* piece proved entirely positive. Praise came from friends and fans alike at his openness. It stunned journalist colleagues who'd known him for years to discover he'd had such trouble coping. Yet, what could have been cathartic and encouraged closer relations only served to underline that they didn't know him as well as they'd assumed. That through all the wealth, style and sophistication on show over recent years, the private man remained the precocious boy, back in the Osterley Park of the 1930s', climbing trees, spying on the bird life, collecting eggs late into the evening and typing in his bedroom his ornithological review. That everything since had been an equally precocious but second-best alternative enforced by circumstance.

1969 would be a year for speechmaking: most of it unwelcome. In the second week of January, he was in his study composing his inaugural address for the forthcoming

Rectorship ceremony when he broke off from typing and pushed himself away from the desk. The infected kidney, once again, blanched within. His local GP was called and adjusted his dosage, allowing him to complete the text the following day. On Sunday the 19th he composed a memo for inclusion in a speech to be delivered at Roehampton three days later. One consequence of his article was an invitation to address the institution's Standing Advisory Committee on Artificial Limbs. As a famous face and regular patient of twenty-three years, he would be a good advertisement for publicising their recent refurbishment. Like a VIP he toured the upgraded limb-fitting centre and lunched at Roehampton House before addressing the Committee on what he'd witnessed. His impressions were, presumably, favourable since he also offered his views on the most effective way to publicise the 'improvements': a convincing stand-in, with Sir Douglas Bader unavailable.

For *Nova*, his other personal column, the tone would be lighter but no less confessional in the face of one who suspected his public image and sussed, quite convincingly, a little of the private man. The cause was a package received from an obsessed viewer. Through the post one February morning fell a multiple-paged thesis from a woman based in Dumbartonshire, Scotland. Emblazoned across its front was the legend THE ENIGMA OF KENNETH ALLSOP. Fascinated by his apparent detachment from his subjects (and compounded, no doubt, by his recent long absence) as much as by his personal style, Ken was flattered but also unnerved by the accuracy of a document he refers to as 'a session of pyscho-analysis *in absentia.*'

While noting his varied interests and talents, she finds suspect the lack of any solid information on him. For her, this makes it '"difficult to know whether we have a man worthy of admiration or one, at worst, whom we should despise." She is forced to the conclusion that I am "an intellectual snob, who really feels too important to waste his valuable time and his genius on the man-in-the-street." Continually, she says, one is "confronted by this discovery of a split personality... Can, in fact, Mr. Allsop himself be sure of his true characteristics?"

Ken's heart-on-sleeve response feels disingenuous but not dishonest.

'My difficulty is that I have a much clearer idea of the person I would like to be than of the person I am,' he admits. Ideally, he'd be the 18th Century Virginian, Colonel William Byrd; 'a plantation owner, trafficker in slaves and country gentleman of a style modelled on the older England of Addison's Sir Roger de Coverley.' Better yet, 'I would like to have been a botanising country parson under the patronage of George II, humbly anonymous and secure in my compact, ordered pursuit of absorbed, personal discovery.'

Ultimately, he concedes the viewer's perspective on him as ambiguous, putting it down to a journalist's unsubtle simplification of major events and 'the over-assertive air which (the polemical writer or TV commentator) may not really feel – or should not...' At the same time,' he defends, 'short of being a know-all, one really ought to know where one stands on basic principles, and be unwilling to compromise.' His advice to others, which he know longer feels able to enact, ending 'Still, Mrs. C., I admit that as my age advances with such dismal speed, my palsied hand can grasp ever less firmly upon convictions it once held.' He appends Oscar Wilde's dictum that "One's real life is so often the life that one does not live."

Such precious introspection was lost on the majority of his women viewers who felt Ken should simply accept his lot as thinking woman's crumpet and that the press's labelling him a 'television personality' was no diminution. 'Why do you argue that your passport calls you 'journalist?'' enquired another in an anonymous letter, 'when, really, you are something so much richer and rare. It is not your feature writing nor your history of hobos, nor your academic honours that we go for. *It is you.* Where would we be without you as our television personality? And, come to that, I wonder how you'd manage without us?'

On the 19th February, the Allsops – minus Fabian, who drove - entrained up to Edinburgh for Ken's installation as Rector the following afternoon. Press and BBC film cameras awaited, decking the University's central hall, the latter for an item to be included in that evening's *24 Hours*. After encircling his new Rector's shoulders with the heavy, velvet robes of office, Ken launched into a prepared, self-indulgent speech on the heady, salient topic of student protest. Typically, he surrounded its pros and cons with allusions, literary and political, which reached out to a subtext asking just what a university education was for.

'It is not...to provide a conveyor belt plant for degrees,' he argued. 'It is, surely, to train minds to test propositions, to sharpen scepticism, to think with discipline but adventurously...' This attempt to convince himself, more than his audience, anticipated the stay at Oxford. He cautioned against the use of violence in defence of a worthy cause.

'Are the principles of liberty and truth at the forefront of the minds of those rebels who would intimidate and silence and close down? And even if they themselves believe so, they should face the grim probability of a backlash of ultra-rightism, which one knows is a powerful potential in the country, not yet clear and consolidated, but explosively near the surface, and capable of being ignited by the sparks which such as Enoch Powell so deliberately make fly. If the young revolutionaries had their way and tried to take over, the result would be even more catastrophic than a victory by them. It would be a victory for the others...'

A full three-quarters-of-an-hour passed before he

concluded with a quote, as a maxim, from George Peele's *A Farewell to Arms*; ' "Beauty, strength, youth, are flowers but fading seen; Duty, faith, love, are roots, and ever green."'

Travel weariness had caught up with Henry and, as at the West Country Writers Conference of '65, he almost nodded off before the speech's end. 'Good, but too long I thought,' was how he excused himself after the champagne party that evening.

What he'd considered his last ever manuscript had just been delivered to Macdonald's after a good deal of re-drafting and his publisher's discovery of a conspicuous typographical error after the initial print run. The relief felt on completion of his *Chronicle of Ancient Sunlight* cycle – eighteen years in the writing - proved almost overwhelming. Elation was expressed in a phone call to Ken from his cottage at Ilfracombe. He said he'd not felt this sure about a work since completing *The Pathway*; a title first published forty years before. He insisted on including a dedication for all the years of unswerving support. (Memories of their recent BBC interview momentarily sidelined). He then wrote to Dan Farson:

'(I'd) got up from my writing table, overcome by emotion, crying out words of grief and amazement while walking aimlessly about the rooms of the cottage - empty except for myself - disturbed by feelings of a lost freedom which also had been a tyranny during the two decades now closed to one.' He highlighted the pride he felt for being born an Englishman, and only now feeling worthy to speak for the men who'd given their lives to the Western Front.

'Everything in Henry's life stemmed from that Western Front,' said Farson, 'after which there could never be such innocence again, though he searched for it always.'

On the morning of the 29th May, Ken opened his final proof copy, complete with the dedication, and became increasingly despondent. 'It produces a sickly distaste,' was all he'd report to his diary. For him, the hyperbolic shock tactics he'd always despised from lesser writers had replaced the former poetry of the prose. Indeed, precisely the kind of writing that undermined his attack on censorship from The Old Bailey dock in November '67: "Am I like that, really? Wanting revenge, because my father raped me when I was a child: was it punishment for coming on him when he was frigging the nanny goat behind the hedge? If I wrote that no one would believe it. Mother found out and I had to sleep with Grannie ever afterwards..." As well as, "animals are shapely, compared with women after twenty-five. Black brassieres and French knickers – trap for John Thomas, Esquire – finally cancer of the breast from too much mauling. *God, I am human bait, nothing more...*"

Less blackly comedic and closer to the bone was his hero Philip Maddison's diatribe, reflecting Henry's own long-held, defensive view of the Nazi:

"Atrocities induce atrocities – all those civilians burned by our phosphorous bombs on German towns – all those Jews *burned in revenge.*"

Ken could only join the chorus of Fleet Street disapproval that accompanied its release. But he couldn't bring himself to commit it to print. The omission, intended in Henry's favour, returned their relationship to one of cool impasse.

On the 25th April, he swept his dark green Aston Martin, box-loaded with research papers and cases filled with expensive clothes, into the car park of Oxford's Merton College. A Fellow arrived to show him to his double-roomed quarters: 'Door 4 into Fellows Quad'; a spacious, sun-facing, white panelled sitting room inset with French-style windows overlooking Christ Church Meadows – where cows grazed in the distance – the outer door opening onto a pathway leading to the Fellows Garden. His bedroom adjoined this.

Returning to the car a student appeared, offering to carry

the ambling celebrity's remaining baggage. This same student would inform Ken of the College verger, who'd show tourists around the site reciting an impressive catalogue of famous ex-students, none of who had actually attended. A passing student, interrupting his flow, might be called out to with "Did your caviar and champagne reach your room all right, sir?"

Blissful surroundings to most were rarely untainted for Ken. That night a Chinese student hung himself. The very next morning Ken awoke to a particularly bad stump attack, followed by a swift intake of numbing *Panadol*. Fortunately he'd been assigned two 'advisors'; a secretary and a scout: a Polish student named Rush who assisted by obtaining those basic utensils required by the individual Fellow: in Ken's case, ashtrays and tumblers. Regular offers of sherry, brandy and good conversation from the other Fellows and occasional student was assured to regularly interrupt his intended studies.

In French Literature tutor Peter Hoy – who told Ken he'd once been the suicide's moral tutor - he found a like-minded consumer of Henry's work. He'd also experienced a 'political dichotomy' parallel to Ken's. Hoy told him he'd been a communist supporter in Paris yet could link Henry to all his 'ecstatic' experiences. By the third day he'd received a good luck letter from Amanda. That evening he unloaded his boxes, the piles conforming to his three literary commitments. These were a foreword to a new edition of *Uncle Tom's Cabin*, a short biography on its author, Harriet Beecher Stowe, for Heron Books, and an educational brochure on the current state of Britain's rural environment - *Fit to Live In?* - for Richard Mabey, editor at Penguin. He'd also brought notes for a fourth he'd been pondering over this past eighteen months, since his controversial interview with Henry: a book on the origins of fascism, which the talk with Hoy had helped re-inspire.

But the imbibing of 'port and Sauterne and various sweetmeats amid the silver candlesticks' was the kind of elitist diversion guaranteed to entice Ken away from the matters at hand. As ever, the challenge would be to please himself and everyone else in the limited time set. Three days in the case of the *Uncle Tom's Cabin* piece. With his record-player set up and playing – pretentiously – 'Goossens with Bach,' he typed a reply to Amanda:

'I'm welcoming this chance of re-orientating myself to a more sensible routine. I was in bed and asleep by 11.30 last night and up this morning at 8 and feel all the better for having had a whole day to operate within... I don't think it can fail to be an enormously interesting and valuable interlude in my otherwise idiotic life...' Sparing her his usual stump attacks, he feigns an upbeat tone on the history of fascism idea:

'I hope I can turn with more leisure to other tasks, the main one being this tenuous idea of connecting 20th century totalitarianism with 19th century pastoral romanticism: the seeds of so much of the Nazi blood-and-soil philosophy, nature mysticism etc. Little more than a notion at present, but it's amazing how ideas mesh together.'

A further stump attack the night before his deadline didn't stop Ken from meeting it. Beyond May Day he began tiring of the formal beauty and trappings of tradition. It began on the second Sunday. A virtual day off, he felt uneasy surrounded by the four dark-suited undergraduates taking breakfast after Holy Communion. 'Pallid, homosex(ual) ambience' he sniffed.

Occasionally, between sessions of his own writing and dictating inescapable correspondence, he'd walk alone – if he could – around the perimeter of Christ Church Meadows. He observed the new intake of students decked out in their long hair and hippy clothes of casual defiance and wondered just how long it would take before the 'sheer weight and power of Oxford's spell' and the experiential awe of getting here conformed them. More often, other Fellows would catch him up and discover his wealth of acquired knowledge. Martin Gilbert, his sponsor, in his final three months, was a regular confidante.

'I was very fond of Kenneth,' he recalled, 'and spent many hours in his company. I learned a lot from him about events and about life. I...considered an hour walking with him around the Meadows as an hour well spent.' Meanwhile, John Roberts, another accompanying Fellow, recalled an occasion where Ken tried too hard to impress. Presiding over that evening's dinner, he witnessed Gilbert introduce 'Kenneth Allsop' to a cleric and one of the eldest Fellows at the College.

'The cleric and he then fell into lively conversation, mostly on matters ecclesiastical. It became evident that KA was getting more and more out of his depth, and the clergyman more and more puzzled. He finally asked KA, 'Where, incidentally, do you hold your canonry?' It transpired he had misheard 'Kenneth' as 'Canon.''

Another, never having owned a TV or read his reviews, learned about him from scratch. Recalls Thomas Braun:

'Only because he had to rest several times during each of those walks did his war injury come up. I was interested to learn from him how the Germans in the 1920s had devised artificial limbs far in advance of the British, but how clumsy and awkward even these had been.' Ken repeated the unfeeling response of his ward sister at the military hospital. Being mutual strangers, Ken's mask remained solidly in place throughout. 'What I admired most about him was his resolute cheerfulness.'

Mid-May: after a day in London for editorial meetings and arguments over dues, the Allsops' celebrated Amanda's 21st with a champagne dinner at The Ivy followed by a performance of *Hair*, during which Ken suffered a further attack: this time from his dormant kidney. The weekend at Braughing was a prelude to nearly a week of commitments up at Edinburgh, for committee meetings, debates and speeches. This meant stopping off at Merton en route. The honour was feeling more like an albatross and Ken had serious misgivings at what he'd taken on.

'Very frustrated at not being able to get to <u>real work</u>.'

Back at Merton on the 4th June, a pale looking Betty arrived with a dual-dedicated letter from Amanda: a thank you for their consistent encouragement in her progress. Ken was especially touched and promised to make time for a large gathering in her honour as an apology for being away. He told Betty he'd just pottered to the last page of Henry's *The Gale of the World* and wondered, guiltily, how he could do anything other than give an honest assessment. Something, for once, he was reluctant to do. That weekend, he drove back to Braughing for his daughter's belated 21st celebration.

That Monday, en route back, he stopped off at Lime Grove for a summons from John Crist and Tony Smith, the new, 29-year-old editor of *24 Hours*. (One of Smith's early editions, later that summer, cannot be allowed to pass unmentioned. If nothing else it highlights Ken's level of buttoned-down solemnity on a job in the face of high provocation. Ken had been assigned to fly to Copenhagen for a three-day series of interviews on the subject of the burgeoning European sex industry. After interviewing a married couple of sex therapists and columnists, he visits the Leo Madsen Studio to watch a beautiful nineteen-year-old girl joining a man and woman for a threesome before provocatively undressing herself. He then moves on to the shooting of a blue movie in a suburban flat. 'There until 3.30 am,' he reports. 'Extraordinary experience. About 25 people there – much hash-smoking and pep-pill swallowing.' Next day, he films a piece to camera in the city's largest bookstore, against a backdrop of pornography sold openly on the stands. Short of doing a piece before a naked couple having sex, the matter-of-fact tone remains in place with no hint of opinion. On the subject of sex, Ken could be as publicly indifferent as he could be shamed by its worst examples. But never amused).

Grist informed him of other changes due for the autumn season, commencing September. While a cutback in BBC funding – and staff - would place him as the overall Presenter for the regular editions, his income would also be effectively halved. Not surprisingly, the extra work this higher profile entailed made Grist's hope of acceptance unrealistic. Ken pondered his options a few days later in a private memo:

'(c) Solution: raising rate per prog. (d) No alternative but no longer to regard *24 Hours* as my first priority... (e) Insist on release from BBC-only clause to accept work offered by commercial networks.' He'd stake his career on the latter being accepted. On the 2nd July, Betty phoned his study to inform him of the BBC's compromise proposal regarding the new contract. Whatever it was would, by his standards, have still left him out-of-pocket. As it was, his chequebook showed only a solitary page within. He told her they'd have to think again.

The following week he was back in Edinburgh for the Summit Meeting of the Scottish universities Rectors. Dundee University's was Peter Ustinov. He'd already had several engaging television encounters with the man he knew to be 'a remarkable journalist with a rather brittle manner.' Ustinov recalled:

'This at a time when Rectors in Scottish Universities were regarded as sinecures. We all decided at almost the same moment – those of Aberdeen..., St. Andrews..., and myself at Dundee, that once we were elected, we would be active or not at all. We began to hold meetings between ourselves, to the consternation of the Vice Chancellors... Since there was an element of taunt in these very constructive collaborations, it suited Allsop's temperament down to the ground. He was a live wire.' A collective agreement arose that they should collect and share information on student representation – seeing where it could be made more effective and enforced - with the help of the honorary Presidents of each.

The summer down south was especially hot that year. With *Fit To Live In?* late for delivery to Penguin, Ken suffered the pained and sleepless nights to spend the dense-aired afternoons writing outside his study. With his chest bared, he'd clip around his neck a metallic ruff, used to reflect the sun's rays back onto his burnished face: a point of stifled amusement to those who saw it. His gun-grey hair, left to grow out, was contrasting silver, and – in keeping with the students he mixed with - he cultivated a broad moustache. But it was all rather too late. The whim-pandering distractions – the too-available wines, dinners and sun-drenched Meadow – had proven too great. Of his three professional and one personal commitment, he'd only completed the *Uncle Tom's Cabin* piece and *Fit To Live In?*'s first draft. The Beecher Stowe was barely half written. His difficulty in finishing it would be a standing joke within the family for another two years. And as for the book on German Romanticism...

On his final evening at Merton, Amanda arrived from Peter Hoy's nearby to attend his leaving dinner. At midnight they shared a cigarette on the battlements, Ken suddenly sad at leaving.

Ken takes over the helm at '24 Hours.' (BBC), 1969.

22
Oct 1969 – Oct 1971: The Allsop Spirit

The elderly man had pulled out from beneath the weight of his wife's expectations and untimely death at sixty-three by marrying, not once, but twice more. Through the ensuing emotional upheaval, the love of landscape art, harboured since his Yorkshire childhood, had never left him. One of two colour snapshots taken the previous year at a local fate, shows him standing proudly by his latest on display and for sale. The old artist is brown-suited and wearing a matching, pre-war style trilby. His blue eyes are still clear and his slender frame upright despite being in his eightieth year.

He was back at home in Harrogate with his third wife, Annie, when, on the evening of the 3rd October, he was suddenly gripped by an internal pain in the region of the lower stomach. A worried Annie called the local General Hospital. The voice at the other end tried to calm the elderly lady and asked his name, which she gave; 'John Allsop.' As the ambulance stretchered away her husband's frail form, Annie then called his only son. Ironically, he'd just had the calmest, most pain-free couple of days experienced in some two years. Back at his Hertfordshire home for the weekend, dinner and TV – watching Paul Newman in the movie *Hud* - had already conspired to take him away from typing his next article. But Annie's call overrode them all. He feared the old boy might not last the surgery set for tomorrow morning.

That day, Ken and Betty sped off in the Aston Martin, the speedometer reaching and retaining 100 mph for long periods along the dual carriageway north. At the ward holding John, his nurse assured the couple that it was a suspect inflammation of the bowel and, with antibiotics, he could be out within a fortnight.

'But of course,' Ken unwittingly pondered, 'he is 81 (sic) and although remarkably alert and active, the mechanism isn't so pliable.'

Ken's own was already overburdened. At Edinburgh three days before, stalemate had been reached between the Rectors and their supporters on one side and Principal Swann with his on the other, on the mooted issue of greater student representation. To a colleague, Ken confided the idea of threatening to resign to break the current deadlock. A kamikaze tool used to good effect in the past. The hope being, with his journalist contacts, Swann *et al* wouldn't dare call his bluff. He used it. Ken and Principal Swann faced each other with stern expressions. No supporter of student power, Swann had called Ken after his previous visit to read out the kind of headline that only served to strengthen his cause. *Student* magazine had printed a clearly partisan article suggesting Swann had somehow caved in to Ken over his resignation threat. Despite this, a compromise was reached, avoiding an inevitable split, along with closure on the issue of admitting the Honorary Presidents.

He and Betty had begun to search for a larger property, back in the country. The increased traffic, less than two metres beyond their front door, and its heightened noise, were determining factors in their decision. And, for once, it may have been mutual. With rare indecision, Ken regretted passing over a mill they'd just viewed in Ashwell but agreed it was the type of property they should concentrate all their energies on finding.

On the 8th October, soon after his arrival at Lime Grove, Annie called to say she'd been told John was to be operated on after all. The next day Ken returned to the Harrogate General. 'Father quite alert and in good spirits but frail and weak of voice.' From Annie's spare room he sounded rather less confident in a letter to Amanda, with whom he had recently fallen out.

'His chances are now slight indeed. I wanted you to know that your message reached him and what comfort it brought him.' As if in search of some assurance for himself he adds, 'You have inherited much of his fierce and affirmative spirit – "the Allsop Spirit," as he called it - but you have unnecessary doubts about yourself and your adequacy to be loved. You should not have these misgivings about yourself. You are an exceptional person...you have no cause to doubt the love Mother and I have for you.'

On the 3rd November, Ken and Betty headed for West Dorset and the promise of a mill house for sale in the remote rural district called West Milton, between Beaminster in the north and Bridport in the south. At Bridport they roomed for a night at The Bull Inn. Here, Ken found another reason for disillusionment:

'The map and one's own memory of the countryside reveal nothing of the overall pollution of towns, villages and cities in between by cheap, nasty building. (sic) Really, the country where we already are is less botched up. There probably simply isn't anywhere to escape to.' An attitude destined to wind up the locals. Next morning they drove to the location in the village of West Milton. En route, Ken realised he could not have been more wrong. The area appeared hermetically sealed from life outside: a thriving, self-sufficient community practising crafts and daily routines dating back to the Saxons. Lovely, semi-hidden hamlets such as Powerstock, Nettlecombe and Loders flanked the area to the east, with Lyme Bay and the East Devon border to the west. The mill house itself justified all they'd seen. It stood on almost eight acres of land with the sale including the cottage close by. Vines and wild, untended plantation scaled its face. With the mill house run by one couple - the Sleamans' – this and its cottage were run by two upper-class dog-breeders – the Madigans' - to whom Ken took an instant dislike though remained typically detached.

En route to two further mill houses in Honiton, South Devon, the Allsops cruised through the scenic route west, up Eggardon Hill 'along the most magnificent of panoramas, across a vastness of country, under huge skies.' The area he found on arrival was too flat and desolate and the properties too small. Back to Wiltshire and a viewing in Devizes. Too urban, he found. 'Indistinguishable from a Watford suburb.' While it demanded some clearance and renovation, the mill at West Milton seemed the only serious proposition.

John Allsop died on Sunday 9th November. He and Betty were awoken after dawn and summoned back to Harrogate in the hope of catching his final breath, but they were too late. Seeing his father laid out on the bed still fails to provoke anything other than the usual detached analysis.

'Difficult to comprehend the line drawn by death without religious feelings. There still remains the strangeness of seeing the life gone from the body – the *person* extinguished.' Before they leave her, Annie gives Ken his father's gold watch and chain and, to Betty, the wedding ring given her by John.

Ken's new ruling status on *24 Hours* ensured a second he'd spend the rest of his life refuting: that of what both public and press were terming 'a TV personality.' Ken would not be held or defined by the medium he saw as a job: a valuable one with ego-stroking perks, certainly, but nothing more. He wanted no part of the celebrity the vacuous term represented – if only because he knew he couldn't avoid it. His return for the autumn season provoked a virtual outcry that typified his position. The steel-grey moustache he'd left to grow at Merton now drooped at either side of his upper lip in a style not dissimilar to that of the camp, English actor, Peter

Wyngarde, then playing Jason King: the outrageously dressed, womanising freelance detective on ITV's *Department S*. Ken's own women admirers were not so impressed.

'I loved you better before, Ken,' sighed one viewer from Swansea. 'He used to be my pin-up boy,' bemoaned another from Stoke-On-Trent, 'but just lately he looks like a cross between an elderly hippie and Neville Chamberlain.' (The 'elderly' hurt even more than the comparison to the former Conservative Prime Minister). Even William Hardcastle - the influential, veteran newspaper editor - began staring more than listening. In a *Radio Times* profile two weeks later – itself entitled 'No Moustaches in *The World at One*' - he admitted,

'tending to be more and more interested in Kenneth Allsop's new *Viva Zapata* ...than in what *24 Hours* is doing.'

Ken's determined silence harboured pent-up anger at such trivial and, worse, *published* comments. He'd never underestimated the necessity of image: only its importance. For his TV audience, he took it in good stead:

'Perhaps women do not fully realise that a man's boring destiny is to stand 10 minutes a day – a solid four months out of his adult lifetime – staring at his own face in a looking glass, while scraping at it with metal. An occasional variation in the topography, a touch of topiary can, I find, slightly reduce the tedium.' For one more specialised, he sighed at what such effrontery signified. 'I am left with an uneasy impression that packaging is more important than content; that what is mostly wanted from television is nightly soothing reassurance that the familiar furniture of the airwaves is in its secure and proper place, unchanged, changeless.'

To help boost *Nova*'s sales – and thank a magazine that, for four years, had offered him a totally free hand – he posed for an advertisement reading the new November issue. Mistakenly, Ken was deemed to be back to his old tricks. The BBC's Assistant Head of Programme Contracts saw it the following week in the *Evening Standard* and blew his top. He pointed out the irony that, in his prior contract, Ken would've been allowed to do the ad, but the relevant 'Clause 6' had since been revised and that Ken's solicitor should have known about this. Awaking, bleary-eyed, from a long evening of funeral arrangements after his father's death, Ken shaved off the jinxed facial hair.

Now presenting the programme every third week, alone and on consecutive nights, it was his name that featured below the title: responsibility shared across the other three weeks between Ludovic Kennedy, James Burke and, making his TV debut, David Dimbleby - eldest son of the late Richard. This was an acceptable situation to a man who so compartmentalised his life. With the average age of the new production team under thirty, he found himself in the unenviable position of BBC Current Affairs elder statesman.

At twenty-four, Tony Summers had been taken on as the youngest producer in the Corporation's history, having joined *24 Hours* in 1966 as a researcher.

'Some of the older presenters were out of kilter with the youth. But Ken never seemed out of kilter. I think he felt he'd more in common with some of us young producers, film directors and researchers than he did with the hierarchical suits.' Summers would soon witness, at first hand, his senior's prowess, as well as his ability to manipulate opportunities to his own advantage.

At the end of one night's broadcast, his front man called over as they were preparing to leave: 'Tony, would you like to come to a reefer party tomorrow night?' At the time, Summers knew there were only two types of environment where this was overlooked;

'There was your poorer student smoking joints – that I recalled from university – and there was the fashionable-thing-to-do types. Ken was definitely in that category.' He recalls arriving by taxi at a rather grand house, possibly in

Hampstead, with his girlfriend - a ballerina - whom he'd earlier introduced to Ken in the foyer at Lime Grove. 'As the evening drew on it was pretty clear that Ken had been talking quite a lot to my girlfriend. I was talking to some others and felt pretty secure about her.' Out of Summers's earshot, Ken expressed his interest by asking her about the specialised type of footwear ballet dancers required when they weren't performing. She replied that they weren't as restricted by style as he might think. Observing a pair of green, high-laced boots worn by another of the guests, she added that she wouldn't mind a pair of those.

Feeling this was as far as he could go with preliminaries, around 1 a.m. Ken came to a decision. He told them he had to get back to Braughing and that, since it was a freezing cold night, would they like a lift? None of them were drunk, but the joints had been doing the rounds.

'We gratefully accepted. We climbed into his Aston Martin, my girlfriend – surprise, surprise – in the front with Ken, leaving me to curl up awkwardly in the back.' Knowing Ken would have to drop them off near - or at - Summers Chelsea flat before heading back to Hertfordshire, the couple stared at each other in worried silence. Their driver was not only heading for the North Circular Road, *his* direction home, but was frowning intently at his windscreen, oblivious of Summers concerns. Missing the exit off the roundabout, their driver then repeated the clockwise journey not once but twice more. 'Finally, he slowed to a halt and said, "Well, I have to turn off here." We got out, peered around, and he shot off into the night. We then both realised that he'd been desperately trying to figure out how in the world to get rid of me, his friend, to be alone with her. Not being able to think of a way, he'd just stopped and dropped us off. The funny thing is that neither I - nor my girlfriend - minded a bit, such was his charm and the awed affection we held him in.' A couple of days later, a large, anonymous parcel arrived by special delivery for Summers girlfriend. Inside, were a pair of green, high-laced boots, precisely the same as those she'd pointed out, admiringly, to him at the party and in her size.

24 Hours was finally broadcast in colour from Monday 17th November. The main items that evening were on the Biafran War and the killing of unarmed civilians in Vietnam.

Three days later, at home, a virus struck him down. What may have only been 'flu, gave him a temperature of 103 and more than usually sensitive jabs on the nerve-ends of his stump. He purposely threw back a handful of pills to try numbing what merely left him drunk. Knowing he'd never sleep, he called his GP who delivered a double injection of a 'morphine-strength' liquid that managed to ease the worst. The doctor suspected he'd developed a benign tumour on one of his exposed nerve-ends, aggravated by the change in his temperature. He advises Ken to see a neurologist, who might be able to isolate the exposed nerve and numb it, permanently, with an appliance of pure alcohol. Not for the first time, Ken is advised to give up smoking. He promises to make a serious attempt.

While Betty takes care of a convalescent Annie, the bargaining begins over the purchase of the grounds at West Milton. Ken confides to his diary that the sums forwarded on his side are all hypothetical. He intends to purchase on credit and hope to claw back the final sum through personal sales and advances from the freelance broadcasts. How logical was his thinking at this time, swallowing pills to fight back the increased stump pain, is unclear.

On the 11th December he attends his appointment with the neurologist at the Essex & Hertfordshire Hospital. He confirms the problem is most likely a *neuroma* on the nerve ending, but with the stump reshaped and padded its easing could be permanent. Ken was both reassured but resigned.

He sighed that his pains seemed to queue up and take turns to affect him after each refit of the suction cup.

Back at the house, viewers came to call. Ken quickly tired of repeating the grand tour, while Betty just as easily ran out of ways to divert visitors' attention away from the traffic roar outside. Over the first weekend of January 1970, they resorted to playing Beethoven, loudly, on the stereo hi-fi in a desperate bid to drown it out. They needn't have bothered since one of the couples, the Fernsbys,' put in an offer. When they eventually pulled out, the James's put in another and they held.

He wasn't due back in Edinburgh for another week when Betty took a call from there, passing on the news that a group of students were staging a sit-in at the university's Empire Bureau in protest against the Afrikaans' policy of apartheid in South Africa. At least, this was the publicly stated line. Though genuinely abhorred, it was also a ripe opportunity for dissent over what they saw as the unfair practice of the staff harbouring secret dossiers on individual applicants. A subsequent break-in at the Applications Department occurred with the intention of publishing their contents in *Student*. Ken, having agreed to an interview, had quotes flung accusingly back at him during the first committee meeting of the year by the Swann-supporting Lord Cameron.

'(He was) implying I had stirred them into action – the Bernadette Devlin of the situation.' Ken insisted the student interviewer had greatly exaggerated what he'd said. A point that *Student*'s new editor, Gordon Brown, believed made Ken's allegiance suspect.

After dinner there that evening, he tried to call Henry. He'd received a letter from Victor Bonham-Carter, Secretary of the Royal Literary Fund, sounding out Ken on the possibility of supporting his application for a Civil List pension he intended taking to Downing Street. Like a lot of friends who'd tried, increasingly, in vain to understand the old man, Bonham-Carter believed him deserving of additional financial support. Particularly after the 'revolting' climax to the eighteen year Philip Maddison cycle and its consequent poor sales.

'Henry Williamson was, of course, his own worst enemy,' he recalls of the man who'd also managed to alienate C. F. Tunnicliffe, Negley Farson, Eve Farson and Ken amongst others. After a further unanswered attempt, several days later, Betty took an evening call from the seventy-four-year-old author just as Ken returned, exhausted, from a second Edinburgh trip. Bleary-eyed, he told her to make the excuse that he was still there. 'How was he?' he asked her. 'Most odd,' she replied. 'Kept telling me his mind was going.' But he'd left a number. Next day, Ken tried it through the morning only to finally discover it didn't exist. A long letter attempting an explanation arrived from Henry in the post. Ken was none the wiser.

'Difficult to know if he is seized by genuine paranoia or really does believe – as he says – that he is being spied on and snooped on.' He caught him in London's Liberal Club the following day, putting to him Bonham-Carter's proposition and sketching out his supporting letter. Henry, his pride deflated more than once by his old friend, grudgingly accepted, but left, shrunken by the feeling he was perceived to be a charity case. Ken's submitted letter, though, is hardly ungenerous. He calls him a 'genius,' not from perfection but his 'intensity of vision of an artist with a purpose' over and above the need to earn a living. He admits to Henry's philosophy and politics being diametrically opposed to his own, adding that this makes his support all the more objective. He is sure that Henry will, one day, be acknowledged as one of the present age's greatest writers.

'It would be good,' he ends, 'if some of that acknowledgement could be accorded him while he is still living and aware of it.'

On the 29th January Ken reached fifty. 'How unspeakably gloomy,' he rumbled with a new self-pity. 'Half a century of fairly futile occupation of this planet; also, increasing sense of fewer years left than have already been consumed.'

The day after, he appeared on Radio 4's *Any Questions*. Although not his first guest appearance on the weekly half-hour of public Q & A, today's edition sat him alongside a woman on whom we can only speculate the extent she might have slapped such sentiment down: the soon-to-be Conservative Minister for Education and future Prime Minister, Margaret Thatcher.

On Wednesday 4th February, his Chancellor at Edinburgh, Prince Phillip, visited the *24 Hours* studio to pre-record an eighteen-minute talk with Ken in his capacity as a public figurehead to launch European Conservation Year. The theme of the interview – checked and cleared by the Duke's staff beforehand to an extent Ken would normally deem unacceptable – was on possible ways to roll back the current tide of environmental pollution. From managing the competing demands of the countryside - through compromises and restrictions - to planting new forests and introducing leisure facilities.

'He arrived with just (his) equerry and cap,' he noted that evening. 'He talked reasonably hard facts – didn't waffle. John Guest (the equerry) much in evidence. All seemed pleased with result – we all watched it run through in colour before he whizzed off in his Rolls.'

On the 20th February he was fitted with a new, adjusted limb from Roehampton. It felt solid and heavier than he'd expected but offered some solace. The jabbing stings had been easing and he was able to tell Sir Eric Riches that he'd managed to remain off of one his more addictive medications for nearly two years and the smoking close to three months. And he felt positive about the move to Dorset. He departed feeling something close to renewed hope.

The remainder of the month and most of March were taken up with haggling over purchase and repairs Ken demanded for The Mill. Mrs Madigan insisted upon delaying until their departure. By the second week of March the contracts had been signed, the process overseen by Ken's former fellow tenant and trainee solicitor at Barwythe, Edward Moeran. On the 2nd April, he and Betty finally took possession, Ken delivering the agreed sum of £2,120 to Moeran personally. Of course, it was a figure he found only *theoretically* acceptable. He'd nothing even remotely close to it in his account. Betty updated Margaret Benenson with the assurance of one whose rock never failed her but,

'I have some qualms about going so far. We have lived in Hertfordshire for so many years but I shall make regular visits to London. Now that the work rota of the programme has changed, Ken spends much more time at home, so we are free to live where we want.' Freer, certainly, with greater mobility all round. 'Tris is working for his finals… Mandy is in her second year (at the University of East Anglia) and is enjoying the course very much. Fabian managed to get into the Camberwell School of Art, which we are very pleased about as it has a very high reputation.'

Contractual repairs and renovations continued, protracted, over the next three months, with clearouts and conversions expected of Tristan and Fabian on their return from college beginning the summer recess. The disregarded swimming pool was cleared of its weeds and adorned with a Romanesque bust, while the brothers also converted the upstairs of one of the outbuildings into a warm, airy room.

Consecutive weeks away from Lime Grove and stable health afforded Ken a little more peace and time to do what he always did best: socialise. A swift morning radio interview at Broadcasting House, followed, in the afternoon, by the typing of an *Evening News* piece in the office of a colleague, allowed for an early evening nap to keep a late evening appointment. On June 8th, Quentin Crewe was throwing a party in honour of his new wife, Sue Cavendish. On his arrival, Ken observed how time marched on with equal speed.

'Like an Antonioni film,' he observed. 'A cross-cut through the worlds of high aristocracy, rich, fashionable and hippy swingers; dress ranged from verdigris DJs' of older gentry and ruffles of younger to Eastern robes and sweaty Mick Jagger t-shirts.' Chatting to his old *Tonight* colleague, Derek Hart, plumper and baggy-eyed, he was surprised by an interruption from Lord Snowdon, who kissed Hart his welcome. As Ken followed Snowdon's receding back, he observed him gazing at a Beatle-haired Malaysian boy. He sounds surprised, distinctly uneasy, and adopts an almost prudish tone.

'Naive of me, doubtless, but I find the flagrancy staggering: I suppose he feels secure among his own Beautiful People.' Kenneth Tynan – his old rival and ambivalent acquaintance - is also there: 'his eyes rolling Proustianly, waiting for someone to insult or strike him,' notes Ken. (In reality, Tynan nervously awaited the London debut of his nude revue, *Oh! Calcutta!*) He is still only forty-three, but with his best years about to trail him. "We'll have to shoot it again," George Melly concluded of the party before they left.

Two days later, Ken makes a personal return visit to Amsterdam: this time with Betty and Ruth Inglis, an American journalist friend, for a pre-arranged link-up with the Edwards. On the second day, they find a club, off Leidesplein, called Madam Arthur's. He notes John's 'glum irritation' at discovering its exclusively transvestite clientele – male strippers and singers - several of whom, built like bricklayers, make suggestive advances to the pair.

'B. wanted to go to the loo but couldn't decide whether she was a *Herren* or a *Damen*. When we got up in the morning I asked her whose clothes she wanted to wear: hers or mine.'

A year earlier, he'd left his three month term at Merton College with a commitment still outstanding; the biography of *Harriet Beecher Stowe* for Heron. By now an excuse for regular, tongue-in-cheek inquiries from his sons and daughter, Ken would do any odd job around the house – painting panels, screwing on doorknobs, or chopping wood for the front room's open fire – to avoid returning to it, boredom having long since set in. Even friends were welcomed round to the incomplete restoration in a bid to stave off a job he no longer believed in. During such encounters he could come off worse, the dearth of stimulation making him less attentive, more anxious and broody over the void in his bank account.

His sense of humour took a mean turn. He started smoking again after nine months abstinence. On the night of the 7th August, he experienced his first stump pains since the move. Unable to sleep, he casually downed a double prescribed dose of his painkillers. The next day, Nat and Pat Solomon made a pre-arranged visit with their eleven-year-old daughter, Clare. The Mill's pool had now been cleared of natural debris and filled with clean water. Away from prying eyes, Ken hobbled out – one-legged - on his crutches, and proudly described the work his sons had achieved. Apart from his attentions, he invited Clare Solomon to test it. Walking to the edge she looked down and shook her head, shyly. Ken smilingly encouraged. After a third refusal, he lifted his left crutch, hit the middle of her back, and pushed her in. He laughed quietly to himself but, on looking to Nat and Pat, saw their expressions set.

'I suppose it was the sort of thing she would expect from her brothers or from other boys in a public pool, but she didn't expect it from an uncle…Certainly, her father wouldn't have done it,' Pat recalled. 'She was quite shy but had earlier shown an instinctive control of the peacocks he owned that he'd never had. Being naturally controlling, I think he took that personally.'

The Mill would soon be completed to the Allsops' specifications. But the ongoing financial demands to pay for it all gave him an idea to fall back on what he'd always done best: from first-hand experience, write about the country he loved. Arthur Brittenden now edited *The Daily Mail*. The paper's political balance had shifted little since Ken's departure in '64, when he'd never remained a subscriber. (Brittenden would be the last such editor under this regime). During his next week at Lime Grove, Ken dropped in on him at his Fleet Street office and mooted the idea of a country column of observations, from walks around Powerstock and the rural region of West Dorset. Brittenden was charmed and suggested a dummy run of three such columns, between 450 and 500 words, over three consecutive Saturdays,' that could be extended depending upon their reception. No final fee was agreed but Ken noted with relief that Brittenden 'will pay anyway' for the trials to commence from the start of September. What he wasn't to know was just how quickly such cordial meetings of bargaining would be dropped, acting as a portent to the dismantling of what he'd taken for granted, to his advantage, for so long.

But, yet again, his body enacted punishment for his excesses. Ken's good leg, that had managed to avoid the wheelchair and – God forbid – a second nerve-pressing tin limb, was under threat. While he'd been tied to the house, his various pressurising jobs – mucking in with his sons and contractors – allied to his rich diet, had done it few favours. His Dorset-based GP was Dr. Michael Hudson. Pointing out the pain rising up from his instep bone, Ken was asked to roll up his trouser leg. Hudson felt around his calf and diagnosed an onset of arthritis. To be certain, he told Ken he'd return next day to take a blood sample to test for possible gout. A blood clot in the calf was confirmed. He had thrombosis.

As the invoices for the jobs completed began arriving, Ken made an effort to sell his now sought after Aston Martin. As consolation, he hired the very latest models from the local garage for test runs. But he couldn't bring himself to lower his sights quite far enough, trying out the sleekest, broad bonneted saloons, including the Jensen Interceptor, Ford Capri and the company's latest Jaguar, the XJ6. But there were no takers for his price. By the third weekend in August, most of the sawing, screwing, hammering and re-painting had ceased to leave a much-needed feeling of calm.

'After dinner we sprawled about in (the) sitting room with a log fire and all the dogs' piled on one's legs, while Mandy read from *The Lord of the Rings*. We looked at old photographs while B. made curtains and M. frayed the bottoms of my jeans – and no telly all evening: v. civilised and pleasurable.'

Personal Choice was about to commence its third series and Ken received a call from its producer, asking him on, and to suggest further likely candidates for interview. He wasn't greatly enthusiastic to comply. But he needed the money and fast. Who could follow Henry? Who else did he know, still living, which represented an important part of his life? Frank Sinatra topped his initial list but this was pure cynicism. He then considered the children's author, Mary Norton, the only other Henry he knew – Moore, the sculptor – and that author who lived not far away, in Lyme Regis, down on the Dorset coast, whose first two novels – *The Collector* and *The French Lieutenant's Woman* - he'd once admiringly reviewed: John Fowles. He and his wife Elizabeth visited the Mill for lunch on the 26th.

'Like them. She...is gaunt and attractive with greying bobbed hair. He's a reticent but v. sympathetic person. I hope he'll be forthcoming enough for the TV int. idea...

He says 31 buzzards were killed with pole traps in Sussex, this year, by gamekeepers. In 5 years at Lyme he's seen only 1 peregrine and, possibly, 1 hobby.'

The 30th was a swelteringly hot Sunday. While awaiting Fowles confirmation, several separate groups of the Allsops' various friends descended upon the refurbished Mill and its garden including Tony Summers with his new wife, and photographer friend, Peter Ryan, among them. The trio had spent the previous day at the Isle of Wight rock festival. Here, Summers witnessed a positive change in his colleague:

'Towards the end, after he moved to the Powerstock mill house, he seemed to appear rather uncharacteristically content. In material terms it was a huge reach for him, financially, but it was the style to which he wanted to become accustomed. So, he struggled to get a better contract by which to pay for it. He'd say, 'I'll have to go on doing this damned television work for quite a bit longer, but this is why it's worth it.' One of the last images I have of him, which Peter Ryan photographed, is of him seated in the garden behind the house in the late summer sun, working and talking.' The close-up, sun-drenched image is iconic. He has put on weight, wears flamingo feathered sideburns beneath his silver locks, and bare-chested, with a forearm across it to his shoulder, the hand holding a perfectly sharpened pencil. He evokes the Greek sun god that Colin Wilson had witnessed in Negley Farson in the mid-Fifties.

Summers himself was forced to stay on an extra day, having gone down with *gastro-enteritis*, picked up at the crowded, mud-drenched festival. Later that day, Ken's two biggest fans, Jenny and Janet 'James,' arrived for tea, driven there by their new husbands. Each in turn snapped colour shots of themselves with their hero and took advantage of the pool. But Ken quickly tired of doing most of the talking, and was relieved when Betty, Amanda and Fabian came out to recharge the conversation.

By late summer, Tony Smith's own contract with *24 Hours* ended. Replacing him was the equally young Peter Pagmanenta. Contracted for just one year, Pagmanenta's mission was to reinvigorate the content. Over lunch, Ken received Pagmanenta's ideas of increasing the quota of broad, human-interest stories over the solely political with enthusiasm. The programme was in danger of repetition. It hadn't helped that unscripted controversies were stoking the anger of an increasingly right-wing Establishment, critical of the impertinent questioning.

Some interviewees were learning how to manipulate the medium to their own, occasionally bizarre, ends. Tony Summers was Producer on the night after the cult Japanese novelist, Mishima, publicly committed suicide, or *hari-kari*. It was a big news day with a large section of the programme to be beamed over from the Middle East on new, not entirely reliable, equipment:

'We were also trying to bring together a visual feed from the USA featuring a politician with one from Tel-Aviv which, then, was particularly difficult to achieve at one and the same time. Ken was to anchor the discussion from the London studio. Since it would take time between a couple of items to ensure both these feeds were ready to go, I wanted a short filler item.' Summers, with Ken and Tony Smith, agreed that this should be on the Tokyo suicide. A young production assistant discovered an Oxford Professor of Literature who'd recently been to Japan and claimed he'd spent the day with the author.

'One would always hurry down for a brief look at the guest in the hospitality room to make sure they weren't drunk or misbehaving themselves. Ken and I met this professor, typically dressed in a slightly shabby sports jacket with leather patches on the elbows. Relieved, we rushed back up to get on with the rest of our work. A filmed item on

Mishima and his astonishing death followed. Then, up in the gallery, I only waited long enough to hear Ken say his opening question and hear the start of the Professor's answer to make sure they were both 'on mike.' This was so I could turn away, assured that Lynn, my gallery assistant, was holding the stopwatch, so I could get on the phone to Tel Aviv and America to make sure we had everything connected at the right moment to go into next item about the Middle East. Within ten seconds, Lynn was tugging at my sleeve. I motioned her away as I was still on the phone but she kept tugging. Finally, she got my attention and I listened to what was being said in the studio. What had happened was that Ken had asked the Professor as his opening question, "Professor, in your view, what was Mishima trying to say to the world by this act?"

"I think, Mr Allsop, what Mishima was trying to say was - 'fuck *you*, fuck *you*, fuck *you*...'" and so he went on. Lynn later told me that he'd managed to say 'fuck,' on-air, for about thirty-five seconds. About twenty-five to thirty of them were uttered beyond the control of anyone other than me! I was regarded, by the 'suits,' as a mischief-maker anyway, and someone who did rash and irresponsible things. I was the one who could, and should, have cut him off after the first one, but I didn't because I was so busy on the 'phone.

After the programme, Ken and I went down to the hospitality room. The Professor had been bustled out by the commissioners and disappeared into the night. Ken and I sat there with the editor and others, knowing that the shit would hit the fan in the morning. And, of course, it did. But, really, neither of us could've helped it.' Summers believes that edition continues to hold the world record for the most number of expletives in a current affairs programme, putting Tynan's solitary use in the shade. Ken wasn't amused, knowing that even referring to the incident outside the studio could further heap contempt upon a programme that, five years on, he still believed in.

Later that year, Michael Hudson was at home watching his famous patient on *24 Hours* when he was witness to the biggest technical blunder in the programmes six seasons. Ken called it 'my worst night ever on TV.' Following a smooth piece to camera on the latest bombing in Belfast, the screen showed a desert shot of marquees run by the Shah of Persia. Later, the intro to the Shah's greeting of dignitaries at the desert scene was followed by vehicles aflame in the Falls Road. 'Ken went ballistic about the incompetence and lack of professionalism of the studio directors,' Hudson recalled. 'My friend and I thought it all hilarious…'

The first *Daily Mail* column – headed under 'In the Country' – was printed on the last Saturday in September. The tone appears pleasingly wry with a slant both personal and social. Relating to a day when the pest controller was called in to remove a spreading wasp colony in the garden, he describes how,

'The officer was a boy, an upstanding, up-and-coming exterminator with a rural Beatles hair-do. Down in our part of Wessex there are still young men who don't train as computer mechanics or hunger to read sociology at Essex University. They follow their fathers and become shepherds and thatchers – and rodent operatives.' Occasionally, the descriptions of the wildlife around his acreage evoke an alliterative poetry harking right back to his initial contributing tread as a teenager for *The Slough Observer*.

'A kestrel breasted the freezing sea wind and hung, wings hooked, in the glinting space of sun and sky, a dark anchor.' And, again, the prey of the hunt he witnesses, makes good its escape, although – from his more elevated pier – his concern at its fate is less intense. 'I am more worn out than the hounds.'

But too often the prose style is long-winded, showily overwrought, and suffers the pretensions of the Georgian parson diarist he longed to be. This is mainly due to his descriptions of the locals, which are remote and caricatured, just stopping short of condescension. Ignorant he wasn't. His boyhood encounters helped here, although his experience of the working class then was rarely positive, based on those he witnessed in the employ of the hunt, or the council, to keep out trespassers like himself. But, the hermetic, rural sanctuary depicted in the Saturday column proved popular enough with the *Mail* readership for Brittenden to give Ken the go-ahead for more.

Those locals living in and working off the sanctuary were gaining a rather dimmer view of their famous new resident and his column. Michael Rudd was a farmer neighbour at Powerstock.

'He arrived here and took it over as his piece of the country without much thought of the people. I think we felt that he was making use of Dorset, to write about it, to make money out of it. (The Allsops') didn't join in very much. He was in town a lot of the time, which didn't help much, and he kept his connections with all his London friends going.'

John Samways was Rudd's farmer neighbour. Ken was passing down the Loders road one day when he witnessed Samways trimming a hedge at is side. Recalling seeing nesting birds within it he fumed and later had it out with the farmer.

'It wasn't really a hedge as such,' said Samways. 'It was really a tall bank growing over and touching traffic. The county council were always on to us about it, so it had to be kept down. When he complained...I explained to him we weren't cutting every hedge off in the district, only that one, and the birds still had plenty of nesting places to go.' Samways added that Ken also dissented over the building of a Dutch barn he'd received planning permission for. 'He put us in the *Daily Mail* the following week...He obviously wasn't a true countryman, otherwise he'd have known that winter fodder's got to be kept dry...'

There were other locals with grievances; one – a historian - accusing Ken of utilising his research as if his own for the column. Michael Hudson has since put his finger on the causes of the antipathy.

'Ken was a tremendous idealist dealing with what were, actually, *national* issues, and that was part of the problem... In the years they lived at the Mill, Powerstock was entirely occupied by people who were Dorset-born, whereas West Milton was largely incomers, retired people. With them he had a sort of ambiguity. He recognised that if they hadn't spent a lot of money on their cottages, half the houses would've fallen down. On the other hand, he resented them because they wanted to turn everything into suburbia, knocking out old windows and putting in nasty front doors.'

Ken found himself fighting for what he believed in from the threshold of his own front door. He hadn't found himself a minority within a minority since Barwythe. He experienced a renewed sense of purpose. In contrast, the TB's latest attempt to undermine it was cruel. As well as the pains in his one good leg, he now believed his good kidney under threat.

During the spring of 1971, Ken was gazing into the Britt – the millstream (or leat) from which passed by his land – and noticed a bubbling and cloudy thickness running through water usually clear. Suspecting someone was wilfully tipping waste upstream, he informed the Avon & Dorset River Authority. Agreeing to look into it, they sent an inspector, a Mr. Clark, who dipped a test-tube into the Britt to examine the sample in their lab. Sounding out a local, Ken was told that it had once been par for the course for residents to tip their sewage here until pipes were dug to redirect the majority out to sea. The N.R.A. assured him the discoloration had been due to natural mineral deposition, dislodged by the natural rise in temperature. On reading Ken's April entry, local *Mail* readers fumed again.

'I worry...about crusty meringues of foam, which float down my little river, What is it? I, again, remember farms upstream where, when churns are being washed out, detergent suds gurgle down the drains and eventually the river.' He manages to seamlessly merge this complaint against his neighbour into an otherwise rather poetic passage. His remoteness was becoming alienating. The lobbying would continue for months until he'd got his second opinion.

In May, David English took over what was being sold as the New Look *Daily Mail*: a transition from broadsheet to tabloid. English had been editing the recently folded *Daily Sketch*, situated in the same Fleet Street building. Vere Harmsworth, the *Mail*'s Chairman of the board and future heir to the Rothermere family Estate, had been grooming the forty-year-old English for some months as the paper's prospective new editor. To repay his master's faith, English's first duty on arrival was to transfer two dozen redundancy notices - from his former *Sketch* office – to his new home, each bearing the name of a *Mail* journalist. That evening of sackings became known as 'The Night of the White Envelope.' George Melly was one of the biggest casualties. He'd been writing the captions to jazz colleague Wally Fawkes's *Trog* cartoon – on and off – since Ken first joined the paper in 1956.

English knew what he was doing even if none of his surviving staff did. *The Daily Mail* – itself losing circulation – would no longer be a mid-market broadsheet but become a tabloid geared to the suburban housewife. Ken's 'In the Country' column was temporarily put at risk. The last thing he needed after having to rely on his freelancing to pay off the bills. Ten days passed before English, through an intermediary, decided it could continue.

'I thought this rather odd and cavalier behaviour, and that I would at least like to hear what D(avid) E(nglish) himself has to say about the column and how it would fit into the new *Daily Mail*.' But no longer were the new breed with him, behind the typewriter and camera. New and younger regimes were about to take-over, elsewhere, that needed journalists with Ken's experience rather less than he currently needed them.

Now accompanying Ken for his 'In the Country' columns were new, long-haired, naturalist friends, like Richard Mabey – his editor at Penguin, responsible for the recent release *Fit To Live In?* - the *Sunday Times* latest recruit, Brian Jackman and his dependable GP, Michael Hudson: each finding their mutual concern for Britain's rural future voiced by a wry and devastating intellect. Dressed in leather bomber jacket, denim shirt, jeans or cords, and with a pair of field binoculars around his neck, Ken evoked both in look, and intent, his younger, post-war self, searching for the elusive little ringed plover around Slough's sewage works. It had become something of a battle-dress; a sign of reinvigorated concern in what he felt must be protected and nurtured. Small observations by others still interested him greatly. John Fowles would phone with updates on returning species not seen in Lyme for years. Jackman would call him from the nearest phone box – between assignments - with a report on a bird of prey just witnessed. Mabey would describe the latest effects of chemical spraying on a particular insect, a nod to Ken for the next reprint.

Despite being well into the new season, Ken couldn't understand the lack of new greenery. On the 7th May he noted,

'Hedges just thru' in partial leaf: most trees are still bare, including the lime and catalpa and the beech saplings. It is all incredibly late.' A local press item on verge spraying across the Arne Peninsular goaded his suspicions. Ken phoned Dorset City Council, demanding to speak to the department responsible for allowing the spraying of DDT in the presence of the Dartford Warbler that nested there. Didn't they know its assumed benefits were still unproven? He then called a local pressure group – 'Care for Dorset' – to hear 'the full, sinister story' of a corporation dig nearby, overseen by English China Clays.

Lieutenant-Colonel Ashley Bond of Creech Grange had sold his ball clay-quarrying firm to the company for £1.3 million in 1968. And, as Patrick Wright wrote in *The Village that Died for England*, 'it would hardly be in the commercial interests of that company – in which Colonel Bond was said to retain a financial interest – to leave the heath unbroken.'

In the Conservative Government's survey report on the ECC's claim, the company's managing director stated how he'd like a lease over the mineral rights of any area released from public ownership for prospecting and research. Rodney Legg, editor of *Dorset Magazine* and former political activist with the right-leaning 'League of Empire Loyalists,' witnessed their operations thus far and described the clay-pit as 'the biggest hole in Dorset... a quarter of a mile wide and seventy-five feet deep.' He predicted the area would be left desolate by the year 2000. Ken witnessed the scene for himself three weeks after his initial call to 'Care for Dorset' and shared Legg's distress. Further correspondence with ECC elicited a meeting with a rep. from the company, sent to calm Ken's mood. On the 19th August they met for lunch at the Hyde Park Hotel. The charming unstoppable object met an equally charming immovable one. In this tone Ken calmly explained that he'd use any means at his disposal to foil them in their attempt to 'strip Arne.'

A further excuse for his detractors to criticise – should they have required one – occurred soon after. *Thrombotic* aches around his buttocks and chest had ensured a return to sleepless nights. On such a night, in the garden and long after dusk, one of a pair of guinea fowls exacerbated his pain by screeching hour after hour up into the darkened room. With Betty away, Ken lifted himself up, hopped naked out into the hall, brought out a rarely used 410 pellet-rifle - kept to ward off such intrusions - and blasted the bird from his bedroom window. Later, one afternoon, the surviving guinea fowl silently reappeared and sat, staring sadly at him through the dining room window, while he and Betty ate.

'It haunts me like a ghost at the banquet,' he noted guiltily, 'making my flesh crawl with remorse.'

More on view was an increasing roll call of expensive, petrol-guzzling cars, roaring at top speed around West Dorset's country lanes. First his long-loved, 1965 Aston Martin, then the rented Jensen, Capri and Jaguar, each feeding an impression of a rich and hypocritical outsider staking a fatuous claim to their land. In reality, this was nonsense; Ken was merely test-driving the latest models from his local garage, and never more than one at a time. (Fatuous in itself, since the British Army had been running another part of the county for military manoeuvres, with the acquiescence of an influential, *local* minority, since the end of the First World War). In this, there was no ulterior motive. And he was becoming increasingly aware of the impotence of his idealism.

'How much is a view worth?' he pondered in his *Mail* column: 'How do you cost account a landscape? Can a computer be programmed to evaluate bird song and the brief choreography of a young beech plantation against a May sky, a kestrel hovering in winter air? Is there a method of reckoning up the percentage in a person's inner replenishment from wild country? No one bothers with these contemptible little sums, not when real money is involved.' He refers to yet another threat to his area of Dorset then being ominously surveyed by a Canadian oil company. 'What does it matter where (oil) comes from and if steel towers are driven into Britain's remaining non-industrial acres... It is Whitehall policy. It is progress. It is modernisation. It is growth. Or is it shrivelling what is most lastingly worthwhile?'

It looked as if long term good would always lose out to short term need; whatever the consequences left in the latter's wake. Ken was finding a sympathetic ear but little else from those representing the CPRE (Council for the Protection of Rural England) and NCC (Nature Conservancy Council) whom he found to be pen pushers of an indistinguishable sort.

Ken was in a state of nervous exhaustion on Friday 1st October following another solo week on *24 Hours*. Four weeks earlier he'd been given notice to quit the Hill Road flat. He'd found an alternative easily enough – 72, Colville Gardens, W11, on the top floor of Trident House – but small re-connections, for the 'phone and door intercom, had been in abeyance for some days. While awaiting a late cab he feared might never come, he began to shake, gulped air through constricted lungs, and felt a cramping in his stomach. In no better state on his arrival at the Mill, Betty checked him into Dorchester Hospital, where he remained, sedated, for the weekend. Next evening, back at the Mill, Betty looked after him. But he was still anxious and unaccountably angry with her. What they discussed isn't known, but Ken blew up to an uncharacteristic degree. It took Hudson's bedside manner and openness to listen to placate him.

There is circumstantial evidence that he was again overdosing on medication at this time, knocking back pill after pill, inflaming the notorious short temper. Betty once told a friend, after his death, that he'd smashed up furniture during an argument. Later, while drinking at their local pub

– 'The Three Horseshoes,' Ken spied an NCC representative there, confronted him with the usual sardonic charm, then exploded into a stream of abuse on his deficiencies as an alleged 'conservationist.' He then rounded on the man as if ready to punch him.

'You really hate me, don't you!' cowered the official. Brian Jackman was with him at the time and not put out by what could be deemed a minor victory. But, the time had come for more affirmative action.

Michael Hudson found his friend severely depressed on his next visit. Examining him, he discovered his blood pressure was particularly low, a clot consequently forming in the *thrombotic* left leg. He arranged for it to be bandaged and prescribed counteracting tablets. Next morning, as sleep had continued to elude Ken, he tried mildly overdosing on pep pills to counter the sluggishness. Though a Sunday, a car came for him to take him to BBC Southampton to record, back-to-back, two editions of a celebrity quiz he'd agreed to chair. Returning to Colville Gardens that evening for the start of his next solo week at *24 Hours*, he collapsed exhausted on the bed. His stump took advantage and renewed its sting. He gazed at it, wearily numb.

'*Another* abscess...*for God's sake!*'

Looking out for marauders – of all kinds. 1972.

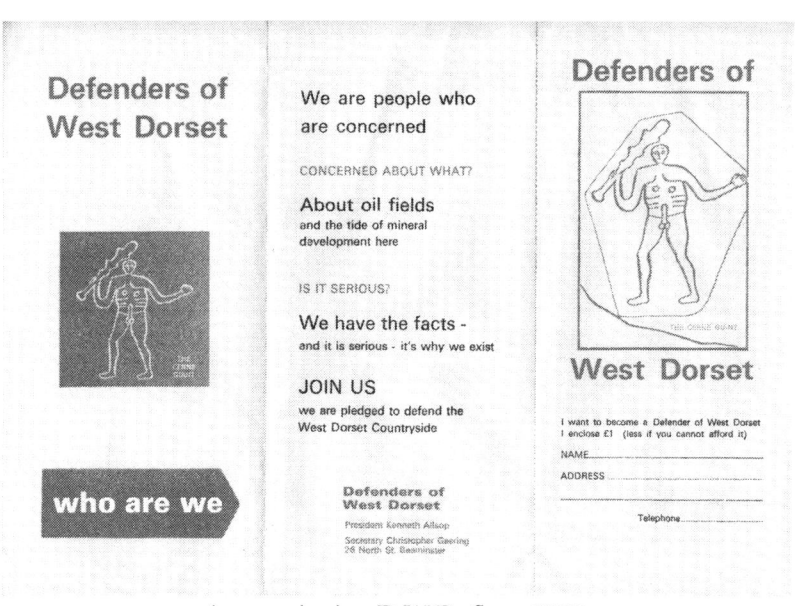

A campaigning D.W.D. flyer, 1972.

23
Oct 1971 – Oct 1972: Defending West Dorset

Ken's determination to continue in the face of such handicaps seems extraordinary. Speculation as to why can't be definitive. Ego and pride, characteristics once dominant, appear subsumed from here on by the sheer *rightness* of a cause for which he was steeling himself to fight. His dilemma is inherent in a discarded, private note, found by Amanda, and written the previous spring on the day after his and Betty's twenty-ninth wedding anniversary. He reflects on the recent past and, for the first time, the possible consequence of years being his own, self-supporting, man:

'I dread the thought of leaving Betty with so little materially and not much in compensating happy memories. I regret to a very melancholy degree that for so long we haven't been as deeply involved in each other as we should and could have been but for my deliberate estrangement because of fears of demands on me that I couldn't meet. And yet I know I've lost so much because of this distancing myself from a person of beautiful spirit and mettle.

How foolish we are. I wish I, and Betty and the children could have lived in conjunction with greater happiness and sense of the moments together. I am possessed by this recognition now of my own insensitivity and impatient indifference to bereavement and the loss of someone near – my mother dying of cancer on that sofa... - and what I remember is MY discomfort, MY distaste for disease, sickness and death. Did I write to my father when my mother died? I don't believe so: nor to my uncle when my

Aunt Pattie died. I remember his bewildered face at the funeral yet, really, it meant little to me. I suppose I'm being cowardly but it is also guilt...'

From now on, he and Betty would make a point of snatching brief walks around the grounds. It was likely, during one such stroll, that Ken confessed to taking her constant support for granted. He vowed they would travel more together, as they had during the War in the years following their marriage. In replying to an enquiry from Jenny James, he sounds as if he has agreed to an imminent fortnight in Crete more for Betty's benefit than for them both:

'Actually, it's the first proper holiday we've had for about three years. It doesn't bother me too much, but I know she feels rather in need of one, as the house seems to have been full of relatives all this summer.'

A couple of days later, Ken was at Lime Grove when Betty called him with news that a tanker had arrived to drain their leat, and that West Milton was about to be invaded by a drilling firm surveying for a suspected source of natural gas. This proved something of a red herring when a little more digging soon revealed the company's true intent. The trespassers operated under the name Berkeley Petroleum. With no public inquiry on the horizon, Edward Moeran suggested he'd be well within his rights to apply for an injunction and to put his protest in writing. He then called Rodney Legg at the *Dorset*, and asked for maximum coverage. Legg promised to make it his lead story in the next issue. Late the following morning, three distant blasts were heard. Two more occurred two days later, with a further series two days after this. An ominous knell that only served to taunt Ken's anxiety. His left calf began to swell up and recede intermittently, placing him, as a precaution, back on the anti-clotting tablets.

By November, he'd charmed the local mayor and his wife into allocating Bridport Town Hall's chamber for a meeting between local protesters and Berkeley Petroleum. Family and visiting friends were roped in to distributing warning letters and leaflets as invitations. Since he knew Harold Evans at *The Sunday Times*, Ken began a concerted letter writing campaign outlining the company's actions and his concerns at their consequences. The *Bridport News* were called, but Ken was warned by a reporter that most of the locals he'd quizzed welcomed the arrival, with the hope of subsequent jobs and trade. One voice was more supportive and something of a surprise. Simon Wingfield-Digby – the local MP, and a Conservative – suggested to Ken that, due to the lack of consultation, the oil company might well have committed an act of trespass. He promised to write to the Energy Minister, Peter Walker, on the dissenters' behalf.

The protest meeting took place from 8 p.m. at the Town Hall on Friday 26th. A recently re-conditioned E-Type Jaguar V12 roared up to the steps - Ken having reverted to type and given up on selling the Aston at his asking price - other cars depositing the Jackmans, the journalist Nicholas Tomalin, Wingfield-Digby, and more than three-hundred supporting locals. Ken found the Berkeley Petroleum's representatives already there when they arrived, seated in pre-arranged order, and led by Lawton-Clark; the company's Texan head. Ken's prosecution was carefully scripted and, to those who witnessed it, devastating. To him, their defence offered nothing new. His own review reveals the new level of fatalism to which he'd sunk:

'This is merely the start of what may be a long, hard and unsuccessful fight.' But Ken expressed a passion that proved infectious. On the evening of Tuesday 1st February 1972, Mike Hudson, with his wife Anne, opened their home to a meeting of like-minds that had attended the Town Hall meeting and those since swept up in the tide of opposition.

The aim was to coalesce a pro-active grouping as a more recognisably formal protest to the Canadian oil company's claim on their land. Amongst the fifty-three that crammed into the Hudsons' Beaminster residence was what Ken pleasingly recognised to be a wide cross-section. Along with his GP, was David Lyon-Smith, a Dorset-based solicitor, and David France, a reporter with *The Bridport News*. France, a former policeman, would find Ken personally supportive during the planned campaign, 'although we were poles apart in terms of experience and intellect.' A subsequent reference from him secured his next two jobs: with *The Morning Telegraph* and as a producer with the BBC. With his high profile and articulate charm, an easily convinced show of hands voted Ken in as President, with Hudson Chairman and Christopher Geering and Mary Gilham as Secretary and Assistant. Lyon-Smith and France – usefully experienced on the committee of six – completed what they'd collectively christened 'Defenders of West Dorset.'

Duties were assigned and delegated. Over the following weeks, DWD leaflets and car-stickers were printed, The Cerne Abbas Giant – the age-old chalk outline of pagan fertility, brandishing club and erect phallus – adopted as the group's logo. *OIL MEANS SPOIL* became its clarion call. Hudson lobbied the Department of the Environment. A cautious, non-committal reply emphasised Dorset County Council's responsibilities but also, should BP require to prospect for longer than their planned three months, they'd be required to submit to them a second application. Lord Southborough was the owner of a Dorchester estate, whose own pile had once come under threat from outside prospectors, despite holding a Protection Order. He sympathised with the DWD's plight but outlined the Council's deference to the invaders in such matters and bemoaned the recent ineffectuality of the CPRE. He ended advising caution that the 'real danger' would arise if oil or gas *were* discovered. Their bid would then become a flood of demands for further drilling which the Government could find morally difficult to decline. Ken wrote again to *The Times*, advertising the DWD, their objective, and asking sympathetic readers to "make any representation" to the Clerk of Dorset County Council. He ended on a typically breathless hard sell:

'The eventual outcome is almost bound to be a public inquiry, and we shall need all the support to be mustered, both to defeat the powerful financial interests involved, and to bring about changes in Whitehall procedures and Westminster legislation to put an end to this random grabbing of resources (over and under the surface) which we should be cherishing.' If not ecstatic, the response was encouraging. Within the week, he'd received £100 in donations. His letter to Dorset County Council reveals a little of the content of the protest meeting the previous November. BP's claim of job creation was to be seriously questioned:

'After the specialist riggers have gone, it is a largely automated process. Even (Lawton-Clark)...had to admit, under questioning, that his scheme could not provide jobs "for more than 15 men" – and those jobs would expire after the drilling was over and the machinery installed.' Looked at nationally, 'our brightest hope of becoming self-reliant, and free from duress from overseas suppliers, is the massive strikes off our shores,' from the North Sea. 'Therefore, ... such a development would seem to be a poor business deal for Britain.' He concluded that the DWD were 'the true patriots,' citing the 1949 Countryside Protection act and its principles he believed they, alone, honourably upheld.

The following Sunday, he and David Lyon-Smith arrived at Godmanston Manor to meet with three representatives of the CPRE to put the DWD's case and lobby their support. Despite Southborough's earlier reservations, and dissent from one, Ken departed encouraged by their reception:

'*Think* we actually did make some impression on them, and that they may re-examine their reiterated belief that oil *doesn't* mean spoil.' Ken and Lyon-Smith had also publicised Sunday 25th June as the date their group would congregate at the Welcome Hill drilling site for their next public protest. The officials cagily agreed to turn up, 'hopefully, mostly, *on our side.*'

Outside the cause, little held much further relevance. He idly followed up a couple of leads for possible arts programmes, but his heart wasn't in it. On a visit to Colville Gardens, a downcast Amanda was driven around outer London for a heart to heart with her father. He listened but was suddenly distracted. Sensing his childhood hunting ground, Osterley Park, close by, Ken made a quick diversion to describe to her what he could recall. His heart sank at what he saw. He'd purposely avoided the incursions built into it over the past four years. He could see why. The route he'd once taken from Wyke Green across the grass, carrying a young kestrel, had gone. The new 'tarmacadam slash' of the M4 motorway sliced through the exact centre, also swallowing the park's once bird-infested lake. He drove Amanda back to London, as bereft as she, but grimly determined to take up an offer, that evening, that would end his six-and-a-half year tenure at *24 Hours*.

John Percival had been pursuing Ken for almost three months. Currently producing *Rich Man - Poor Man* - a series of fifty-minute documentaries on the ways rich countries exploited the poor – Percival had been asked to follow this with a weekly environmental series on topics accessible to a wide audience. Christopher Brasher, its initiator, had risen to Head of General Features. Percival recalls:

'Brasher was an admirer of Iain Nairn – a journalist fashionable at the time. Nairn's stuff was well written, but it was 'environmental' only in the broadest sense, with pieces ranging over subjects as diverse as Forestry Commission plantations and the ugliness of most modern architecture. His approach was cosmetic, not radical, whereas I was an environmentalist of the deepest green.' *Rich Man - Poor Man* reflected this campaigning streak, covering topics such as pollution, high consumption and habitat destruction.

'I knew that what I was saying was not likely to go down well with the authorities, both inside and outside the BBC. I also knew that my ideas were radically different from Iain Nairn's. But I was not going to pass up the chance of editing a weekly programme on environmental matters on BBC1.' Ken was his first choice, having 'great presence and integrity as a broadcaster,' and - sensing parallel views - his recent publicity drive confirmed Percival's instinct. A provisional title was chosen: *Us*. This skirted any charge of elitism while cleverly embracing its audience. To Ken, it would come as a blessed relief: in more ways than one.

The latest contretemps with the BBC over his contractual obligations had been running some two years. It began innocently enough. A note about a repeat fee for an extract, broadcast on Radio 4, from a *24 Hours* interview was mistakenly sent c/o his agent. The Talks Booking Manager explained to Ken he hadn't been advised to forward it anywhere else other than his TV agent, but understood his embarrassment and apologised. Soon after, Ken was sent a contract for his new Radio 4 book programme – *Now Read On* – bearing an additional footnote stating all payments were to be made payable to this same agent. Exasperated, he wrote back stating that the service this particular agent rendered was solely over approaches made by a producer or department interested in using his services or to negotiate a new proposal and not those rendered already. The Talks Booking Manager returned a new contract copy, appropriately amended, adding that he needed clarification as to whether every detail like this should be cleared with him in future before the contract was signed. Ken thought this might be wise.

That same year the BBC's Natural History Unit in Bristol invited Ken to write the script and commentary for an edition of their second channel's nature documentary strand, *The World About Us*, entitled 'The Wildlife of New York City.' Initially enthusiastic, a mutual unease grew, over the coming months, into wary ambivalence. On their side, scheduling for the American filming became nightmarish as the BBC bosses failed to prioritise a series deemed 'educational'. On Ken's, the answers he awaited over his contractual queries were increasingly protracted by bureaucracy and his own follow-up questions.

The Bristol Unit's editor found himself unwittingly roped into the debacle early the following year. In conversation with Robin Scott – Controller of BBC2 – the editor asked if Ken could be approached to participate. Scott was in favour providing he was given enough to do. Kenneth Allsop was an expensive commodity. The editor suggested two major and two 'less important' commitments only, to cover the next two years, since he was doubtful the Unit could afford him for more. Ken was also being considered as link-man for a cheap, safe and cheerful entertainment programme called *Top Ten*; also to be produced by the Unit, the following spring, for BBC1. (He'd been winging it, down in Southampton, on such light fare). The object of their discussion had concerns of his own. His argument being, since the reduction of his fee for *24 Hours* forced him to make up the deficit by freelancing, the BBC's insistence on counting this TV work under the one, original contract negated the point in doing it in the first place. On top of this, Peter Pagmanenta had reason to suspect his one, pressurising year with the programme was expected to be its last, leaving Ken suspended, mid-contract. To Grist, he suggested doing an Arts programme if this should occur and not be shackled to Current Affairs alone.

By October 1971, he'd phoned Paul Fox with his grievance, asking for an assurance that, should *24 Hours* change, his freelancing would be considered as additional to his guaranteed sum. Like Grist, Fox was not yet in a position to promise anything.

'I emphasised that the proposed contract was a reasonable one and that it assured him earning for two years.' In other words, never mind his increased cost of living, Allsop should be thankful he had a job! Before Ken stormed out, Fox did offer one concession: 'Payment for programmes not *networked* on BBC Television (i.e. regional opt-outs) would be *additional* to the £8,500 guarantee for the second year.' He could do no more. A not unreasonable offer that Ken appeared not to hear. He'd still consult his solicitor. He then called the Assistant Head at Contracts who related, by memo, what they'd discussed:

'Allsop feels he is being very poorly treated after all his long service... I told Allsop I felt it was only reasonable and business-like...to leave the programme commitment open in the second year (and) that you were guaranteeing his income whilst possible changes in Current Affairs programmes were being considered... Allsop "after all his long service" asks for the assurance suggested and that the financial guarantee for the second year should be for those programmes. Any money he earns from programmes in the regions or radio should be additional to the £8,500 guarantee.' In response, his boss's blunt dismissal reflected a long festering antipathy between himself and Ken:

'If Allsop has been offered a fair fee for the services required, then he must either accept or refuse.'

But an unexpected trump card arrived, inadvertently, by David Dimbleby's sudden resignation. The second *24 Hours* presenter, after Michelmore, to require bodyguards, recurring threats came from the IRA over alleged anti-Republican bias during a recent interview. *Yesterday's Men* –

an unsentimental look back over the troubled years of Harold Wilson's Government – caused a furore from the Labour Party, and most vocally from Joe Haines, the former Prime Minister's Press Secretary, that only added to the unwanted pressure. Though sympathetic to Dimbleby's plight, the loss of such a key member of the team at the end of 1971 placed Ken in a fortuitous position. What if *he* threatened resignation? The Head of Contracts would have to compromise. But it was now the day before Christmas Eve and he wouldn't return until the 4th January. Ken's agent called an associate who agreed their treatment had been intolerable and would sort it out. Ken finally put his name under the 1971 contract on Monday 3rd January 1972; the Head of Contract's reaction to this on his return to Lime Grove was not recorded. But Ken had run out of such victories. In the eyes of the new, economy led, management, he had blotted his card – indelibly - for the rest of his television career.

Then, he was used to being an outsider. He'd been one all his life. The uncertain space in his current contract's second year offered him the chance to put his own case and speak his own mind, for the first time on TV from *within* the Corporation. After relating to Paul Fox his wish to end the contractual uncertainties, he resigned from *24 Hours*, with effect from the new programme's May debut.

With as much uncertainty hanging over his contractual future, Peter Pagnamenta, as editor, transferred with them. A joint statement was issued to the press:

'We want to show that the environmental issues affect all of us all the time – in the jobs we do, the houses we live in, the food we eat, the air we breathe... Some of the problems tackled will arouse gloom; we believe they needn't spell doom. We want to put forward positive and constructive ideas and arguments, not only for halting the deterioration of our environment, but for improving it – and to get across to the people that they have the power to do this if they exercise it.' It ends on the announcement that Ken was to leave *24 Hours*, and return for its final week in the last week of July. Shown the contract, he was understandably happy at the fee of £250 per programme – his current wage – but balked at its intended transmission from BBC Manchester. With a sigh, he picked up a pen and scrawled in a heavy hand, '+ *covering necessary travelling expenses.*'

On Friday 28th April, Ken arrived at Lime Grove to prepare his last, regular appearance on *24 Hours*, having already surpassed a thousand editions. Awaiting him was a large gathering of current and former staff, one of who handed over a giant, signed card, a bottle of scotch with whisky glass set, and demands for a speech. The programme, sadly, showed how little had changed since 1965, centring on a discussion on the latest US Army atrocity in Vietnam.

Next day he flew out to New York for a week's filming and commentary for *The World About Us* team. This represented the third year for the 'urban wildlife' project he'd first committed to back in the spring of 1970. On returning he'd heard that *The Sunday Times* had been trying to reach him with a view to offering a regular environmental column. He was surprised to find the caller was Peter Crookston, who Ken had known since the early days of *Nova*, and due for promotion as *The Sunday Times'* editor at Features, under Harold Evans. The offer was for *two* weekly commitments: a country column and an urban angled piece called 'Look!' If cleared by Evans, the fee could be significant – compared to what he'd been getting for more recent, freelance journalism – and, in range of topics, he'd have carte blanche: 'I'm delighted.'

Us was re-titled *Down to Earth*: a reflection of the BBC's discomfort at even the merest hint of alliance. Transmission from their Manchester studio guaranteed a further trial for Ken. Each Wednesday morning, a chartered eight-seater plane – a Dove – would fly them from London Airport to the northern city where they'd remain until the evening, 'live' broadcast. Percival recalled a journey, typical but for a lose comment that revealed Ken's state of mind:

'Ken and I would usually sit next to each other. We'd talk about a wide range of subjects – natural history, Third World issues, domestic politics. Looking at the forces ranged against us, and the seeming impossibility of winning the environmental argument, I sometimes sympathised with those who took more extreme measures against big, vested interests. I remember saying to Ken; "Can you ever imagine dying with a gun in your hand?" "Oh yes," he said. "I think about it every day." I was imagining a fight to the death against the guards around Sellafied. Later, I realised that Ken's interpretation of what I'd said was probably very different.'

Freed from the shackles of working as a team, Ken made his intent clear from the outset.

'He was quite demanding,' reflected Percival. 'Most of the presenters I'd worked with up to that time were content to grab any unoccupied desk in an office and make temporary use of it. Ken insisted on his own office, even his own secretary. I found him guarded, protective of his own status, sometimes irritable, and easily angered if he did not get the co-operation and back-up he felt he needed. On the other hand he was always loyal to the programme, even when under intense pressure, and, as far as I know, loyal to me.'

Fired by the ignorance of governors he suspected wouldn't take the issues too seriously, Ken relaxed within his small elite circle of like minds, becoming a much friendlier colleague. But the mutual goal was to change minds, not preach to the converted.

'At the time, young people were still lost in a confused miasma of student politics and druggy hedonism, while their elders were preoccupied with making money and building careers. Ken believed in the sanctity of the truth as he saw it, and determined to try putting the environmental agenda across to a larger audience.' To this end, Percival acquired the services of comedy actor and campaigner, Spike Milligan, journalist Gillian Reynolds, and Labour councillor Anne Clwyd. Reports from the weekly series' magazine format ranged from the residents assocation complaining of the noise from the new Battersea heliport to those from the dissident scientists – of the newly founded 'Friends of the Earth' – about the nuclear contamination around Sellafield. Controversy could not be avoided. Mock commercials were filmed as inserts, including one for Fairy Liquid, where an infant asks her mother why her hands are so soft. The shot cut to hands covered in scabrous sores with the effluent from her drain running down to the local river. The company concerned were not amused and complained. The only regret arose from the idea of an award of a blow-up, plastic banana for the worst environmental decision that week.

During the second week, 'a fanfare of showgirls in toy soldier uniforms paraded the banana, which collapsed on the final trumpet blast. We awarded it to Peter Walker, the Environment Secretary, for opening Spaghetti Junction on the M42. We pointed out the effects of lead pollution on local children from the exhausts of all the extra vehicles that would use it. I was carpeted the next morning by Paul Fox and threatened with the sack.' During the meeting with Percival, Fox went so far as to threaten the series' with cancellation. Percival reported back to Ken that he'd persuaded him otherwise but that they were now 'being watched.' Ken conceded that the Plastic Banana Award to Walker might have overstepped the mark, 'more because it was juvenile, than because he thought it undeserved.'

But relations between Ken and the BBC hierarchy were deteriorating beyond repair. No sooner had he left his presenter's seat at *24 Hours* than he was typing a considered snub of the series treatment over recent years for their in-house magazine, *The Listener*. His self-confessed 'valedictory tribute' was innocently reflective over its first half. Conceding his lack of balance, he then argued against the second-rate status by which it had been treated from the outset. That it had 'always scraped by' on a budget meagre compared to programmes of a similar genre and that its irregular time-slot mitigated against it holding a regular audience; that it 'has always been the BBC's moveable snack bar.' That 'if there was an over-run (by the previous programme) *24 Hours* was run-over.' Hardly shocking in retrospect, but it served to reinforce the BBC's impression of him as a dissenting loose canon, who harboured his concerns for public consumption. *The Evening Standard* leapt on the article, headlining its TV section with KENNETH ALLSOP RAPS BBC. Internally, there was concern that not everyone in the Features Group had known of Ken's intention, with this banner deemed particularly embarrassing to the Director General, Charles Curran, who'd been his first editor at the paper a generation before.

On Sunday afternoon, 25th June, the DWD's official protest gathered at Berkeley Petroleum's drilling site at Welcome Hill. Chris Coneybeer - today a reporter for BBC South - was David France's right-hand man on the story for the *Bridport News*:

'I vividly remember the discussions and arguments publicly aired and hotly debated in the town. You could hear them in the newsagents in the early morning, in the shops during the day, in the bar of the Bull Hotel at lunchtime or in the offices of the *Bridport News* at any time. Acquaintances, friends and strangers - everyone had a view on the subject. The most contentious issue seemed to be not so much the subject of the test drilling itself, but whether it was right that an outsider and, worse, a *northerner*, should take such a prominent role in a local debate, *and* have the cheek to be telling those of us who lived there what to do. Others welcomed the huge impact that such a figure had on the debate, refusing to yield from his position of defending the countryside and providing far more force to the environmental argument than anyone else living locally could possibly have done.

It was a classic argument: the likely effect on jobs and the economy versus the likely effect on the environment. Around that time, the national economy was usually in some difficulty and many felt that if any oil was found it should most definitely be exploited. But, at the same time, there was a growing realisation of the critical value of the environment and the need to protect it: money-versus-nature. The arguments often became quite emotional. It might be argued they set the pattern for the following decades.'

Both Ken and Betty had made regular, covert forays to the site over previous weeks. Betty bringing her camera and taking a single shot to keep the Defenders up to date on BP's progress. Come the day of the protest, the assembled were stunned into silence by the sight of the tall, iconic, steel rig towering over them, a servile yellow crane dormant at its side. Despite local and national press making up a significant crowd, initial reaction was not dissimilar to a fancy dress party mistakenly arriving at a genuine wake. The Defenders had arranged to turn up in mock-funeral garb: the women in lace veils, the men in top hat, winged collar and frock coat. Ken's appearance, striking enough *sans* hat, not dissimilar to an Edwardian father-of-the-bride. Each wore a black armband, with South Dorset's long-serving, long-shanked former MP Victor Montagu - latterly Lord Hinchingbrooke - standing sullen vigil by an empty coffin showing two legends painted in white upon either side. On one:

'WELCOME HILL, IN AN AREA OF OUTSTANDING NATURAL BEAUTY, DIED OWING TO LACK OF PROTECTION FROM GREED, STUPIDITY, EQUIVOCATION AND NAIVETY.'

On the other:

'HERE LIES AN AREA OF OUTSTANDING NATURAL BEAUTY: DIED OF SICKNESS, WHICH THE WESSEX COUNTY COUNCIL AND OTHERS DID NOT SEE FIT TO PREVENT.'

Hinchinbrooke gave a speech from a hastily arranged platform followed by Ken, stripped to his shirtsleeves with serious intent. Covertly, Ken would add a romantically loaded account of events to the book version of *In the Country* he was then editing. But, despite the encouragingly mixed turn-out of 'the potter, the earl who renounced his peerages, the farm worker and the retired Naval Commander,' he concedes, 'we by no means represented unanimous opinion, for not marching with us were those who had the sniff of money in their nostrils... who like the sound of our slogan OIL MEANS SPOIL for its secondary meaning.'

Indifferent, as usual, to his public appearances, a small BBC news crew had also been present to film a short insert of the marchers. Once again, the BBC almost wilfully positioned itself into being appalled. Aubrey Singer, the Head of Features, had seen that evening's news and wrote a disappointed letter to Ken at home. He'd found his appearance, gliding passed in his Jaguar, as 'rather disturbing,' and questioned how he could reconcile being anchor-man on *Down to Earth* with 'taking part in such demonstrations.' Surely, he could see that anyone he interviewed from now on would be bound to consider him a partial observer. Did he plan to take part in further demonstrations during the remainder of the series?

'If this is the case,' concluded Singer, 'we'll have to seriously consider whether or not we alter your role in the programme.' Ken was understandably outraged by the letter. In a phone conversation immediately after, Percival informed him that Charles Curran had complained to Singer that he'd also found his questions to Peter Walker – on the previous edition – 'biased and leading.' Ken vowed to 'deal firmly' with them both. After returning a 'sharp reply' to Singer, the Features Head offered a conciliatory, if ultimately futile, chat at which Ken insisted his position on the oil issue could not change.

It was in this aggravated atmosphere that Ken returned for *24 Hours* final week in mid-July. The nostalgic look back with Michelmore, Ludovic Kennedy and David Dimbleby–advertised in that week's *Radio Times* – was scrapped by the team, on the day, for something more typically hardnosed. Its valediction faded out on a shot of a Protestant couple burying their two sons: further victims of the Northern Ireland Troubles: a parallel with Ken's final May edition showing little, politically, had changed.

A few hours before this broadcast, Ken attended the office party. With him, he'd brought a blow-up of a personally supportive letter received from Sir Hugh Carleton-Greene – the former Director-General – that he proceeded to pin to a nearby wall. On the other side of the room, behind the crowd of inebriated laughter, he noticed the cropped-headed, burly frame of BBC1's Controller, Paul Fox. Having caught his eye, he repeatedly signalled to him to read it. But Fox would not take the bait. He just returned a smile, inscrutably saturnine, that Ken could only return. In some respects, Fox was, emotionally, the antithesis of his employee. While Ken was totally reactive, Fox's business-like ability to keep his counsel for the longer term good made for an edgy relationship, making him tough to read and as wily as his name. Ken could never really get a handle on him, making the relationship polite, business-like, but often ambivalent. The association with John Percival hadn't helped, as Ken discovered at a subsequent conciliatory lunch meeting days later after the cancellation of *Down to Earth* – a mere eight editions in total - had been confirmed. Percival himself has reason to maintain the distance.

'Paul Fox took the programme off the air before it finished its run. The ostensible reasons for killing the show were that it was poorly made, tasteless, and ill informed. There may have been some justice in all these accusations, but the real reasons had more to do with the political pressures, and the attacks engineered by big business. I was not sacked, but I was not offered any further work on my existing contract, and it was made plain to me that I had blotted my copybook for all time.' Soon after, Percival left London to found an organic smallholding in Somerset, his next contract from the Corporation confirming his demotion. Yet, his association with Ken would unexpectedly re-emerge long after he'd gone.

Ken received the impression from his lunch with Fox that his old employer wanted him to remain with the BBC. He'd gained this impression from Fox leaving open an option for a second environmental series, though almost certainly minus Percival. But Ken irritated Fox's colleagues for the last time when, in August, he casually admitted to *The Daily Express* what was, to him, simply the case: that – as far as he was concerned - his regular TV appearances had come to an end. Meantime, Ken would only continue on a one-off, contract basis, recording an uneven mix of *Conversation*'s for Sunday afternoons with the likes of British film director, Ken Russell, ageing stage actress Dame Edith Evans, classical guitarist and Dorset friend, Julian Bream, and – portentously – the Bishop of Salisbury, George Reindorp.

Early in the Second World War, soldiers of the British Army and Royal Air Force were billeted in the South Dorset village of Tyneham, snug within a valley of that name. By November 1943, the increased military manoeuvrings and counter strategies against Hitler forced Churchill's War Cabinet into requisitioning all available land for the purposes of training. The unobtrusive, tranquil disguise Tyneham represented, allied to its coastal access, made it an ideal plot for field exercise. Their reluctance to leave tempered by a mutually shared patriotic duty, the villagers were given a month's notice to quit. They understood that they could return to their homes once the need for the build-up had passed. Churchill, himself, had promised. With compounded insensitivity, their D-Day would be a mere six days before Christmas.

On arrival, the soldiers found a sad, heartfelt note pinned to the front oak door of St. Mary the Virgin, the local church:

Please treat the church and houses with care. We have given up our homes, where many of us have lived for generations, to help win the war to keep men free. We shall return one day and thank you for treating the village kindly.

But the Ministry of Defence had stubbornly maintained control of the valley for military exercise, beyond 1945, and beyond Churchill's death twenty years after that. Most of the former villagers had long since given up the ghost and made new lives within and beyond Dorset's boundaries, while a stoic few held fast to the war leader's pledge, anger festering and dormant at the wilful dismissal of a principle. As a constant recourse to that pledge they named themselves The 1943 Committee.

One such was John Gould: born in the region and bred there since the First War, working class, and so virtually deemed a communist in the eyes of both the village's and MOD's middle-class elite. But credit stemmed from his determined refusal to leave back in '43, his gaunt-featured, woollen-capped appearance making him the reluctant representative of the most stubborn, principled dissenters.

According to Patrick Wright in *The Village That Died for England:*

'Gould spoke of Kenneth Allsop with...admiration "Oh, he was fantastic, he was, he was really for Tyneham."' Gould had been present at the latest in a long line of '43 Committee protests held against the Armed Forces continued presence, in the village's sole car park on the last Bank Holiday of August 1972. Rodney Legg was also there along with the grudging presence of the Tyneham Action Group, from which he'd earlier been acrimoniously ousted as its first leader in a blue-rinsed coup. Their shared goal appears to have been to 'liberate' former public buildings for public usage, including the local post office. The police, tipped off by a turncoat, had other ideas.

'We were very close to being in the Black Maria,' recalled Gould. 'Very, very close.' But, this occasion at least, ended in uncertain failure.

By now, Ken's personal notoriety on the subject of conservation was attracting the attentions of those considered the enemy. Two weeks before the Grand National, the DWD made their first visual protest at Welcome Hill, as a precursor to the main event in June. There, Lawton Clark arrived to assure the protestors that the survey would soon finish at the time promised to the Government, when they would then pull out for good. All departed totally unconvinced.

Unwisely, BP's President then tried appealing to their President's good nature. His old *Tonight* colleague, Alan Whicker, had as many friends in the business community as out, one of whom happened to be Geoffrey Keating: Head of

Public Relations at the company.

'Geoffrey said, "Look, BP has hired a train for a party to go the Grand National at Aintree for the day. Do you think you could bring Allsop along as well?" He obviously wanted to try to influence Ken. We spent a day on their train, having a good time and a lot to drink.' Ken did confess to enjoyment of the misspent afternoon, quaffing endless refills of champagne, the race meeting itself turning into a numb afterthought – as did Keating: 'The BP people were an extremely pleasant and agreeable crowd . . . *of brain-washers*.'

Just recently, the Central Generating Electricity Board wrote inviting him to be their 'principal guest' at the opening of a nature trail through an industrial zone and marked by the symbolic planting of a tree. Having been given *carte blanche* by Evans and Crookston at *The Sunday Times*, Ken, for his first article, took complete advantage. Hearing of BP's bid to extend their survey, he replied that,

'honoured though I was, I could not accept,' but added: "If you were asking me not to plant a symbolic tree but to fell an actual pylon, I would be up there like a shot." I don't think the CEGB should be allowed to get away with trying to prettify their stupendous record of uglification with a sprig of Japanese *prunus*, or whatever it was. I hate the CEGB with an ineffable hatred.'

Through all this, and quite out of the blue, the former *24 Hours* reporter, Michael Parkinson, personally invited Ken to appear on the second season of his peak-time, Saturday night chat show. Since Ken would be back in Dorset and writing his *ST* column that day, the recording date was set for the Friday. Usually, guests were chosen because they had some personal product to plug. Occasionally, the names were big enough, alone, to sell the programme. It was a mark of Parkinson's respect and growing cachet that Ken was now considered amongst the latter. For the broadcast, he arrived in the trademark pinstriped three-piece suit, over a shirt of small blue and white check and tie of daffodil yellow. The interview itself is informative, if not personally revealing, Ken seemingly calling the shots. He is asked why he wrote *The Bootleggers*. He startlingly contrasts the logical ethics in America's economy:

'Here you have a society, an economic system, which believes implicitly in total free enterprise, and the gangster is the ultimate development of this idea. He's a man who will push ruthlessness and competitiveness to any final length. He uses bullets – most businessmen wouldn't – but the ethics aren't all that different, I think... He has a romantic aura about him. He's the man who just goes – recklessly - a little bit farther than your legitimate, commercial operator...'

Parkinson later asks if the terms 'conservation' and 'environmental issues' haven't become boring to a lot of people, relating this to the recently pulled *Down to Earth*. Ken doesn't disagree, but adds:

'We got an immense response, and I've never done anything in journalism which brought the kind of response we had there, which was a great flood of letters saying...' (Becoming animated) '"What can we do because there's a motorway going through my back garden," "they're cutting down a wood here," "they're going to start mining in this bit of relic countryside, which is all we've got left in this area." This showed immense concern, immense agony of mind, because people don't know what to do and they recognise the pressures coming from every direction... Are people bored with it?' (Very guardedly relates question to the BBC itself). I think, perhaps, people in control of the programmes felt that it didn't achieve the kind of viewing figures they would like... It's a difficult one, but I feel that if two or three million people are responding to a programme, it is an important programme...'

Asked what 'protections' existed to prevent such things, Ken replies that, despite the presence of some two thousand environmentally related organisations, there is little co-ordinated sense of what could be done for the future.

'I'm not just concerned with the countryside, (but) the quality of the surroundings in which we live, and they're as much urban as rural. Let's not forget that 85% of our population live in cities or suburbs. But to them I believe the countryside is as important as to those who *live* in the country. It should be integral and all of a unification (sic) because, I think, we need the countryside. It is replenishment. It's something that Man needs. A spiritual need...'

Parkinson moves him on to define his duty as a journalist. Ken quotes Wilbur Storey who once ran *The Chicago Times*; "to print the news and give 'em hell."

'He should be a sceptical man, not content with soft answers. This goes for television and written journalism.'

He rates the underground press for keeping this maxim alive for the past decade.

'I believe in *spilling* the beans... not *selling* the beans, which advertising is very much concerned with, and one of the pressures that leans heavily upon journalism in both media.'

Ken is then goaded, with a knowing smile from Parkinson, into reacting to the long held perception of him as a 'television personality.':

Ken: '*Not* in my presence! (Laughs) I really hate the word. It's so vapid. I'm a person and I'm a journalist. I'm *not* a personality.'

MP: 'I accept that... but you were once voted, I might add, The Fifth Most Handsome Man in Britain! How did that grab you?'

(Some women in the audience burst into supportive applause before he can answer).

Ken: 'Where were you on the list, Mike?'

MP: 'I was nowhere, mate!' (More laughs).

Ken: 'Yes. That's an accolade I'll wear with pride for the rest of my life... *Oh God!*'

Parkinson ends by asking him which of his disciplines as a journalist give him most satisfaction. Ken pauses for a few seconds as he considers. His response highlights the self-centredness of writers:

'Crouching in solitude late at night over a typewriter putting words down. This is where the greatest satisfaction is. Writing is a misery, a solitary occupation, as you know very well. It's not a pleasurable thing to do... but I like producing things from myself; particularly images, and trying to illuminate things that have struck me. It's that dreadful word "communication"... Trying to say "this thing matters because" or "this struck me as being important in this way." And it's being your own man, really. That's the most important thing. And not trimming, and not temporising.' (Smiles)

MP: 'Kenneth Allsop, thank you.'

Like the few great journalists, with preparation Ken spoke very much as he wrote - with a considered, cool authority. He could skilfully elaborate his point - often over-elaborate - without ever entirely leaving it. But the man is never revealed. We get the view but not the perspective. The charm, but not the soul. He is intellectually righteous but never, outwardly, emotionally honest. To his closest friends this remained his unresolved legacy. It also ensured that his word, upon any issue, was final.

24
Oct 1972 – May 1973: Out of Time

It was almost like old times. On the last Sunday in October, Ken was able to mix business with pleasure by combining a stay at The Grey House on North Devon's Ventian Sands with a journalistic commitment; in this case to profile his old friend, Dan Farson, for *The Sunday Times*. En route, he noted the changes to once familiar scenes; past the expanse of Saunton Sands, the downs he and Betty had crossed during their honeymoon thirty years before, and Croyde, retaining a 'homeliness' despite the presence of caravans and mobile homes.

After Eve's death in 1963, her son was told via her will that the house had been left him. The Allsops previously visited the new owner the following summer but, other than one or two brief encounters in Fleet Street, he and Ken had become increasingly estranged. While Ken's output had grown significantly, Dan's was in free-fall. Drink was the culprit along with his growing reliance upon it. The once freckle-faced, blonde-haired boy had ballooned out to middle-aged, purple-flushed corpulence. He'd taken a young lover - Peter Bradshaw - handsomely Germanic blonde in appearance, but with a squandering, addictive personality to which the disciplinarian Ken was about to take an instant dislike.

'Despite his constant jibes at Dan as the fallen TV star, Dan merely treated him as a naughty child.' As Ken set up, they reflected on the past. Dan saw that his friend had become a victim of his own success.

'Ken confided in me that he was unhappy if he made less

than £1,000 a month, which was a lot of money then and a considerable burden.' This echoed what he'd told Colin Wilson on their last meeting the previous year.

'He said that it would be impossible for him to go back to the days when he had no money, and write more of the books he really wanted to write. He had become too accustomed to driving a sports car and having a bottle of whisky in the cupboard.'

After a repetitive intake of wine during the interview, they repaired – without Bradshaw – to a local pub, where Dan moved on to the brandy. Ken was disheartened to see a masochistic tendency through his old friend's stupor, getting an apparent kick out of his boyfriend's leeching. 'All very sad and sleazy,' he noted. After the next morning's hangovers, he and Betty left, stopping briefly at Ox's Cross to see if Henry was in, only to find the gate closed and the 'in residence' sign up. As they drove on to Bristol and an appointment for another voiceover, Betty, at least, could not have known that they would never return – together - again.

Three weeks later, Ken attended an art exhibition at The Queen's Elm: a bohemian pub based in Chelsea, frequented by writers and artists. Across the small, crowded bar-cum-gallery, Ken clocked his old idol with his daughter, Sarah. They hadn't met since the Literary Fund bid two and a half years earlier. Fearing another possible scene, he quickly looked away - too late - as the old man strode into view, smiling, and clasping him to kiss his cheek. Although now in his seventy-eighth year, with bags beneath his large, dark eyes and hair and moustache a snowy white affecting him the appearance of an avuncular barn owl, he remained upright and erect in carriage. Barry Driscoll, Henry's last, personal illustrator, was also there. The three men left the exhibition for more intimate drinking elsewhere, Henry striding off ahead. Ken looked almost wistfully after him. Driscoll recalled: 'As we walked along, searching for a taxi,

Ken said, "look, he moves like a young man."'

Mid-November saw Ken in discussions with a young, boyish-featured BBC producer with a viable idea delivered in solemn, measured tones. Will Wyatt didn't come with the baggage of experience that had so tainted Ken's reputation in the eyes of his elders. He and his assistant invited Ken to a Chinese restaurant in central London to discuss the idea of him presenting a possible twenty-six week run of a broad-based media show, where his only commitment would be the pilot. Hearing that, if successful, it would be broadcast from the plush Television Centre in Wood Lane rather than the hothouse of Lime Grove was the icing on the cake. It may have been such 'pros' that made the 'cons' more digestible. He could expect no pay increase for a once-weekly appearance in a twenty-five minute slot scheduled late on BBC2: a channel then generally considered an art-house backwater. Then, he had greater priorities.

The first *Edition* went out on Wednesday 3rd January 1973. Feeling not entirely dissimilar in format to *24 Hours*, it began as it intended to continue, with the emphasis on the press behind the scenes. Another reunion took place. Tom Hopkinson - who'd left *Picture Post* in December 1950 just as Ken was starting – was brought in to discuss the legacy of *Life* magazine, its contemporary that had just folded. In a way a second took place when Ken was hurriedly introduced to his new reporting colleague, Chris Dunkley. Only later would Dunkley discover that his training as a reporter mirrored Ken's almost exactly, starting on *The Slough Observer*, first as a 'cub,' then second-string film and theatre critic, then paper's primary critic as he'd been after the War.

A week later, Ken was in his flat, writing an article on the peregrine falcon for his next *Sunday Times* article, when he experienced an epiphany that evoked memories of his kidney failure of 1968. Suddenly overcome by tiredness and an inner chill, he pressed a hot water bottle to his back, wrapped himself in a pullover, overcoat and grey blanket and desperately downed four large whiskies. But still he felt cold, despite the warmth from the radiator. Experiencing a panic of loneliness, he got out his diary:

'If this is the onset of another bad betrayal of the body, it is the last I will take. The thought of death is a refuge and yet is unbearable. So much which is so dear, never to be seen again – unthinkable, and yet I constantly think of that likelihood. But there must be a maximum of pain and debility with which anyone can put up with reasonable dignity and self-respect: my limits are very clearly demarcated in my mind. A thing – life – can be clung onto too desperately – until it becomes despicable...

...to have been trying to write about the peregrine – such perfection and flair and nobility brought down by our foulness, our poisons, with which we make money – doesn't leave room for self-pity. They die with nervous co-ordination, so finely and delicately attuned, destroyed by the *dieldrin* and *aldrin* persistent toxins, so that their stoops are misjudged and they break their necks on the ground. There wouldn't be much to regret in leaving this loathsome, scientific Belsen we've made of the world.'

As Ken saw his health in terminal decline, others were taking up his cudgels, including the newly formed 'Friends of the Earth.' It was a representative from the ecological pressure group who directed Ken's attention to a London-based, ore-mining company, that would form the basis of his next *Sunday Times* article. Instinctively, Ken viewed Rio Tinto Zinc (RTZ) as another Berkeley Petroleum only, worse, on an international scale. Some initial digging of his own unearthed a small mystery far closer to home. BBC Enterprises – the Corporation's marketing wing – had sold prints of a recent *Horizon* documentary on RTZ and their surveying for copper in Snowdonia National Park to two separate bodies, 'Friends of the Earth' being one. Having refused to take part in the programme itself, only the live, follow-up debate ensured an unanswerable distance in the eyes of their detractors. Questions became necessary when, after the programme went into syndication, the first body received a request from BBC Enterprises to destroy their requested print, while 'Friends of the Earth' were asked, separately, "for purely contractual reasons," to return theirs. When each failed to respond, directly, to the request, the order was subsequently rescinded. Clearly, the BBC had become nervous of the documentary's final cut after pressure exerted from a vulnerable RTZ. They had already been investigated by ITV's *World in Action* team, whose scheduled report on them drilling forty-eight boreholes in the forest of Capel Hermon without planning permission failed to materialise in certain regions. Ken wrote how,

'difficulties arise for Nosey Parkers who question their business operations. RTZ's £24 million level of annual profit...derives from enterprises in all five continents – such as extracting zinc in Australia, nickel in Rhodesia, copper in the *Transvaal* and the Soviet Union, diamonds in South Africa, uranium in Canada and bauxite in Brazil.' (With the issue of black apartheid a virtual taboo at this time, the African references would incense the company). With current technology, 'the legacy, expert opponents estimate, will be "enormous devastation" on a scale so far seen only by Bougainville villagers whose reluctance to vacate their ancestral land above the mineral caches was overcome by police using tear gas and clubs.'

Within a fortnight of publication, *Times Newspapers* received a writ from RTZ claiming libel over Ken's claim that they, in any way, were profiting from Rhodesia. Behind Ken's back, his paper printed an assurance that he had not intended to suggest RTZ had been sanction busting there and apologised if the contrary seemed clear. Mildly put out by this show of submission, he could not believe the subsequent capitulation in the High Court on the 10th April. Ultimately, the defence agreed with RTZ's prosecuting counsel:

'There were, in the column, a number of passages which could be taken as impugning the integrity of RTZ in the conduct of its business and, in particular, implying that the company had, at various times, tried to suppress legitimate comment and criticism of its activities.' He could not believe it when *The Sunday Times* apologised to RTZ and paid the company's costs.

Berkeley Petroleum, meanwhile, had still to depart from site 'Nettlecombe No. 1,' West Dorset. The DWD understood them to be taking advantage of the earlier confusion over precisely what they were surveying for by citing the possible presence of other minerals, equally worthy of oil. Before judgement came through on his RTZ article, Ken attempted a tie-in with his ongoing beef against BP. As DWD President, he wrote to *The Times* that,

'as mining and extractive companies press ever more heavily upon Britain's National Parks and scheduled countryside, (BP) is, after an interlude following its abortive drilling in the Thomas Hardy country...now returning.' He claims to have heard Lawton Clark – at the April '72 public meeting – promise no geographic extension to the site while, paradoxically, his British spokesman had added that he'd only been talking about oil, and "not to carry out further surveys." Ken ends by calling all residents in the possibly threatened, neighbouring towns to look out BP 'reconnaissance squads' and remember that they can legally bar such intrusions.

Four weeks later, the DWD held their first annual general meeting, this time at Bridport's regularly invaded Bull Hotel. A turnout of fifty saw Mike Hudson, as Chairman, introduce their President and his review of the past year. He confirmed the unreliability of BP's statements on their intentions and the need for continued vigilance. The good news was that landowners across Beaminster had taken Defenders concerns on board and resisted bids for further surveys in the north region. He paid tribute to Simon Wingfield-Digby MP for his publicising them in the Commons and, in reference to RTZ, 'Friends of the Earth' for their 'help and advice,' and announced DWD's bolstering affiliation to the much-criticised Council for the Protection of Rural England. Ken then announced a broadening of their mandate, encompassing threats to local transport, closure of village schools, and 'the establishment of an early warning system' in the light of undisclosed planning changes. Echoing his *Parkinson* interview of the previous October, Ken emphasised that the DWD was not opposed to change for changes sake but to 'wholesale industrialisation of the countryside' unconnected to the needs of those living in the area. A belief extending way beyond the confines of his local audience.

Ten days after the embarrassment of the High Court verdict on his *Sunday Times* article, he and Betty flew to the continent whose mention spawned the RTZ writ. A man from the Wildlife Youth Service – linked to the World Wildlife Fund – had invited one hundred and three London-based children and their guardians for a once-in-a-lifetime, week-long, eight-hundred-mile coach safari across the plains of East Africa. Ken and Betty rode with them on behalf of the paper.

'The star objective of the trip was Nakuru, (near Nairobi): 10,000 acres of alkaline water daubed pink by the million-and-a-half flamingos, which feed in its shallows,' he wrote. 'This ornithological spectacular...is endangered by encroachment of the adjacent industrial town and its sewage effluent, and British schoolchildren through their WYS sections are now nearing their £30,000 fund-raising target to help to buy an insulating buffer of land encircling the shore.'

With Nakuru in view, Ken sent Nat and Pat Solomon a card: 'Fabulous sightings of elephant, lion, cheetah, etc... and multitudes of birds. *Mau-Mau* situation now satisfactorily pacified. Love K & B.' (*A reference to the Kenyan rebels' then fighting for independence). For once, the authorities had their own ulterior motive for Ken being there; tourism could only return once the fighting was over. One he was happy to acquiesce in, his own being his ongoing rehabilitation with Betty. On returning, they immediately set to making plans for their next expedition together. Where else had they yet to explore? In the short term, Ken set his sights on observing the bird life in the Welsh valleys: a reachable district he'd still not seen. Betty unexpectedly trounced him in the cosmopolitan stakes by half-jokingly suggesting she'd yet to scale the Andes. The reaction was positive.

With the *Phillips* home videocassette recorder still a year away from the marketplace, Ken had been forced, since February, into spending his few, free windows commuting to BBC Bristol's Natural History Unit and the *World About Us* team. Their three-year-old promise to work around his tight schedules had backfired significantly, leaving him unable to shoehorn the timing of his commentary into that of the re-edited wildlife footage shot in New York the previous April. Huddled, in taut-muscled irritation, over his typewriter between the Grand Spa Hotel in Clifton - just outside the city centre - and his study at The Mill, rewrite after rewrite squeezed themselves out of him, in evermore overwrought, literary language. Yet, the style was ultimately singular and remarkable for one TV documentary.

'Deeply frustrating,' he wrote to them on the 21st March, with what he prayed would be the last draft. 'Excluding and junking 80 p(er) c(ent) of the material – and ideas – fighting to get in. But I hope you'll think this measures up to (and fits) your pictures.' He was sadly mistaken. Three weeks later he tried again. His hotel expenses were, consequently, building up, leaving the Unit open to the promise of his infamous temper. A surviving memo of the 19th April confirms that they took the bulk of responsibility for his 'torrid time.' It ends: 'Kenneth Allsop...says that this is positively the last film ever to be made by him, and that he will not come to Bristol anymore.' The sender hopes for better relations in future since 'talent like that doesn't grow on trees!' A placating dinner at his hotel with 'everyone letting off steam' avoided the real possibility of him walking out before post-production had finished. To avoid him seeing his name connected with *this* bill, she asks that he be reimbursed for the whole of the meagre sum 'without saying another word.' The final cut of the film was hastily scheduled for broadcast on Sunday 20th May: just five weeks after wrapping.

Early in the month, Ken took delivery of his latest modified limb from Roehampton. A broad rubber band had almost been the sole stabiliser of his last, the socket from the new, looser but more comfortable. He wondered aloud if, after thirty years, he'd finally found his 'Cinderella' of legs. He appeared in good spirits to Clive James – *The Observer*'s new TV Critic – who passed him on the other side of the glass partition in the foyer of Television Centre during the next Wednesday afternoon rehearsal for that evening's *Edition*. Clocking each other, they stopped in their tracks and mimed their mutual reasons for being there.

'It's the kind of semaphore one tends to develop in order to transmit information through the teeming hubbub of a telly office,' James recalled. Ken suddenly halted, self-conscious, mid-flow. 'After a few seconds he reminded me of the absurdity of what we were doing by shaking with noiseless laughter. He looked very alive.' The news Ken received on arrival at the studio was deflating if not entirely unexpected. Robin Scott was now the Controller of BBC2 and demanded certain changes: one of which was Ken Allsop, who remained a budgetary liability. An equally deflated Will Wyatt broke the news to him over lunch. *Edition* would return in the autumn - but with another presenter. Ken sympathised with his position, 'bending to the dictates of the grey maggots, which inhabit the 6th floor woodwork.'

Again, Ken was live to an ulterior motive. He'd been criticised, by a relatively small number of viewers, for referring to Greece as 'a military dictatorship' in a recent report. The BBC's fear of the personal perspective, as he saw it, doled out such punishments with further demotion. But, as a sop to his temperament, Mike Fentiman, Wyatt's Executive Producer, offered Ken an equivalent post on a planned, forty-five minute, monthly book version of the programme, which he provisionally accepted though pondered with little interest. His contempt for the management now reached an all-time low, citing them in his diary as 'dangerous fools' he was loath to having to deal with. On hearing of the meeting's outcome, Scott distanced himself from sole responsibility. But there was no love lost between himself and Ken. He sent a memo for Fentiman's attention:

'My understanding was that we were all in agreement that he was not adding anything particular. That his initial, slightly superior, attitude towards the programme and the team had not gone down well with them, and that it was difficult to operate with him because of the limited amount of time during the week which we could devote to the programme.' He then claimed that the decision for Ken's sacking was Wyatt's alone and that he'd only responded in kind as part of the consensus. Scott ends that he'd be willing to see Ken to furnish him with the facts as he saw them if required. Ken, trustful of his producer, called Scott's bluff. A date for the conciliatory meeting was set for the Wednesday after next: the 23rd May.

Relations between Ken and Henry had eased enough over drinks after the Queen's Elm art exhibition for Ken, once more, to actively seek out the old writer. He and Betty had not attended a West Country Writers Conference in eight years, when Henry had donated his second batch of papers to Exeter University. So, with only the next *Sunday Times* piece to research the following Monday, the couple took the weekend off and headed West.

At the Rougemont Hotel they found him. Henry told them he was awaiting a friend. She turned out to be a student at the University named Melanie. Out of her earshot, Ken asked him if the relationship had yet been consummated. Henry solemnly responded that it hadn't and was anxious as to whether he could still perform. Genuinely impressed by his condition, as he was, Ken told him not to worry on that score. But Henry wasn't so sure. 'I wake up with the horn only about once a month,' he cautioned sadly. Later, at the opening ceremony, Henry – in his capacity as honorary member – was invited by President Christopher Fry to get up and say a few words of welcome to the attendees. Henry responded with a dubiously unverifiable account of finding himself at a New York speakeasy with fellow writer in 1930, and being "shaken down" by gangsters. Ken had heard something like this before but noted the embroidery:

'So that, when the door burst open and a swarthy mobster said, "I'm Scarface Al Capone!" HW growled back "And I'm Tarka the Otter!" causing the gunmen to fall back in disarray.' After, the Allsops drank late into the evening while Henry cut a lonely figure, imitating the cuckoo and narrating further, unrelated stories from his War.

On returning to Dorset, Ken sank back into another

depression; one he'd been holding at bay since January. Writer's Block ensured a lack of inspiration. On cue, his new leg, of which he'd still remained hopeful for technology's ongoing advance, proved once more unreliable. Its' loose hydraulic suction offered inadequate support, cornering him into returning it to Roehampton for further modifications.

Only two plausible articles presented themselves. The first concerned the local village of Tyneham and an update on the campaign against the military range. Renewed doubt swung into view regarding its future. An understanding that the land would be returned to the nation under National Trust care appeared under threat. Recent correspondence between the staff of Geoffrey Rippon, Secretary of State, and Arthur Latham, Labour MP for Paddington North, pointed to deferral of the decision to acquire the Purbeck Hills in which it sat to an interested third party. A subsequent letter referred to a further proviso: that, since 1954, an understanding was set that agricultural land, no longer required by the Government, would be offered back to its former owners. So, any return would be provisional and piecemeal. The second was based in Wales and the red kite breeding ground he'd heard of and was itching to observe. To his irritation, he could not manufacture an angle. It was only when he heard of the two Cardiganshire-based men, up on a charge of theft of eighteen ravens' eggs, that he found his excuse, for the breeding ground was in the same part of the country.

Camped in caravans at Devil's Bridge, the Wildlife Youth Service were on land run by the Forestry Commission, and maintained by wardens from the Royal Society for the Protection of Birds. Ken would defer to the latter for the research he needed on both topics while they'd also offer their services as guides on his arrival. The long weekend visit reinvigorated him: birds of prey descending on him and Betty as if for their benefit alone. A sparrow hawk came into view above them as they left West Dorset, driving out toward Bridport Lane. On reaching Wales, no sooner had they pulled up at the side of the mountain road short of the shire, than Betty drew his attention to a grounded golden eagle, two hundred yards ahead. It stayed in sight for nearly ten minutes before swooping majestically away for further prey.

The couple witnessed their first two kites, on separate occasions, next day. The Sunday Ken described as 'a red letter day.' An RSPB warden accompanied them to an abandoned lead mine the Allsops had passed on a couple of occasions but never visited. Ken was eager to visit what he'd been told was the only peregrines' eyrie in the shire. ('And 1 of only 6 or so in Wales.') No sooner had they parked and climbed a hillock to the observation post than they witnessed, circling above them, a pair of kites, a pair of buzzards, a falcon, tiercel and kestrel. Ken couldn't move. He wrote breathlessly, 'All morning there were magnificent views of birds singly and simultaneously...gliding and ringing...' It didn't get better than this. Like the boy in pre-war Osterley Park, he went to bed late that night having completed his notes in an excited rush.

Before leaving Devil's Bridge on Monday morning, he couldn't help trying for one last sighting of the peregrine. Pulling in just passed the lead mine, they didn't have to wait long. He thought he saw it crouched on the edge of the eyrie, with one from the pair of the prey-birds seen previously then arcing across the top of the cliff away and then back. 'Felt satisfied and full of delight for them.'

The 'Wildlife of New York City' broadcast showcased its unfortunate three year gestation. Ken's narration over the year-old footage is as overly dense and literary as a first draft of one of his novels returned by Campbell Thomson twenty-five years before: great in itself, but more as episodic radio than one-off TV. It requires at least a second swift viewing to absorb all he describes. 'I've just been chatting to a bird,' he states to camera, exiting a phone box after the title sequence. (No unscripted diversion on his sex life, this, but a statement of intent). He goes on to make telling connections, showing just how the city's bird and insect life utilise such man-made contraptions as makeshift habitats - including cockroaches networking amidst the wiring behind his receiver – to the blissful ignorance of the surrounding tourists.

It is hypnotic and revealing but, possibly, too rich a wordplay for a Sunday evening in these pre-home video days. But its subject matter was unique for its time and, if returned to since by David Attenborough and others, remains the flawed blueprint. The only occasion where a tighter schedule for Ken might have produced the pearl.

His article on Tyneham had been published that morning. In it, he sneers at the sanctioned bestowal of 'paper garlands' and its listing as a Site of Special Scientific Interest and Grade of '1' by Nature Conservancy. 'None...has been a serious obstacle to the guided missiles of Chieftain Tanks, which ranged into crags where peregrines once nested...' It is only after he reads the piece in print that he discovers unexpected cuts. 'What is lamentably lacking is centralist idealism – and that should not be a naive word to use in these times of beleaguered countryside.' A series of obsessively meticulous phone calls to *The Sunday Times* follow from The Mill on Tuesday morning, against a backdrop of overcast sky and drizzle mutating into heavy rain. Assuming they were sanctioned by Harold Evans and his deputy 'who, ever since the RTZ article, seems to go over my stuff with (an) x-ray,' he calls the latter who agrees to see him on Thursday. Ken then calls Rodney Legg at *Dorset Magazine* – who'd helped in the research – with an apologetic explanation and a series of directives. Legg later recalled that

Ken sounded typically 'chirpy and the absolute epitome of charm.' He continues:

'What was unusual was the content and the instructions, down to the dictation of a letter, to be sent in by proxy, complaining about an omission which had been edited out in his article about the Tyneham tank gunnery ranges in the current issue... he went on for about an hour and a quarter, spelling out just what he felt about this issue and that, and was probably ticking of a list as he went, and interspersed superfluous apologies for things that had not been done or might be taken wrongly.' Ken then rang Roehampton to inform them of the lack of suction in the knee joint, a new lining for which he is promised will be sent for. He also calls the *Scott Merriott* company and orders a medlar tree with a weeping crab for the garden, though is disheartened to hear delivery will not be until November.

Ken's movements beyond here can only be speculative. Just before dusk he gazes idly at a tree-creeper on his front lawn and five male blackbirds feeding at the back. 'No territorial defence apparent,' he noted of them. That evening, he and Betty enjoyed a pre-birthday meal and drinks with Amanda, whose twenty-fifth was due next day. Externally, at least, Ken appeared to both in high spirits, though suddenly flagged, drained of energy, before turning in.

In the morning the sky remained overcast as rain poured in an unrelenting blanket. Around 8 a.m. Betty left The Mill with Amanda to catch a coach to London and a birthday treat at the Chelsea Flower Show and a show that evening. Her father had been invited but it was a Wednesday and so another *Edition* was due for rehearsal that afternoon. Ken heaved himself up from beneath the sheets and sat on the side of the bed feeling pain in all the old places, with an additional exhaustion before he could even dress. A momentary silence pervaded the house. Suddenly, the front door latch was thrown back and the housekeeper, Greta, of the Powerstock-based Pitcher family, let herself in to begin her chores. Initially, she thought her employer might already have left for London. But she soon heard a familiar creek from the upstairs passage and the floor of his study. Greta Pitcher recalled what followed.

'Before I left, Kenneth was in the kitchen and asked me to close the shutters, there, and in the dining room, and lock the back door. I did this as requested as I assumed he would be leaving for London, later, as Betty had told me.' As she departed, Ken locked the front door behind her and took the downstairs phone off the hook before ambling back up to his room. She'd concluded that 'Kenneth seemed a little quieter, a little more distracted than usual.' Just before 8:45 a.m., still debilitated, he returned to bed to continue working from there. From here he came to a decision: the one he'd been ruminating on for several months. Rolling a fresh sheet of paper into the typewriter on his lap, he tapped out: '(My dear) I am sorry to cause you this last distress...'

That afternoon: the taxi driver had been waiting in the station car park for more than an hour. For his fare to be late without calling was out of character. Will Wyatt thought so too, but advised him to wait for the next train, just to be sure. When their man hadn't arrived on this, Wyatt felt something was seriously wrong. He called the *AA*. Had there been any accidents or hold-ups on the road route, he'd asked, in case he'd decided to drive himself? No, there'd been no obstructions. By afternoon's end the team at Television Centre were collectively edgy. Wyatt then called the police, telling them how uncharacteristic it was for their man not to give notice of his intentions. They promised him they'd investigate and took the absentee's address. PC David Emmett - a constable from the local constabulary - arrived at his home and saw a familiar looking Jaguar parked in the driveway...

...at that moment, John and Elizabeth Fowles had been driving around *La Rochefoucauld*, Northern France, when they pulled in to look over the small town's famous chateau. Fowles recalled that as they crossed the bridge that spanned the river running before it, something caught his eye, immediately above.

'It was a swift, hanging suspended from some high telephone wires over the water. There were boys fishing and the bird must have taken a fly off the end of one of their lines. The hook was in its gullet, the gut somehow wrapped round the wires. There was absolutely no way to rescue it. Repeatedly, the poor creature flapped, winnowed a frantic foot or two up, then fell again and was jerked to a stop. Out of nowhere, the thought of Ken drifted into my mind: how I would have to tell him about this when we returned home, how he was the one person who would feel the same acute distress we did.'

The following week, in another part of the country, he'd discover the awful truth of what had occurred in his home county on that day. Having just collected a rare orchid – the woodcock (or *ophrys sphegodes*) – from the region, he returned to re-plant it in his Lyme Regis garden in his name: a subsequent seed of an idea for his friends.

Two hours later PC Emmett returned with another officer and Greta Pitcher. They tried the front door. Discovering it locked, Greta produced her key and led them around to the back. Opening the door to the main bedroom they saw him; sitting up in bed, in his pyjamas, and with his silver-locked head slumped forward on his chest, the dark, deep-set hunters eyes shut. No pulse could be found. Ken was still, cold, and had been dead for the past eight hours. He was fifty-three years old.

'The left leg was raised and a clipboard was resting against (it),' Emmett reported. 'The clipboard was held in the left hand and a ballpoint pen was grasped in the right hand.' The Constable saw an open book by his side: *The Collected Dorothy Parker*. Two passages were underlined. 'There is nothing good in life that will not be taken away,' and 'Mrs Parker can find no other means of dealing with the pain of being.' The suicide letter he'd typed for Betty's attention that morning was also before him, but would not be referred to in the Press for some time; suicide remained an odd point of taboo in 1973. But, the cause of death confirmed itself clearly on further inspection. On the bedside cabinet were a small plastic bottle containing the remnants of all he *didn't* swallow - two blue and red and one black and purple painkilling capsule. The rest of his medication was found, untouched. The inquest would show that he'd ingested four times the minimum lethal dose. 'Acute barbiturate intoxication.'

'We were in a very difficult position,' Will Wyatt recalled. 'We couldn't say anything about it on air – not until the family had been told – and the police couldn't get hold of them because they were on a coach returning to Dorset. So, we had to be quite mysterious on the programme. The journalists in the studio sensed something was wrong and we said "Look, do you think you could keep a lid on this for a time?" We certainly didn't want the Press to be the first to tell the Allsops that Ken had just died.'

The morning after, Brian Jackman was at home with his wife, Sarah. Anne Hudson phoned to break the news.

'She said that she and Mike were going around to consol Betty, and perhaps we would like to join her. We drove down to The Mill on a May morning made even gloomier by the unseasonably dull, wet weather, and went into the kitchen where all five of us just sat around and wept uncontrollably. I suppose it was partly because his death came as such a shock; an untimely bolt from the blue.' A fellow *Sunday Times* journalist, Jackman took possession of the notes Ken had been making before the last overdose: his final piece was to feature the story of the prosecuted egg collectors with a tie-in on the peregrines' eyrie - the last ulterior motive.

Meantime, the obituary Jackman produced typified what was already being perceived by many as the legacy of a romantic. 'Here, under the great limestone prow of Eggardon Hill, among the buttercup meadows and plunging lanes, was he happiest.' He recalled one of their last meetings. 'Uncharacteristically, we were talking about death barely a month ago... We had been watching a pair of barn owls. Driving back, the talk turned to Scotland, where I had recently found the bones of a red stag on a lonely hillside. "That is how I would like it to be for me," he said. "For my body to be laid on the summit of Round Knoll. For my bones to be picked clean by the foxes and the crows. To return to the great circle which is the wheel of life."'

But Ken's threat of suicide was far from uncharacteristic. John Percival could vouch for that. If nothing else, the Dorset diaries revealed the ever-widening chasm between Ken's public and private personas: the charming, relentless, man of action alongside a martyring, insecure melancholic. His legacy to family and friends was equally mixed. The funeral - at Powerstock Church - was set for Tuesday 29th May. The weather, as usual, was as it had been on the morning of his suicide: portentous grey with perpetual rain. Inside, George Reindorp, the presiding Bishop of Salisbury whom Ken had interviewed for *Conversation* just a few months earlier, introduced Amanda, who read aloud the strangely salient Hardy poem she'd chosen; *Afterwards*:

'When the Present has latched its postern behind my tremulous stay,
And the May month flaps its glad green leaves like wings,
Delicate-filmed as new-spun silk, will the neighbours say,
"He was a man who used to notice such things..."?

If I pass during some nocturnal blackness, mothy and warm,
When the hedgehog travels furtively over the lawn,
One may say, "He strove that such innocent creatures should come to no harm,
But he could do little for them; and now he is gone."'

Along with the predictable turnout of old Fleet Street colleagues and rarely seen relatives, came Henry, carrying on from where he'd left off at The Rougemont. Standing tall, aged and vague in the pulpit like a waning lay preacher John Allsop SR might have once known, he prefaced his own tribute by bemoaning a current urinary infection to an embarrassed silence. Julian Bream – the classical guitarist and another Dorset resident – then played a lilting refrain before the congregation filed out up the winding path to the open grave. During the subsequent, rain-drenched burial, the quiet was suddenly shattered as Amanda broke down, sinking to her knees with a loud, moaning wail, and – with Reindorp reciting the last rites - had to be restrained from a desperate lunge at the descending coffin. A heart-rending, almost Gothic, scene the attendees would not easily forget. Betty remained silent behind dark glasses, being pole-axed and withdrawn for several days. Yet, small reminders of Ken's other past impressed themselves. Surprising by their presence were Jenny and Janet 'James,' his biggest female fans, who'd made the journey down from Luton. Another wreath for the deceased bore the name of a woman unknown: the sharpest reminder to Betty to maintain composure.

'Mr. Pencil,' Summer, 1970.
(Photo copyright Peter Ryan)

Epilogue:
The Irrepressible Peregrine

Like a long held intake of breath finally released, thirty-one years of stifled deferring came to an abrupt end. Shirley Williams draws an ecological analogy:

'Betty pulled out from under the huge impact of Ken's personality and began to flower... We thought when Ken died that she would be crushed. She was for a few weeks but then began to climb out, almost like a plant that's had a big tree over it, which begins to grow when the tree's cut down. She joined Amnesty International, where she became very lively and bold. She began to find her own intellectual capacity, her own attractiveness as a person, and became quite forceful. When she was married to Ken it was very much a supportive role; a case of not saying very much at all when he was there. You only knew her when you had private conversations with her at the edges of life; not the full occasion like a party or function... She'd do very little talking while Ken would talk unstoppably, and very fascinatingly, seizing all the attention.'

Tributes emerged from friends who'd felt, for too long, they'd missed too much of his time. Trevor Philpott led them on *Midweek - 24 Hours*'s successor – with a particularly moving look back, tremblingly defiant in tone. Peter Black interrupted his intended *Listener* article with an admission:

'His notion of a holiday was to write a book... His writing was an expression of his energy: it would have been better if he could have cut out every other adjective, but then it wouldn't have been Allsop. You couldn't meet him without thinking that the naturalist was the Allsop he wanted to be, and that, in becoming a successful and rewarded journalist, he had... been carried past his destination.' Peter Lewis, a former colleague at *The Daily Mail*, confirmed:

'Despite his glamorous and amorous adventures... the real Ken was the one who belonged in the country and observed and described it so intensely. He did everything intensely. He always seemed in a hurry, even in the small hours after a party, to drive back there.'

Alan Brien recalled an emanating charisma, how being in a room with Ken was akin to standing before a roaring fire. Dennis Buckle, a business colleague of Nat Solomon's, had only just met Ken, through him, at a dinner. He'd been caught, instantly, by the duality in the persona:

'The warmth of his personality...contrasted so strongly with the rather stern, austere figure he cut in his television performances. His wit and shrewdness made him quite a man, and when one remembers it had to fight its way through a curtain of great pain, one can only salute his great fortitude.' Grudgingly, the BBC printed a token valediction in the *Radio Times* from one of his women fans. 'I shall miss his personality on my television screen,' she wrote – a final irony.

As the Defenders of West Dorset sank into receivership through a debilitating mix of winded sorrow and mounting debts, the danger arose of Ken's campaigning spirit sinking with them. The medlar tree he'd ordered hours before his death - delivered respectfully early and planted behind his coffin after the funeral - hardly constituted a fitting memorial. The desire for one of greater significance and public notice was a feeling uniting those left behind. John Percival left his Somerset farm to meet Rodney Legg. Jackman and Mabey came together for discussions. John and Elizabeth Fowles returned from France ready to articulate the feeling the others already being shared. Mike Hudson joined a reinvigorated Betty and convalescent Amanda to complete a nine-strong committee in Ken's name.

Initially, mother and daughter each cited Eggardon Hill as the most obvious choice for official commemoration. Since they'd first discovered this chalk land prehistoric fort, en route to The Mill, in the autumn of '69, it remained Ken's favourite site for watching the peregrine wheel before the setting sun. The committee contacted the landowners with a view to purchasing fifty per cent of the site. However, according to Legg, the asking price for the Hill was the same as that for Dorset's arable land, making £42,000 an unreachable figure, even from their pooled funds. Added to this was the likelihood of another conservation agency using and abusing public money for its maintenance. Then, mid-September, Legg received a call from the agent of one Baroness Wharton. ' "Would you consider an island?" he said.' The agent had written to Betty, just three days before, informing her that Steep Holm, situated in the Bristol Channel, was already being run by a private trust whose lease would be up for renewal in six months time:

'The Baroness wishes to sell the island, she thinks to someone, or some group...who would perpetuate its present use as a bird sanctuary and as an unspoilt site for botanical research...It occurred to me that, though not in Dorset, it might well be an appropriate memorial to your husband in view of its ornithological interest.' When Betty put the proposal to the rest of the committee, a few hearts quietly sank, suddenly threatening its unity. Jackman spoke for the dissenters that he thought it worth holding out for Eggardon and that, as far as anyone knew, Ken had never actually *seen* Steep Holm. It was only when Betty threw back that *she* had, from Penarth, during her stay with him in Wales that progress on the issue seemed certain.

Extra funds still had to be raised to secure the bid, when, from a bout of renewed publicity, the young composer, Andrew Lloyd-Webber came forward, offering the

Committee half the proceeds from the imminent preview of his third major musical, *Jesus Christ Superstar*. By now, Amanda and Legg had become an item and threw themselves into making plans for its purchase. Another bridge to its coastline formed when the Fowles's voiced what they saw as its potential for botanical research, sealing a majority in both influence and numbers. Returning from the first, unsteady boat trip, Fowles showed Betty an outline of what he believed to be the island's three greatest assets. That it was a breeding sanctuary and migrants' resting place, a possible site for botanical experimentation to improve its unbalanced ecology, and a future wildlife park for visiting small groups to pay, solely, for maintenance. Allied to his respected status as a novelist, his growing knowledge of the landscape proved crucially influential in their successful purchase and redevelopment of the island.* Fowles was still patiently listing the island's flora and fauna a generation on.

*Rodney Legg wrote at length and in detail about the trials of obtaining and maintaining Steep Holm in a series of locally published books through the 1980s' and 90s'.

Ken underestimated the efforts of others, like him, to defy the corporate pollutants. While his energy unavoidably waned, there remained much to fight for. Laws restricting the use of DDT and Dieldrin would be passed within five years of his death. Far from heading for extinction, his beloved red kite and peregrine subsequently flourished in the most unexpected of eyries, including the highest man made alcoves of urban city centres. Due not only to wildlife friendly alternatives, but the campaigning efforts of the RSPB, the Bird of Prey Trust, and other committed, rural specialists run as publicly accessible sanctuaries, significantly influencing Government legislation.

The exhausted melancholia Ken sank into at Dorset –

revealed in the diaries – proved fatal, assuring the descent into oblivion to the exclusion of all others. A freelancer to the end, he turned inward, making his own decision as judge, jury and executioner; the suicide's silent prerogative. What he took for granted, to the end, were his strengths. He always considered journalism secondary to what he'd once believed his true vocation as a novelist. A view - instilled by John and Mary - which never entirely left him. But his gifts as a journalist were significant.

As a communicator through the new medium of television, he took advantage, adding a dissenting weight to his instruction. From his high profiled position, he was the first to span the divide between pro and anti Establishment, enlightening the public to a degree more worthwhile than the sensitivities of those colleagues inevitably sacrificed en route, and from a point of access younger, like-minded dissenters could never attain. The consequent legacy was broad and bore fruit. In the grey, buttoned down, post-war Fleet Street of the 1950s, his discerning acceptance of pop culture as a credible equal to 'high' culture became the norm; cable TV, digital TV and I.T. ensuring today's consumers (a word he'd surely have hated) enjoy an ease of access to each.

At the BBC, *Newsnight* replaced *Midweek* with a more opinionated, cynical and demanding line in questioning politicians that followed Ken's lead. More than thirty years later, *Down to Earth*'s openly critical agenda remains in isolation, with neither *Country File* nor the wildlife pages on the BBC's own website showing the courage of any particular conviction. As he once feared, the beans are being sold rather than spilled.

In print, *New Internationalist* - debuting only weeks before his death - took up the RTZ issue in light of the loaded court case he'd lost, and flourished. While, across America, this trade-off maintains his memory where he is best known as the author of *The Bootleggers* and *Hard Travellin'*; considered the seminal works on their subjects and, at the time of going to press, his only titles still in print.

While works of non-fiction, they form part of a legacy that contradicts his belief – typed in that final letter to Betty – that he'd produced little of lasting value. When due to start on *24 Hours* in 1965, he'd regretted the consequence of 'live' TV, in its immediacy 'wiped out of existence like a smear from a window pane.' But hadn't he made his bed, and defined himself, by being driven through necessity? He mourns the consequent lack of time: time to write of his personal involvement with Henry, time to write the 'origins of fascism' book, and those wasted hours at Merton. It was, after all, *only* journalism. 'Less effort and time on instant consumption stuff, more on what might have mattered a bit more for a bit longer.'

Those he will miss recall the many stolen hours of leisure that took up such time. In jazz and its appreciation: George Hilton at Oxford Street's 100 Club during the War, Christopher Lucas during that revelatory fortnight in New York, Chicago and New Orleans in the late Fifties, at home with the Malberts.'

He assumes Betty and himself as representing 'the last generation' lucky to witness the land as it stands. 'We are the predators and killers,' he recalls of that joyous air show on their last weekend in Cardiganshire. 'Not those peregrines, for they and the few of their kind which survive, *but not for much longer*, live exalted lives, true to their nature...' Like them, his life was never to be a burden to others. He asks her not to feel at all responsible for his imminent act, that it's his 'internal decision.'

Amongst the notes openly left that day were those recalling his early life; another prospective reflection discarded by time. They show him, unaware, that he was not the last of a kind, as he'd feared, but the first of a new breed, on the brink of a rapid, social change being reaped to this day.

'I suppose that's what I've always felt to be,' he concedes in the final letter, 'on the edge, but preferring it to the safe centre...it's a better observation point than being part of the mass in the middle; precarious, but where you can hold on to some identity.'

BOOKS BY KENNETH ALLSOP
(Original releases excluding reprints and contributions to collections)

Adventure Lit Their Star, Latimer House, 1949
The Sun Himself Must Die, Latimer House, 1949
Silver Flame, Percival Marshall, 1951
The Daybreak Edition, Percival Marshall, 1951
The Leopard-Paw Orchid, Quality Press, 1954
Last Voyages of the Mayflower – A Story of the Pilgrims' Ship,
John C. Winston Co., 1955 (USA only)
The Angry Decade, Peter Owen, 1958
Rare Bird, Jarrolds, 1958
The Bootleggers – The Story of Chicago's Prohibition Era,
Hutchinson, 1961
Scan, Hodder & Stoughton, 1965
Hard Travellin' – The Hobo and his History,
Hodder & Stoughton, 1967
Fit To Live In? - The Future of Britain's Countryside,
Penguin Education, 1970
Harriet Beecher Stowe, Heron Books, 1971
In The Country, Hamish Hamilton, 1972
Letters to His Daughter, (Edited by Amanda Allsop)
Hamish Hamilton, 1974
One And All, Alan Sutton Publishing, 1991
Letters from My Father, (Expanded edition of LTHD)
Alan Sutton Publishing, 1992

*

Acknowledgements

I'd like to thank the following people for their time and contribution to this book:

Betty Allsop; Fabian Allsop; Tristan & Rosie Allsop; Michael Barratt; Dr. Sarah Bendall; Margaret Benenson; Natasha Benenson; Alan Bennett; Derek Bond; Victor BonhamCarter; Thomas Braun; David Brend; Alan Brien; Dr. Angus Calder; Richard Cheffins; John & Roslyn Chillingworth; Chris Coneybeer; Gillian Cooke; Dr. Bob Cooper; Kenneth Corden; Elizabeth Cowley; Geoffrey Cox; Betty Creak; Kenneth Creak; Brian Dowling; Chris Dunkley; John & Marjorie Edwards; Jan Fairer; John Fowles; Sir Paul Fox; David France; Christopher Fry; Sir Martin Gilbert; Jennifer Godfrey *(nee* JAMES); John Grist; George Hilton; Iain Hilton; Godfrey Thurston Hopkins; Michael & Anne Hudson; Angela Huth; Ruth Inglis; Brian Jackman; Antony Jay; Audrey Jungworth *(nee* ALLSOP); Cynthia Kee *(nee* JUDAH); Robert Kee; Rodney Legg; Peter Lewis; Christopher Lucas; Peter Marler; John McLaughlin; George Melly; Cliff Michelmore; Sir Alasdair Milne; David Mitchell; Dr. Desmond Morris; John Moynihan; Michael Peacock; John Percival; Greta Pitcher; Dr. John Roberts; Grace Robertson; Peter Ryan; Anne Scott-James; Rae Sebley *(nee* JEFFS); Ned Sherrin; Alan Sillitoe; Anthony Smith; Nat & Patricia Solomon; Dorothy Stainforth *(nee* SNOXELL); Anthony Summers; Olivier Todd; Wendy Trewin; Leslie Tunks; Sir Peter Ustinov; June Watkins; Alan Whicker; Katharine Whitehorn; Baroness Shirley Williams; Richard Williamson; Colin Wilson; Will Wyatt.

With grateful thanks to:

BBC Information & Archives; BBC Natural History Unit; BBC Written Archives Centre; BFI; *Bridport News;* British Library Newspaper Library; Rt. Hon. Gordon Brown; John Brown; Dennis Buckle; Campbell Thomson & McLaughlin Ltd.; Chris Cook; Corbis Images; Alan Coren; Sarah Newcombe and Marlow Roberts at Trafford; *Daily Mail; Daily Telegraph;* Yuri Doric at

Trafford; *Dorset Magazine;* Anne Double; Barry Driscoll; Edinburgh University; *Evening Standard;* Estate of Daniel Farson; Richard Fitter; Michael Foot; Fredericks Foundation; Friends of the Earth; General Register Office; Barbara Gordon; *Guardian;* Helen Gurley-Brown; HRH Prince Philip; Estate of Tom Hopkinson; Hounslow Library; Hulton Getty; ITN Archive; Clive James; Kenneth Allsop Memorial Trust; Leeds Central Library; Haven Lutaaya; Deirdre Macdonald; James Marshall; Merton College, Oxford; National Sound Archive; Paul Newman (Index); Northam Bookshop; *Nova; Observer,* Estate of George Orwell; Michael Parkinson; Queen Mary Hospital, Roehampton; *Radio Times;* RAF Innsworth, Glos.; Paul Routledge; Alan Sked; *Slough Observer;* Neil Somerville; *Spectator; Sunday Times;* Sussex University; *TV Times;* Tophams Picturepoint; *Tribune;* Russell Twisk; Roxana Tynan (Estate of Kenneth Tynan); Michael Websell; West Country Writers Association; Anne Williamson (Estate of Henry Williamson); Patrick Wright; *Yorkshire Evening Post* and all defenders, past, present and future.

*

Front cover photo courtesy of BBC STILLS LIBRARY / Tristan Allsop.
Author photo, copyright Jeremy Pakes.

Cover layout by Chris M. Corney. Cover designed by The Author.

Index

Acland, Richard, Christian Socialist Movement, 181
Adelphi, magazine, 248
Alexander, Patrick, 214, 260
Algren, Nelson, writer, 394-395

Allsop, Amanda, daughter of KA and Betty, 233-234, 250, 256, 281, 286, 321, 361, 362, 379, 381, 393, 395, 409, 412, 430, 431, 446, 448, 451, 455, 470, 488, 523, 527, 528, 534

Allsop, Andrew, (Tristan), eldest son of KA and Betty, birth 208, problems 211, 229, 286

Allsop, Audrey, John Jr.'s niece, 61, 157

Allsop, Betty, nee Hilda Creak, 142-145
       pregnant, 188
       Common Wealth involvement, 180-197
       birth of Andrew, 208
       birth of Amanda Susan, 234
       birth of Fabian, 261
       year 1964-65, chapter 18, 381-385
Allsop, Fabian, youngest son of KA and Betty, 261-262, 345, 348, 381, 393-394, 409, 430-431, 449, 464-465, 470

Allsop, John Sr., site manager, 28-29, 30, 45

Allsop, John Jr., father of KA, 27, 31-32
    appearance, 39
    co-operative society, 40-46, 56
    move to London, 41
    first world war, 47-52
    promotion, 53
    move to Onslow Village, 57
    move to Meanwood, Leeds, 59-60
    move to Spring Grove, Isleworth, 60
    local politics, 67-69
    open offices, 74
    economic depression, 75-76
    move back to Beeston, 128
    living alone at Bushey, 287
    illness, 454
    death, 457

Allsop, Kenneth
    birth, 55
    appearance 59, 61
    attendance at Wyndham & St. Andrew's College, 63
    first 'sexual tremor', 63-64
    boyhood interests, 64
    jazz, theatre and painting, 76-77
    diary, 78-80, 89
    friendships, 78
    ornithology, 80-81, 111, 113
    pulp magazines, 82
    early literary efforts, 83
    holiday in Devon, 84
    Pitman's private school, 85-87, 108
    work as shorthand and copy typist, 111
    reads *The Lone Swallows* by Henry Williamson, (HW), 89, 109
    schoolboy impressions, 92-93
    Poppy, girlfriend, 108, 136
    first ventures in reporting, 114
    postcard from HW, 115-116
    writings for *The Slough Observer*, 115-118, 121-128, 209, 211-212
    joins staff of *The Bicycle*, 118-120
    enlists with the RAF, 136

stationed at High Wycombe, 137
St. Regis Hotel, 139
meets, courts and proposes to Betty Creak, 142-145
sylvan days, 147-149
Leighton Buzzard, 146, 151
No. 5 Radio School, Oxford, 163
leg problems, 161, 164-168
diagnosis of Boeck's Sarcoid, 170-171
invalided out of the Services, 176
new home in Highgate, 186
amputation of leg, 191
fitting of artificial limb, 206-208
move to 10, Marish Court, Langley, 210
North Devon and Cornwall holiday, 217-218
Barwythe Hall, 239-264
intent to become a novelist, 243
taken on by *Evening Standard*, 250
car crash, 255
wins the Llewellyn Rhys Memorial Prize, 262-263
moves to Alder Cottage, Old Welwyn, 273
death of his mother, Mary, 283
pain from stump of leg, 294
holiday with HW
television years, 321
middle-age image anxiety, 349
moves into rooms in St. John's Wood, 385
'24 Hours,' 399-423
application for literary study at Oxford, 429
installation as Rector of Edinburgh University, 442-443
'nerve ending' problem, 462
violent stump pains, 414
arthritis diagnosed, 469
severely depressed, 482
depression and suicide, 521, 525, 527
funeral, 529

Works

The Ascending Circle, 154, 158-159
The Man Who Could Float (ss), 185
The Egotistical Dog (ss), 185
Stories of Smirril, Whitestar, King and Jasper, 201

Martin Chadwick, 201-203
Pobbles, 230-232, 254, 260, 262
The Sun Himself Must Die, story collection, 10, 233, 259
The Murder of David, 245
Adventure Lit Their Star, novel, 247-250, 260
Silver Flame, novel, 262, 276
Mooney, (*The Daybreak Edition*) Fleet Street satire, 276
'Franco's Secret Weapon,' article for Tribune, 294
Leopard-Paw Orchid, The, novel.
Last Voyages of the Mayflower, novel, 287-288
Rare Bird, novel, 335
The Angry Decade, study of the Angry Young Man, 340, 342
The Bootleggers, study, 363, 405, 414, 434, 505
Hard Travellin', study, 17, 410, 416
'On Living With Pain,' article for 'The Spectator,' 436-438
Fit to Live In?, study, 450, 451, 478
Harriet Beecher Stowe, biography, 466
In the Country, essays, 467, 472-473, 475-476, 479

Allsop, Louisa, *nee* Hustwaite, wife of John Sr., 29, 31
Allsop, Mary, *nee* Halliday, wife of John Jr., mother of KA, 36-37, 4, 58, 128, death, 283
Allsop, Sam, 27, 28
Allsop, Samuel, grandfather, 29
Allsop, Tom, 27
Allsop, Tristan, eldest son of KA, (see Foreword), 15-18, 345, 381, 393, 395, 399-400, 431, 432, 465, 539
Allsop, Walter, brother of John Jr., 28, 29, 32, 34-35
Allsop, William, 27
Amoore, Derrick, producer of '24 Hours,' 389, 400, 402, 404
Armstrong, Louis, jazz musician, 326
Astor, David, 322
Ayres, American soldier, 171-172

Bader, Douglas, fighter pilot, 296
Barratt, Michael, TV presenter, 401, 414, 428, 435-437
Barwythe Hall, residence of KA, Chapter 13, 239-264
Basrah, 49
Batley, 32, 34
Batty, Peter, TV reporter, 370
Baverstock, Donald, BBC producer, 337-339, 343, 353-354, 356 358, 366, 369, 373, 378-379

Bayley, Peter, editor, 257, 287
Beardsley, Aubrey, artist, 185
Beeston, 36-37
Behan, Brendan, playwright, 329-331, 346, 368-369
Bell, Neil, author of 'Cover His Face,' 171
Benensons' and Tennysons,' 'Gurneys' joint residents, 344-345, 347-348
Bennett, Alan, 30, 360-361
Berkeley Petroleum, protest against, 485-487, 498, 515
Binyon, Lawrence, poet, 169
Birch, Lionel, 303
Blair, Eric, (George Orwell), 136, 260, 303
Black, Peter, journalist, 326, 531-532
Boeck's Sarcoid, KA's inflammatory disease of the leg, 170-171
Bond, Derek, film reporter, 337
Bonham-Carter, Victor, 462
Bonham-Carter, Violet, 203
Bouchier, Christopher, friend of KA, 140-141, 146, 362
Book Man, The, ITV series, 339, 345
Bramley, 32
Bradshaw, Peter, partner of Dan Farson, 510
Brasher, Christopher, BBC head of features, 490
Bream, Julian, guitarist, 529
Bregman, Buddy, film producer, 385
Brend, David, friend of Tristan Allsop, *16*
Brentham, 42
Brien, Alan, journalist, 326, 367, 379, 532
Brittain, Vera, mother of Shirley Williams, 381-382
Brittenden, Arthur, 'Daily Mail' editor, 467, 468, 473
Brown, George, foreign secretary, 408
Brown, Gordon, 461
Bruce, Lenny, KA on controversial comedian, 367
Buckle, Dennis, colleague of Nat Solomon, 532
Burton, Richard, 410

Calder & Boyars, publisher, 415
Calder, Angus, 181-182, 382
Cameron, James, journalist, 269, 271-272
Capone, Al, gangster, 80-81
Capote, Truman, novelist, 403
Cardington, KA's impressions of, 160-161
Carleton-Greene, Sir Hugh, former BBC Director-General, 500
Cartland, Barbara, novelist, 414

Castle, Ted, editor of 'Picture Post,' 277, 279
Causley Charles, poet, 310
Charles, Ray, singer, 366
Chataway, Christopher, 322-323, 325
Chillingworth, John, photographer, 269, 295, 297, 402
Chillingworth, Roslyn, 402
Cockburn, Claud, journalist, 433
Common Wealth, political party, 180-197, demise, 193-197
Common Wealth Review, 185
Coneybeer, Chris, journalist and BBC reporter, 497
Connolly, Cyril, 311
Conversation, BBC TV series, 500, 527
Cooper, Dr. R. A., 401-402
Co-Ops, 39-55
Corso, Gregory, author and critic, 364
Cowley, Elizabeth, TV editor/journalist, 357-358, 370, 387-388
Cox, Geoffrey, ITN, assistant editor, 322
Crawley, Aidan, KA's boss at ITN, 323, 325
Creak, Hilda (Betty), 131-133
Creak, Pat, Betty's sister, 131, 181-184, 189, 208, engagement to Nat Solomon, 253
Crewe, Quentin, journalist, 326, 428, 465
Critics, The, BBC Radio series, 406
Crosland, Tony (Anthony), Labour MP, 284
Curran, Charles, editor of 'Evening Standard,' 250, 500

Davis, Miles, *12* 350-351
Day, Robin, broadcaster, 322, 323
Deakin, John, photographer, 312
De La Mare, Richard, 104
Dewsbury, 32
Dimbleby, David, BBC broadcaster, 493, 500
Donne, Peter, recording producer, 322
Dorothy, girlfriend of KA, 204-205
Dowling, Frank, editor of 'Picture Post,' 279-280
Down to Earth, BBC TV series, 494-495, 498, 499, 500, 504
Driscoll, Barry, 510-511
Drummond, Jock, editor, 292
Duffield, Christine, girlfriend of HW, 219
Duncan, Ronald, writer, 310
Dunkley, Chris, journalist, 511
Durham Prison, 374-375, 378

Ebenezer Methodist Chapel, 30
Edition, BBC TV series, 511, 512, 518, 519
Edwards, John and Marjorie, friends of KA, *16*, 390-394
Edwards, Robert, editor of 'Tribune,' 291, 297
Emmett, police constable, 526-527
English, David, editor of 'Daily Mail, 475-476
Everybody's, magazine, 268

Fainlight, Ruth, poet and wife of Alan Sillitoe, 348
Farre, Rowena, novelist, 331-333
Farson, Daniel, journalist, 305, 312-313, 328, 510
Farson, Negley, author, 112, 277, 308-309, 313-317, 322
Fawkes, Wally, ('Trog'), DM cartoonist, 476
Fitter, Richard, author of 'London's Natural History,' 205, 214, 228
Fitzgerald, Dr., surgeon at St. Anthony's Hospital, 190, 191
Foot, Michael, 291, 297
Fowles, Elizabeth, 469
Fowles, John, novelist, 469, 526, 533
Fox, Charles, journalist, 404
Fox, Paul, BBC programme controller, 403, 493, 497
France, David, 486, 497
Friends of the Earth, 496, 514
Fry, Christopher, playwright, 386

Gardner, Mike, colleague of KA, 155, death of, 156
Gilbert, Martin, 424
Godfrey, (James) Jennifer, Luton girl fan, 413, 529
Goldie, Wyndham, 379
Goldfinger, James Bond movie, 392
Goodenough, Jack, Betty's first fiance, 132
Gould, John, member of 1943 Committee, 503-504
Great War, The, BBC TV documentary series, 372
Great West Road, see Chapter 4, 72
Grierson, Harry, sherry company rep., 292-294, 298-302
Grist, John, head of BBC current affairs,, 436-437, 449, 539
Gurley-Brown, Helen, author/journalist, 375-377
'Gurneys,' KA's Hertfordshire home, 345-347, 363, 380-382, 404-409

Haley, Bill, rock n'roll star, 326
Hajula, Terry, 348
Hamilton, Gerald, 315

Haines, Joe, journalist, 493
Hardy, Bert, photographer, 269, 271
Hart, Derek, TV reporter, 353, 370-371, 378, 465
Hewitt, Charles ('Slim'), photographer, 269, 278, 284
Heygate, John, friend of HW, 97-102
Highlight, BBC TV series, 338
Hilton, George, friend of KA, 15, 141, 142, 146, 171, 362-363, 536
Hitler, Adolf, 99-103, 220
Hodder & Stoughton, publisher, 416
Holbeck, nr. Millshaw, parents of Mary Halliday move, 58
Hopkins, Bill, author, 315
Hopkins, (Godfrey) Thurston, photographer, 269
Hopkinson, Tom, editor of 'Picture Post,' 268-269, 271, 273-274, 511
Horizon, BBC TV series, 513
Horsforth, 29
Horwich, 36
Hudson, Dr. Michael, KA's Dorset GP, 469, 473, 475, 478 481, 516
Hulton, Sir Edward, 'Picture Post's proprietor, 268, 278-80.

Illustrated, magazine, 268, 275, 304, 339
Inglis, Ruth, journalist and friend of Allsops', 467

Jackman, Brian, journalist, 477, 527
James, Clive, TV critic for 'The Observer,' 517-518
'James,' Janet, 413, 529
Jay, Anthony, 370
Jazz, 'What is This Thing Called...?' first jazz article by KA, 211
Jeffs, Ray, publicity manager at Hutchinson, 329
Jenkins, Roy, Labour MP, 284
Johnson-Smith, Geoffrey, TV interviewer, 342, 353
Jones, Aubrey, Latimer House, 244-245
Jones, Ted, friend of KA, 253, 255
Judah, Cynthia, journalist, 269, 382

Keating, Geoffrey, head of public relations, 504
Kee, Robert, journalist, 269, 277
Kennedy, Robert, brother of John Fitzgerald, 434
Kerouac, Jack, beat writer, 341, 342
Kester, Simon, ITV producer, 339

Langley, village, 210
Lasky, Melvyn, co-editor of 'Encounter,' 396

Latimer House, publishers, 231, 244, 250, 259
Lawrance, Frank, editor of 'The Slough Observer,' 113-114, 154-155, 158, 213, 230
Lawrence, T.E., 95, 97, 362-363
Lawton-Clark, head of BP, 485, 487, 503, 514
Leader, The, magazine, 267, 280
Legg, Rodney, Dorset author and environmentalist, 485, 532-534
Lennon, John, 387-388
Lewis, Peter, journalist, 532
Life, BBC TV series, 426, 429
Lilliput, magazine, 280
Lime Grove Studios, passim, 336-388, 402-493, 511
Listener, The, magazine, 15, 496, 531
Loache, Ken, film-maker, 410
Lockwood, Margaret, actress, 336
London Natural History Society, 205
Lucas, Christopher, journalist, 340, 342, 536
Lyon-Smith, David, 486
Lyons, Sir William, chairman of Jaguar Cars, 366
Lyttleton, Humphrey, jazz musician, 297

Mabey, Richard, nature writer and editor at Penguin, 446, 476
Macdonald, Deirdre, media writer, 356
Mackenzie, Bob, political analyst, 404
Magee and Schimanski, 'Picture Post' journalists, 270-271
Magnusson, Magnus, TV presenter/reporter, 379, 387
Mailer, Norman, novelist, 364-365
Mais, S.P.B., author/critic, comments on the Great West Road, 72
Malbert, David, journalist, 16, 284, 536
Manchester Guardian, The, 369
Mangeot, Sylvain, editor of 'Picture Post,' 290
Marchant, Hilde, 'Picture Post' journalist, 292
Marler, Peter, botany student, 214, 227
Martin, press association editor-in-chief, 246
Mason, James, actor, 336
Massine, Leonard, dancer/choreographer, 343
May, John, friend of KA, 139
Melly, George, 367, 466, 476
Merton College, Oxford, 442-451
'Messrs. Pawson Brothers,' Morley, 28
Mexborough, West Yorkshire, 27
Michelmore, Cliff, TV presenter, 355, 365, 389, 401, 404, 412

Midweek, BBC TV series, 531
Miller, Arthur, playwright, 341
Miller, Jonathan, author and entertainer, 338, 360
Millshaw, Mary Halliday's village, 39
Milne, Alasdair, TV journalist, 338, 353
Mishima, Japanese novelist, 471-473
Mitchell, David, journalist on 'Picture Post,' 277, 282
Moeran, Edward, 'Common Wealth' candidate, 186, 192-193, 258
Moeran, Nadine, wife of Edward, 206, 235-236
Molloy, Joe, (see Chapters 8 & 9) ,363
Monitor, BBC TV arts series, 342
Monk, Thelonius, jazz musician, 367
Monroe, Marilyn, 341,
Montgomery, John, 399
Moore, Dudley, comedian and musician, 360
Morley Carnival, 35
Morley stone, 27
Morris, Desmond, zoologist, 427-428
Morris, Mr & Mrs, proprietors of the Plough Inn, Evesham, 151
Mosley, Oswald, fascist politician, 220, 316
Moynihan, John, journalist, 364
Muckle brothers, 344
Muggeridge, Malcolm, 346-347, 432

Nakuru, lake near Nairobi, 517
Nairn, Iain, journalist, 490
Neill, A.S., progressive educationalist, 433
News Illustrated, magazine, 268
Nova, magazine, 15, 431, 437, 440, 458, 494, 540
Now Read On, BBC Radio series, 489, 493

Obank, Kenneth, 297
Odetts, Clifford, playwright, 282
Oh! Calcutta!, (see Kenneth Tynan), 465
Old Grey Whistle Test, BBC TV music series, 400
Osborne, John, playwright, 311
Ossett, 32

Pagnamenta, Peter, BBC producer, 470, 491, 493
Panorama, BBC TV series, 322, 328, 330
Parkinson, Michael, TV presenter, 414, *Parkinson* chat show, KA's appearance on, 503-507, 515

Parrinder, E.G., ornithological expert, 250
Pearson, Hesketh, biographer, 358-359
Percival, John, TV producer, 489-490, 495-496, 501
Percival Marshall, publishers, 276, 287
Personal Choice, BBC TV series, 417, 429, 469
Peto, Michael, photographer, 297
Pettifer, Julian, TV journalist, 369, 401
Philpott, Trevor, 269, 290, 532
Pierce, John, junior manager of 'Picture Post,' 288-290, 303
Powerstock Church, funeral of KA, 529
Priestley, J.B., author, comments on the Great West Road, 72, 181
Pudsey, 32
Picture Parade, BBC TV series, 337
Picture Post, magazine (see related entries)
Pierce, Peter, editor of 'Picture Post,' 279, 281, 288,290, 303
Pitman, Robert, 413-414
Prince Phillip, HRH, 463, 464

Randall, Mike, editor of 'Daily Mail,' 377
Ray, Johnny, singer, 326
Redgrave, Michael, actor, 282
Redhead, Brian, 369-370
Rexroth, Kenneth, beat poet, 341
Rhys, Mrs. (pseudonym of Jane Oliver), 263
Rich Man - Poor Man, BBC TV series, 488
Richardson, Tony, film director, 348
Robertson, Fyfe, journalist, 269, 281, 387, 401
Robertson, Grace, photographer, 269
Rose, Dr., and Gadsby, Mr., germ warfare discussion, 434-435
Routledge, Paul, writer, 433
Ryan, Peter, photographer, 469-470
Rudd, Michael, Dorset neighbour of KA, 475
Russell, Ken, film director, 502
Ryan, Nancy, (see Alan Brien), 326

Salinger, J.D., novelist, 366
Scott, Joy, tenant of Barwythe, impressions of KA, 242
Scott, Robin, controller of BBC2, 519
Searchlight, ITV series, 347
Singer, Aubrey, BBC head of features, 500
Sillitoe, Alan, novelist, 348
Slough Natural History Society, 217

Slough Observer, The, 115
Smith, Tony, BBC producer, 470
Solomon, Nat, husband of Pat Creak, impressions of KA, 254, 274, 468
South Korea, reporting on the war, 270
Spectator, The, magazine, 415, 437, 439
Spooner, Len, editor of 'Illustrated,' 304
Startup, Ronald, 'Picture Post' photographer, 278, 291
Steele, Tommy, pop singer, 326
Steep Holm, island in the Bristol Channel, 533-534
Stewart, Joy, fiancée of Colin Wilson, 312, 315-316
Student, magazine, 462
Summers, Tony, TV producer, 459, 470-471
Sunday Times, 15, 21, 24, 110, 244, 432, 436-437, 477, 485, 493-494, 503, 509, 512, 514-515, 519, 523, 527, 540

Taylor, Elizabeth, actress, 410
Tempest, alleged father of Samuel Allsop, 29
Thatcher, Margaret, 463
This Nation Tomorrow, BBC TV series, 372
This Week, ITV series, 322, 328
Thomson, Christine Campbell, KA's first agent, 215-216, 232-233, 235
Tinniswood, Kay, (pseudonym), features writer, 327, 355, 366, 399
Tomalin, Nicholas, 485
Tonight, BBC TV series, 336, 338, 353-380
Tonight Productions, (BBC), 371
Top Ten, proposed quizmaster appearance for KA, 490
Trethowan, Ian, political analyst, 401
Tunks, Leslie, (see Chapters 8-12)
Tunnicliffe, C.F., illustrator, 463
Twenty-Four Hours, BBC TV series, 399-423
Tynan, Kenneth, theatre critic, 350, 353, 367, 465, 471
Tyneham, Dorset village, 502, 521-524

'Us, '(working title for 'Down to Earth'), 489, 493
Ustinov, Peter, playwright and actor, 360

Van Gogh, Vincent, 311-312
Van Loon, author of 'Lives,' 171
Vitali, Mirek, Portugese doctor, 295, 414

Walker, Peter, energy secretary, 486
Wareham, A.C., editor at 'Daily Mail,

Watkins, Gordon, journalist and TV producer, 288
Warhol, Andy, artist, 409
Wheatley Housing Act, 62
Wheldon, Huw, BBC producer, 342-343
Whicker, Alan, 338, 370, 389, 504
'Wildlife of New York City,' 490, 493, 516, 522
Wildlife Review, BBC Radio series, 427
Williams, Dorothy, 403
Williams, Shirley, Labour candidate, 381, 401, 431, 531
Williamson, Anne, daughter-in-law of HW, wife of Richard, 95
Williamson, Henry, author, see Chapter 5,
    influence on KA, 89-92,
    appearance (1935) 95
    letter from KA, 97
    enthusiasm for Hitler, 97-102
    Allsops' visit, 219-222
    letter to KA, 247
    reviews KA's first published novel, 248
    'fascist' meetings at Stiffkey, 252
    1953 holiday in Devon, 307-316
    'The Golden Virgin,' (novel), 333-336
    West Country Writers Conference, 385-387
    'Lucifer Before Sunrise,' (novel), 411
    'Personal Choice' int. with KA, 417-423
    completion of CAS, 443
    Queen's Elm, 511
    reunites with KA at Rougemont Hotel, 519
    attends funeral of KA, 529

Williamson, John, son of HW, 96, 218
Williamson, Loetitia, wife of HW, 96, 97, 219, 386
Williamson, Margaret, daughter of HW, 96, 218
Williamson, Richard, fourth son of HW, 96, 97, 333-335
Williamson, Robert, son of HW, 96
Williamson, Rosemary, daughter of HW, 96
Williamson, William ('Windles'), eldest son of HW, 96, 97, 218
Windows & Ladders Ltd, post-war charity, 203-204
Wintour, Charles, deputy editor of 'Evening Standard,' 305, 326
Wintringham, Tom, 135-136
'Wildlife of New York City,' 490, 493, 516, 522
Wilson, Colin, (see Introduction, 9-14), 310, 315-316, 330, 339, 511
Wilson, Harold, prime minister, 324,

Wolfe, Tom, writer, 409
World About Us, The, 490, 494, 516
World in Action, ITV series, 513
World of Books, BBC Radio series, 373, 403, 406, 408, 411
Wuthering Heights and 'Jane Eyre,' 157-158
Wyatt, Will, BBC producer, 512, 527-528

Yesterday's Men, BBC TV series, 491-492
Young, Mr & Mrs, friction with the Allsops,' 210-211, 216, 227, 234

Zefferelli, Franco, film director, 410

Printed in Great Britain
by Amazon